The Education
of a
Correspondent

HERBERT L. MATTHEWS

The Education of a Correspondent

GREENWOOD PRESS, PUBLISHERS
WESTPORT, CONNECTICUT

TO MY NEPHEW

2ND LIEUT. ROBERT ALLEN MATTHEWS,

KILLED IN ACTION, APRIL 25, 1944

*"A man may as well die young,
having died for a purpose,
than live a whole life without one."*

My thanks are due, as always, to *The New York Times,* in whose service I passed the years described here, for permission to use material which appeared in the newspaper. I must also thank *Town and Country* for the right to reprint an article. The quotation from "The Masque of Plenty" is taken from *Departmental Ditties and Barrack-Room Ballads* by Rudyard Kipling, copyright 1899, reprinted by permission of Mrs. G. Bambridge and Doubleday and Company, Inc.

CONTENTS

CONTENTS

Indian Course

Post-Graduate Italian

The Education
of a
Correspondent

The Pupil

I HAVEN'T yet succeeded in convincing myself that I ever should
have been a newspaperman, least of all a war correspondent, but,
then, I drifted into the game by accident. When I answered a
want ad back in July, 1922, in *The New York Times* signed
"PUBLISHER" and asking for a secretary-stenographer, I believed
and hoped that the publisher in question would be one of the
book concerns. For I am a bookish man by nature, and was
meant to live in an ivory tower—which until that time I had
done. Indeed, I kept one foot in that instinctive home of mine
for years afterwards, until my affections were transformed by
marriage and children and a painful but steadily growing ab-
sorption in world affairs. But, then, as head of a family, it still
does not make sense to go sticking my nose into danger year after
year and asking more of my Guardian Angel than a man has a
right to ask, since he has but one life to live.

The lesson is an old and trite one, but we all have to learn it.
The life that civilization imposes on us is only a veneer. A man
must go to meet his fate, wherever it may be, whenever it may
come. The urge to go out and fight, to pit one's strength and
wits against the forces of nature, to seek adventure, risk life and
take joy in comradeship and danger—these are deep feelings, so
deep that even I who love life and family and luxury and books
have yielded to them. But I still say that it all means nothing if
one cannot at the end turn back to where the heart is, and in
that warm place seek to put into thought and language the
lessons that have been so hardly learned.

Meanwhile, one has to carry on. The urge to turn one's back
on this unhappy and turbulent world is, to a varying degree, in

every man. For anyone so unsociable and introspective as I am, the desire is sometimes overwhelming, which is one reason I often feel that the newspaper game was not meant for the likes of me. However, it is always a comfort to feel that anybody can be a newspaperman. Journalism has always attracted young graduates—like myself in 1922—trained for nothing in particular, with no technical or professional knowledge, but with a belief that they can write. Actually, it is a profession like any other, and one of the most difficult to learn. To reach anywhere near the top one must go through an apprenticeship longer and harder in its way than that of a doctor, lawyer or engineer, and if one has not gone through the mill from bottom to top, there is always something lacking—not the least being the respect of the old timers who have done so, and who know the necessity of experience in newspaper work.

With me there was no choice. I had neither the intention nor the desire to become a journalist. At Columbia University they tried hard to get me to stay there and teach in the Romance language department, and in the years that followed I often wondered whether I had not made a mistake in turning down the offer—academic life has many attractions. My reason was a simple one; I knew I should make a very bad teacher, being shy and unsociable. Above all, I hated and despised stupidity more than anything else in this world—and I still do. So I knew I should never have the tolerance, the patience, the humanity, the pity and the kindliness which a good teacher needs and is born with. I suppose I lacked the presumption, too, for I was acutely conscious of how pathetically little one learns in college—and I never relished that sort of teaching which keeps just one step ahead of what the pupils know.

So it was just as well that I got kicked into journalism through the back door, or entered it like a child who is tossed into the water and has no choice but to learn to swim. The "PUBLISHER" in that advertisement I answered was the personnel officer of *The New York Times,* who was looking for a secretary-stenographer for the Assistant Business Manager, Edwin S. Friendly, now Business Manager and part owner of *The*

Sun. My knowledge of French, Spanish and Italian, of medieval history and literature, and especially of the works of Dante, and all the other odd bits and scraps of learning I had taken much pleasure in acquiring, were at that time and for some years to come of no use whatever to me. Later, with refinements and additions, they all became parts of my stock-in-trade, but the only thing that counted then was the fact that for some odd reason, which is still obscure to me, I had learned stenography and typing. My head was in the clouds, but the stenography and typing were like two good feet on the ground, good enough to help me in earning $25 a week and a job on *The New York Times.*

Those were miserable years, the three I spent in the business and advertising departments, although now I can look back on them as part of the valuable milling process I have gone through. But had I stayed I would have made a much worse business man than teacher. The urge to get away into real newspaper work was more than a mere floundering effort to reach solid ground, and more than mere ambition, although there has always been plenty of that. Looking back, I can see now that I was always, more or less unconsciously, striving to get beyond the easy, level shore and climb the storm-covered mountains where life is truly lived and where our struggling world makes its history.

In that I was only responding to a natural urge, of course. The yearning is in every man's heart, but most men have other tasks in life and have to take their adventure and history vicariously. I have been a lucky man, for it has been my fortune to be in the midst of great events. All I can claim are some special aptitudes for which I deserve no credit—the training of a body in sports throughout my youth, an education that, curiously enough, proved especially adapted to my work, and an inexplicable love of soldiering, with its comradeship and dangers.

Perhaps, too, there is involved a question of degree of feeling. With me, these natural longings have been very acute. I was first aware of them in World War I, which ended when I was 18 years old, but not before I was able to get into it and over to France, albeit I arrived just too late to see any action.

I was no different in my emotions from hundreds of thousands of other youngsters of the same age in that war and this one, but the point of interest is that they did not seem consistent in one who had lived a pampered, secluded life in which the outer world had little part. What was special in my case, however, was my constant indifference and my ignorance of the political issues of the war and the peace. I had responded to the common emotions of unthinking patriotism, fanned by anti-German propaganda which I swallowed whole. But, above all, there was an intense urge to seek what is bombastically called glory, to fulfill all youthful dreams, to emulate in some modest way the heroes of old that I had been reading about all my life, to win the respect of others, not for any scholarly achievement, but for physical prowess—to be, in short, everything that I had not been.

None of these dreams came true. I was no hero, just a generally unhappy, homesick boy who reached the Tank Corps center at Bourges, near Langres in eastern France, just too late to see any action. I hated the regimentation of army life without action and thanked my stars when I escaped being sent with the occupational force to Coblenz. During the five months of my waiting to be shipped back home, the "Big Four" were settling the peace of Europe—or, rather, preparing the basis for this war—but I was not interested. I could have read the French newspapers, but did not. I would not even try to speak French, although I had studied it in high school, and I returned home knowing almost nothing of France and caring less.

Does any of that seem shocking to you? It should not, because virtually every lad in this later war, from India to Italy and back to the United States, to whom I have talked or about whom I have heard, is just the same. We Americans are not a politically minded race, and our education is almost completely lacking in sound political training. The last thing I was capable of doing then was to conceive of war as an instrument of politics, which it is. The appeal was to my emotions, and for many years thereafter I lamented the fact that I had arrived too late to see action and would probably never know how well or badly I could respond to danger and terror.

There was always that sense of frustration, that unfulfilled dream, that longing to break away from the comforts of life and civilization, and I thought that I would, like the proverbial virgin, die wondering. How I hated listening to other young men talk of their fighting experiences! It made me writhe inside. How everlastingly true is that gibe of Henry IV at Crillon:

"Hang yourself, brave Crillon! We fought at Arques, and you were not there!"

Later, a professional element was to be involved in my thoughts, for to miss a good fight meant to miss a good story; but in those days I was thinking of myself only, and about my own frustration. I need not have worried, although I had to wait seventeen years—years during which life developed normally and happily enough, and wars and the thought of war seemed remote.

Yet the lives of all of us in that period were but a preparation for war, consciously or unconsciously, and neither I nor anyone else was going to escape the test. Only for me it came earlier than for other Americans, and one war was to lead to another, and through them all I have had my joys and sorrows, my great days and my black ones, and now I am full to the brim with the bitterness.

Human nature being what it is, I love to think of the joyful days, when life seemed more full and intense or else just more satisfactory than I ever dreamed it could be. There was that day in the Spanish Civil War when we—Ernest Hemingway, Sefton Delmer of the *London Daily Express,* and I—took Teruel, or at least. we as good as took it. Just a little while ago, although seven exciting years had passed, Hemingway and I agreed that that was the greatest day of our lives, and so it ever will be.

And then there was that starry evening on the edge of the Salt Plain in Dankalia during the Abyssinian War, when it first came to me that my dreams were really being fulfilled and that my instincts had not lied to me, and that men were really born to fight and suffer and die, and glory in doing so. I was out with a flying column on a dangerous mission, and only one other correspondent was along, Luigi Barzini, Jr., of the Milan *Corriere della Sera*. This is what I wrote of that evening:

"We dined out under the stars in the light of storm-lanterns hung from a nearby tree. The food was excellent, and there was a last precious *fiasco* of Chianti, brought from Assab, to wash it down.

" 'What more could a man want?' I thought to myself as we stretched out lazily on the ground afterwards, too replete to do anything but puff our cigarettes in silence. Good food, good wine, good fellowship, sentimental music played by a portable gramophone, the half moon spreading a mild glow about the camp and the spirit of adventure pervading all . . . I thought of Paris and the daily grind, with feet stuck under a desk and bowed shoulders poring over newspapers. It amused me to think that lots of people were feeling sorry for me at the moment—poor, misguided people, who have never learned why men are willing to give up the luxuries of civilization, and leave sweethearts, wives and children for a life of hardship and danger."

That was a beginning, and I was not concerned then with ethical or moral problems. They grew with time and experience and thought as the wars took on a political shape, and the wanton, wicked, vicious quality of the suffering imposed on others seared its way into my heart. Yet, every now and then it is impossible not to respond to that profound joy of battle, which we poor, accursed human beings will never lose. And even in this war, in days like those which preceded the fall of Naples, and in Marseilles, I have felt it again, like an unholy reminder of primitive forces.

I still say, as I did years ago, "Let him who loves life, risk it," for it is only in danger, and in surviving it, that one can learn how good it is to be alive. Allow for a bit of exaggeration, since I never meant that one should risk life needlessly just to give a perverted zest to life; I only meant that one will never realize how precious life is until danger, whether it be from bullets or illness, threatens to take it away. Where the personal element enters is in the use of the word "needlessly." Some newspapermen think it worth while to risk their lives for a good story;

others do not. Maybe the others will live longer; perhaps not. A man, as I remarked before, must go to meet his destiny, and it may come in the crash of an airplane over an enemy target or it may come as he crosses Times Square. I can see no other way than to go ahead and do one's job.

I have lived longer than I have had a right to, considering the events of these past ten years, but others have gone down almost at the first encounter with death. I am not questioning why it should be so—why I should be alive and my nephew, Second Lieutenant Robert Allen Matthews, should have been killed, after a month or two of action, on his twenty-second birthday—because in war you have to take what comes to you, and this life has made me a little weary of thinking why, or at least I am not in the mood these days to do so. After the war is over, if I am still alive, there will be time enough.

So the joys of battle and campaigning have been and are, in ever-increasing measure, dissolving into suffering—the world of suffering which I have seen and the gradual weight of it which has turned war into a weariness of flesh and mind, a sort of numbness that must suffice to shut off tragedy and pity. Yet emotions and brain go on working, and out of the fiery crucible of war after war there has been forming in me an attitude toward life and, above all, toward the ways in which other men—dictators, statesmen, diplomats, politicians—are directing the lives of individuals and nations.

It has been, as life should be, an education, and I hope, in the literal sense, a liberal one, for it has impelled me from an ivory tower of political ignorance and cynicism toward a conviction that the only way of life worthy of a moral, thinking man is in liberalism.

I find myself unable to apologize for the slowness, the lateness, the reluctance with which I arrived at some degree of political education. The omniscience that so many journalists assume has always seemed silly and illogical to me. There is no royal road to knowledge or wisdom in a profession dealing with the most complicated forces of life. It should seem perfectly obvious that newspapermen, like other human beings, make mistakes, and

yet how seldom does one find a willingness on the part of correspondents, and even more so on the part of their agencies and
newspapers, to admit having been wrong about a particular
story or situation! Political knowledge is not intuitive. It is
reached by an exhaustive process of trial and error, of patient
accumulation of facts that are judged and studied and pondered
over and then placed in their proper perspective. Into it should
go a knowledge of the past and of the judgments regarding it
which students and philosophers have made.

This is a "counsel of perfection," of course, and to expect to
find perfection except in rare individuals faced with a particular
situation that they have studied is asking the impossible—but,
then, the solution is still a simple one. We have a right to expect
a certain amount of humility where knowledge is lacking and a
constant effort to improve the sources and degree of that knowledge.

The important thing is not the making of errors but the persisting in them, and trite though that statement may seem, it
is one of the truly vital considerations facing the world today.
The problem of whether a man is to be punished for his political
beliefs in the past is agitating minds in every country in the
world. One must first make the distinction between political
beliefs, and crimes or misdeeds committed in the name of those
beliefs. The crimes should be punished, but one cannot have
any pretense to liberalism and then seek to deny any man the
right to think and follow whatever political creed he believes in,
as long as he and others like him follow a course of action that
may, for brevity's sake, be called legal.

It is easy for the young in age or mind to be quite sure of their
political beliefs, but if they have not reached that assurance
through a painstaking process of living and thinking, they deserve no hearing and no respect. You find that type of mind
among young Communists, for instance, who may have lived
the hard way and the right way, but whose reading has been
confined to Marxist literature or whose attitude toward other
literature is such that they approach it with closed minds. The
blind acceptance of any doctrine, whether it be democracy, Com-

munism, Fascism, or some other ism, does not entitle a man to claim virtue, even though such belief may place him on the side of righteousness in particular situations.

To have been anti-Fascist through an understanding of the meaning of Fascism and the evils which were inherent in it is one thing, but to be anti-Fascist because you are a Democrat, Communist or Socialist is no more praiseworthy than to be anti-Moslem because you are a Christian.

I have always envied those who are sure of their political beliefs or religious feelings. They possess a comfort which those of us who seek faith and knowledge through observation, study and reasoning can never attain. I learned my politics the hard way, and although they may still and always be mistaken, at least they have a basis in life and experience as well as study. As far as I am concerned, knowledge gained through living in and with events and pondering upon their meaning is the only knowledge that has any value, and it is inherent in the process that one's attitude should be subject to change under the impact of those events. The only wisdom that can be cheaply won is borrowed or guessed at or accepted from others, and as such it contributes nothing to the sum total of human knowledge.

True journalism, like true historiography, is not mere chronology, not (to cite Von Ranke's famous definition of the purpose of history) "simply to describe the event exactly as it happened," but placing the event in its proper category as a moral act and judging it as such. It is too glib to say of newspapermen that they are writing history. Those of us with our noses to the daily grindstone are not writing history when we describe the events we see or hear; we are merely providing the material for history. It is only afterwards, in the summation and analysis of what we have written, that the meaning of the events and their place in the continuous and ever-changing web of life become clear. That knowledge has to be fought for and won on the only battlefields where victory has any meaning: in the midst of all the contending forces—political, military, economic, and religious—which are shaping the world we live in.

As Benedetto Croce wrote, one cannot stand outside events

"and move as in a void. It is necessary to pass through them, to feel the impact and the agony which they generate in order to stand above them, rising from suffering to judgment and knowledge."

And so, I repeat, I make no apologies because once I thought I admired Fascism, or because not so many years ago I was ignorant of and indifferent to the political forces which were preparing this holocaust we are living through. If you were wiser than I, you have my respect, but I rather suspect that if the vast majority of you were honest with yourselves you would have to admit that you were no more aware of what was happening and shaping up than I was. Perhaps the realization came later to many of you than it did to me; perhaps some of you still do not know what it is all about. After all, do not forget that the statesmen who controlled our destinies knew so little and had so little wisdom that they brought us to this pass. Nothing is so cheap and easy as wisdom after the event.

If I am daring enough to put down here the educational process through which I went, it is primarily because I feel that it was the normal and natural one for many other millions of misguided people like me who had to be dragged protestingly through the mill of the gods. It merely so happens that my profession and my good fortune took me to places where great events occurred and put me in touch with the men who were both the instigators and then the helpless puppets of the forces that they loosed upon the world.

Already one can see only too clearly the shape of things which threaten to come after the war if we do not realize the errors of the past. One can see the lines of thought which persist, the attitudes that merely shift color and appearance without actually changing their form. If I here present a *mea culpa* it is in the belief that my mistakes were, and still are, the common ones, and if I have rectified any of them, others may do the same. The only way to avoid a repetition of error is to recognize the error, and the only way to conquer indifference and ignorance is to have some valid reasons for belief in what is right. And, to come back to where I started, the only reasons that can have any validity are those based upon "the impact and the agony" generated by events that are lived through with understanding and moral judgment.

The "agony" is real—at least, the process has been for me, as painful and painstaking as drawing a silk thread from a cocoon. As I said before, all my instincts were toward seclusion and study and, above all, toward the past considered as something detached from the present and hence having the quality of a dream. It was not easy to reach the stage I did reach, finally, in this dangerous decade, of feeling that this is not simply the day and hour in which I must, perforce, live, but it is the one above all that I want to live in and make the most of. It is not that I have any desire to say, with Faust: *Verweile doch, du bist so schön*, for, the Lord knows, this is far from a beautiful moment, but because I feel the challenge of these great and terrible events and because it is better to contend against great forces than to live in a placid world, and because, anyway, my turn of mind no longer permits me to consider myself, even in imagination, as destined to live in any other situation or epoch.

Elementary wisdom, to be sure—but often the simplest dictates of wisdom are the hardest to learn and to accept. My college career seems to have been, now that I look back upon it, as much an escape from life as a preparation for it. I went to Columbia University after my discharge from the Army, partly because I was not prepared or willing to become a part of the world and I hoped for a job with some book publisher, partly because I wanted to remain in my own fictitious world of books. Even when on *The Times* I kept fighting against the tides that were carrying me toward the hard realities of the shore. After two years I switched over to night work so that I could return to Columbia for a postgraduate course aimed solely at winning a fellowship that would take me abroad for more study and less practical work. I won the fellowship—two, in fact—and I did spend the year 1925-1926 abroad, mostly in Italy, studying—of all things!—Dante and medieval history and philosophy.

That year was a crucial one for Europe and the world, but at the end of it I could have told you precious little about what had happened. In Italy, where I spent most of the time, it was the year following the Matteotti affair, the murder of the Socialist deputy by highly connected Fascist thugs which almost wrecked the Mussolini regime in its infancy. The Duce had recovered from the blow and was in the process of carrying out that remarkable transformation of every phase of governmental and social work which before the end of 1926 made him not only the dictator of Italy but the head of a state which had all the characteristics we now know as Fascism.

It should have been the year, above all others, for anyone aware of the forces operating in the world to be in Europe and keep his eyes and ears open, but I have only the vaguest recollection of political affairs then, nor do I recall ever having read any Italian newspapers. That does not mean I absorbed nothing about Italy and Italians, because I did, and it served me in good stead later, but the knowledge I acquired was not of politics.

In France, where I spent a few months, I was so little aware of what was happening that I failed to change my dollars when the franc was down to two cents, and thereby shortened my sojourn in Europe. When the time came to go to London for a final month in Europe, the clerk in the Paris office of Cook's said: "You don't want to go now, do you? There is a general strike on and you wouldn't be comfortable." I agreed, and waited until the strike was over.

So when I got back to New York and saw Arthur Hays Sulzberger, then vice-president of *The Times,* and he asked me what I wanted to do, I replied that I would like to get into the Book Review department. Fortunately, there was no place open there at the time, but Frederick T. Birchall, Acting Managing Editor, was looking for a secretary to work at night and I reluctantly took on the job.

That put me into the News Department and began a forceful education in the things that were really happening in the world. I could not feel interested in them, as such, or in their effect on the lives of nations and individuals, but the personal equation was a simple one: I wanted to get ahead and make money, and I always had a desire to write, and some talent in that direction.

Thus began a natural progression: reporter, rewrite man, copyreader, and since I had been abroad and theoretically knew something about Europe, I ended up on the cable desk. I was there one evening in the spring of 1929 when Mr. Birchall bellowed across the room for me to come over to his desk. He had a proposition which set my heart rejoicing. The Carnegie Endowment for International Peace, in conjunction with the Japanese Government, was organizing a junket for eighteen newspapermen chosen from important newspapers throughout the country. It was to last five months and include Japan, Korea, Manchuria, and northern China. *The Times* had been asked to send a representative, and for some reason which still rather baffles me Adolph S. Ochs, the publisher, had picked me. Certainly, I could be easily spared, and no doubt he wanted to choose a young man who had some promise.

Those were fantastic months. There never has been a junket like it in the newspaper game, and there probably never will be another comparable to it in length, expense, and luxury. It seems ironical, now that we are at war with Japan, to think of an effort being made to create good will and understanding between our two countries, but the idea was surely a laudable one, even if still-born and futile. I had no faith in international peace, even then, but the skepticism was at that time based on a mixture of cynicism, indifference, and shrewdness. I had read too much history to be able to conceive of a world without war, and I have, at least, always had a practical bent which fastened my mind on the possible and the present, to the exclusion of Utopias of any kind. I was even then vaguely groping toward a knowledge of how governments are run, whom they are run by, and what to expect of men responding to and acting upon forces which do not permit any great deviation from certain basic principles of an essentially conservative nature.

Not that I had become really politically conscious at that time. What I responded to, above all, was the charm and hospitality of the Japanese. I confess to being naive in that respect, and I know I shall remain so all my life. If someone is nice to me I always take it as a compliment and as an expression of amiability and goodness, so long as it does not take the form of flattery or is very obviously an effort to "sell" something. The Japanese were nice, and I still see no reason to believe that the individuals who entertained us were not themselves quite sincerely hospitable, whatever nefarious reservations some members of the government may have had. I was willing to believe that war between our two countries was always a possibility, but I could not connect my hosts with that war, nor could I conceive of such men perpetrating the cruelties which we now connect with the Japanese. That was before the invasion of China, and what little Japanese history we knew depicted the people as brave, chivalrous, straightforward fighters.

We took for granted their economic and political penetration of Korea and Manchuria, and, indeed, admired their progressive spirit as evidenced by the South Manchuria Railway, the development of Dairen, Harbin, and Chungking. I do not recall anyone in the crowd following the simple logic that an effort to dominate the whole of China would ensue and, in time, inevitably lead to a clash with Great Britain and the United States. In fact, I believe it is a fair statement to make that after visiting Peking, Tientsin, and Shanghai, and then returning to Japan, everyone of us went back to the States much more sympathetically disposed toward the Japanese than toward the Chinese.

Only a short time before, Chiang Kai-shek had gained control of northern China, although the young Chang Hsueh-liang still maintained a nominal and precarious autonomy in Manchuria. The Generalissimo, in fact, came to Peking or Tientsin while we were there and gave us a banquet. I vaguely recall that the speech he made afterwards had us smiling cynically, for it was bombastic and made claims far beyond the reality. It was foolish to compare the literal truth with his statements and then reach the conclusion that he and the Kuomintang movement were not great and representative forces in modern China. It took years for me to realize that a situation has to be judged by the real forces which shape it, and which are a compound of many factors, political, military, economic, and moral. The words that are spoken by the statesmen representing those forces may cloak, or even deny, the realities, as we discovered in the course of time with Hitler, but it took the world, as well as myself, a long time to learn that simple truth.

At any rate, I really believe that not one of us was properly moved, at that time, by the Chinese struggle for national sovereignty or unity. I know I returned to the cable desk with a hodge-podge of ideas that showed little understanding of the true factors involved. Nevertheless, one always absorbs a great many facts and a great deal of atmosphere which may be confused and misplaced at the time but which later, in the wisdom that comes with and after events, can be put in their proper places; and that, for me, was the primary value of the junket to the Far East in 1929. I could, in the following years, reach into that grab-bag of knowledge and pick out the factors which counted.

My mind, in those years, was acting like a sponge, gradually, instinctively and almost automatically absorbing material. To do my work properly I had to achieve a certain coherency, so as to handle stories from foreign countries with some degree of intelligence, but the trouble was that I had no first-hand knowledge of what was happening anywhere, and without such knowledge there can be no valid basis for judgment. My year in Europe had been so pleasant and satisfactory that I wanted to go back and live there, and I was strengthened in this desire by my wife, Nancie, who was English. The motives were personal and professional and were not based upon any great interest in world affairs nor on any comprehension of the developments—positive in Italy and Germany, negative in England and France—which were shaping up for the catastrophes to come.

We went to Paris in November, 1931, sailing on the Hamburg-America Liner *Albert Ballin,* and were as charmed by the German officers and a young passenger, of the type which we knew later as typically Nazi, as I had been by the Japanese a few years before, and for the same reasons. Later, looking back, we were aware of having seen in miniature the drama that soon was to be enacted with sickening and disastrous effects in the whole of Germany. There was a wealthy young German Jew aboard, who threw his money around ostentatiously, "made passes" at the pretty women, including those later to be designated as "Aryan," and in general was a little loud, a little too friendly, and not too dignified. We enjoyed him, and attended his parties and would have thought nothing of it if our young pre-Nazi friend had not been so bitter and almost vicious about his "non-Aryan" compatriot. At the time it seemed nothing more than the resentment of a well bred man toward a *parvenu* whereas it was, of course, an example of that racial intolerance which Hitler was to use with such terrible effect.

The economic depression of the early 30's was the all-absorbing topic of interest, but the contributions which it made to the final catastrophe of this war are still hard to evaluate. In those days everyone thought in terms of possible social revolutions, and yet it was not the radical but the reactionary forces which triumphed everywhere. Anyway, it is axiomatic that people in the midst of economic distress do not think along political lines, however easily they may respond to them and be manipulated by demagogues who use promises of more bread and better jobs to further their own striving for power. In the straitened circumstances of home—the *res angustiae familiares* of Dante's poignant phrase—there is little incentive to play politics. Only theoretical Marxists were translating economic factors into politics, doing so without much regard to logic but at least with resultant convictions that placed them on the side of righteousness when the crucial test began in Abyssinia and, above all, in Spain.

The rest of us thought of economics in terms of our daily, personal lives. Those years of 1931 to 1935, which my family and I spent in Paris and its suburb of Garches, were the years in which our children, Eric and Priscilla, were born, and during which I was "second man" in the Paris bureau of *The Times*. Years ago a similar situation drove Walter Duranty to Moscow; in my case it was another good incentive driving me toward Abyssinia and war correspondence.

Meanwhile, I concentrated on economic developments merely to find an uncontested field where the stories were good. That was an excellent example of how newspaper work contributes to history, without in itself being history. The files of my dispatches could, I am sure, provide a great deal of factual material for those seeking light on the economic factors which played their role in the degradation of France. There you will find the sad story of a rapid budgetary collapse, only thinly veiled by the deliberate and shameful efforts of French politicians to disguise the facts. There you will find scandals, of which the outstanding one was the Stavisky affair. The permutations and combinations of so-called "high finance" fill many, many columns. So do innumerable stories on war debts and reparations—although that was primarily our stupidity, not France's.

All of it is material for history, since it helps to show the seething rottenness under the thin crust of respectability that the politicians of the time precariously maintained. Now and then the rottenness would break out, as it did in the Stavisky scandal, and, above all, in the riots of February, 1934. The moral decay was well represented by the political leaders. Men like Georges Bonnet and Pierre Laval were more conspicuous by degree and opportunity than by any fundamental difference from the others.

Those years could not help being an education—but an education, like ordinary newspaper work, can only supply the material. The important thing is what you do with it, what conclusions you reach, what judgments you make. Anyway, politics is an art; it is not a science. You cannot take the facts and add them up as you do a column of figures, to reach an exact total. In politics, the conclusions are to a large extent matters of opinion and belief. No matter how strong one's convictions are, they are still incapable of proof. Although no one in his right senses could excuse a Georges Bonnet, there are thousands of Frenchmen right now who are sincerely convinced that the policies of Laval and Pétain were not only sound but honest, and they have reached that conclusion with much the same material from which you and I have reached an opposite opinion.

Moreover, what most people normally do is to reserve judgment—or, even more commonly, they make no effort to get any of the facts. One is inclined to forget that the average person was not placed in the necessity for taking sides until this war came along—at least, he did not feel the necessity. My own reaction, in those years, was a cynical acceptance of an immoral state of affairs, immorality being the natural thing. I could have no illusions, since I was too close to what was happening, but the conclusion to which I jumped was that government is like that, and whatever one did, men like those who were ruling France would continue in power. The only thing to do was to shrug one's shoulders and base one's calculations on the strength of the men involved and the forces at their disposal. The moral condemnation could remain, but not the will to do anything about it, and a moral condemnation that remains abstract, that does not form the basis for a positive judgment, let alone for action, cannot stand up in a world where one must fight constantly against the forces of evil and gain strength in the fighting.

All the same, if cynicism and inaction are reprehensible, stupidity is even more so and I was not being stupid when I talked and wrote about the weakness and hypocrisy of the League of Nations, and the strength and progress of Japan, Italy, and Germany during those years. It always serves some purpose to call attention to realities. A good deal of our troubles today are the result of illusions harbored by worthy people who refused to face those realities. And the statesmen, primarily the appeasers, who fostered those illusions in a desire to use them to further national and party ends were even more to blame.

We shall see all these factors at work as time and these pages unfold. As far as I am concerned, I still consider my position on a question like that of Manchuria, then to the fore with the occupation by the Japanese and their subsequent withdrawal from the League of Nations, as more sensible and valid than the futile protestations of the idealists and the more or less hypocritical compromises of the statesmen.

I remember talking at the time to a French Socialist deputy, who argued that the League should adopt sanctions or make some stronger protest than was being made to Japan. "While you are talking," I said, "Japan is doing things. What you say will have no effect upon her. As far as I am concerned it is worse than a waste of breath; it is a confession of weakness." On that basis I reached the not too illogical conclusion that the action of the Japanese was less reprehensible than the gestures of their opponents. Moreover, I refused then to admit the validity of any question of ethics, basing my refusal on the belief that the Japanese action was the sort of thing one must expect of one nation or another at all times, that it was therefore natural and normal, and had to be accepted as such or met with the only reply which could have any validity in the circumstances—force. Since we were not prepared to apply force, let us realize that our protests were merely formal expressions of condemnation for the historic record, and of no practical use.

I still maintain that my position was fundamentally sound. In those years of 1931 to 1936 the issues did not touch me personally, and where I later felt willing and anxious to combat the forces which were acting evilly, I was then content to be a mere spectator, to applaud success because it was success, and to refrain from any moral judgment.

That was more or less the way I felt—without analyzing my feelings—at the time Mussolini began the Abyssinian adventure, which was to set off all those explosive forces leading inexorably to the second World War. The right or the wrong of it did not interest me greatly—not any more, let us say, than they did Laval, Eden, and the Standard Oil Company. Premier Laval, for instance, gave the Duce the go-ahead signal as early as January, 1935. British interests were imperial, and if they were also moral, the British statesmen demonstrated in the appeasement years to come that morality was an impulse to action only where it served their interests. And everyone knows what the American oil interests did during the fake sanctions period.

The invasion was going to take place whatever I did. It is the glory of American journalism that, within certain mildly restrictive limits, it can and does present "what happens" to the best of its correspondents' abilities, regardless of the moral factors involved. Judgment is left to the editorial writers and the readers. I was a journalist, and this was going to be a great story, probably the greatest since World War I, and as I spoke Italian and knew Italy I felt entitled to cover it from the Italian side.

I was, in the Dantesque sense, "in the midst of this, our mortal life," and quite capable of a hard campaign. All the old dreams were surging up, the lure of adventure, the longing to go to strange, far-away places, to face danger, to distinguish myself, to be anything but a "second man" in the Paris bureau living an uninterruptedly humdrum existence. I little realized then that I was embarking, not on one adventure but on years of adventure, on a whole career of danger, hardships and loneliness— the loneliness that any man must feel away from the ones he loves. But they have been great years, full and rich, and I would not exchange them for a lifetime of ease and safety.

Abyssinian Course

The First Lesson

I TAKE it for granted that you who are reading this were anti-Italian and pro-Abyssinian during the conquest of Ethiopia, which shows that your heart was in the right place. Of course, you were not Italians, for they, with a small percentage of exceptions, were more or less enthusiastically behind the Duce and for the most part convinced of the righteousness of their cause. We are dealing here, again, with forces and principles that are incapable of rigid definition. You—and I, too, for that matter—say that the attack on Abyssinia was a cynical and immoral deed, because it was unprovoked, because it violated freely accepted treaties, because it infringed upon the modern principle that countries have a right to govern themselves, because it was an example of the worst sort of imperialism, and there are lots of other becauses. On such bases we have a right to brand the conquest as immoral, but, having done so, one feels a possibly malicious urge to ask: "So what?"

Remember that you were pro-Abyssinian for some or all of the reasons mentioned above, plus a natural sympathy with the underdog, but remember, too, that your Government, and the British and French and other governments, did precious little to help the Abyssinians, except for some farcical sanctions which did Mussolini more good than harm. In fact, the United States, and particularly the American oil interests, actually worked to deprive the League of Nations sanctions of what little validity they might have had. Moral indignation in a righteous cause is praiseworthy, but if it takes no practical form it does not mean much.

Moreover, you have no right to pass any judgment without

first coolly weighing both sides of the case. Suppose, for argument's sake, that we become the devil's advocate.

Italy was the last, and weakest, power to grab African colonies. England and France above all, but Germany and Belgium, too, had seized all the richest portions of the vast continent except Abyssinia, leaving to Italy the barren and unhealthy strips of Eritrea and part of Somaliland. In 1911 she was able to wrest Libya from the tottering Ottoman Empire, on the flimsiest of excuses, but Libya was hardly a prize package, being nine-tenths desert.

It was argued by her opponents that what seemed natural in the dark ages of the nineteenth century, when the whole world was wickedly imperialistic, was now inexcusable. The world had outgrown such barbarism in its progress toward morality. The Italians, who are only human beings, felt that it was easy for the British and French to be moral about the colonial question after taking all they wanted, and if the world had changed in such matters in the twentieth century, how was it, they asked, that the British seized the German African colonies after World War I? The argument was very much along the lines of "if you did wrong, I am entitled to do wrong, too," but, nevertheless, it is well to keep in mind at all times the fact that nations are run by individuals, and individuals must be expected to have normal instincts, desires, and emotions. The fault is partly original sin.

In the case of Italy there was the impulsion of a large and expanding population crowded into a small and poor territory, which needed outlets for its surplus of people and yet found the doors of rich and lightly populated countries like the United States closed to her. To be sure, Mussolini deliberately made matters worse by doing everything possible to increase the population and by actually encouraging emigrants to return to Italy. However, that particular moral condemnation which he and Fascism deserve still does not alter the fact that over-population was natural and inevitable.

The Italians also had on their side arguments of what might be called "historic impulsion." In 1896 an Italian army had suffered a costly and humiliating defeat at the hands of the Abyssinians under King Menelik. It not only put an end to Italian aspirations in that part of Africa, but left a shameful blot on Italian military history. There, again, human nature must be given its due weight, and it was only human on the part of a later generation of Italians to wish to seek revenge.

This is no place for going into an involved discussion of Italian foreign policy, but it should be pointed out that Mussolini was picking up an old thread of colonial expansion, broken when Francesco Crispi retired from politics at the end of the nineteenth century, and so strong was the impulse toward expansion that Giovanni Giolitti, who was anything but an imperialist and war monger, felt impelled to yield to it in the seizure of Libya in 1911, and the Duce, himself, had to reverse all the beliefs of his youth, in which he had opposed the Libyan War and sneered at Crispi's designs. It is easy to demonstrate that any Italian aspirations to re-create another Roman Empire are not only anachronistic but are just as impossible as bringing Caesar Augustus back to life, since this is another world we are living in and history does not repeat itself, despite the popular saying. However, to deny the validity of what Georges Sorel would have called "the myth" of the Roman Empire would be silly. It will continue to return as a force impelling Italian regimes toward adventures like the conquest of Abyssinia. There it is, and if you want to be realistic you must admit the strength of the impulse, and if you make that admission you are, to a certain, if slight, extent explaining and even implicitly excusing the Italian action.

There are, of course, many other and less excusable reasons for the war, such as the common one of diverting attention from a deteriorating internal economy and that of seeking war for war's sake, but what I am doing at the moment is arguing for, and not against, the Italians. In that connection there is one other argument to advance—the utilitarian one. Italians pointed to the backward state of Ethiopia, to the misery of the inhabitants, to the existence of slavery, to the tyranny and oppression which characterized what little government there was. These were un-

deniable, and it is just as undeniable that in the five years succeeding the war the Italians did bring a measure of civilization
to Ethiopia, and the country made more material progress in
those few years than it had in many previous generations. If you
believe that it is justifiable to reach a moral end by immoral
means, then you have to give some credit to the Fascists. You
can argue, of course, that the same end could have been achieved
by other and more admirable means, but, if so, you are denying
the moral validity of a lot of history including, since we have
brought the matter up, the immense and varied benefits brought
to the ancient world by the Roman Empire.

All this is merely to demonstrate that even so apparently clean-
cut an issue as the conquest of Abyssinia was not nearly so
simple a proposition as it seemed. Only rarely in history is anything pure black or pure white. The Italian case may have been
weak—and I think it was—but no one had a right to pass judgment on it without considering it and without remembering
that elementary principle of historiography, which is that you
cannot be categorical about international politics. There are no
valid laws; there are only changing customs, generally accepted
practices and beliefs, and you, as an individual, cannot say:
"That action is right (or wrong)." You can only say: "I think
that action is right (or wrong)."

It never would have occurred to me, during the Abyssinian
War, to disagree with the moral condemnation passed by most of
the world upon Italy, because it was based upon universally
accepted principles of what is right and wrong from an ab-
stractly ethical viewpoint, but I chose at that time to deny the
validity of the moral issues involved, on the basis that everyone
directly concerned—opponents and Italians alike—was doing the
same thing. If you start from the premise that a lot of rascals
are having a fight, it is not unnatural to want to see the victory
of the rascal you like, and I liked the Italians during that scrim-
mage more than I did the British or the Abyssinians.

That was a personal reaction, for which I still make no apologies. Where I—and so many, many others—went wrong was in
not giving due weight to the consequences of Mussolini's making

Fascism "an article for export." These consequences could have been foreseen, although they were not inevitable. But there you had to start from the premise that Fascism was an evil, and I had not yet reached that point. I was merely at the stage where I was saying: "I do not want Fascism for the United States, but if the majority of Italians feel it is the government they want, they are entitled to it."

It is only by looking back, with the wisdom that comes after the event, that one can give to the progression of Fascism the inevitability of a Greek tragedy. You did not have, at that time, valid reasons for saying that Italy, Germany, and Japan must inevitably get together, clash with other powers, and bring us and every other country into a world war. At least, I could not see the elements of future war in 1935. I did in 1936, when Italy and Germany began intervening on the Franco side in the Spanish Civil War, and I was one of the first publicists to proclaim the fact and issue a warning on what was coming, but by then the issues were clearer.

In 1935 it was still fashionable to laugh at Hitler and think of him as a clown and, of course, Mussolini was even more a subject for mirth. Napoleon, in his time, was ridiculed also, but that did not make him any the less great. Human beings are incorrigible in such things; they transfer personal characteristics to the level of their next door neighbor, whose ridiculousness counts—in the neighborhood. It would be nice to think that human beings have such a sense of humor and of the esthetic that they could laugh men like Hitler and Mussolini off the stage of history before they could do any harm. But that is so far from being true that millions of Germans and Italians could not see the ridiculousness in their leaders, and many other millions—quite properly, from one viewpoint—did not care.

I bring up the subject because I happen to be one of those who felt supercilious and civilized, like the society folk who looked at "The Hairy Ape" in Eugene O'Neill's play. And, strange as it may seem now, Mussolini felt the same way about Hitler when they first met. That shows how natural such feelings are. It followed that if you felt that way about the leaders you felt that way about their regimes. They were hard to take seriously, and anybody who looks back on those years of 1933 to 1936 will surely realize how much Fascism and Nazism were being underrated.

Now you can see that the Fuehrer's entry into the demilitarized zone of the Rhineland was only the first step in a progression that ended with the invasion of Poland. Now you can put that first move into a larger picture which would contain the Japanese penetration of Manchuria and China, the "Black Biennium" (1933-1935) in Spain, and the Italian invasion of Abyssinia. You can agree with the Spanish philosopher, José Ortega y Gasset, who wrote: "The direction of society [in Europe] has been taken over by a type which is not interested in the principles of civilization."

That is the picture of the period we would draw now; it is not the picture that was being commonly or even universally drawn then. Fascism had its tenth anniversary in October, 1932, and it had, in internal affairs, a good deal to show of a constructive nature. Even granting that it was only a façade, it still looked attractive to Italians and the rest of the world. The Duce had words of peace on his lips then and for another three years. In 1934, great European statesmen—Ramsay MacDonald, Sir John Simon, Von Papen, Goering, Dollfus—all made tracks to Rome. Premier Daladier paid homage to the Duce as a man of peace. The four-power pact of Italy, Germany, France, and Great Britain was signed in Rome on July 15, 1934. Earlier had come the "Rome Protocols" of Italy, Austria, and Hungary, and in April, 1935, the Stresa Pact in which England, France, and Italy expressed their desire to reach an international accord on the reduction of armaments.

That was the picture at which most people were looking. Few could go behind the scenes to learn that the era of appeasement had already begun with the French and British refusing to give Mussolini any assurances at Stresa that they would lift a finger to help Austra if or when Hitler made his expected move in that direction. Few were aware of the fact that they were already exercising appeasement toward the Duce, himself, who, at the time he signed the Stresa accord, was feverishly building up large forces in Eritrea and Somaliland with which to invade Abyssinia.

This is all very confusing, no doubt, and perhaps a little dull, but it was part of an education—yours, as well as mine. Laval was cynically indifferent to what was going to happen. Eden, and many others, thought the Duce was bluffing, that the League of Nations, the pressure of world opinion, and the British fleet in the Mediterranean would stop the Italians. The newspaper world was so unprepared that it took one of the worst beatings of the century.

I was on the train from Paris to Rome on October 2, 1935, when the great *"adunata"* was held in all the cities, towns, and villages of Italy, and Mussolini announced from the balcony of the Palazzo Venezia that Italian patience was exhausted, and long-suffering, civilized Italy was being forced to take measures against those dangerous, wicked savages. It was the fable of the wolf and the lamb all over again, but the Duce was never squeamish about insulting the general intelligence. He fooled enough people for his purposes and, on the whole, there was more directness and less hypocrisy on his part than representatives of democracy were to exercise in the coming period.

My own sentiments at the time were purely professional. All I cared about was to get to Abyssinia as quickly as possible, and I was willing to leave the moral issues to the moralists. I will never get over a profound conviction that only acts count, that only the possible is worth trying, that life is adaptation and compromise, that common sense demands we should make the best of a bad world. No Utopias, no myths and no bunkum! If I failed to take up cudgels for the lamb in this situation (which it was not my business to do, in any case) at least I did not contribute at any time in the war to befuddling the issues by ignoring, distorting, or hiding the realities.

No one dealing with those realities could take the League sanctions seriously. Indeed, if anything at the time called for a debunking process, that was it. British public opinion was genuinely and profoundly aroused on behalf of the Ethiopians, which suited the Government's policy, since Empire issues of great importance were involved. It must never be forgotten that the Abyssinian War was a three-cornered struggle whose European angle was a clash between the British and the Italians. Abyssinia lay athwart the Cape-to-Cairo route; it contained the source of the Blue Nile, in Lake Tana and, in general, was strongly subject to British influence. The Italian invasion was the first of many successful twistings of the Lion's tail and the first practical demonstration that the moral fiber of the British ruling class had deteriorated seriously. The loss of British prestige was one of the important results of the war, and the failure of sanctions was the first blow.

I was anti-League in those days on the same old principle that the League was an example of trying the impossible and under the shelter of proclaimed ideals was nothing but an instrument of the great powers, particularly England and France. Now I would admit that in spite of its handicaps it did more good than harm and made some advance toward a desired internationalism, but in 1935 I could see, and I wanted, nothing but nationalism. Anyone who closed his eyes then, or who closes his eyes now, to the overwhelming strength of nationalism as this second World War ends, is going to move just as far away from reality as the League champions did at the end of the last war, so there is no need to apologize too much for years spent in ridiculing the Geneva effort. If those who felt as I did can be accused of lacking idealism and faith, the others are open to the criticism of being the dupes of the more practical statesmen and presenting the world with a resounding failure of the international ideal.

Sanctions unhappily provided a good example of how the League of Nations worked. They were ratified by fifty-two states on November 18, 1935, a black date in European history, for sanctions unified Italians behind the Duce by providing a motive for patriotism and a common grievance against the world. Sanctions started Italy on the path that was to lead to the Axis and convinced Mussolini of the need to pursue a program of economic self-sufficiency, disastrous in its consequences.

And the sanctions were all for nothing, since the Abyssinians did not profit in any way. They were not furnished with arms and Italy was not deprived of the only materials which could have affected the course of the war—oil, coal, iron, steel, and cotton—which were carefully excluded from the sanctions. Brazil, Germany, and Japan had already quit the League and the United States was never a member, so they were not bound by the sanctions and made the most of the situation. It was all of a piece with the bluff that the British Government was making in the Mediterranean, where it ostentatiously concentrated a part of its fleet. Mussolini was already so sure of what soon was to be called "appeasement" that he could safely laugh inwardly at the fleet, and in public take credit on behalf of Italy for daring, determination, and military strength.

I cannot see that those of us who laughed with the Duce at the British and the League were to be blamed very much, even though it may have been a case of two wrongs not making a right. At least, there were more honesty and common sense, and less hypocrisy, on our side. On board the Italian troopship *Gange* we all read bulletins about the League as if we were reading spirit messages from another world. It never seemed to occur to any of the soldiers around me that anything Geneva decided could affect them or their task in Africa, and obviously they were right.

A moral issue of another sort arose at the end of the year, with the publication of the so-called Hoare-Laval proposal. That was a compromise which would have left the Negus with a central nucleus of his Empire and at the same time given Italy a large part of Abyssinia. Public opinion in England rose vigorously against it, led by the press and a chorus of howls from the world at large. So, in the name of morality the Abyssinians were deprived of their one chance to save a part of their territory. Britishers still talk with pride of their defense of right and justice on that issue, blandly overlooking the price which the Ethiopians paid. If the world is going to be run on that sort of morality, God help us all! The only defensible attitude at the time was to say: "Yes, this is an immoral proposal put forth by two especially cynical politicians, but in the circumstances we shall have to sacrifice abstract moral standards, since our intention and desire is to help the Abyssinians. We cannot serve the cause of justice by harming them."

However, that was too much to expect of human nature, especially as the outside world persisted in blinding itself to the realities of the situation in Ethiopia. After the war ended everybody said: "Of course the Italians won. They had a push-over. The Abyssinians never had a chance." Which conveniently overlooked the fact that during the campaign these same people swallowed with gusto the tall tales that came out of Addis Ababa and refused to believe the simple, first-hand accounts that we were sending from the Italian side.

That was my first lesson in the difficulty of convincing people of truths that they do not want to believe. (My education in that respect was even more discouraging in the Spanish Civil War, but, at least, by that time I knew what to expect.) One can take some comfort in the knowledge that "truth will prevail" in the long run, but only too often the damage has already been done. Eden himself sadly admitted in the House of Commons after the Abyssinian War that "there was a miscalculation by military opinion in most countries that the conflict would last very much longer than it has in fact done." Yet the most elementary trust in the neutral journalists who were following the campaign would have convinced anybody that the Italians were going to win without too much difficulty.

Our primary handicap lay in the fact that few people wanted to believe us, since their sympathies were with the Ethiopians. There would have been little harm in that if the Abyssinians had restricted themselves to a truthful presentation of events and, instead of claiming victories or denying defeats right up to the end, had shown the world the desperate nature of their predicament.

After the very first encounter, at Adowa, correspondents in far-away Addis Ababa sent lurid accounts, furnished by the Abyssinians, of a counterattack by Ras Seyoum, who surprised the Italians in their sleep and "made a carnage among them."

All that the boys on the spot could do was to send a true account of the casualties: six Italians, twenty-five Askaris killed, seventy wounded in all corps, in the whole Adowa engagement. Yet on October 6 one of the most important and serious of the London Sunday newspapers had this to say: "The casualties on both sides have been very heavy. One estimate puts the losses as 1,300 Ethiopians and 700 Italians killed."

One factor, of course, is the incorrigible belief on the part of editors and the public that when there is a censorship the truth cannot be sent. As a general statement, nothing could be more false. Censorship can prevent the sending of news from a particular spot at a particular time, but it cannot force correspondents to send falsehoods. When reputable correspondents examine a situation on the spot and make positive statements about it, those statements can be accepted whether they have gone through a censorship or not. If errors occur they are due to the mistaken judgments of the correspondents, not to the censor.

These elementary considerations are singularly important in a world which depends upon newspapers, magazines, and the radio for its news. Of course, there are only too many fakers in the game and they do a distressing amount of faking, which consists in claiming to have done things and to have been in places where they were not, and presenting second-hand or imaginary information as eyewitness. That is another, and also very important, problem to which you have no other guide than your knowledge of the reliability of the correspondent and his organization, as well as your common sense. However, the faking of news concerns particular incidents and does not affect the presentation or validity of the general news coverage of a big story like a war.

In Abyssinia (and later in Spain) there were two versions of the same developments. First, there were men working often on the spot, while the other side rarely got away from Addis Ababa and there were no eyewitnesses with the Ethiopians in any of the battles. Moreover, the events as they unfolded proved the veracity of the Italian version.

Take, for instance, the first battle of the Tembien, which oc-

curred in January, 1936. Ras Kassa and Ras Seyoum launched a
heavy attack against the Italian center near Hauzien, with the
the laudable purpose, from the point of view of good strategy,
of cutting the liaison between the right and the left of the
Italian Army, massed at Axum and Makale, respectively. They
came very close to success and inflicted heavy losses on the
Italians, but in the end they failed. Marshal Badoglio told us
about it afterwards, and we talked to some officers who had been
in the engagement. Any experienced newspaperman knows the
extent to which he can trust his sources, and he becomes a
judge of character in that respect. We ascribed the story to
Badoglio and our other sources, and we believed them. Addis
Ababa broadcast a version of the battle as a great Ethiopian
victory.

The public had the choice of believing one or the other version or reserving judgment, and for readers far away the latter
choice was the sounder. Then as the course of the war unfolded
itself within a few weeks and the truth of the Italian version
became apparent, it should have effected credence in future
stories of the war. Instead, the public in general went on believing the Ethiopians and discrediting the Italians—or, at best,
refused to believe either side.

This is not a question of personal pique. The problem involved is too serious. In the case of the Abyssinian War this attitude on the part of the public did tremendous harm to the
side that most people wanted to help, and in Spain the results
of a similar attitude contributed its part to the preparations
for the second World War.

Lest anyone think I am exaggerating about Ethiopia, let him
consider what happened almost at the end, when Dessye had
been taken and we were all on the final march which was to
take us unopposed to Addis Ababa within a few weeks. Our
caravan halted on the road one night, and we listened, over a
field radio set, to the news broadcast from London. It had been
reported, said the voice, that Dessye was occupied by the Italians,
but since Addis had denied it, listeners were cautioned to reserve
judgment. It was admitted that the Abyssinian position was

"rather difficult," but that concession was followed by an account of a battle which had supposedly taken place just north of Quoram, where a large force of Ethiopians had attacked the Italian army and had presumably halted its advance. We thought it over, and realized that this mythical battle was taking place on the exact spot where we were peaceably spending the night!

It was amazing, later, to realize that even at that stage people did not know that the war was virtually over. The lesson for me, as a newspaperman, was a discouraging one. The first categorical story I sent, in January, that the Italians were unquestionably going to win the war, resulted in my being labeled as a Fascist, probably in the pay of the Italians. In the Spanish War I was a Communist getting Moscow gold. In India I was, at the very least, the dupe and probably the tool of the British. Such is life for a newspaperman, but since the accusations always cancel out in the course of time, no harm is done to the individual. It is the reader who loses out by getting a false idea of a situation, because an objective account of it disagrees with his conceptions and desires. And because the truth is not believed and the facts are not faced, the cause of right and justice is inevitably harmed, as it was in Abyssinia.

I have been, throughout my career, an exponent of the necessity for getting news on the spot. Once I got abroad it took me very little time to learn that a situation cannot be understood safely and properly at any distance from the sources of what is happening. For instance, when you are in Paris you cannot know what is going on in Brussels, nor can you stay on a frontier and cover events in the capital of the neighboring country. No news that is not first-hand is worth any more than the source to which it is ascribed. It would amaze readers to know how inaccurate are the reports picked up at any army headquarters during a campaign. Only soldiers and correspondents actually at the front know what has happened, and they merely know their own restricted sectors. It is not until all the frontline stories are collated that a true picture can be drawn—and by then, days have passed.

I, and others in the same game, have isolated ourselves, in the past decade, for long stretches from the world, so that at any given moment we would have had only a fraction of the general news which you read in your newspapers—but, at least, what we have is solid. For the most part it will not make the front pages, which are reserved (to take the case of war corresponding again) for the man at headquarters who gives you a complete picture, embroidered by the material of handouts and often embellished by an imagination which is not hindered, as in the case of the front-line correspondent, by the hard facts. Such stories do not even provide the material for history, which historians will get from official communiques and from a collation of eye-witness accounts.

This is a digression, a sort of lesson in journalism, but one worth learning, and it is pertinent to the subject under discussion. If you, as readers, could not be in Abyssinia covering the campaign, you could, at least, have given your credence to those chroniclers who saw things with their own eyes. In the case of that war, it is true that, largely for geographical and technical reasons, those of us on the Italian side were able to follow the campaign at first hand, and those on the Ethiopian side were not. It should have been elementary common sense to trust our version more than the Abyssinian one, particularly as the course of events bore out the truth of our accounts.

The turning point in the war, which should have opened all eyes to what was coming, was the battle of Amba Aradam in February, 1936. It was the first great battle of the war, and it was decisive. Some of us were lucky enough to see it, and I want to tell you about it in the next chapter, to emphasize the points I have been making, but also because it gives a good idea of my own attitude toward war in general and the Abyssinian War in particular, and it was an interesting step in my education.

A good deal had happened before that battle. The *Gange* landed at Massawa, Italy's fetid, desolate Red Sea port. This was my first contact with the discomforts of war and the tropics. At 18, before the effects of civilized life soften body and spirit, one has a resilience which makes army life relatively easy to bear, as even I discovered in World War I. To step into the fiery hell of Massawa at the age of 35 was another thing, but it taught me again that my instincts had not misled me. The miseries that often came in the years of wars which were beginning then never had the effect of canceling out the joys and satisfactions of war corresponding.

Abyssinia gave me its peculiar trials, as well as the normal ones. Most of the war was fought on the plateau at heights of 6,000 to 11,000 feet. So near the equator, the rarity of the atmosphere is so intensified that in terms of strain on the heart, lungs, and nerves, the effect was comparable to that of an altitude of 10,000 to 15,000 feet in the temperate zone. The difference between midday and midnight was often as much as 70 degrees. In Dankalia and on the seacoast I was to encounter temperatures as high as 140 in the shade; it was so hot that one gasped for breath, but I never minded heat very much. The intense cold of the nights on the plateau was much more bothersome to me.

So was the dust. One hears much about the role of mud in wars, but the other extreme of dust is equally common and very distressing in its way. The campaign in Abyssinia was fought in a constant cloud of dust which choked and blinded one and covered clothes in layers. One has to live through wars to discover what an astonishing amount of punishment the human body can take. I often wondered how lungs could stand up under the quantities of dust that have to be swallowed. In the invasion of Italy, from the Salerno beachhead up to Naples, we lived in a world of dust.

My own peculiar phobia is the common, ornery fly, and yet for a decade fate has tossed me into the most fly-ridden portions of the globe, and, of all such portions, Ethiopia takes the prize. War has no horror for me greater than that. I have had lice and bedbugs and fleas and similar pests galore, and have borne them philosophically. The ants and the cockroaches of a tropical country like India can be intensely annoying, but they do not give me the shudders and creeps. I have lived in the filth of camps and amidst the stink of dead bodies and could take them stoically, but I never could stand flies.

In a sense, I feel like adding bad food to the list of the

horrors of war, because I love food dearly and have a delicate palate. One of the things I am living for is to go back to Paris in peace times for lunch at La Rue on the Place de la Madeleine, or for a *chateaubriand* at the Cochon d'Or or pressed duck at the Tour d'Argent or *tripes à la môde de Caen* and one of Albert's inimitable salads at Pharamond in the Halles. And always some delicate French vintage wine, the only wine that is worth drinking in this benighted world. Yes, indeed, these are things to live for! So can a man wash away the pain of these years, even if only momentarily.

But they will taste so much better for this long deprivation! That, for me, has always been the saving grace of these many campaigns—that and a naturally good appetite which provides the necessary sauce for disguising the worst of food. When I used to come out of Spain during the Civil War after four or five months of campaigning, the food was better for me at Cannes, Nice, Paris, or London than it was for any of those gourmets who had been eating it all along.

I must say that usually I had enough to eat in these wars. The American Army in this conflict is extraordinarily well fed as armies go, much better fed now than we were in the first World War. The food is frequently unappetizing and it does get monotonous, but it is healthy and quantitatively satisfying. In Abyssinia we lived out of cans of food. Those were the days before vitamin pills, but I do not recall anyone suffering for the lack of them.

My one and only trial from hunger was on the Danakil journey I made in November, 1935. I was out with an Italian flying column on a perilous journey across Dankalia and up to the plateau, flanking the main army under General Santini, which was parading down to Makale. We were ambushed in a gorge half way up, fought the most sanguinary encounter of the war to that date, and escaped massacre by the narrowest of margins. From the time the battle began, many of us were separated from the supply train, and we had to go on for four days without food and with little water. It was a hard march, but when it ended there were bowls of minestrone, large hunks of meat and bread, with wine and coffee to wash it all down. I have rarely eaten with more gusto, and at the end I was none the worse for wear.

That battle in Ende Gorge, incidentally, was my baptism of fire—seventeen years after the World War ended, a long wait, but the results were satisfying, for I was no more afraid than I should have been. Fear under danger is the natural emotion; courage is will power and the control of one's nerves with which you hold that fear in check and act contrary to its dictates. Now and then, in moments of great exultation there is a joy in battle and danger which sweeps away fear, and those are great moments in a man's life. I felt it often in Spain, and a few times in Italy and France. It is the caveman coming out, I suppose.

There was little physical danger in Abyssinia, except for that ambush in which there was only one other correspondent, an Italian, beside myself. The circumstances of the war were such that battles had to be followed from observation posts and field headquarters. The casualties of the war were due to disease and nerve strain, not bullets, shells and bombs, of which the Ethiopians had little. The Battle of Amba Aradam was typical of the way in which those of us who stuck it out through the long weeks of confinement in Asmara covered the war.

Marshal Pietro Badoglio, who took over in November, found things in a dangerous mess. This was due to Mussolini's desire to make a Fascist war of it. He put General Emilio de Bono, Quadrumvir of the March on Rome, in charge, with results that were almost catastrophic. Before the Marshal arrived we could, and did, go where we pleased—to the original front of Adigrat, Adowa and Axum, to Makale, and even, in my case, out of the country to Khartoum in the Sudan.

To be sure, there was not much to be seen in Eritrea and what little of Abyssinia the Italians held. Places with lovely names like Adi Ugri and Adi Qualà were nothing but squalid, filthy native villages. Even an ancient center of culture like Axum had come so far from its early glory that almost nothing of interest remained. The romance of the tropics is rarely on the surface—and only too often it is nonexistent. I remember our first disillusionment when we got off the boat at Massawa; we had been looking for something exotic, and perhaps wicked, such as Hollywood had led us to believe was to be found in all ports east of Suez. Asmara, neither African nor European, was just as bad.

Romance there is in plenty in tropical lands, but it is subtle. It penetrates the senses in odd ways; it is a delicate, musky perfume, a palm tree against moonlit waters, a bronzed and glistening body, the flash of a vividly colored bird, the languor of a soft sea breeze on warm nights, the near brilliance of the stars over sandy wastes.

Abyssinia had all that, but you were more conscious of it down on the Red Sea coast or inland, where the Sudanese desert spreads to the foot-hills of the plateau. Up there on the roof of Africa is some of the most stupendous scenery in the world—if that be romance. I have seen much that the world has to offer in that regard. I have flown over the hump of the Himalayas from Assam into China and once straight up to Kanchanjanga, second highest mountain of the world, and gazed from there at Everest. In Afghanistan I looked up at the Pamirs which, indeed, form "the roof of the world." And, yet, I would give the palm to Abyssinia.

After I returned to New York from Ethiopia I was often asked to say what the region looked like, but I could only babble incoherently of deep bowls and chasms, of fantastically shaped *ambas* and jagged mountain ranges, of flat sands, lava beds and stretches of lovely, rolling green. There was something stupendous about that great eroded land, into one small corner of which the whole Grand Canyon of the Colorado could be put. A majestic and fantastic land that any nation might be proud to conquer and desolated to lose.

I was to see more of it in those seven months than any other correspondent—or any Italian officer, for that matter, with perhaps a few exceptions. But there was that deadly period of ten weeks, while Badoglio was getting ready, which we had to spend cooped up in Asmara. That is the sort of thing which tries a newspaperman's soul—ten weeks without a story worth writing or, on many long stretches, without any story at all. We started that stretch with well over one hundred correspondents, and ended it with about twenty.

Only one human interlude broke the monotony, Christmas Eve on a hospital ship in Massawa harbor. That was the first of all those Christmases away from the three whose place is where my home is. On Christmas Day an engagement was fought in the Tembien. An Italian column was ambushed and a number of men were killed as it fought its way out. A priest stopped to give absolution to a wounded man, and as he knelt, an Abyssinian dashed up and split his head open with a heavy scimitar. Peace on earth, and good will to men! But there has not been a Christmas of peace since that day.

The Marshal was almost ready by mid-January, and he called us down to his headquarters at Enda Jesus, across the valley from the towering mass of Amba Aradam. There we spent four weeks roaming around and meeting with some mild adventures on odd occasions. And there, on February 10, 1936, the Battle of Amba Aradam began.

The Battle of Amba Aradam

I F YOU have not seen a battle your education has been somewhat neglected—for, after all, war has ever been one of the primary functions of mankind, and unless you see men fight you
miss something fundamental. The Battle of Amba Aradam gave
me an important part of my education, being the first major
battle that I saw. But it was also a factor in the education of
the world, as it was the first fight of any importance in the west
since the end of World War I. Besides, it had that sort of symbolic importance which gives a decisive quality to some battles.
For those who had eyes to see, that victory meant a great deal;
it decided the question of who was going to win the Abyssinian
War, and the winning of that war permitted the next adventure,
in Spain, which, in turn, led smoothly and horribly into the
second World War.

So I want you to see Amba Aradam as well as I can describe it.
By the time of the battle there were only three American correspondents and one English left in Abyssinia—Reynolds Packard
of the United Press, Edward F. Neil of the Associated Press,
Christopher Holme of Reuters, and I. I was sharing Packard's
amazing tent. It had been acquired at Jibuti, and was possibly
the most expensive and intricate little tent in history. It was a
complete departure from the ordinary in looks, shape, and com-
ponent parts, and no one ever learned the combination of it
except Packard himself, who generally got nervous prostration
setting it up and taking it down with the aid of a platoon of
soldiers.

They began by taking a few dozen metal bars and constructing
first a top and then a hexagonal set of walls. That resulted in

something like the steel framework of a miniature cathedral. Then a covering of heavy green cloth was swung over it and fastened down by any number of spikes in myriad little holes running round the bottom. The next step was to hook the inside intricately into place. It was a one-piece affair which fitted snugly around the framework, and covered the whole ground space inside. That, said Pack, made it snake-proof. At night you tied yourself in, with much complication, and trusted that no sudden call of nature or attack by Ethiopians would necessitate a quick escape, for without a sharp knife to hack one's way through the walls there was no swift way out. By day the inside flap was rolled up, and the outer one was supported, like an awning, by another intricate combination of steel bars, ropes, and spikes. In the center, on the top, was a shining metal ball which, with fitting magnificence, capped the apex of a truly wondrous structure.

It had taken Badoglio a long time to make up his mind. That methodical, cautious way of working, that insistence on having every detail prepared in advance, helped to make Badoglio a good general, but in the most critical time of his career and that of modern Italy's—the forty-five days between the fall of Mussolini on July 25, 1943, and the armistice of September 8—it was to prove a handicap from which his country suffered cruelly.

Ras Mulugheta and his force had to be blasted out of Amba Aradam; fortunately for the Italians he waited until every single detail of the marshal's plans was ripe. We correspondents were getting bored and filthy sitting around waiting for something to happen. Bridge was our salvation, and we stopped playing only long enough to eat and sleep. And at last, on February 9, Badoglio summoned us all and announced that on the following day he would begin his operations. We were getting what I thought then was remarkable service, for he not only patiently explained to us his general plan of battle, but promised us that we should watch it from the same observation posts as he did, and that each evening he would have his Assistant Chief of Staff, General Cona, explain the events of the day. In Spain we developed a much better technique for covering battles; it consisted in following up the "briefing" by going into action, more or less, with the troops. That is the technique adopted by all conscientious war correspondents in World War II, but it had not been developed so early as the days of the war in Abyssinia.

Badoglio explained that the battle to come would be fought exclusively by white Italian troops, with no Askaris taking part except as a reserve force which he did not expect to use. Pitted against the 70,000 Italians of the Sabauda, January 3d, Sila, March 23d, and Val Pusteria Alpini Divisions, with the Assietta and First Eritrean Divisions as reserve, was Ras Mulugheta's force, which the Italians estimated at 80,000. It was an exaggerated guess, I should imagine, but there was no possibility of getting an accurate figure. Judging from the way the battle and the casualties worked out, and adding substantially to the understatements from Addis, I should say there were at least 50,000 Ethiopians on and around the *amba,* which had been heavily fortified. It was an immensely strong position by nature, and the Abyssinians had had several months to systematize it and build trenches. Strategically it was vital to them, for it commanded the only good passage to the Tembien, and they had been using it steadily as a base of operations. So it was obvious that they were going to throw every ounce of their strength into holding it. The plan of battle involved two masses making a pincer-like movement around Amba Aradam and joining at the town of Antalò on the southern slopes of the huge mountain.

We woke to the roar of the bombing planes on Monday morning, while the full moon still hung high above Amba Aradam. So the curtain rose in spectacular fashion, and yet it was a dull day. We were up at Badoglio's observation post as soon as the light came, shivering in the early cold and munching bars of chocolate that I had dug up in Makale. Like the cannon and the shells that were blasting the sides of Aradam, they had come all the way from Italy. The Marshal's post was on Amba Gheden, just above Doghea Pass. To the right it commanded the whole valley of Gabat, and to the left a series of low hills overlooking the Plain of Buia, while directly in front was the depression which hid Shelikot and the eastern end of Amba Aradam around which ran the road that led south to Amba Alagi.

At the zero hour of eight the Sabauda Division on our left moved forward some ten miles, occupying without incident the low line of hills over the plain. At the same time the January 3d Black Shirts went through Doghea Pass at our feet, halting a few miles short of Shelikot. From our post we could see interminable lines of soldiers and thousands of heavily laden mules crawling like so many lazy ants down the valleys and up the hills, while the roads behind us were choked with trucks. Every road and every path was "one way," except for some dozens of inhabitants of Shelikot who, warned by the Italians, came through the Italian lines to safety. On the flying field behind us the reconnaissance and bombing planes rose by the dozen, flew high over head, and gyrated above the *amba* like a swarm of flies. Returning pilots would report, and the telephone would soon ring on Amba Gheden. It was always the same story—intense activity on the *amba,* as well as around the town of Antalò behind it. We knew then that Mulugheta's force was not retreating, but preparing feverishly to meet the Italian advance.

It was rather boring. By noon, both wings of the "pincers" had reached their objectives without a shot being fired, and we were told that the show was over for the day. So we continued the battle over the bridge table all that afternoon at our camp at Enda Jesus.

That night it rained heavily, and every day that week it rained hard, greatly impeding the Italian advance and making conditions there much more difficult for every soldier, as well as making the problem of supplies extremely complicated. It was an extraordinary occurrence, for the "little rainy season" was not due, and heavy rains were exceptional there at that time of the year.

It gave us something to complain about, too, as we slithered along the road to Doghea Pass. The artillery was getting under way in full force with a heavy barrage laid down by the 149's, 105's, 75's and 70's on the upper mass of Aradam. Right at the pass there was a battery which we watched for a few minutes, until the noise became distressing. Later I learned they were using tear-gas shells. As far as I know, that was the only time gas was used during the battle. As in all the big battles, once they started there was no need for gas, which would, in any case, have proved dangerous to the Italian troops as they advanced.

It is well known that the Italians used mustard gas on other occasions during the war. This was stupid of them, because it made little difference to the outcome, and rightly brought down worldwide condemnation on them. I myself could not see the logical objection to using gas in warfare, and after what we have witnessed in the present great conflict there is even less basis for its condemnation. However, it is instinctive to want to see wars cleanly fought, and gas is a dirty weapon. The objection is sentimental, not logical, for the world has ever recognized that "all is fair in love and war."

The roar of the guns was a sound that never stopped for five days, except during the nights, for an enormous line of Italian artillery was heavily engaged at all times. Badoglio was a fiend for artillery. He brought shipload after shipload down from Italy, while foreign military experts scoffed. And then he won battles with them.

But there was no fighting of importance on Tuesday, and we soon got bored again. The Sabauda, to our left, carried their line further south, while the January 3d, just in front of us, made a remarkable two-and-a-half-hour dash across the Gabat, swarming through and around Shelikot, and then climbing the lower eastern end of Aradam to the village of Taga Taga. There they occupied a prominent mound, which became famous in the campaign under the name of the "Priest's Hat," for it was there, the next day, that the bitterest fighting of the entire battle took place. The Ethiopians made no effort to stop them, and when we ran into Badoglio that evening he expressed himself as highly pleased with his army's "perfect discipline, order and speed across an extremely difficult terrain." However, the enemy still held their position, making it more and more evident that they were prepared to fight it out.

But they did nothing to make life interesting for us that day, and we spent most of the time playing bridge again. Battles were fought much better in the movies, it seemed to us. In fact, the four of us (Packard, Neil, Holme and I) conspired to oversleep the next morning, and let our more conscientious colleagues get a two-hour start. To vary the monotony, we were all spending the morning at an observation post which went under the name of "l'Albero Isolato." By some freak of nature, a magnificent *euphorbia candelabra* had taken seed and flourished exactly at the top of an *amba* that dominated the whole western approach to Amba Aradam, with a sweep that carried the eye far over to the Semien on our right and the Tembien to the northwest behind us. From there we were watching the pincers' right wing, composed chiefly of the Sila Division.

Stationed at the post was a battery of 77's, while another was at the foot of the hill just to our right. They amused us for quite a while.

In front of us, the Sila Division was moving across the valley of the Gabat and then crawling up the other side toward the Plain of Zalcabà which gave access to the western end of the *amba*. The day's objective was a hog's back that ran for miles along the edge of the plain. The previous day the right wing had not moved. The Ethiopians had expected them to come on and had concentrated a heavy force on the hog's back, which dominated that whole sector and provided an advantageous position. However, discouraged by the artillery bombardment, and seeing no Italians come, they withdrew. So the next day, when the Sila did advance, the Abyssinians were caught by surprise and the ridge was virtually undefended. We watched the men and mules crawl painfully up its steep side, expecting from moment to moment that they would be forced to deploy and fight their way up, but they reached the top before a shot was fired. The enemy hastily threw a force against them, but half-heartedly and too late. As a result, the Sila won their objective with a loss of only nine men.

The colonel in command of the post had, very nobly, invited us to share lunch with him. It started to pour, giving us an added incentive for joining him. A shelter had been rigged behind the hill, with a telephone for the colonel. He and the rest of us were conquering an excellent mound of fetuccine, which Packard named "Amba Spaghetti," when the telephone rang. The colonel put down a forkful, and groaned: "Why can't they leave me alone?" He picked up the phone, listened for a moment, and finally said, testily: "Don't bother me; we'll see later." Someone asked what was the matter. "A concentration of Abyssinians was spotted in the village of Dansa, near the ridge," he answered, "and they want me to disperse them."

And then we had some native beef. The colonel cut himself a juicy morsel and was just lifting it to his mouth when the telephone rang again. "*Accidente,* blankety-blank-blank," said he; "this is terrible." Once more he picked up the telephone, and angrily inquired why he was being disturbed. This time he answered, unhappily: "Oh, all right, I'll be up." It was the superior command on Amba Gheden, asking why Dansa was not being shelled. The colonel looked sadly at his uneaten meat, sighed, and left us.

In three minutes our shelter shook to the roar of the batteries, and I wondered idly, between mouthfuls, how many Ethiopians would not have died, and how many would not have been wounded, if they had only let the colonel finish his plate of meat. It was my first realization that war is truly like a game of chess in which men have no more value than inanimate pawns.

The rain was coming down in torrents when we went back to our post of observation. The only shelter was a little open shed which had been set up to camouflage the telescopes of the colonel and his staff. They probably thought it was more important to look through the glasses and tend to their jobs than to take care of us. But the battle was far away and did not seem at all real, whereas the rain was very wet indeed. Packard, Neil, Holme and I looked at one another with a common thought:

"How about going back for a game of bridge?" said I.

Does this seem very frivolous to you? And yet the battle before us was a great one, gallantly fought on both sides. We played bridge while men suffered horribly and died, but we had plenty of historic precedents. There was a French correspondent who resented our frivolity. He seemed to feel that if the soldiers suffered we should suffer too, but he himself reduced the principle to the absurd by refusing to take shelter during a heavy shower because so many thousands of soldiers would be unable to do so. We did not like him, and we were all for suggesting that he should go out and get himself shot, just to be thoroughly logical.

While we were fooling around the Isolated Tree, the heaviest fighting of the battle was taking place at the "Priest's Hat," where the January 3d Blackshirts were fiercely attacked by the Ethiopians under cover of the morning mist hanging over the top part of Amba Aradam. It was a bitterly fought, hand-to-hand engagement, in which the Italians lost ninety men. Gradually, the enemy, fighting viciously step by step, were pushed back toward the upper levels of the *amba*. It was slow, exhausting work for the Blackshirts, who pressed on all morning. At 1:30 Badoglio, receiving reports and watching the course of the battle through his powerful telescope, decided to rush up reinforcements, and two battalions of Alpini—Italy's finest troops and ranked with the best mountain fighters in the world—swarmed up the eastern end of Aradam. Joining the Blackshirts beyond the "Priest's Hat," they broke the Ethiopian resistance, permitting the Italians to reach their objective, the Plain of Enda Gader, by 4:30. They then held the whole eastern side of the *amba* up to the immense, fortress-like top.

The Ethiopians had fought with ferocity and disdain of danger, having as many as 25,000 men involved against an equal number of Italians, without counting the reserves. For the first time in the war the enemy had brought up guns. They had two batteries, composed of six and four 75's respectively, which they used with surprising skill, disabling some Italian machine guns. General Cona, telling us that evening about the day's fighting, lifted his hat in symbolic tribute to a gallant foe.

The Sabauda also moved forward again, reaching their objectives without trouble as early as nine in the morning. By evening the Italian pincers had made a tactical junction of their two masses in front of the *amba*, but the enormous top had still to be taken, as well as Antalò and the whole southern side of the mountain.

During all that night it rained heavily again, while Packard and I slept snugly in our warm tent. The next morning Badoglio decided that enough was enough, and he gave orders that the troops were to rest for two days—if the Ethiopians would let them. Meanwhile, the engineering corps was to repair the damage to the roads. The rain had almost ruined communications, for even the main artery of communication from Adigrat was not then prepared for the rainy season. Trucks, instead of taking four hours to Makale, were taking twelve, while all the roads and paths just behind the front had become quagmires. Moreover, the troops were exhausted, for they were fighting on a steep and very rough terrain at an altitude of 7,000 or 8,000 feet. On Wednesday alone 129 Italians had been killed and 275 wounded.

So Thursday and Friday were devoted to consolidation of positions, entrenchment, the bringing up of more artillery, the repairing of the roads and paths, and guarding against surprise attacks by the Ethiopians. In fact, one such occurred on Thursday afternoon at Adi Acheiti, when about 2,500 Abyssinians, armed with machine guns and light artillery, attacked the 46th Infantry of the Sabauda Division, on the left. The waiting Italians, however, were in entrenched and fortified positions, and they beat the attack off easily, with the loss of only eighteen killed and sixty-four wounded. The Ethiopian losses were many times heavier, perhaps as many as 300, for the obvious reason that the assault was made against machine gun and artillery positions in their usual mass formation.

Time hung so heavily on our hands during the interval that we organized a trip to Shelikot on Thursday afternoon, between bridge games. As we rolled down to the level of Shelikot we noticed a group of men digging up the ground, and fresh crosses stuck on loosely packed mounds. A representative of the official Luce Photographic Service was with us and wanted to take some pictures, so we stopped our cars and walked over.

These were the dead of Amba Aradam, brought down from

the mountain that will forever tower above their graves. A shallow trench was still open, and a half dozen bodies had been laid side by side. Two soldiers had just started to throw the earth back on them; the first figure was completely covered, the second half so. There were burlap rugs over the faces, but the bodies were still dressed in torn and dirty uniforms, red now with blood. The emergency dressings on their wounds were still in place, for these were men who had been fatally wounded, and who had lived only long enough to reach the field hospital, and there die. Five or six other bodies, in the terrifying limpness of death, lay on the ground outside the trench. Every body was shod, even in the ditch, and every pair of feet stuck out, some of them crossed, with an apparent nonchalance that was infinitely pathetic.

We stood there, in silent and embarrassed tribute, for a few moments. These soldiers had come far from their homes and families and had died in a hard-fought victory. I felt then that it was as good a way to die as any—and yet, the pathos of it! If they were prepared to die, we who lived and who shall perhaps die far less well another day, could at least pity them.

The chaplain was telling the Luce photographer, in a voice bitter with emotion, of the horrible wounds that the Ethiopian bullets made. They were dum-dums, he swore, dum-dums, and he went feverishly from body to body, pulling back the pitiful remnant of a shirt to show where one bullet had crushed a man's chest, and uncovering a torso to show where an arm wound had made a man bleed to death. The white face grinned up at us from its last agony. He who had been covered with earth (it seemed forever) was brought again into the warmth of the sun.

And then we moved on. None of us said anything as we got into our cars and started to drive the few hundred yards separating us from the edge of Shelikot. Then Holme made a remark that was to be the *faux pas* of the war, as far as the journalists were concerned. He was riding with Packard and an Italian journalist, Pier Luigi Barbato, who was later to go to the United States and write vicious, lying propaganda against Americans. Turning to Packard, Holme said: "If only Mussolini could see that!"

Barbato almost burst down the door in his frantic effort to get away from the contaminating presence of poor Holme, whose mind had only been dwelling on the pity of what he had seen. The Italian had thought of the glory and heroism, and only incidentally of the human element involved. To him it was nothing short of sacrilege to intimate that Mussolini would be sorry he started the war if he saw a dozen corpses.

Knowing Mussolini as we do now—the man who was wantonly to sacrifice hundreds of thousands of lives and plunge his country into the worst ruin of its history—Holme's remark stands as the most pathetic piece of mistaken characterization I have ever heard. It was the old, unhappy and ever-recurring story of the good man believing that the evil one must think as he does, and it was, too, an unwillingness to believe in the force of evil. Carry Holme's erroneous way of thinking into international politics, and you can explain much of what has happened since 1935.

We were a mixed lot of journalists down at Shelikot—half Italians, half foreigners—and there was quite a furor at the place where we were halted, near the village. It was just as well, in a way, for it permitted us to look without too much horror at the scene before us. I, for one, was not yet inured to death and suffering. I was still sentimental about them, which was as foolish for a war correspondent as it would have been for an army doctor. Now I can look upon the dead with relative indifference, but I resent many of the things which have caused those deaths —and that is what is important.

At Shelikot, we had stopped about thirty yards short of the field hospital. Several trucks had backed into the open space alongside it, and dead bodies were being loaded into them like so many sacks of corn. An officer was hastening and encouraging the nerve-racked soldiers who were performing the task. Standing, waiting to be unloaded, were about twenty mules, and tied over the side of each in burlap bags, with feet and heads hanging down, were other bodies. Every body was shod, and every pair of feet stuck out with that same ironical nonchalance.

One body was being pulled gingerly off a mule by two soldiers, as we watched. They let the feet touch the ground, and then drew the upper part of the body toward them. The head jerked back helplessly, and the burlap wrapping fell off, disclosing a livid and bloodstained face. One of the soldiers shuddered, and let his burden go. It sagged limply to the ground.

"*Corraggio! Corraggio!*" shouted the officer.

More mules were arriving, and my eye followed the line of gray-brown animals and horribly inert bodies, wrapped in sacking, as they came from high above, where the "Priest's Hat" gave them a mute benediction. Slowly, in single file, the mules wended their way down the mule-path—as strange a funeral cortege as I have ever seen.

General Cona that evening explained to us the measures that were being taken to keep Ras Kassa and Ras Seyoum bottled up in the Tembien with their forces. It was imperative that they should not be permitted to make a junction with Mulugheta, or fall upon the Italian rear. In the beginning, full preparations were made to meet the attack, but it never materialized. The Emperor had ordered Kassa to go to Mulugheta's aid, but he did not even try to do so.

On Friday I took a bath, the first in two weeks. Packard and I emptied the tent in the morning, swept out an astounding amount of dirt, put his portable bathtub in it, and then sat down and waited for the water. All morning we waited in the sunlight swarming with flies, but the water never came. Just after lunch a few of us dashed down to Makale on a foray, and made an excellent haul: gin, vermouth and bitters for cocktails, chocolate, caramels, biscuits, oranges, ham, and cigarettes. Decidedly, the war was becoming more and more civilized as time passed. At 4:30 the water-tank truck drove into camp, and, despite the fact that the air had turned cool, I took my bath, closing the tent well and lighting three candles for heat.

Then, it being Valentine's Day, I wrote a letter to Nancie, and afterwards we played bridge and drank cocktails and ate and slept. And then the Italians won the Battle of Amba Aradam (or, as they called it in their official histories, the battle of Endertà, referring to the region of Abyssinia where the fight took place). That was Saturday, February 15, 1936. These two days of rest

had bored us immeasurably, but they gave the Italians a valuable
breathing spell. The Ethiopians seemingly took them as a definite halt in the Italian advance, if not as a victory for their side.
For them, Adowa, in 1896, was the classic type of battle, and
they took it for granted that in every succeeding battle they
would have no trouble whatever in routing the Italians and
mutilating them to their hearts' content. They kept on thinking
that until the Italians marched into Addis Ababa.

When, at the zero hour of seven on Saturday morning, the
Italian artillery opened a crashing fire against the positions of
the Ethiopians, the effect was obviously disconcerting, for the
enemy were unable to decide upon a course of action for four
hours. At eleven o'clock, however, it was possible to note that a
definite decision had been made. We were then at Badoglio's
observation post on Amba Gheden, and we could hear a sudden
burst of fire that spread until the whole *amba* seemed alive with
the noise. But the fighting was ten miles away from us at the
nearest point, and we could see nothing. Late in the afternoon
Cona explained to us what had happened, paying an ungrudg-
ing tribute to the courage and surprising tactical skill of the
Ethiopians. They had based their action upon the huge natural
fortress which the top of the *amba* made, dividing their forces
into two masses facing the two Italian wings, and they had
placed the strongest units nearest to the western end of the *amba*.

Badoglio was finally closing the pincers with the January 3d
going around the left, or eastern end of the mountain, and the
Sila around the right. Meanwhile, the Sabauda and the Alpini
were making a great sweep around the back of the *amba*, from
the left, toward Antalò, at the foot of the southern slope of Aradam. It was a sound conception whose success was inevitable,
given the troops and matériel at the Marshal's disposal. The
Ethiopians fought stubbornly and ferociously, but at no time
was the issue in doubt. They yielded only step by step, and the
battle raged almost until sundown. When the sun finally sank,
all the Italian objectives had been gained, and Ras Mulugheta
and his shattered forces were in wild flight southward. At five
o'clock the Alpinis marched into Antalò, and half an hour later

the March 23d Blackshirts, who had cut through to the left of the Sila Division, scaled the then unoccupied summit of the *amba* where the Duke of Pistoia, their nominal commander, planted the Italian tricolor.

The Battle of Amba Aradam was over, and the twilight of the Abyssinian Empire had begun. The Ethiopians had fought bravely but vainly. Faced with a devastating artillery fire utterly foreign to their methods of warfare, they never flinched. Their leaders had displayed considerable skill in tactics, and they had all given their best. But it was not good enough, and to us who had seen the battle it was quite obvious that the beginning of the end of the war had arrived. Kassa and Seyoum were bottled up in the Tembien, faced with the necessity of either withdrawing hurriedly or waiting in their turn to be smashed. They waited.

It was six in the evening, just as it was becoming dark, that Badoglio walked up to where we were standing; his face was beaming with joy, and his arms opened in an embracing gesture.

"You have brought me luck," he said, in a voice almost choked with emotion. "That mountain which was lying on our stomachs has been won, and the enemy is in flight toward the south. But you may be sure that the Negus, in some deep cavern, is concocting a victory bulletin at this very moment. You have noted the boldness of our maneuver, which has shown that Italian soldiers have good legs and marvelous hearts. And now write freely what you have seen. I wish you all good evening and good appetites."

He was essentially right about the Negus, as a matter of fact.

"A denial that Italy had won a sweeping victory on the northern front was telegraphed to the Government today by Ras Mulugheta, Ethiopia's Minister of War," wrote the Associated Press correspondent from Addis Ababa on February 18, three days after the battle ended. "He said there were several skirmishes last week in which the Italians lost heavily and thirty-one Ethiopians were killed and seventy-five wounded."

Other correspondents, including our own, wrote similar stories from Addis, but that night we were still naively of the opinion that, as we had witnessed the battle ourselves, people would accept our accounts and realize what had happened and what was going to happen to the other armies of the Emperor. Alas, that was too much to expect! Even so acknowledged a military expert as Captain Liddell Hart, of *The Times* of London, wholly missed the importance and significance of the battle. This he did in the articles he wrote for his newspaper and *The New York Times*. Writing in the latter, he said:

"Lacking any impartial witnesses, can we penetrate the present rosy haze by the cold light of reason? . . . On examining the map, the distance they [the Italians] had advanced in six days appears to have been barely four miles. . . . There is no hint here of a decisive victory . . . Even if the Ethiopians are utterly shattered, nature could still be counted on to offer resistance to the Italian 'steamroller' that makes talk of victory sound extravagant. A battle becomes 'decisive' only when it can be followed up and its strategic fruits reaped."

The issue containing this article arrived in Asmara after the Italians had taken Amba Alagi, had defeated Kassa, Seyoum, and Immeru, and had occupied Gondar!

But the Battle of Amba Aradam made a grand story, whether anybody believed us or not, and that night I wrote three columns' worth, which was carried by plane to Asmara on Sunday morning, whence it was radioed to Rome, telephoned to Paris and wirelessed from there to New York for the Monday morning paper. It was a wonderful break for me, since there are no evening papers in New York on Sunday, so the accounts of the agency correspondents could be used no sooner than mine. Moreover, Italian papers do not print on Monday morning, so even Italy got from New York the first news of the victory.

No newspaperman could have asked for more—unless he was the sort who might feel that even the best story in the world was not worth the triumph of evil. However, anyone who felt that way would not be a good newspaperman. We journalists do not bring about such situations any more than a doctor causes illness. Just as the latter feels professional pleasure in contem-

plating and treating some dreadful disease or injury, so we journalists are inclined to deal with stories as if they had no ethical
content. The value of a story, in point of news interest, has nothing to do with the moral factors involved. If a newspaperman
takes joy in handling a "juicy" murder case it is not because he
approves of murder.

I am belaboring the point because it is one that readers so
often forget or refuse to see, and I myself feel rather touchy
about it, because I have so often, in my career, been accused of
serving an interest or a country because a factual, sincere presentation of a situation proved favorable to that interest or country.
This is especially true of those readers whose hearts or interests
are involved in one of the authoritarian political or religious
structures of our times. Such criticism is all a mixture of ignorance of journalistic practice, an inability to understand that a
man can have his personal opinions but still put them rigidly
aside in presenting the facts of a case, and behind it all is that
very human sentiment, "If you aren't for me you are against me."

That a journalist has, at all times, his bias and his sympathies
is certain, since he is only a human being. That those feelings
color his choice and presentation of news, without his being
conscious of it, is also obvious (and I may say that this is true
of editing as well as of writing news). It all boils down to the
impossibility of achieving perfection or complete precision, and
we journalists could write as many books on that subject as the
philosophers have written.

I am not writing such a book; I am merely defending an
honorable profession against dishonorable or ignorant criticism,
and if I am choosing this place in my book to do so it is because
in writing about Abyssinia I presented an attractive picture of
a morally ugly subject. You may have wanted me to portray
nothing but the injustice, the suffering of the Ethiopians, the
immorality and wickedness of the Italians. Had I been covering
the war from the Abyssinian side it would have been within
my province to do so insofar as I confined myself to facts and
not opinions or imagination. But I covered the war from the

Italian side, and the description I gave of it was as correct and honest as I knew how to make it.

My story of Amba Aradam was my first description of a big battle, and I have given it here just about as I wrote it then, so that you can see how I felt as well as how the battle was fought. My heart may have been in the wrong place, but the description was sound and so were the deductions which I drew. Those who did not believe me were not only being misled; they were playing into Fascist hands, for the only way of saving any of Abyssinia for the Abyssinians was to recognize the hopelessness of their plight.

Remember that this was the first step in the progression that was to lead to the second World War, and there were lessons to be learned. Some were obvious at the time, some were obscure. It was interesting to note that the chief German "correspondent" was an officer of the Reich's General Staff, a certain Captain Strunk whose dispatches were really the reports of a military observer. It was significant, too, that the only Spanish correspondent should have been sent by the right-wing, monarchist *El Debate* of Madrid, representing interests that were dickering with Mussolini and Hitler even before the Abyssinian war ended. The man was Bermudez Cañete, who was killed by Anarchists on the streets of Madrid in the early days of the Civil War.

Marshal Badoglio represented another thread which was to run through the succeeding years. It was his military skill which won a quick and decisive victory but, curiously enough, what counted most for Italy in the long run was not his ability but his character. One description I gave of him in my book, *Eyewitness in Abyssinia,* while inadequate in itself, is still revealing:

"One such encounter [with Badoglio] was just after the Battle of Sciré," I wrote. "He called us into his tent and proudly showed us a Hotchkiss machine gun which had been a personal gift of Haile Selassie to Dedjasmatch Bieni, slain at Amba Uork. He was as pleased with it as a child with a new toy—but a rather spoilt and conceited child. He alone among all the Italian commanders was never generous to the foe he defeated. I do not mean in what he did, for he was just and wise, or in what he wrote in his book, but in what he said to us. There was not a battle in which he did not afterwards say something sarcastic about the Ethiopians and their leaders, and I never heard a word of praise about them from his lips from the beginning to the end of the war. Yet, he was not the rough, uneducated type of soldier; he was a charming, cultured man, who had been in the diplomatic service for many years. Tough and courageous he certainly was, and a military genius probably without a peer in the world today. He did not lack a sense of humor, although his wit was always rather barbed. Perhaps he lacked the milk of human kindness."

In some ways the Ethiopian War was misleading. It led many to overrate the Italian military machine, which had not been properly prepared for such an effort. Having been a complete success, as far as it went, it gave the illusion that the Italian Army could do much more if called upon. And the man who was being deluded more than any other was Mussolini.

He was having his first clash with the British—and getting away with it. The appeasement era, that most shameful of all periods in British history, was under way, although half-heartedly and negatively. Mixed in with appeasement were still many elements of British pride and decency, but the weakness of the opposition to Italy, the willingness to compromise, and, above all, the simple fact that Italy won and England lost were all to play, unhappily, a role in encouraging not only Mussolini but Hitler.

There was something about the British attitude of smugness, self-satisfaction and hypocrisy, in those appeasement years, that was so irritating it was impossible not to take a malicious pleasure in seeing the Lion's tail properly twisted. The British deserved what they got—but all of us, all over the world, suffered for it, and our role should have been, rather, to encourage those elements of greatness in the British structure and character which were always there and ready to come out—as they did, finally. I should add that it would have been well, also, to consider the motes in our own eyes, as well as the beams in the

British. After all, we Americans did our bit to help appeasement along.

In Abyssinia, the outstanding symbol of challenge to Great Britain was Gondar, which is near Lake Tana, the source of the Blue Nile, and hence a point of great strategic importance in Africa. It was taken under the nominal leadership of that clown, Achille Starace, Secretary of the Fascist Party, who missed no opportunity to heap sarcasm upon the British. The capture of Gondar, the defeat of the Negus's last army, and Hitler's entry into the Rhineland all came within a short space of time, and they were signposts pointing toward disaster.

On April 10, 1936, I flew down to Sardo, the Sultan of Aussa's summer capital in the heart of the Danakil Desert, and from there, the nearest point yet reached to Addis Ababa, it was easy to predict that the war would be over "within a month." Yet, just about that time Anthony Eden was earnestly insisting on the necessity for reaching a peaceful solution in conformity with the Covenant of the League of Nations, and without granting Italy any territorial concessions. That was either hypocrisy or lack of information on the true state of affairs, and in either case was inexcusable, since there was still time to save a part of his territory for the Negus.

My personal reaction was, I confess, happiness that the campaign was drawing to a close and I could soon go home. That element of selfishness is a natural one. Much as I hated to see the Spanish War end the way it did in 1939, I could not help being relieved at seeing the end of a period of danger, discomfort and nerve strain.

I went into Addis Ababa with Marshal Badoglio at four on the afternoon of May 5, 1936. Two nights before, at Termaber Pass, I had written that "my thoughts kept turning to the conquered, for whom our coming meant the end of an ages-old independence. They had fought in defense of hearth and home and country, as fiercely and courageously as they knew how. They had lost, and an era was coming to an end."

Of Addis I wrote: "There was nothing spectacular about it— no shouting, no excitement, no cheering crowds, not the slightest ceremony. Yet it was one of the great moments of modern history, and it lacked no genuine element of drama and color. The setting was an imperial capital in ruins—buildings still burning, the stinking dead still lying about the streets, gutted houses and stores gaping blackly and emptily at us as we drove by . . ."

I wrote an article from Addis Ababa about the resources of Abyssinia and what the Italians hoped to get out of it, and in a letter to my wife I said I "wished them luck," which I did. I was still isolating the war in Ethiopia as a historic as well as journalistic event. For me the adventure was over. I thought it was for Italy, too, and that Mussolini meant it when he said that he wanted twenty-five years of peace to develop its rich possibilities. Had it been that way, one could have condoned, on a practical and utilitarian basis, the conquest of Abyssinia, since it would have been the best thing that ever happened to that ancient country. Indeed, the Italians did wonders, with slender resources, in the next five years, and the Negus eventually went back to a country better and richer than the one he left.

However, there were many other factors involved that I, and others who thought as I did, were not taking into account or did not know about. There were the personal ambitions and delusions of Mussolini, the internal difficulties of his regime, and, above all, a whole complex of world factors that made him and his country just a poor bark, driven helplessly before the storm. Mussolini, like the sorcerer's apprentice, had set in motion forces which he could not begin to control.

Abyssinia finished nothing, but it started a great deal. I had gone through it rather heedlessly and cynically; nevertheless I had learned much, even more than I realized at the time.

Spanish Course

The Spanish Course Begins

I HAVE to keep emphasizing that I learned the hard way. The lessons had to be driven in, on the spot, and almost literally by getting knocked on the head. We all have our "roads to Damascus," I suppose. "The light of truth is always a gleam or a flash," as Croce says. My "conversion" came in Spain, but it was infinitely more than that. I have already lived six years since the Spanish Civil War ended, and have seen much of greatness and glory and many beautiful things and places since then, and I may, with luck, live another twenty or thirty years, but I know, as surely as I know anything in this world, that nothing so wonderful will ever happen to me again as those two and a half years I spent in Spain.

And it is not only I who say this, but everyone who lived through that period with the Spanish Republicans. Soldier or journalist, Spaniard or American or British or French or German or Italian, it did not matter. Spain was a melting pot in which the dross came out and pure gold remained. It made men ready to die gladly and proudly. It gave meaning to life; it gave courage and faith in humanity; it taught us what internationalism means, as no League of Nations or Dumbarton Oaks will ever do. There one learned that men could be brothers, that nations and frontiers, religions and races were but outer trappings, and that nothing counted, nothing was worth fighting for, but the ideal of liberty.

Today, wherever in this world I meet a man or woman who fought for Spanish liberty, I meet a kindred soul—Constancia de la Mora and Gustav Regler in Mexico City, Ernest and Martha Hemingway in New York, Don Juan Negrin and Hans Kahle in

London, Randolfo Pacciardi in Rome, Robert Capa in some front line—and nothing will ever break that bond, for it is stronger than tempered steel. In those years we lived our best, and what has come after and what there is to come can never carry us to those heights again. I, in my own field, have never done such work as I did in Spain, nor do I ever hope to equal it. We left our hearts there. If here I can re-create some days of tragic glory and make you feel, with me, what it meant in this dark world, I shall be content, because then I will have repaid, ever so slightly, the debt that I owe to a noble people and to those generous souls who flocked thither from all over the world to fight and die that liberty might live.

But we must first set what happened in its proper framework and then, like a moving picture, keep pace with the political and international events of which it was not only a part, but a deciding factor. To say now that the Spanish Civil War was the opening battle in Europe of World War II is a truism, but when a lot of us said it back in 1937 and 1938 few would listen. In the prologue of my book, *Two Wars and More to Come,* which I finished in Madrid in the Autumn of 1937, I wrote:

A civil war is the smallest thing that is happening here on the Spanish Peninsula. This conflict could be written in so many terms— a struggle of the Left against the Right, of the proletariat against capitalism, of democracy, republicanism, Socialism, Communism and Anarchism against Fascism, of Russia against Germany, England against Italy.

Why are so many good and ordinarily intelligent people blinding themselves to these facts? How is it that so many Americans do not realize that those sit-down strikes [in France] are just as much an expression of the forces that have been unleashed in Spain as the Civil War itself? How is it that England, whose Empire is at stake, does not yet realize that the Loyalists are fighting her battle as well as their own? Is it possible that there are still people who do not know that the Spanish War is changing the face of the earth? Has the world gone mad, or just we newspapermen and writers who seem to be preaching in a wilderness of indifference and ignorance?

The ancients had a phrase for it, "Whom the gods would destroy they first make mad," and the collective madness of those appeasement years was a willful blindness to the truth and its implications. Those of us who wrote from the Republican side were "Reds," or at least so biased that our accounts could not be trusted. We lacked "objectivity" or "impartiality" or some such virtue that would have permitted us to ignore any problem of right or wrong, good or evil. It was the same old error which readers and editors will always make and which will forever continue to plague the chronicler who, being human, must have his feelings and opinions; in condemning "bias" one rejects the only factors which really matter—honesty, understanding, and thoroughness. A reader has the right to ask for all the facts; he has no right to demand that a journalist or historian agree with him.

However, this is stirring up old and dead embers—and anyway, we all have had our revenge. What a sardonic pleasure it was, in the fall of 1944, to read in Sumner Welles's book, *The Time for Decision*, that "of all our blind isolationist policies, the most disastrous was our attitude on the Spanish Civil War . . . In the long history of the foreign policy of the Roosevelt administration, there has been, I think, no more cardinal error than the policy adopted during the Civil War in Spain." I have no recollection that Mr. Welles talked or acted in that way during the conflict, but it is gratifying to know that he felt that way. At any rate, few would question the judgment now.

So, the Spanish Civil War meant something of world-wide and enduring importance, and you cannot understand what happened afterwards unless you place it in its proper historical perspective. For history, along with nature, abhors a vacuum. The war cannot be isolated from the historical stream that started flowing before the Romans established their lasting province. Nations are like individuals; they bear the marks of their ancestry and their childhood. The causes and effects make an endless chain, and one might despair of producing one or two links if it were not possible to say that the composition is always the same, except that sometimes there is more or less of gold or dross.

The Spaniard is a Latin—but with what a difference from the Frenchman or the Italian! It makes only for confusion to call him a Latin, even if his language belongs in that group and if Roman culture left an indelible imprint on him. Primarily he is a mixture of Iberian and Celt, but the Arabs, or Moors, invaded Spain in 711 and remained there until Ferdinand and Isabella expelled them in 1492, and they, too, left an ineradicable mark. And for four centuries Jews were numerous and influential —so much so that even their expulsion in that same fateful year for the world's history failed to prevent a strong Jewish strain from coloring the Spanish character.

So there you have the primary elements in the Spaniard. The Iberians and the Celts were tough fighters, and it took the old Romans two centuries to conquer them. The Romans brought order, discipline, culture. The Orientals added another type of culture, with grace, learning, romance. And then Catholicism put the final stamp of rigidity and faith that conquered a world.

Those were the materials with which history worked, even modern history. That was the heredity which shaped the Spanish character, and the environment of geography, and of world affairs, did the rest.

It all went to form an individualistic people, deeply and instinctively religious, with a dignity and distinction which the masses fully share, but at the same time quick to violence, uncompromising, passionate, spontaneously revolutionary. In their great days they conquered much of the world for Catholicism and for gold. The Church gave them a philosophy suited to their temperament, but when the clergy betrayed them they sought other philosophies, in vain. So they have been a lost people, divided among themselves, an easy prey to the more ruthless and efficient nations who reconquered the Spaniards' world for materialistic reasons. The masses have been betrayed as in no other country—betrayed by their monarchs, their Church and their Army. They have sought little, and have been persecuted for seeking it. Bettering their lot, making progress, educating themselves—these were made crimes. Yet it was the upper classes who really needed education. They should have taught themselves the principles of government, the place of an army and a church in an enlightened state, the social obligations of the rich toward the poor.

Back of this twentieth century was another of some progress but much pain. It began with Napoleon's invasion, and continued with unending civil strife. The Spanish Fascists like to call it the century of liberalism, using the word with all the contempt that liberalism is supposed to merit. By that they mean such things as internal disorders, the upheaval of the masses, the spreading germs of democracy, the weakening of the Monarchy and the Church, the beginnings of popular education.

A glorious war was fought and won to begin the century; Spaniards call it the War of Independence, and the English know it as the Peninsular War. It was the Spanish people who, with Wellington's armies, defeated the French; it was not the upper classes, the Monarchy or the professional army that did it. (In those days the clergy was on the side of the people.) The masses who called Joseph Bonaparte "Joe Bottles" and who rose spontaneously to fight seven years of guerrilla warfare were the conquerors who so drained Napoleon's strength that his enemies elsewhere in Europe were finally able to defeat him.

All through the Civil War which ended in 1939 the Spanish Republicans thought of the earlier conflict and conceived of themselves as fighting a second War of Independence. The first time they won the war and lost the peace; this time they lost the war, but they have not fought in vain. The symbol for both conflicts might well be the Cortes of Cadiz in 1812, convened by the people and dominated by liberals, which gave Spain a liberal constitution. It was lost to a reactionary, stupid, perfidious and wicked king, Ferdinand VII, supported by the Church, but the memory remained to play its part throughout the nineteenth century, as the last Republican Cortes of Figueras, in February, 1939, will remain to inspire Liberals and Republicans in this century.

The Liberals of Ferdinand's day, betrayed by their King, turned to the Army, and, to Spain's unhappiness, brought in the system of *pronunciamientos* and the role of the Army in politics. Their motives were upright but the results were deplorable, especially as the military were soon to be found on the reactionary side, where they have remained to this day. And so began a series of *caudillos* and a series of civil wars. One picks periods like 1833-1839, 1870-1876, 1936-1939, but those were times when the intensity of the internal strife led to great and more or less equal forces taking the field.

The reign of Alfonso XIII was a relatively peaceful and prosperous one for Spain. Born a king posthumously, he attained the age for reigning on May 17, 1902, and he held the throne for twenty-nine years. Alfonso was a man of keen intelligence and autocratic will; he was patriotic, charming, unstable, and impulsive. He wanted to be the Bourbon despot in a country which had outlived that stage in its history. He sought to base everything on the throne, and hence the saving of the dynasty was his prime motive. Being Spanish, he believed the way to do so was through force and guile—the Army and the Church—aided by a corrupt political structure which deprived the masses of any honest part in government and gave the King absolute control over the Cortes and the Cabinet.

It was a system which did not work well even in the eighteenth century; how could it do so in the twentieth? Alfonso had no feeling for liberalism or democracy; his was the line of the French Bourbons, not of the German Hanoverians. The modern twist it took was to make him what we call today a politician. The Government and the constitutional structure failed, and the solution for the ensuing evils was sought not in their reform, but in a withdrawal into greater despotism, backed by the Church and Army. The vital thrust of the people trying to rise above the rotten structure that had been imposed upon them was thwarted by military force and clerical obstruction, aided somewhat by the landed aristocracy and big business. So the liberal movement seethed below the surface, until, in 1931, it exploded.

Many books have been written about Spain's internal problems, and they all tell the same story, whether written a few centuries ago or today. The country is fundamentally agricultural, and agrarian questions are always the knottiest and most important for Spanish statesmen. The fault was primarily due to the large landowners, whose *latifundia* date back to the expulsion of the Moors, when great holdings were awarded to the military and the religious orders. In the former case the lands were acquired by the nobles. Subsequently, no matter what happened at times to their political power, they never lost out, because of the grip which their feudal holdings and rights gave them. The great estates of the Church were broken up and sold to the aristocracy by Mendizábal in 1837, but this did not prevent the Church from accumulating enormous riches in mobile possessions, until it became the largest capitalistic group in Spain.

That whole problem of the Spanish Church is an unhappy one. There is no escaping the fact that the Spanish clergy defended the material possessions of the Church at the expense of the spiritual. They shamelessly cultivated the rich, through whom legacies, gifts, and political power were gained, and too often they worked by intrigue and flattery. Their strength (until the Second Republic) started with the Crown, since the kings were brought up by priests and found powerful support in the Church. They had the women on their side, for the Spanish woman's conventual upbringing and relatively secluded life make her especially susceptible to religious pressure. Among the men, the middle classes—the so-called "lay Jesuits"—whose interests were material rather than religious, were a strong source of support for illiberalism. Then there were regions like Navarre which have always been deeply Catholic and where the Church could count on virtually unanimous support.

The Church was largely to blame for the backwardness of Spanish education, and if the state schools were not much better than the clerical, at least they tried to be tolerant and intellectually neutral. It was the Jesuits who had a firm control of the majority of private and religious schools. In studying the abuses of power which led Spain to disaster, one returns again and again to the Jesuits. It is not a case of blaming them for everything, nor of painting them as black as their cassocks. They did much good but they did infinitely more harm, and one needs no better proof of what the Spanish people have thought of them than the constant efforts made since 1767 to drive them out of Spain. On six different occasions, the last in 1936, they were ousted—and they have as often returned. One of the first things Franco did was to restore the Jesuits to their former privileges. One cannot attribute these expulsions to the wickedness of Spanish nature or to original sin. They were the result of grave abuses against which the people revolted, sometimes violently.

To be sure, other religious orders, with the honorable exception of the Franciscan, must be charged with the same abuses. The chief indictment against them was their unshakable habit of seeking and accumulating wealth, which was bad both for the country's economy and its political structure. As late as 1931 the Jesuits controlled about one third of the national wealth.

Despite all the ponderous weight of authority and riches of the Church—and partly because of it—opposition grew, as it had to grow in a world which elsewhere had shaken off the secular yoke of the Church. Unhappily, it too often showed itself in violence—a violence that is entirely to be deplored, but which nevertheless ought to be understood. It was not only an expression of desperate, passionate hatred; it afforded the only weapon which the peasants and workers knew how to use.

When, in the first days of the Civil War, thousands of churches were burned, and monks, nuns, and priests killed, the world was properly horrified, but it made the mistake of thinking that such actions were a new and terrible invention of the "Reds." Actually, it is an "old Spanish custom," which in modern times began in 1834-1835. During the "Tragic Week" of 1909 more than seventy churches and religious edifices were burned in Barcelona alone.

It is a terrible manifestation of disorder, and one can predict that it will be recurrent so long as the abuses continue and the collective madness which leads to anti-religious violence is not cured by reform.

The Church always had the support of the Army. An organization which, by its essence, stands for discipline and order cannot tolerate mob violence, nor should it do so. However, in any other country it might have been expected to show some understanding and appreciation of the social and political causes behind the violence—but not in Spain. The Spanish Army (by which is meant the officer caste) has played a contemptible role in modern times. It was wretched in its fighting abroad, and vicious in its internal politics. No other army in Europe was quite so disgracefully inefficient and corrupt.

The dominance of the army began in Napoleon's time. From Castaños (the victor of Baylén) to Franco, the progression is clear and unvarying—the same kind of men doing the same things, some good things but more bad. The civil wars are theirs and the colonial wars, too, and they want peace only after they have won their wars. Their claim to power is military victory, not brains, wisdom or even political skill. Their fetish is order. Hence, the popular, labor and social movements, with their inevitably radical trend and violent fringe, must be suppressed ruthlessly.

All these generals opposed regionalism, for the Army was essentially an organ of unity. Its patriotism has been nationalistic. But regionalism is one of the fundamentals of Spanish history, a natural result of Spanish individualism and the geographic structure of the Peninsula. There has always been a tug-of-war between Madrid and Barcelona, and between Madrid and Bilbao, for instance. It is not a coincidence that the two strongest separatist movements—the Catalan and the Basque— occur in the only sections of Spain with highly developed business interests.

That whole question of business interests and natural resources has inevitably played a vital part in Spanish history. Most of the invasions of Spain have had the mines predominantly in view, and the late Civil War was no exception. Hitler admitted this frankly in public speeches, while the British and the French "non-intervention" on Franco's behalf did not lose sight of mining investments. Spain never reached the "trust-busting" stage, although the Civil War did a temporary job of it in Republican territory. Something needed to be done, because the big industrialists, especially in Catalonia, were examples of the worst type of capitalist. They fought, by brutal repression, any improvement in wages, hours, or social conditions—and brutality was met by brutality.

Catalonia was therefore rich ground for Anarchism with its insistence on "direct action." Madrid, less industrialized and less urban, could better afford to embrace the more gentle, reformist policy of Socialism which, anyway, was more suited to the Castilian character. It took a constructive program to appeal to Castile's traditional instincts and feelings, a program that was authoritarian, centralized, institutional, pessimistic. The Catalan and the Andalusian, being by nature optimistic, romantic, and violent, were more apt to choose the destructive line.

The only solution for the problem which the successive governments ever seemed to try was repression by force of any manifestations, even peaceful strikes. Some governments actually provoked terrorism, in order to crush the revolutionary spirit of the masses. After all, it was so much easier to suppress rioting, church burning, and assassinations than to reform the conditions which brought the workers to a state of desperation! There was always enough genuine, explosive rage against the forces of oppression to frighten the middle-class business man, but never enough, thanks to Government, Army and Church, to bring about his reform or defeat. So there were long periods of labor troubles, violence, strikes, incendiarism, even uprisings, and it was in such a fiery crucible that the Spanish labor movement, with its political and social manifestations, was formed.

Anarchism, Socialism, Republicanism, Communism—these were the movements which were later fused into the Popular Front. They are all familiar labels which foreigners have thoroughly misunderstood—partly because the movements were complicated by internal factions and schisms which made any clear-cut definition perilous. Yet without some understanding of what each group did or tried to do, modern Spanish history is meaningless.

Anarchism is as much a Spanish phenomenon as the Inquisition; neither was invented by Spaniards, but both found fruitful soil only in Spain. Contrary to popular belief, the philosophy is not idealistically violent. It starts from that most pathetically noble of all precepts, that men are essentially good. Hence you do not need institutions like State or Church and Army, and capitalism must be destroyed.

The basis for the belief is "the sovereignty of the individual," and that, for one thing, helps to explain why the Spaniard found Anarchism so congenial. The search is for individual freedom, or "libertarianism," as the Anarchists called it. Therefore one must fight against any and every oppression, and especially against the "unholy trinity" of state, religion, and capital. State and capital are to be supplanted by confederations of free communes or municipal councils. There is to be a planned economy of the forces of production—a sort of municipalized syndicalism. Where Communism says: "Each one gives according to his capacities and receives according to his necessities," Anarchism says, "each one gives and takes what he wants, and that presupposes abundance and love."

Such aims can only be achieved by "direct action"—strikes, sabotage, or even, if necessary, violence. Theoretically, Anarchism "abhors violence," but as Errico Malatesta, the Italian Anarchist who had his greatest following in Spain, said, "government oppression and capitalist exploitation are typical forms of organized violence." Hence, the worker "opposes force to force." In the day of revolution "popular vengeance is terrible and inexorable," but "terror is a danger that brings out the worst and least responsible elements." (How true that proved in the Civil War!)

The progression—from strikes to sabotage to assassinations—seemed natural. Responsible leaders always deplored and fought against the trend, with the result that they were being continually pushed toward organization and even into politics, despite the essentially apolitical basis of the movement. In order to have a practical organization through which to channel activity and with which to fight, the movement picked up Sorel's Syndicalism toward the close of the nineteenth century. The more proper designation for the movement, since that time, is Anarcho-Syndicalism. It did not achieve any genuine organization, however, until 1911, when the CNT (the *Confederación Nacional de Trabajo,* or National Labor Federation) was formed in Barcelona. As the movement became more aggressive and violent, the need for determined leadership was felt, and so the FAI (the *Federación Anarquista Ibérica,* or Anarchist Federation of Iberia) was formed in Valencia in 1927. That was the setup which caused so many headaches in the Civil War.

The part the FAI played in Spanish history was evil, but at least it satisfied a natural need. No one can understand what has happened in Spain without appreciating the strength of the eruptive force that seethed just below the surface at all times— a blind, mass fury induced by centuries of abuses. Franco put the lid on again, but the forces are still there.

Anarchism was not an accident in Spain; it was the answer to a genuine instinctive urge of the Spanish character. The philosophical appeal was to that strong individualism which is at the basis of his temperament. The Spaniard does not merge naturally into a society or a state. His instinct is to absorb, not to be absorbed. You cannot make an automaton or a piece of machinery out of a Spaniard. Neither the authoritarian Communism of Moscow nor the dictatorial Fascism of Rome and Berlin suits his character.

It has been said that every Spaniard is an aristocrat. Certainly, he is a being apart from his fellow men. He is egocentric, not social; practical rather than idealistic. His response is to something which has a direct personal appeal, such as Anarchism, rather than to a call for the submergence of his individualism in the State, as Fascism or Communism demands. Political ideologies mean less to him than do the leaders who personify them, and yet no race is so responsive to the idealistic appeal of religion. Hence, if a leader or a movement can be invested with a religious aspect, it enhances the possibilities of success. If the banner of Christ can be raised by any cause, it will win the average Spaniard. There you have one explanation of Franco's victory.

One might ask what all this has to do with Anarchism, but

the point is that when a Spaniard feels himself driven away from his Catholicism he does not become a Protestant; he becomes an Anarchist or a Communist. He wants all or nothing. The deep, religious underlying strain of his character impels him to project his personality like a sharp silhouette against "the white radiance of eternity." He is not at home in what Madariaga calls "the middle stretches in which social and political communities lie." Anarchism catches him at the individual end of those two poles, the ego and the universe, and his response to its appeal is instinctive. Of course, when the time comes to give reality to the abstractions of Anarchism he is only too likely to find that, in spite of everything, society impinges on his individualism and he cannot live in a vacuum. Nevertheless, the philosophical appeal is deep and haunting.

Socialism has the same appeal to the democratic, politically-minded Castilian that Anarchism has to the more hot-blooded Andalusian and Catalan. Students of Spanish politics have often been confused by the foreign tags which the various movements took. German Socialism, French Syndicalism, Russian Communism, Italian Fascism—these are the banners under which Spanish workers have fought and died—and yet each one of those "isms" came out, in the end, as something peculiarly Spanish.

The Socialists, through their UGT (the *Unión General de Trabajadores,* or General Union of Workers) controlled nearly two million workers, yet the percentage of those who could be considered good Marxists was infinitesimal. The bulk of the party and the direction of the UGT were controlled by the so-called "Left-Wing Socialists" under Francisco Largo Caballero. They were reformist and opportunist—more like "Social Democrats"—who generally hoped to work through parliamentary and constitutional methods. Largo Caballero was a big, bluff, hearty demagogue, without much intelligence himself, but directed, behind the scenes, by one of the keenest political brains in Spain, Luís Araquistain.

However, the leaders of the Socialist Party itself were a group of mildly liberal, petty bourgeois Republicans. They were men

from Spain's small middle class, generally intellectuals who followed some profession, or who, like their leader Indalecio Prieto,
were primarily politicians. They played a great role in the Republican movement and the Revolution of 1931 and then supported the Republic through thick and thin. They still called
themselves Socialists, but in any other country they would
simply have been labeled "democrats." Most of them, including
Prieto, gave the impression that they had never even read Marx,
nor did they care to hear much about him. They were suspicious
and fearful of the left-wing element, which gave them and the
Republic a bad name abroad and permitted the enemies of
Spanish democracy to call them all "Red." Except for Largo
Caballero's brief and unhappy fling in the early months of the
Civil War, they were the ones, with Communist and Republican
support and an ever-growing majority of their own party behind
them, who ruled Spain until the end of the Republic.

The Communists had no importance when the Civil War
started, but were able to take the leadership away from all the
Left parties by the simple expedient of dropping their revolutionary program for a loyal and competent support of the democratic Republican elements. Considering the popular belief
abroad that a large and powerful Communist element engineered
and ran the war, it is almost amusing to write about the movement now that it is all over. It began in 1921, when a small
group of Socialists broke away, but for ten years the Communist
Party hardly existed. Even in 1936, when the war started, there
were only about 50,000 members, with sixteen deputies in the
Cortes, which was more than their popular vote entitled them to.
Not even in the war did they develop a single, first-rate political
figure; what genius there was went into the military field.

However, before leaving the subject I should mention that
dissident offshoot which was to play such an evil part in the
Civil War, the POUM (*Partido Obrero de Unificación Marxista,*
or the Workers' Party for Marxist Unification). It was a conglom-
eration of Trotskyists and dissident Trotskyists, dissident Communists of various shades and schisms, revolutionaries who did
not know where else to go, foreign exiles, chiefly German, many

sincere patriots who were unable to join the other parties, and many spies, traitors and Fascists who found it a safe and profitable haven in the storm.

One may well ask, "Where and what were the Republicans who made the Republic?" The question is largely answered by saying that all the parties I have been describing—and especially the Socialists—were the champions and supporters, in varying degree, of the Republican movement. However, there was also a Republican Party—or, rather, parties. In its modern form it was reconstituted in 1903 as the Republican Union, under Nicolás Salmerón and Joaquín Costa. The latter was one of the four important figures of the "Generation of '98," and the only one with energy and political foresight. It was, indeed, the intelligentsia who revived republicanism in Spain after the disastrous experiment of the First Republic in 1873.

By 1905 there were thirty Republican deputies in the Cortes, but they soon split and had to begin again. The Republican Union remained, but it took second place to the Republican Left, which Manuel Azaña came to lead at the time of the Revolution of 1931. By that time there was a whole crop of Republican parties. Spanish politics has never been structurally simple, and the Republicans were typical of its complexity. Nevertheless, they did all want a republic, and 'when the time came they worked together to bring it about. Then they split up and helped to bring it down again—which was also typical.

However complicated the pattern may have been, it was shaping slowly and steadily toward upheaval and then disaster. Another *Caudillo* came along in September, 1923, to put the lid on for seven years, until the mixture became so strong that the lid and he were blown off together. The case for General Miguel Primo de Rivera y Orbaneja, Marqués de Estella, was not nearly so black as the Republicans liked to paint it. As always in Spain, the situation was complicated by many factors with abuses and good intentions on all sides. The really valid charge against Primo de Rivera is that he acted to keep a vicious system in effect against the will of a majority of the people, who at first were led to support him on the basis of false hopes.

Alfonso XIII, like Victor Emanuel III a year before, made the fatal choice of dictatorship. For that he stands condemned before posterity and for that he lost his throne. The dictatorship had a credit balance on material progress, but it so happens that the Spanish people do not value the products of modern civilization so highly as does that sort of foreign visitor who was then applauding Mussolini because the trains ran on time in Italy.

Meanwhile, the Monarch who had said, "Since I was born a King, let me govern," had long since found that the reins of government were out of his hands. Primo de Rivera left in disgrace for Paris on January 28, 1930, and died there on March 16— after which the people of Spain forgave him, with a magnificent public demonstration at his funeral. After all, he had meant well and accomplished some good things. Anyway, he was dead, and what was left of public resentment was turned against the King.

The revolutionary and Republican flood was already bursting through the weakened dam of the Monarchy. The King had only the Church, the aristocracy, a nucleus of high army officers and those industrialists and middle-class business men who were frightened by the revolutionary sentiment behind the Republican movement.

As a means of gaining time, municipal elections were held on April 12, 1931. No one thought of them as anything more than a step toward the republic. Instead, resounding Republican majorities in the cities sealed the doom of Alfonso. As the last Premier, Admiral Juan Bautista Aznar is supposed to have said, "Spain went to bed a Monarchy and got up a Republic." More or less spontaneous Republican demonstrations were taking place throughout the country. The red, yellow and purple flag of the Republic blossomed from innumerable windows.

Alfonso made a creditable decision not to fight it out. "I do not wish a single drop of blood to be shed for me," he said. When the Duke of Maura drew up a document in which the Monarch renounced his throne, Alfonso revised it skillfully, but it was in vain that he wrote: "I am King of all the Spaniards . . .

I do not renounce any of my rights." Those were the sentiments upon which the monarchists placed their hopes for years (and still do, on behalf of the son, Don Juan), but for Alfonso in Italy, at race-tracks, casinos, cabarets and balls, there was only the empty title of "Your Majesty."

The Second Spanish Republic was a colossal failure. One would not be serving history by ascribing all the blame to the internal forces of reaction aided by international Fascism. Yet, even if the disaster was to a large extent self-induced, one cannot deny that the effort was a noble one which deserved to succeed. It failed because it tried to set up a liberal, democratic republic, on nineteenth-century lines, in an era whose most typical expressions are the party tyrannies of Italian and German Fascism and Russian Communism. Moreover, it tried to impose this structure on a people unprepared for such a change. Looking back on it now, one can appreciate the fact that it was a fine expression of the best Spanish aspirations, and for all its faults it had more ingredients for happiness and satisfaction than had the international Fascism which was already spreading from Italy to Germany.

After all, how could the republican leaders know that a plague was going to sweep over Europe as destructive as the "Black Plague" of the fourteenth century, and that it would soon engulf Spain? How could they know that the other democracies of Europe and America would stand by—and even help their enemies? The weaknesses and faults which brought down the Spanish Republic are the same which permitted the German hordes to sweep over the European continent.

It would have needed a generation to bring Spain up to the level of its constitution—but Spain was only to have four and a half years. The leaders were liberal and progressive, and a majority of the people wanted a republic, as they showed in the supreme test of civil war, but the dynamism and determination were at the extremes of radicalism and traditionalism, and the clash of those two crushed the moderate elements in between. Spain did not want a middle-class republic. The workers and the peasants were asking for a revolution; the Church, the feudal landowners, and the Army wanted a return to their old privileged days.

Now that we have the perspective, one can see the relentless progression toward tragedy—the same progression that brought destruction and death to all of Europe.

Two years of well-meaning, but muddling, quarrelsome, inefficient, weak liberalism were succeeded by two years of reaction, known to history as the "Black Biennium." The twenty-seven months between the elections of November 19, 1933, and February 16, 1936, were a period of stagnation, corruption and constantly changing governments; of chaos in the Cortes, disorder in the country, reaction and provocation from the right, and a proletarian uprising cruelly and viciously repressed, but which triumphed in the end. It was pre-Fascism on the Austrian or Portuguese model, in which Church, Army and landed aristocracy were in control.

The revolt of the Asturian miners in 1934 was one of the great working-class uprisings of modern history. The Republican Revolution of 1931 had been bloodless, but the bloodshed was merely postponed. Now came the climax of which other riots and strikes had merely been the prelude. Here was Spain's "Commune," the dress rehearsal for the tragedy of the Civil War. The full truth about the Asturias uprising will never be known, because of the censorship that was imposed and the veil which the Army drew across the horrors it perpetrated. The so-called "Red" atrocities received full publicity, along with a fair amount of exaggeration, so there are no mysteries on that score. But granting all these atrocities, the reprisals had a disproportion, a cruelty and a sadism of which even earlier Spanish history offered few examples.

It is one of those incidents, like the bombing of Guérnica in the Civil War, which will continue to stink in the nostrils of history, however deeply the perpetrators try to bury them. The best that apologists abroad could offer was that most shameless of all half-truths: "Both sides were guilty of atrocities." It was to become an old story in the Civil War. On the one hand is the mad, impassioned fury of mobs or laborers brutalized by a wretched life. On the other is cold-blooded, deliberate cruelty, or what was worse in this case—the condoning of a truly animal brutality by Moors, brought into Spain for the first time in twelve centuries and used against Spaniards in the very region where Pelayo began his reconquest. Nothing could have been more appropriate than that the men who called in the Moors should have been Generals Franco and Goded.

The proletarian forces were defeated, but as Engels had written, "defeated armies are good schools." It was better to have fought and lost than to have accepted defeat as the German Socialists did the year before. Asturias had staged a "preventive putsch" of enduring value to the world proletariat. For the first time, Spanish Socialism had fought with the laborers as a whole in a revolt against Fascism. That is why it was, in a sense, a dress rehearsal for the Civil War, of which one must also say that it was better to have fought and lost.

It was in the next summer—August, 1935—that the Seventh Congress of the Communist International made its historic decision to change world-wide tactics from "united front at the base" to "Popular anti-Fascist Front on the basis of the united proletarian front." Much ink flowed during the Civil War, and has flowed since, over the directives of the Comintern. Since a Spanish Popular Front was formed, with Communist support, it was argued on a *post hoc* basis that the Popular Front was the result of the Comintern congress and that it was fated to end in a purely Communist revolution. The truth is that the Spanish Communists were numerically small, had little influence until after the Civil War started, and were divided among themselves. The Left Republicans and Socialists also claimed primacy for their advocacy of the Popular Front idea, and with better right. The simple fact is that all the Left parties—and not only in Spain—appreciated the fact that it was a splendid idea. But because they adopted it does not mean they placed themselves in the hands of Moscow.

Unfortunately for history, Russia would like to get credit for having done much more for Spain than she did. In my opinion, the "workers of the world" have cause for criticism of Moscow for starting so late, doing so little, and withdrawing help so early in the game.

The elections of February 16, 1936, swung the country back to the Liberals and Leftists, and a social revolution began—not a Communist or an Anarchist or a Marxist revolution, but a Spanish proletarian revolution which alarmed Manuel Azaña and his bourgeois following as much as it did the vested interests. It was confused, adolescent and essentially evolutionary. It was in no sense an organized, deliberate attempt to overthrow the Republican Government. No one will ever know what it may have led to, but one thing is certain: Azaña was no Kerensky. His danger was from the right, not the left.

The Government had ambitious and noble plans, but there was to be no peace to afford time for internal development. The weeks and months that followed were full of strikes, riots, and mob scenes in all parts of Spain. A lid had been lifted by the election, and the violent elements always to be found in Spain were unable to control themselves. The workers remained in the streets. Unfortunately, the first victims were, as always, the churches. The Government did little to stop the outbreaks, hoping that they would die out of themselves.

The tidal wave of Fascism was rushing onward. It was in March, 1936, that Hitler took his first important step toward shattering the whole existing structure of Europe, by moving into the Rhineland. Looking back after the Civil War, the Republicans realized that a ruthless repression, in Fascist style, might have saved Spain. Line up men like Franco, Goded, Gil Robles, Lerroux, Calvo Sotelo, against a wall, and shoot them—that was one solution of Spain's ills. But it was a Fascist or a Communist solution, not a liberal, democratic one. The Republican leaders were never to lose their pathetic belief in the justice of their cause and the importance of international esteem and good will. Instead of good will they got "Non-Intervention." They made a historic record which provides one of the very great pages in the history of democracy—but they lost Spain.

That is the now traditional dilemma of democracy. It cannot fight totalitarianism with its own weapons without abandoning democratic practices, all rules of international law and decency, all easy-going, liberal ways, all individual freedom. Worst of all, it cannot count upon other democracies for help until they themselves are directly threatened.

In Spain, Fascism took the form and name of Falangism, and in the pre-Civil War period I am writing about, the really predominant element was the paid gangster. By then, Spanish Fascism had come out of its political party stage into the open field of revolutionary combat. There was a definite preparation for class warfare, in which all the feudal interests joined. The forces they represented and with which they worked had backing, money, organization and leadership—everything the scattered and quarrelsome Left organizations did not have. Defeated in the February elections, the reactionaries were now triumphantly returning by extra-legal, undemocratic methods. Where the Right as a whole (with the notable exception of the Army leaders, who were already plotting a new *pronunciamiento*) might well have fought the conflict out on a parliamentary plane, the Fascists brought the issue into the streets. When they had created a complete state of chaos, the Army, backed by Italy and Germany, stepped in—and the result was a civil war.

The international significance of what was happening took months to penetrate to the public. What was being planned proved to be even more than a civil war; it was a European war on a minor scale, a dress rehearsal for the great war to come. In it, the Axis tried out successfully the policy and arms which were to lead it in temporary triumph over the whole European continent.

The Italian conquest of Abyssinia, completed on May 5 of that same year, 1936, encouraged Fascists and reactionaries everywhere, and nowhere more than in Spain. Britain and France had been humiliated for the first time; there were to be many other times. Mussolini was, of course, even more encouraged, and his decision to give active help to Franco and the other generals who were linked to the Fascist and Carlist movements was doubtless made then. The Duce was interested in the Mediterranean—*Mare Nostrum*—while Hitler was looking forward to the day of his great conquest of Europe. A republican, democratic, liberal or radical Spain meant an enemy to Germany, an ally for the France and England which Germany was setting out to destroy. Moreover, there were material riches, in Spain and Morocco, which Germany coveted. On June 8, 1939, after the war was over, the *Voelkischer Beobachter* put forward the revealing thesis that the formation of a Popular Front government in Spain, which enjoyed the sympathy of the democracies, was alone sufficient to justify the intervention by the authoritarian states. The true meaning of the Spanish struggle had always been clear in the minds of the two dictators, as many official revelations later proved. It was a struggle between the Fascist states and the "pluto-democracies"; in other words, an exact parallel to the World War which began in September, 1939. However, the democracies refused to fight over Spain.

Internally, as was shown by documents seized in Madrid and Barcelona after the conflict started, the uprising was to be military in character. The result was to be a military dictatorship, which would abolish democratic institutions, Marxism, and regional autonomy, without going so far as Fascism. The Army, the Carlists, the Falange and the Cedistas all had divergent plans and aims. However, the technique, as far as the Spanish Army was concerned, was to effect a pure military seizure of power, followed by "the restoration of order," "exemplary punishments"; in short, another *pronunciamiento* like so many others, only this time carefully planned with foreign help. Franco and his generals soon learned, however, that a straight *coup d'état* without popular support could not succeed alone, and it was then that Falangism, or Fascism, was called in to provide a political framework.

These generals and their supporters claimed to have documentary evidence that the Left revolutionaries had intended to rise in May but had postponed their move to the end of July. Hence—and this is the great argument which conservatives and clericals all over the world were to adopt—the "patriotic" officers and men rose "to save the honor of Spain and rescue her from the Marxist policy of the Popular Front," as Franco put it. Fortunately for

Spain and for world democracy, the people—almost unaided by
their foolish, bewildered, unprepared Government—rose, blindly,
desperately, spontaneously, as they had not done in Spain since
Napoleon's hated forces invaded their country. It upset all the
Rebels' calculations, and those of Mussolini and Hitler.

And so the Spanish Civil War began. The mechanism was set
in motion on July 17, 1936, in Spanish Morocco when a number
of regiments rose to Franco's call to arms. The revolt spread to
the Peninsula the next day. After days and weeks of confusion, a
pattern began to shape up, with a majority of the people supporting the Government. But Franco and his Moors, better
armed, disciplined, were already getting invaluable support from
Germany and Italy. They moved northward toward Madrid,
while three other columns moved down from Navarre and Leon.

The masses fought in the streets of the capital, burned
churches, stormed the Montana Barracks, and through blood and
death saved Madrid for the Republic and for a record of undying glory. Barcelona, too, had its great day and its one claim to
glory in the whole Civil War. The preservation of the seaport
was effected by an effort which showed the spirit and determination of the workers when called upon for the spontaneous sacrifice of their lives in street fighting, where every man fought for
himself. This time the Anarchists were in their element, and they
fought alongside the ordinary Catalan. It was only later, when
discipline, patience, and sacrifice for a common cause were asked,
that Catalonia could not or would not respond.

This is no place to enter into the controversy about atrocities
in general or the Spanish Church in particular. It was all a sorry
and heart-sickening business, which was misrepresented by those
who painted a pure black or white. For what it may be worth, my
own analysis, briefly, came to this: Violence on the Republican
side, in most cases, was sheer mob fury and hooliganism, for passions were roused to a hysterical pitch, and the worst elements
of the population had a free hand in the first few weeks. Because
priests have been invested by tradition and feeling with a sacred
character, the comparatively few deaths inflicted on clerics made
an immensely greater impression on the world than did the

deaths of the many thousands of workers in Seville, Saragossa, Pamplona, and other Rebel cities who were killed simply because they belonged to the UGT or CNT. For one who values human life for purely human reasons the one crime was as great as, or greater than, the other, but, of course, society did not consider it so, and the Republicans received a black characterization from which they never recovered. It was one of the diabolical and baffling and aspects of the conflict that the wholesale and horrible crimes committed by the Rebels were condoned when no worse and even lesser crimes by the Republicans aroused the horror of the world.

As an insurrection, the movement had really failed in the first week of the conflict, but as an international conflict it was only beginning. One half of Spain was pitted against the other half, plus Germany and Italy, with Russia still out of the picture and the democracies either passive or, as in England's case, helping the rebels. Only a few persons behind the scenes in Rome and in Berlin, and in the high ranks of the Rebels, knew that not only a civil war but a European conflict was beginning, although none of them dreamed how long it was going to last. There, in Spain, a door was opened wide to Italian Fascism and German Nazism. All Europe, and, also, we in the United States, were to suffer the consequences.

Telling the story from a personal viewpoint, I am anticipating a great deal in this chapter. So far as I was concerned, I realized nothing of all this when the conflict began, and was only interested from the professional point of view since I liked my taste of war corresponding in Abyssinia and felt that *The New York Times* should use me in the new war. However, I was putting myself in the path of the storm, and it was inevitable that in its crash of thunder and lightning my own little world should have to face a test. You have read here some of the intellectual and emotional results of the lessons Spain taught me. Now, by describing some of the adventures I went through, I want to show you how and why my ivory tower was destroyed.

Glory at Teruel

I ADMIT being highly susceptible to personal contacts, and this is a weakness in a newspaperman. It makes me wonder how long it would have taken to convert me if *The Times* had sent me to the Franco side, instead of to Madrid. As far as the issues were concerned, I was in a state of what Samuel Johnson would have called "stark insensibility" when I first arrived in Valencia toward the end of November, 1936. I had yet to learn what later became for me the cardinal principle of journalism—that in order to know what is happening you must be on the spot. The fault was partly personal, for I live inwardly and have no faculty for putting myself in the place of the other fellow, who is far more likely to be a normal, average human being than I am. It was necessary, for my education, to be thrown into the Spanish maelstrom, and I shall always be grateful to destiny in general and *The New York Times* in particular for the opportunity.

It caught me up, quite literally, like a storm. I should never be able to pick a day or an incident of which I could say: "This has torn me away from my roots and taught me the intensity and joy of a life lived fighting for ideals." I remember that in my first dispatch from Valencia I caught dimly some inkling of the heroism and the glory that Spain was to mean. It was atmospheric rather than precisely factual, for Valencia was far away from the fighting and from Madrid, which was always the true symbol of glory. There was where I really was swept off my feet—I and so many others from odd and far-flung parts of the world, for it was just at that time that the International Brigades were coming into their own.

The Spanish Republican Army had to be improvised, for the

officers had almost all gone over to Franco. There was no discipline, organization, or central command, and while there was plenty of enthusiasm and courage there were precious few arms. Officers rose from the ranks through proved ability in the field. Discipline had to be spontaneous at first and then accepted as a necessary evil. A quartermaster corps had to be created; also war industries, and transportation. The process was the familiar one which the French and the Russians went through in their revolutions. It was the hard way but a good one—and meanwhile the Spaniards needed help.

It would take too long to analyze what the appeal was to each man who went to Spain from the New World and the Old, from oppressed countries, from havens of refuge, from Communist cells and universities, from mines and offices. The Internationals would make another book—and have, indeed, made many books, some of them famous, like Hemingway's *For Whom the Bell Tolls* and Alvah Bessie's *Men in Battle*. This is mainly my own story, but part of my convictions came by contagion from the Internationals, the finest group of men I ever knew or hope to know in my life.

They were the ones who first taught me that in our lives and in our century the crusading struggle of the world is against Fascism, whatever form it may take and wherever it appears. They fought because they were convinced that this world would not be worth living in if Fascism triumphed—and for that I, too, will fight as long as I am alive. I will, later on, want to make a distinction, for my feelings are crystallizing into a hatred of totalitarianism in all its forms, but in those years the enemy was Fascism, and for the time being we will leave it at that.

Spain had already become what Azaña later called "the first battlefield of a world war." The full measure of the international immorality to which we descended in this era was demonstrated in the Spanish Civil War. The Rebels were helped; the legitimate government was hindered. The formula was "Non-Intervention," and the primary blame is England's. It was England which proposed "Non-Intervention" and which persuaded France and the United States to follow suit; England which winked at and condoned and lied about the open intervention of Italy and Germany; England which throttled the League of Nations every time the Spanish Government brought the question up at Geneva.

We in the United States betrayed our democratic traditions, as Sumner Welles later admitted. Outwardly it was the French Popular Front Government of Radical Socialists, Socialists and Communists, which took the initiative in proposing "Non-Intervention" on July 25, and the depth of rottenness and cowardice to which French statesmen had descended was demonstrated by the fact that Premier Léon Blum, a Socialist and a Jew, was the sponsor for the policy. The cause of French democracy received a blow from which it has not yet recovered.

Italy and Germany poured men and matériel into Spain from the very first days, but the policy of ignoring that fact was never wholly abandoned. At best, the fiction that both sides were receiving equal help was steadily fostered. Actually, until October, 1936 (the conflict began in July), not a rifle or even a bullet had gone in from Russia, nor was a Russian plane to be seen in the Spanish sky. Stalin joined the "Non-Intervention Pact" on August 10, 1936, and maintained faith until, on October 23, Maisky, the Soviet Ambassador in London, told the "Non-Intervention Committee" that Moscow "could not consider itself bound by the 'Non-Intervention' agreement to any greater extent than any of the remaining participants." Then, at last, Soviet matériel began to reach Spain. It was paid for—and well paid for—in Spanish gold throughout the war, and was for the most part transported in Spanish ships.

I will not here go into the involved facts and figures of how much help each side got during the war. It will suffice to quote this one sentence written by Sumner Welles, who can surely be trusted not to exaggerate: "The assistance obtained by the Loyalist forces [from Russia] was only a token compared to that obtained by Franco."

Certainly the injustice, the cynicism, and wickedness of "Non-Intervention" were one of the important factors in opening my eyes and stirring my emotions. That was a negative factor; the

Internationals and, above all, Madrid, were positive. Spain has had many a great and glorious siege in her history, especially during the Napoleonic invasion, but the siege of Madrid yields to none of them. It was a martyrdom, but one that was accepted with grace and dignity, and even with gaiety. The Madrileño was touched to the depth of his soul by that attack on his hearth and home, on the things that counted most to him as an individual. Tragedy was to him, as to all true Spaniards, the normal rule of life. He knew how to suffer and die, and if death came sooner from shell or bomb, then it had been so fated. In the centuries to come, Madrid will be to Spain what London and her high bravery during the German "blitz" will be to England.

To live in Madrid in those days was a rare privilege. And we knew that Madrid would not fall; we alone knew it who were there at the hub of a skeptical world.

It was in Madrid that I learned, once and for all, the necessity for being on the spot, to know what was really happening. "Trust as little as you can to report; examine all you can by your own senses," wrote that most excellent reporter Samuel Johnson to his friend Dr. Staunton. I gave a rather spectacular demonstration of my new conviction on February 11, 1937, when the Rebels drove up the Jarama River and officially announced that they had cut the highway to Valencia and taken the Arganda Bridge. To disprove the report required a drive under machine-gun and mortar fire down the highway and across the bridge—but I did disprove it. Although, naturally, I could not have known it, the lines then established remained unchanged for the rest of the war, so I might say my story had a permanent value.

The Battle of Guadalajara, in which the Italian expeditionary force was routed, also gave me an opportunity to contribute material to history, although not even my home office believed me at the time. When you put together all the elements—all the cynicism, immorality, timidity, and cruelty that formed the background of the Italian intervention—your heart must leap when you think of Guadalajara. I still believe I was right when I called it the "Baylén of Fascism." Baylén, in southern Spain, was Napoleon's first defeat, a turning point in his triumphant career, only realized in after years by historians. After Baylén he was to win many victories, but the spell had been broken. Guadalajara was Fascism's first defeat, and it, too, was followed by triumphs, but the world saw that Fascism could be fought and beaten. In vain Mussolini called it a victory, boasted how Italy won the war for Franco, displayed the strength and numbers of his military establishment. The mask was stripped off at Guadalajara.

Strategically, the whole course of the war was changed for the Rebels. Any hope of getting Madrid was temporarily abandoned. At Germany's suggestion it was decided to clean up the northern provinces first. They were cut off and helpless, low in ammunition, troops and food, and the result was never in doubt. We all knew that Mussolini could not swallow this affront to his pride and to Italian prestige. We knew he would have his revenge, or burn himself up in Spain. General Miaja, with his native shrewdness, was cautioning everybody not to become too elated. I remember someone saying to me later that I and all the rest of us who had advertised the Italian humiliation to a delighted world had done the Republican Government a great disservice, because then Mussolini obviously was forced to redeem himself. It was the old fallacy that the chronicler creates history.

I had moved into the Florida Hotel in March—the month of Guadalajara—and there was a brilliant group of journalists present to watch a Loyalist attack on the Casa de Campo. There were Ernest Hemingway, Sefton Delmer of the *London Daily Express,* Henry Buckley of the *Daily Telegraph,* Martha Gellhorn of *Collier's,* Virginia Cowles, John Dos Passos. We watched the battle from a much-battered apartment house on the Paseo de Rosales, which Hemingway christened "the Old Homestead." That was the first show which he and I covered together, but by no means the last.

Madrid, amidst many other happy memories, has that one for me, too—of great days with a man who exemplifies for me much that is brave and good and fine in a somewhat murky world. Ernest Hemingway is great-hearted and childish, and perhaps a little mad, and I wish there were more like him—but there could not be. He and Marty Gellhorn (later Mrs. Hemingway) and I, and the long drives, and the cold nights at the front, and the scrappy meals cooked in the room at the Florida while the Germans blasted shells in and around the hotel, and the gramophone played a Chopin "mazurka"—those were good days.

But one day stands out above them all, the day that Ernest and I, and Sefton Delmer, too, took Teruel. All through the autumn of 1937, in Madrid, we waited for that great Rebel offensive which, according to Franco and his sympathizers, was going to end the war. Instead, it was the Government which launched the offensive on December 15, and it proved one of the most amazing and satisfactory developments of the war. Teruel, high up on the edge of the Universal Mountains, was the Rebels' best fortified city, the place from which all map experts had predicted Franco would drive down to Valencia.

We could not believe it was a major offensive, but it had to be seen, so on the 17th Hemingway, Delmer and I drove to Valencia. Early on the morning of the 18th we were at the headquarters of Colonel Hernández Sarabia, commander of the Army of the Levant, who was acting under the orders of General Vicente Rojo, Chief of the General Staff. Those headquarters were to become familiar in the next few months, but for me they never lost their romance or picturesque quality. The railroad to Valencia goes through many tunnels on the way to Teruel, and under one of them, just beyond the station of Mora de Rubielos, the Republican command put a train. The engine stuck out at one end and a car or two at the other, but the rest was as snug and safe from bombing as any place in Spain. To come from the numbing cold outside to the overheated Pullman cars was one of the unforgettable sensations of that offensive. As we walked up to the train that freezing dawn, we found some soldiers seated around a fire, heating oranges; and that was our breakfast.

Sarabia was out at one of the field posts, they told us, and we finally located him out on top of a mountain overlooking the whole field of battle. Nothing in that whole campaign impressed me so much as the incredibly bad weather in which the battle was fought, and I am sure that for military historians that will be the feature most worth study. It was the cut of the wind which was so especially distressing. Nothing was protection against the icy blasts that came shrieking down from the north, penetrating any amount of clothes. Our eyes filled with constant tears from the sting of it; our fingers swelled and became numb, and all feeling went out of our feet except an overwhelming iciness. We gasped for breath, and could not stand in one spot to look through our field glasses, for the wind buffeted us like a prizefighter boring in. The touch of the binoculars to our faces could not have been more agonizing if we had taken two pieces of ice and held them against our eyes. That wind had been roaring down at 50 miles per hour throughout those four long days of battle, during two of which there was heavy snow while everything under foot turned to ice. And through it all, day after day, Loyalist soldiers had fought steadily forward and Government planes had taken the air again and again to strafe Rebel positions. Teruel was lots of things, good and bad, but it was, above all, a triumph of human material and modern aviation under the most trying conditions imaginable.

Sarabia, former Republican Minister of War, one of the few truly loyal officers of the old Army, was always the soul of courtesy and friendliness. It was a fine war from that point of view in Government Spain. Down in his warm dugout the Colonel showed us on his own maps just what had happened since the troops had moved forward at 7:10 on the morning of the 15th.

The more or less enthusiastic crowds of ill-led, ill-equipped, unco-ordinated militiamen had at last been whipped into an army whose bulk was made up not of the volunteer but of the conscript. The fatal lack of officers and non-coms had been partly made up by the officers' training schools. Matériel that had been bought from every country in the world, including Germany and Italy, and bootlegged at high prices—except from Russia, which charged normal prices—was being supplemented in considerable proportions by the output of Spanish factories. The foreigner had ceased to play an important role, and the army that took Teruel was 100 per cent Spanish.

Four army corps, fully 90,000 men, with all their matériel, had been gathered quietly and thrown into the battle without the Rebels showing any sign that they realized what was coming. The Teruel garrison was neither reinforced nor warned, and Enrique Lister, on the right, repeated his feat at the Brunete offensive during the summer and by ten in the morning had stormed Concud, just off the main road behind Teruel. At the same time an Anarchist division moved up on the extreme left to take Campillo and close the only other egress from Teruel.

Snow had begun to fall at 9 o'clock that morning, and the next day the weather became so bad that men died of the cold, waiting for orders to charge, while casualties from frost-bite ran into the thousands. Lister hung on and fortified his position; the left wing pushed slowly up, to close the circle behind Teruel, and two columns from the southwest and northwest gradually fought their way forward, hindered not so much by the Insurgent troops as by the weather. On the 17th a blizzard cut communications with Lister, and in desperation the Government made plans to throw a "life-line" down from Montalbán on the north. But the next day the weather cleared, and the right-center pushed forward to make a juncture with Lister at Kilometer 179 of the Saragossa highway.

While we were in Sarabia's dug-out Lister was repelling a fifth counterattack, for, as always, he had the vital position. Negrín and Prieto came up as we were leaving, both very happy—Prieto particularly so, for he had staked much on this offensive, and as he was Minister of National Defense, upon him had been imposed the burden of preparation and decision. That was one of the curious and unfortunate things about the Government side. There was no commander-in-chief, no Napoleon and—England being what she was—no Wellington. The old Army men were not good enough; the new still lacked experience, and neither trusted the other. So it remained for a rotund Socialist politician, who had never seen a military treatise, and who had no particular faith in victory, to direct the military destinies of the Second Spanish Republic. Already he had weakened the morale of the Army by his anti-Communism, and now he and that timid soul,

Vicente Rojo, his chief of staff, were to lose the fruits of the Teruel victory by failure to act courageously and decisively.

However, on the afternoon of December 18, we could not know that. The military objectives were clear: to forestall the planned Rebel offensive by creating a diversion, and to force Franco to make a big counter-offensive on ground of the Government's choosing. The first step was to take Teruel, and the attack was being carried out splendidly. We rushed back to Valencia to get our stories off by courier to Madrid, and by dawn of the 21st were back at the railroad train under the tunnel. It was to be the greatest day of the war for the Republican arms, and—quite incidentally—one of the greatest days of my life. The three of us (Hemingway, Delmer and myself) were joined by Mathieu Corman, a mad Belgian correspondent, and we had the rare privilege of accompanying the front-line troops in the victorious assault of a great city. For this time it was the central column that had to smash up the Sagunto highway and into Teruel itself.

Since our previous visit, the pass of Puerto Escandón on the highway had been forced, and the powerful position of Pancho Villa, above it, had been turned so quickly that the Rebels had to flee or be cut off. That left the towering hulk of Mansueto Hill, with its massive steel and cement fortifications, and a whole stretch of rolling hills on either side of the road for the last four miles, to be taken. Corman, who indicated that he was more or less directing the battle, said he would take us to the right places and people, so we put him in the back of the car and drove out along the Sagunto road.

Troops and armored cars were stretched out ahead of us. No one knew where the first lines were, since it was a fight of maneuver in the open, but just before we reached Puerto Escandón a truckload of troops being brought up for the attack passed us, and we trailed along. There were youngsters in that car, white and nervous as troops are before battle, but they grinned and waved to us and shouted, "See you for lunch in Teruel!"

On we went to Kilometer 9, where a battalion was massed, preparatory to moving forward. There we had to leave the car and walk ahead, knowing that when we came under fire the

Rebels would let us know it quickly enough. But nothing happened for three kilometers, and we had almost persuaded ourselves we could keep walking that way into Teruel. The Loyalist artillery had been maintaining a constant fire against Mansueto, which towered on our right, and we knew that had to be the Government's first and chief objective. It did not seem possible that the formidable position could be taken in one day, and we gave up hopes of entering Teruel. There had been virtually no rifle or machine-gun fire, so we knew the attack had not started. It was at Kilometer 6 that the last lap of the offensive began.

Soldiers were strung along a ditch on the right of the road and on the crest of a ridge that rose still further to the right and swung until it faced Mansueto over a gully that had the railroad line at the bottom. Behind the center of this crescent was a loyalist machine-gun nest on a dominating mound. One cannot mistake first lines. They are written on every face and in every gesture. The time was eleven in the morning, and the fearful weather of previous days had turned clear and so warm that all the snow had melted. On that score, and for one of the rare times in the war, destiny certainly favored the Loyalists, for if it had been a worse day they would never have reached Teruel that evening.

Firing began on our left, and we saw khaki-clad Loyalists moving forward steadily and ruthlessly over the broken ground. Never once did we see those lines fall back; never once did we see the Rebels counterattack.

As we could not obtain a good view from the ditch, a group of us decided to climb to the machine-gun post. That was the first of many times during that day that we came under direct machine-gun fire, and it was one of the worst, for as we went up the ridge we exposed ourselves to fire from less than a thousand yards. The machine-gunner was either nervous or a bad marksman, for somehow he managed to miss us all. Five minutes later we had the satisfaction of seeing him and his comrades break for the rear as the Loyalists moved up on them from the left. That, too, was a process we were to see repeated many times during the day.

At 11:20 the fight for Mansueto began, so we ran up to the crest on the right, hoping to see the action from there. It was a foolhardy move, for the Government troops had orders to open up a heavy fire with small arms against the Rebel lines across the gully, and the Insurgents, whose main body had already begun to retreat, covered the maneuver by laying down an equally heavy machine-gun barrage. The troops were protected by shallow trenches, but we had only the crest of the hill to shield us. It meant flattening ourselves on the ground, and there were several periods when veritable sheets of bullets crackled so close that to raise our heads off the ground might well have meant death. Two soldiers were killed nearby from head wounds, which is what one gets in such fighting. In quieter moments, Hemingway showed a reluctant conscript how to unjam the bolt of his rifle with a stone, while Delmer took photographs of the process.

When the fire slackened we moved still further to the right, and there came upon two Rebel prisoners, white-faced, unshaven, with that hunted-animal look which prisoners usually have. They had been treated well, were assured that this late in the war Loyalists did not kill prisoners, and even received bread and jam from the scanty stores of food available. Their worst scare came when Corman decided that a man with a face like one of them could only be a Falangist and asked the soldiers to shoot him—in vain.

From that spot we could see the charge up Mansueto Hill, and changed our minds about the impossibility of taking Teruel that day. Nothing could stop those troops as they swarmed in three deployed columns up the eastern slopes of that half-mountain. Two dogs frisked ridiculously about in front of one of the advancing columns. But it was a grim business; up above, Government artillery continued to pound at the crest of the hill, and already Rebel troops began to break, abandoning marvelously strong positions.

It could be only a question of time, and we wanted to go on toward Teruel with the soldiers who were moving ahead of us. It was 12:30 and they had an hour's headstart, so we went up the Sagunto road. Here was the body of a Rebel who had died in a last counterattack during the previous night. His face was gray, for he had been wounded in the head, and his left arm hung stiffly in the air as if, even in death, he had tried to give the Fascist salute.

The highway went through a gully, swung around, dipped to a little bridge, and there, on the other side, in the midst of this battle, was a family of two girls and their parents. The man rushed up to us, pumped our hands joyously and slapped us on the back, while his wife beamed and chattered happily. Perhaps they thought we were the Russian General Staff they had heard about, but their happiness seemed genuine, and they pressed some excellent anisette upon us, to drink to health and victory.

A little later we came to a barricade which the Insurgents had built well but placed badly, so that it gave them no respite. A battered, bullet-riddled car stood beside it, looking as if it would never run again, but at least it was the first booty. We climbed over and moved down a little further to Kilometer 3, and there was the first line again. Corman almost got us all shot as we barged up, for he had a live grenade in his left hand and a pistol in his right, and since we were dressed in civilian clothes and in the front lines, we could scarcely have seemed more suspicious.

The line spread out along ridges on both sides of the road, with fire coming from the right, where the Rebels still held a corral and part of Mansueto. We watched the corral being vainly attacked by a small group of men who again and again got up, and even went in to throw hand grenades, only to be forced out each time. Sterner measures would have to be used, for it was an important position.

Another advance had been made, and we could see the troops ahead of us at Kilometer 2.5. It was a ticklish job reaching them, for up on Mansueto some expert use was being made of machine guns and rifles with telescopic sights. However, we reached the spot safely just as soldiers lining the road ditch and other troops on both sides got the order to move on that corral and on a signal station next to the railroad track on the left. We crawled up behind them to a vantage point offered by a slight rise in ground. The firing was very heavy, but it was worth the risk to see those waves of men dash forward, so determined, so steady. Those on the left got it worst. While I watched two men went down as they were crossing an open field a hundred yards away. One got up, staggered forward—not backward—for five yards and then slumped down again. Two others had been left motionless behind them on the edge of the field, while still another crumpled limply as he reached the further end.

Then the first mortar shell came over. It was from an 81-mm. gun, and well aimed. It landed 50 yards to our left, slightly behind us and full upon two men lying in the grass. As the black column of smoke shot up, one man ran wildly out of it, unhurt but momentarily crazed. Then I saw him turn in a half circle and join his comrades in a charge toward the Rebel positions. That was a soldier if I ever saw one. His comrade was dead.

Then more mortar shells came and bullets and more bullets, and we had to move back to the road where the side of the ditch protected us. I looked at the top of Mansueto and saw a line of Loyalists moving along its crest. It was 1:40, and it meant Mansueto was falling.

But perhaps the Loyalists could not take it all that day. We waited there one hour, two hours. A motorcyclist went back to get our food from the car; it was shared with hungry officers and soldiers who likewise killed a precious bottle of Scotch. At 3:45 Government planes came over, a few dozen bombers and chasers which spread their destruction and went. The sun was getting low, and once again we began to doubt whether Teruel could be taken that day.

Then the soldiers shouted gleefully: *"Los dinamiteros! los dinamiteros!"* Two truckloads drove up, and out came the toughest and happiest soldiers it has ever been my lot to see. These were the cream of the soldiery, men whose only arm were hand grenades strung in their belts and in pouches by their sides. They were the men who entered towns and "dynamited" their way forward in close fighting. They formed in columns of three, and marched down the road with a zest and swagger that showed clearly enough how they felt. A few hundred yards ahead they turned left and deployed, moving forward to Kilometer 2. The last phase of the day's battle had begun.

The artillery had been moved up to accompany the advance, shells booming and shrieking ceaselessly over our heads. Shots from the mortars were coming our way, too, and there was one expert sharpshooter on Mansueto who would not permit anyone to show his head over the ditch without placing a bullet so close that one could hear its crack. That was a soldier, too; his life was doomed, but he wanted to sell it dearly.

At 4:25 a battalion moved across from Kilometer 2 toward another house and signal station, and we walked down the road to watch it better. The sun was sinking, and the men made a thrilling picture as they surged forward. As they began to attack, a Rebel gunner slammed a mortar shell exactly in the middle of them. A good gunner, that man.

About 4:30 we heard heavy firing down on the edge of Teruel, and although we did not know it at the time, it was the dynamiters making their charge upon the city. As well as I can recall, it was at the same historic moment that an Insurgent machine gunner opened up a burst on us that came desperately close. We piled up behind a big tree, and waited for other things to distract him.

It was already twilight, and our last opportunity to get into Teruel that day, so we moved on, without drawing much fire that time, and at a turn in the road came upon Teruel a thousand yards ahead! Through field glasses, in the gathering darkness we could see dynamiters rushing into the first streets and the flashes of their bombs in the houses. On both sides of the Sagunto highway, hundreds of soldiers were deploying along the final crest. The great moment had come—one of those dramatic moments in history and journalism. We stood watching for a while, but when at 5:25 an armored car drove up and the driver leaned out to shout: "You can get up to the Plaza de Toros," there could be no more waiting. We had shaken off Corman some time before, and there were only the three of us. However, to go in alone would have been foolhardy, for three civilians wandering about in an embattled city in the dark could expect little mercy.

The problem was solved for us a few hundred yards down the road, by our finding two officers, one Spanish and the other a Bulgarian named Stefan. The latter deserves special notice, for he was the only foreigner we came across during the entire day; Teruel was taken by the Spanish Popular Army under Spanish command. So we strolled along as darkness descended, taking a fork in the road that led down into the San Julián quarter, a poor working-class district. We almost stumbled over the body of a Loyalist lieutenant who had had the bad luck to be killed when victory was literally in sight. We carried his body over to the side of the road so that it should not be run over.

And then a little way, and we were in Teruel. Off to our right the shrill chattering of women could be heard, so we cautiously made our way behind several houses in the direction of the sound. Any window, any house might have a desperate soldier prepared to go down fighting, and that knowledge was made more terrifying by the darkness. We crept into a backyard, and the Bulgarian officer forced open a door that led into another yard. One by one we entered on tiptoe and listened, and it was only then that we heard many male voices which had not carried as the women's voices had. The officers drew their revolvers, and after a whispered colloquy decided to work around the house and come on them in the street. We followed silently as they crept close to the wall of the house and suddenly turned into the street. We were almost mobbed, but not by desperate Fascists. These were men and women who wept for joy to see us. They embraced us, shook our hands until they ached, patted and prodded and slapped us and poured out a flood of incoherent but happy talk. It took a long time to make them realize that we were not high staff officers, Russian or otherwise, and had nothing to do with the taking of Teruel, but it did not make any difference. When I told a little girl that I was an American she laughed hysterically and repeated, *"Norteamericano!"* many times, as if it were the funniest thing she ever heard.

For six days, anxious but safe, they had lived in their cellars, and now they were very happy. One woman brought out a pitcher of newly made wine, dark-red and tangy, with a touch of the wine-skin taste.

And so the day ended. It was dangerous to be standing there. Two mortar shells broke very close, and stray shots were landing around us. The officers ordered all the civilians back to their houses, with the strictest orders not to stir out until daylight. Then we walked back. Every so often heavy bursts of fire inside the town showed that some poor devils were selling their lives dearly, but for the most part it was quiet. We had one really dangerous moment as we walked up the road toward that first crest where the Loyalists were strung out waiting for orders to go in. We had been ahead of the front-line troops, although behind the dynamiters, but, naturally, civilians coming out of Teruel must be Fascists! We could not expect soldiers—and nervous ones at that—to realize that we were foreign newspapermen, in such a place and at such a time. I thought they were going to pull those triggers, but we threw up our hands and talked fast.

They did not go in until the next morning, so we had scooped even the military. We were tired, having left Valencia at four in the morning and going hard ever since, but the greatest story in the world is worthless unless it is in the newspaper. The car was nine kilometers back, but at the barricade we found the broken-down automobile, and it proved booty indeed when it worked. We reached Valencia at midnight, and I spent four tired hours writing my dispatch and starting it off to Madrid by courier. I myself thought it the best story of the war and one of the best in my career, but a few days later I received a sharp cable from the Managing Editor saying that there was a war on in China and other big doings, and I should keep that in mind. My dispatch (which was exactly as I have written it here) was hacked down to half length and buried inside the paper. But that was a day's work, and it is good for a man to have lived such days and to be able to look back on them.

We took a few hours' rest that morning and went back to Teruel where some 6,000 of the Rebel garrison and civilians had taken refuge in a half dozen big buildings like the Seminary, the

Gobierno Civil, the Santa Clara convent, and the barracks of the Civil Guard. The Bishop of Teruel was among them—a hard man, from his reputation, and one who had favored the terrible Fascist repressions of the first days. The Government treated him well, but he was later murdered by Anarchists during the retreat into France.

The town could, and should, have been quickly cleaned up and the terrain for miles around cleared of Rebels, but there again Prieto bungled. He wanted to spare as many lives as possible on both sides, and so for seventeen days the heroic garrison was permitted to fight on while Franco launched counter-offensives. To be sure, there is nothing more dangerous in warfare than cleaning up a city, for you are dealing with desperate soldiers firing from shelter at close range. In the case of Teruel there were not only such deadly marksmen as the Civil Guards, but there were underground passages, connecting the important buildings, through which soldiers could retreat.

We went up three days running, watching the civilians pouring out in pitiful groups and columns and the soldiers gradually cleaning up all but those stubbornly defended buildings. Our riskiest venture was to accompany a tank that was dragging a 6-inch gun to fire at 300-yard range against the seminary. Three streets had to be crossed that were dominated by fire, one from only 150 yards away. It was a case of sprinting desperately, one by one, and doubled over in order to make as small a mark as possible. One man was shot in the stomach and two others were killed in maintaining liaison. But the gun was rolled into place and we watched it blast away at the seminary, gradually bringing down the façade.

We saw tanks and armored cars maneuvering and firing until snipers and machine-gun nests were silenced; machine-gun crews being rushed on to roofs and high angles; dynamiters making the last charge while windows were kept under streams of fire to protect their advance; soldiers creeping up from every side to dash into houses. Sarabia was made a general. The Gobierno Civil was set afire, and it made a tremendous blaze. There were dead bodies all over the place, bodies of men and of mules, and there was no time to clean up the streets. Then it was Christmas Eve, and we spent it driving up to Barcelona. It was a great and joyous Christmas for Loyalist Spain, the second of the war, and my second in Spain.

Hemingway left us there, and on the 28th Delmer and I were back in Teruel, with Robert Capa, whose fame as the greatest of all war photographers was solidly established in that war. He was, too, one who lent the warm light of a brave and lovable character to that tragic scene.

The *Guardia Civil* barracks had been captured the night before, and we arrived in time to see about 350 guards being led out of the city. Later we saw a small group of Civil Guard officers coming out. The lieutenant colonel was a heavy, flat-faced, brutish man, his face so brutal that I shall never forget it. In war, at least, one can shoot the people who deserve to be shot. Those Civil Guards had betrayed the militiamen going to relieve Teruel at the beginning of the war and had killed every one of them. So Teruel then became a Rebel city, with its salient pointing threateningly at the coast, and the Spanish proletariat chalked up one more account of hatred against the *Guardia Civil*—which was here being settled.

The first big Rebel counter-offensive started that day, and made steady momentum. Lister held at Concud, but the left wing weakened and the Insurgents drove in toward Teruel. On the 31st, half of La Muela, the dominance just to the south, was lost, and Rojo rushed up Gustavo Durán's division in a blinding snowstorm, with the cold so intense that Durán later told me one of his officers dropped dead while he was talking to him. Communications were being crippled; the Government airfields were buried in snow and ice, while the Rebels', lower down, were still free. The Insurgents began the New Year by claiming Teruel, and some dishonest journalists on their side actually dated their stories "Teruel," with circumstantial accounts of how the city was relieved and the joy of the inhabitants. In Barcelona, even at the Ministry of War, there were long faces, for communications were down and one could believe the worst. So Capa and I went to Teruel to see.

It meant a three-day journey over snow-blocked roads along which was the worst traffic jam since 2,500 Italian trucks had piled up for four days before Termaber Pass on the way to Addis Ababa. About 45 miles up from Sagunto there is a steep pass called Puerto Ragudo, which is nearly 4,000 feet in altitude, but we encountered trouble long before that, since the pass had been blocked for two days and the hundreds of cars that came along were stretched out in a serpentine column fully ten miles long.

The snow had caught the Government unprepared just as heavy reinforcements of matériel were being rushed up to the front, and it became locked there in a temporarily unbreakable grip. Fortunately, technicians and workmen had arrived and were clearing the snow away, breaking up the ice with picks, forcing slower cars over to the right to let others pass them; at the top, where the road was particularly steep, tractors with cranes had been placed to drag the vehicles up the last stretch.

My car started the three-mile climb at eleven in the morning and we got over the top at 7:30 in the evening. The interim was a confused and rather agonizing nightmare of heaving, straining, grinding upward yard by yard, with the car swaying from side to side and the wheels unable even to turn on the slippery surface. We were bruised from innumerable falls, since it seemed almost impossible to keep one's feet for more than a few minutes; we were blue with cold, and famished and terribly tired, but so was everybody else, and somehow we all sooner or later got to the top of Puerto Ragudo.

Our reward came when, after we had coasted down to Barracas, some Carabinero officers with whom we had become friendly on the way up invited us into their headquarters for the night. That meant a cheerful, blazing fire in a peasant's hut, a marvelous feast of dried, salt codfish, bread, wine, and coffee, a pleasant chat on war and women and home, and a few hours' sleep, rolled up in a rug before the smoldering fire. It is for such things that men sometimes love war.

And then in the morning we were off for Teruel, wondering whether we should be able to enter the town. The Rebel stories had so impressed me that I did not dare to drive my car into the city. I left it two miles off and walked the rest of the way. But there it all was, and the soldiers laughed when I told them what the Insurgent communiqués had said. The road was battered; dead mules and broken vehicles lay about; the buildings had been still further smashed and ground down by shells and bombs, but all was quiet. The Rebels' drive had got them to within a mile or two of the city on the southern side, but they were pushed back, and the lines held, so the danger was over.

The Civil Governor's building had just been mined, so Capa and I ran around there to see what was happening. The whole top part of the façade on the side facing the bridge over the Turia had collapsed, leaving what appeared like a mound of beams, broken walls, and cement. Up the side of it Loyalist soldiers were swarming to the attack, and we scrambled up after them. The building was alive with rifle fire, pistol shots, and grenade explosions, and it needed some cautious maneuvering to recognize what corners not to go around and where not to poke one's head.

We came up at about the third floor, and the Rebels were on the floor below us. They shot upward, while the Republicans shot down or threw hand grenades in a setting made fantastic by the destruction of almost every wall and ceiling of the building. Shouts of *"Viva Franco! Viva España!"* came up clearly while cursing militiamen answered with shots and bombs. Once a song floated upward amazingly from that doomed place underneath, and a soldier next to me paused just as he was about to draw the pin of a hand grenade and throw it. "They are singing!" he said in a stupefied tone. I do not know what the tune was, for I was too greatly moved myself by hearing men sing in such a place.

Th stairway rose a few steps, and led into a corridor that swung around to the left. We edged up and around by the wall, peering into room after room where, with slight variations, the same dramatic scene was being enacted: men, crouched at windows or openings in the walls, firing down or throwing hand grenades.

In the last room a tragedy was enacted in our presence. A

Loyalist had broken a hole through the floor that gave him a bead on the room below, and there he waited. While we were standing in the room next door, we heard him shout: "Here's one for you and one for Franco!" and he blazed away twice with his revolver. From the room below came a scream, followed by a confusion of sounds, half weeping, half moaning from pain. We ran in, and the soldier who shot cried to us: "*La granata! la granata!*" pointing down as if to get us to bear witness. In truth, when I peered down for a second I did get the picture of a youth with a grenade clenched in his right hand, which was held over his head, so I ducked back quickly before realizing that he must have been crazed with fear and did not know what he was doing. It was his end in any case, for the Loyalist pumped four more bullets into him in the next second.

"Rather terrible, isn't it?" I said to the captain in charge, who was standing next to me.

"But he was right!" he answered, implying that war, after all, is like that, and newspapermen have no right to come around and be critical.

That was my sixth visit to Teruel, and I was to make four or five more. Back in Barcelona I said good-bye to Luís Quintanilla, artist and fighter and friend, who had served his country well, and was now going to New York to exhibit his hundred great drawings of the war. On January 7 the last refugees in underground Teruel surrendered honorably under charge of Lieutenant Colonel Rey d'Harcourt, the Military Governor. His heroic resistance was rewarded by contumely and charges of cowardice from the Rebel high command.

The counter-offensives kept coming, and against them two International brigades were used, the 15th, with the Americans and the English, and the German 11th, with the Canadian Mackenzie-Papeneau, in reserve. I found them all on January 13, strung alongside the Alfambra road under some of the many tunnels where the railway line ran; they were lousy, but healthy and relatively happy. Captain Milton Wolff was on the brigade staff and Captain Philip Detro had come back to take command of the Lincoln-Washington. I remember vividly the long talk with Detro and Fred Keller, for it was the last time I was to see Detro, that lanky, six-foot-four Texan, and hear his soft, courteous voice; he was wounded on the 29th, lingered for some months in Murcia Hospital, and died. That was the last day on which I saw Captain William Titus, poet and playwright, for he, too, was marked for death. Doctors Barsky and Eloesser were doing their jobs right on top of the lines, as usual.

Teruel looked safe then, but much more was to come. On January 18 the counter-offensive was resumed in still greater force, and once again it was broken, this time thanks to the 11th (German) Brigade, which held the keypoint of El Muletón, a sharp spur dominating the western bank of the Alfambra River just north of Teruel. They and the 15th had been "loaned" by the Polish Communist General Walter, and were the only Internationals used. The defense of El Muletón was one of the great pages of the war, so far as the Internationals were concerned. The 11th lost the hill, but faced the heaviest attack of the conflict to that date, and made the Rebels pay so heavy a price they had to stop and organize still another drive.

The Americans had been brought down to the edge of Teruel itself, where I saw them on the 21st, and again on the 30th after the Insurgents for the second time announced their destruction. To be sure, the brigade had forty killed and 200 wounded. They estimated that at the height of the attack there was no five-yard square that had not received its shell from German artillery. In fact, the Rebels were using such quantities of matériel—particularly artillery and aviation—and their casualties were so high that we all felt sure that, whatever the fate of Teruel, Franco would not be able to take the offensive for a long time. That was a mistake which we were to repeat after the Ebro, too. There was no miscalculation of Franco's (and Mussolini's and Hitler's) expenditure of men and matériel, but what we misjudged was the amount of matériel that Italy and Germany had sent in. It did not matter how much the Generalissimo used up in his counter-offensives—so far as that war was concerned his supply was relatively unlimited. And matériel counted far more than men.

The artillery work was superb at Teruel, for the Germans

were doing it. On that visit of January 30 Delmer and I had
proof of it driving in and out of Teruel. It was breath-taking to
see the accuracy with which they were laying down three-inchers
on the road. But, as it happened, Barcelona was having a worse
time of it that day than Teruel. The terrible series of bombings
that was to make Barcelona a martyred city by the end of the
war had begun on January 15 with five raids that were concentrated on the outer edge of the city. However, on the 19th and
30th the raiders came into the center of town, using delayed-fuse
bombs that for the most part ranged from 250 to 300 kilos each.
Both the Italian and the German air forces did a lot of experi-
menting during the war, and that was one of their more "successful" experiments, although an even greater one was to come in
March.

Take as an example the bombing of Barcelona on January
30, 1938. Perhaps you do not know how delayed-fuse bombs
work. Here is the damage that one did, far inside the city. The
San Felipe Neri refuge for children had been a Catholic school
and church, in the heart of old Barcelona, with walls a good
yard thick and rising from narrow streets. You could not imagine
an apparently safer refuge, but, to make sure, the children had
been trained to go down into a crypt underneath the church
when the air alarm sounded. It was like the fire drills that we
hold in American public schools, and that Sunday morning the
children dutifully filed down the stairs into the refuge. There
were a few stragglers and lazy ones, and they lived—about fifteen
of them. Most of the other bodies—158 in all—were never recovered, for they were buried under an appalling amount of
wreckage. The hole in the church roof where the bomb entered
was hardly larger than a four-inch dud shell would have made,
and had the bomb exploded on contact nothing would have happened to the children. However, that was where the delayed-
fuse proved its efficiency, for the missile continued its plunge
until it landed directly on the ceiling of the crypt, and then
exploded.

There were just two bombing raids on the 30th, but the identi-
fied dead were 350—and then there were those unidentified, those

buried in the wreckage of buildings, and those who disappeared. I had just returned from Teruel as the second raid ended, and to me the war there seemed clean and wholesome compared to that horror of destroyed apartment houses, of mutilated bodies (some long and some pitifully short) side by side in the morgue, of screaming women and children trapped in rooms from which there were no stairs down, of the wounded whose spirits as well as bodies seemed broken.

One never could say how many were killed in such raids. When a seven-story apartment house, for instance, is driven into the ground with every single man, woman and child in it buried underneath, how are you to know the number of victims? I saw many such houses. They smelt bad for a long time. That afternoon I saw 108 bodies lying in a morgue; sixty-one were of children. One was a girl about a year old. She had tiny earrings; her cheeks were red, and her eyes were open in a bright, perky stare, so that you knew she was dead only because of where she was lying and because her eyes did not waver.

When you have seen such things you do not forget them easily, and one of the satisfactions of the war was to describe them as I saw them, not quite in all their blood and horror, because it is against journalistic tradition to go into too much detail about human bodies, but with enough detail to stir the reader's imagination. In that way one knew a little what war was like, and how civilization was brought to Spain. The symbol of that bombing was to me, as I wrote at the time, the little old lady at the head of the line of bodies in the morgue. She was well dressed, in black, with a dainty lace collar and a rather expensive comb in her hair—not a working woman, just an old lady of a good, middle-class Catalan family. Death had caught her protesting at the pain and horror of it, somewhat as the lava from Vesuvius had caught the Pompeians, petrifying their gestures for future record. She had raised her arms and twisted her body, and then the whole house had come down on her, taking life away but infinitely multiplying the power of expression that permitted her to say in death more about bombs than any number of books like this could tell you.

Of the wounded I remember especially that list of ninety who had been admitted to the clinical hospital in the morning. The last entry was, "A woman who cannot speak."

Of course, such victims are the incidentals of a bombing. Neither Franco nor the Italian pilots deliberately chose such targets. Bombing is done for two reasons: either to destroy definite military objectives or to terrorize and demoralize the rear-guard. If you accept the "totalitarian" theory of waging war (which we have all had to do) the old lady and the baby were also military objectives. There is no picking and choosing. And let no one ever deceive you about so-called "precision bombing" from high altitudes. Dive-bombing can, under favorable conditions, be precise, but high-altitude bombing never is exact.

You want people to say, "We will pay any price to end this horror." You want soldiers to feel that it is not enough to be brave and ready to give one's own life, since that will not spare the lives of wives and children. Fortunately, the human spirit is stronger than bombs or the logical minds of totalitarian theorists, and the Spanish war proved it before the "blitzes" of World War II. The bombings in Spain caused untold misery and suffering and death, but the hatred and fury they aroused prolonged the war; they did not shorten it.

Out at the front, Teruel was gradually being lost. Rojo did not dare to engage his reserves; his troops in the line were badly distributed and terribly tired; and, worst of all, matériel was running desperately short. A third counter-offensive was launched in the middle of February, 1938, with an overwhelming amount of matériel. It was a pincer movement to the south and north of the city. The left wing forced its way to the bank of the Alfambra the first day and then moved behind Teruel to Valdecebro on the 20th. Then it crossed the Sagunto highway, meanwhile bringing pressure from the west and forcing the Republicans to fall back across the Turia. That picturesque swashbuckler, El Campesino, had been ordered to hold Teruel with his 46th Division until the end, to cover the retreat of the other units. With characteristic daring he waited until the circle around Teruel had virtually closed, on the 22nd. Then, that night, he got his men together, placed his tanks in front, and literally blasted his way out through the Rebel lines to safety, with all his guns and matériel.

A few minutes later the Ministry of National Defense in Barcelona issued the following communique: "The high morale of the Republican troops was unable to overcome the accumulation of German and Italian matériel gathered by the Rebels as a result of the advantages afforded them by the policy of 'Non-Intervention,' which can record among its victories this most recent one of the evacuation of Teruel."

The Insurgents had taken two months and four big counter-offensives to regain what the Government took in six days, but it was worth the price they paid, both in prestige regained and in the weakening of the Loyalist forces. The Popular Army had put up a glorious show, but the odds against it were too great. The outstanding figure on both sides was the big, burly former stone-cutter from Galicia, Enrique Lister, whose capture and defense of Concud proved him one of the great divisional commanders of the war.

The 15th Brigade hovered around in the last days of Teruel, but were not thrown in after Segura de los Baños. Then they got 700 new additions—American, Canadian, British, and Spanish—and a well-earned rest which was not to last long, for Franco, Hitler, and Mussolini were preparing the drive to the coast.

Since it was expected that the offensive would bring victory to Franco, the British were busy laying their plans for "after the war." The exchange of "commercial agents" in November, 1937, was followed by overtures to Mussolini and Hitler in which a willingness to sacrifice Spain was clear. Lord Halifax went to Berlin late in November but was met with a rebuff, so Chamberlain turned toward Rome in the endless and always futile effort to split the Axis. It was "appeasement" coming into bloom, but opposition developed in an unexpected quarter. Eden wanted Italy to show its good faith by first withdrawing troops from Spain. However, Mussolini had said that Franco must win, and he could not win without continued Italian help. It therefore followed that Eden would have to be sacrificed and Il Duce per-

mitted to supply the Rebels with all the men and matériel necessary for this "final" offensive. On February 20 Eden resigned. On
March 9 the Aragon campaign started, and, with its success
assured, Chamberlain went to Rome to sign the "Easter Pact."
The only difficulty was that the war did not then end.

"Appeasement" had by then become a nightmare for all those
who could see where it was leading the world. I had long since
lost any quality of indifference or amorality about international
politics. Spain was proving the best of all schools, and despite
the bitterness of the knowledge acquired, I had learned the joy
of comradeship in battle, the satisfaction of sharing the tribula-
tions of a fight in a great though losing cause. It so happened
that "I loved the games men played with death, where death
must win." That was personal, and selfish, but not unnatural,
and, after all, Spain was the most suitable place in the world to
feel the joy in man's tragic struggle against the forces of evil.

Tragedy at Barcelona

TERUEL, for all its heroism and logic, had failed. The attack
had been well planned and carried out; the defense was brave
and tenacious but badly handled. However, the tragedy was in
the mistaken conception. In ordinary circumstances the strategy
would have been excellent—to strike before the enemy did and
force him to fight on ground of one's own choosing, thus exhausting him in a fruitless battle at the temporary sacrifice of
one's own strength. But Franco could not be exhausted; his resources, like the contents of Thor's horn, stretched back to a
relatively limitless ocean—Italian and German matériel strength.
It was a simple matter to replace the matériel the Generalissimo
used up in his counter-offensives, and he even had fresh Italian
troops who had not seen action since the northern campaign.
The Germans had sent in more planes, artillery, ammunition,
and technicians to strengthen the Condor Legion.

Meanwhile, the Government was truly exhausted, and, thanks
to "Non-Intervention," had no means of replacing the matériel
used up. There were enough troops, although there was a lack
of good officers and non-coms. And then there was treachery,
skillfully organized by the same Germans who had prepared
Caporetto. The effect behind the lines was devastating—and the
gangrene reached as high as Prieto's staff.

A war that had been second- or third-class suddenly took on the
dimensions of the World War, so far as one side was concerned,
while the other remained weak. The old formula was proving its
validity: one-half of Spain could not defeat the other half plus
Italy, Germany, and England.

On March 9, 1938, the drive to the coast began when the Insurgents struck at three points on a 60-mile front with the main axis pointing at Hijar. The Loyalist line crumpled like paper. The Rebels, using great mobility on a wide front, found it a simple matter to thrust columns of tanks or Moorish cavalry into the open spaces, once the opposing line had been broken, so that any point or sector where a stand was made could be flanked. The Government never had enough matériel or good troops to establish a solid line. General Sebastián Pozas, commander of the Army of Aragon, had shamefully neglected the question of fortifications. The weather remained perfect throughout the whole offensive. So, all in all, the wonder was not that the Rebels reached the coast, but that they were unable to win the war then and there.

The Italians were having an easy and triumphant time of it to begin with, but they had hardly got started when Mussolini received a fearful shock as Hitler marched into Austria. That was part of the price which Il Duce was to pay for Spain. He had tried desperately to finish it off quickly and be prepared, but Guadalajara had ended that hope, and there was Italy still making a huge and weakening expenditure in Spain while Hitler calmly marched down to the Brenner Pass.

I have no space to describe for you that disastrous retreat to the coast which was to split Loyalist Spain in two. I followed it day by day, unhappy and nervous, for there is nothing in war-corresponding so dangerous as to feel out a retreat with non-existent lines. Every evening, back in Barcelona, I was able to send my newspaper the full and tragic story of the day, for I had discovered (I am confessing this for the first time) that if my Paris bureau telephoned me at a certain hour, the Spanish censor who usually listened in would be out to dinner. The trick was never discovered, and I used it again during the even more disastrous campaign which ended the war in Catalonia. I have never considered myself under any obligation to hold back news, however much it harms the cause or the country I favor, so long as I have given no pledges of secrecy.

One of the things which most impressed me during the break-through to the coast was the mass flight of civilians before the oncoming Rebels—not a new sight in Spain, and one that was to become terribly familiar in Europe in succeeding years. There were few things sadder or more significant in that whole horrible Civil War than the anxious and weary flight of peasants, carrying their children and their few poor household goods in carts, on mules, or simply afoot. Thin, pitiful streams of men and women struggled stoically forward to an uncertain and unhappy future, gradually converging into the mass that ultimately poured into France. There was never a more expressive plebiscite against Fascism.

But that period was to provide an even more important example of the horrors of modern warfare, for it saw the first blitz of a great city—Barcelona. In the Abyssinian War I had developed a stupid contempt for aerial bombardment, simply because the Italians did very little of it. So I came back from Africa convinced that the public had an exaggerated idea of the destruction which airplanes could cause. Madrid and Guérnica had made me change my mind.

The destruction of Guérnica on April 26, 1937, during the Basque campaign, will forever rank as the prototype of totalitarian bombing. There one had the systematic and complete obliteration of a town far behind the front lines—which was going to be taken without difficulty anyway, since the Loyalist troops were routed. It happened to be a road center, although not a very important one, but was in no other respect a military objective. Few troops were quartered in the village and there were no factories. It was, however, the historic and sentimental capital of the Basques, older than Bilbao, with its sacred oak tree that symbolized the undying quality of Basque democracy. It was the heart of Vizcaya, and to smash it was to break the heart of the Basques. That was the "military objective" at which the Germans aimed.

The attack was machine-like and systematic. Each section of the village was taken in turn at about twenty-minute intervals, and for the first time incendiaries were used on a large scale. The fires they started permitted the Rebels, in one of their later contradictory accounts of what happened, to say that the Anarchists set fire to Guérnica. Innocent or dishonest newspapermen were shown houses with their four walls standing, and they were told that only fire could have done that, although it is a commonplace sight, after a bombing, to see houses so gutted, with their walls standing.

Guernica is a landmark in journalism because of the veil which the Rebels were able to throw over it and the confusion which their false versions caused outside of Spain. However, history cannot be fooled in the long run. The Basques will pass the story on to their children, and to their children's children as long as the Basque people live on this earth. The confusion which Franco and his American Catholic sympathizers caused did not survive the war.

"The destruction of Guérnica was not only a horrible thing to see," wrote G. L. Steer, *The New York Times* correspondent in Bilbao, in his remarkable book on the campaign; "it led to some of the most horrible and inconsistent lying heard by Christian ears since Ananias was carried out feet foremost to his long, central-heated home."

But as an experiment in totalitarian bombing it was a complete material success.

I had seen some fearful bombings in Madrid, but there was no blitz in the form in which we now know it. The capital had its own special form of calamity in the incessant shellings by the ring of German artillery around the city. I lived through and wrote about so many of them that the feelings they aroused became dulled, and it used to take all my ingenuity to find something new to say about them. The terror, destruction, and death were never less for Madrid, but for newspaper readers it was merely another shelling, and one got used to reading about such things. The callousness to suffering which World War II has made a commonplace, began in Spain. A newspaperman cannot sustain indignation or horror in others, and that was why the Rebels were able to ignore public opinion in their bombings and shellings. The first few times it was embarrassing to them that the civilized world was shocked and horrified by what they did, but Fascism knows that the way to deal with public opinion is to tell it lies and then to forget about it.

The penthouse which I and Sefton Delmer had on the edge of the Retiro Park in Madrid provided a spectacular observation post for the night shellings which were so frequent in the autumn of 1937. There never was rhyme or reason for them, no system, no particular objective; it was totalitarian warfare along Italo-German lines. The idea was to strike terror into and break down morale in the rear guard. The terror was there, but to the eternal glory of Madrid it must be stated that the morale never wavered.

When I was not on my terrace watching the flashes of the guns along the whole horizon beyond the Manzanares and hearing the screech of the incoming shells and feeling that sick sensation in the pit of the stomach, which means that you are afraid, I was in Hemingway's room at the Florida Hotel. A little crowd of us used to gather there nearly every evening—Evan Shipman and Martin Hourihan (American Internationals then recovering from wounds), Martha Gellhorn, Almuth Heilbrun (widow of a doctor in the International Brigade killed outside Huesca), and any American friends who happened to be in Madrid on leave. Hemingway was certain that he had a "dead angle" and that we were safe in that room. It was a good thing to believe, anyway, so we would open the windows and turn on the Chopin "mazurka" record, just as they did in *The Fifth Column*. Indeed, that was the time when the play was being written, and the ideas came in on those 3-, 6- and 9-inch shells which frequently shook the Florida to its foundations, but somehow never reached our room.

By March, 1938, we thought we knew all about bombing and shelling, but we were innocents. It took eighteen raids in forty-four hours on Barcelona to show us and the world what a weapon the airplane could be. Until the next war it remained the one classic example of what modern bombing could do to a city and the human beings in it. No people in mass had ever been called upon to suffer the physical and spiritual torture which the inhabitants of Barcelona endured in that maddening stretch of time during which bombers of a foreign nation which had no quarrel with Spain inflicted punishment on a defense-less city.

It began at 10:15 on Wednesday evening, March 16, 1938, under a full moon that seemed to hang in the center of the sky. That meant the raiders had excellent visibility, while the city's searchlights were paled under the glow. In any event, the anti-aircraft defense was so pitifully inadequate that nothing could be done to stop the attacks. Prime Minister Neville Chamberlain (and therefore all the others) had refused the Government's plea to be allowed at least to buy anti-aircraft guns which they would guarantee to use only in the rearguard.

We could see even that night—or rather hear—wave on wave of planes coming over, for the same ones could not possibly have gone back to Majorca and returned so quickly. Only later, in Italy, did I learn that they came from Italy itself and from Sardinia, as well as from Palma. Understand that, to a considerable extent, this was an experiment. The air force had to teach its pilots how to make long raids, and besides, there was a new type of bomb to be tried out.

Between 10:15 and two in the morning there were eight raids, but it was not until the morning of the 17th that the full horror of what was happening penetrated the city. At night only those in immediate contact with the bombs and their destruction could know their message, but in the daytime you saw it with your own eyes, and it seared the eyeballs so that however much you tried to forget or however long you lived, the picture could not be erased. During the night we sat in the darkened offices of the press censorship, hearing the throb of the engines, the roar of the bombs, the crashing of houses and the tinkling of glass, trusting that the next bomb would not land on us and that the lights would go up and the telephone be restored long enough to permit us to get our stories over. We knew the bombs were being scattered all over the city; that the planes were flying too high to choose objectives; that an appalling amount of death and destruction was taking place. But you have to see things to feel them with full force.

The next day, St. Patrick's Day, I and a million others saw things which Dante could not have imagined. Bombs can do more horrible things to the human body and spirit than the most fiendish tortures can devise. I did not get up for the first raid at 7:40, but when the next came at 10:25 I drove immediately to the center of the destruction, and what I saw made me realize that newspapermen had a mission that day: to tell the world what bombing means. My pen was dipped in blood for that dispatch.

I had been seeing the effects of bombs for more than a year, but it was immediately obvious to me that this was something different—not the ordinary high explosive, not the delayed fuse, but something intended to fall in the streets and break out flat, killing a maximum number of people. One bomb dropped in a square at the foot of the Paralelo, a busy cross-section in the lower part of the city not far from the port. The trees around had been snapped off a few inches from the ground; one would have thought they had been sawn off, but for the roughness of the break. It does no good to throw yourself down, when that type of bomb falls near you. I could tell where each person out of thirty or forty killed there had been standing, because of the isolated pools of blood. A street car had been wrecked, and everyone in it killed or wounded. A truck was still burning, and something black and shriveled that had been human had just been taken out and placed in a basket.

And then there was the noise—ambulances dashing up with men on the footboards blowing whistles, women screaming and struggling hysterically, men shouting. Up the block a house was burning fiercely. And all around, all over the city, everywhere I went were wrecked houses, dead, wounded and those intangibles of fear, horror, fury, mental and physical torture. The attacks were in one sense haphazard, for the bombs were dropped at random, without specific objectives. However, there was an obvious plan to be certain that every part of the city, from the richest quarter to the poorest, received its full measure of tragedy. It was not necessary to send many planes each time. The fearful damage done in the 1:55 P.M. raid on March 17 required only five Savoia-Marchetti bombers. That raid alone bore within itself more terror and ferocity than any previous raid in aviation's history.

The planes came along the axis of the Calle Cortes, a wide, fashionable avenue that cuts across the center of Barcelona. At a given moment one plane dropped two or three bombs (the Spanish experts could not determine how many) of the new type and of a size that could not have been less than 500 kilos each. At the same time, a number of 50-, 100- and 200-kilo bombs (the kilogram is 2.2 pounds) were released by the planes. The effect was like that of a combined earthquake and tornado. The best guess that could be made afterwards was that they were liquid-air bombs, for the destruction was caused by concussion and not by fragmentation of the bomb-casings. No pieces of casing were recovered, indicating that the shells were thin. The buildings on one side of the street were literally blown away, so that one could see through into the next street. One of the houses on the other side, which stood on a corner, was considered the strongest building in Barcelona, of huge blocks of stone around a steel framework six stories high. The part facing the spot where the bomb had fallen was torn apart, and blocks that could not have weighed less than a few tons each were scattered over a radius of two hundred yards.

The Paseo de Gracias cuts across the Calle Cortes at right angles, three blocks down. People standing at that intersection were bowled over like ninepins; some died through collapse of their lungs. Limbs of trees, six or eight inches thick, were torn off their trunks; nearly every window, from the Plaza Cataluña to the Calle Majorca, crashed. A little nearer to the scene, lampposts were blown down, trees torn up by the roots and set afire. A loaded bus which had been close to the main explosion was a grotesquely twisted mass of iron; the passengers had disappeared. Everywhere around were those viscous masses of blood which showed where human beings had been. A haze of smoke and dust hung over the scene for hours, as did an acrid smell of powder or some other chemical.

It was sheer madness. I happened to be eating lunch with

Delmer's wife in the Hostal del Sol, which was about five blocks up toward the Diagonal, but fortunately not in a direct line. The windows bent in toward us, and the whole building shook exactly as if there were an earthquake. We were unharmed and others had been killed, but there never is any reason in a bombing—particularly totalitarian bombing of that sort—why you should not be the one killed. You feel that always, and it is nerve-racking. Any unusual noise makes your heart jump—horns of cars that sound like sirens, the banging of doors, the roar of automobile motors. I even saw a cat jump as if from an electric shock when a shopkeeper suddenly lowered his blinds. Bombs make a rushing, whistling, screaming sound when they come down, and that was what we kept hearing, sometimes actually, sometimes in imagination.

You see so many freakish things and they add so much to the horror! It is all horror, and one gets dazed from it—blood over pavements, bodies, all black and red, that seem the creation of a diseased mind; men, women, and children buried alive or screaming, in the wreckage of their houses, like trapped animals. I never saw so many weeping women. There was a house where nothing remained on the fifth floor except some clothes hanging on a rack. In another place the corner of a kitchen had somehow escaped, and we could see that the housewife had not had time to wash the dishes before she died. I saw a guard pick up somebody's finger; I saw a pool of blood topped with a man's beret; I saw an automobile whose occupants must literally have disappeared into the air. It was all a nightmare—the dead piled in trucks, gangs of salvage men digging in the ruins, stretchers stained red, street-cleaners sweeping up human fragments, a cock crowing lustily from atop a wrecked building, smoke, dust, powder—and blood everywhere, thick, sticky pools of blood, splotches and drops of it; wherever one looked there was something stained with blood.

I watched them take two wounded persons out of a building wrecked in the first bombing on the 17th. Both had been completely buried. The woman was screaming so weakly that we thought it was a child until they extricated her limp body. She seemed dead then, but they rushed her away to the hospital. The other was a fifteen-year-old boy. By some miracle he had not been crushed, although one could see that from his hair down to his bare feet he had been completely buried. His body did not seem to have been hurt, but something else was, for he could not control his movements or the twitching of his face or his shuddering.

The hospitals were quickly overcrowded. They were already burdened with wounded from the Aragon front. Every autobus had been commandeered for ambulance purposes. Men stood on the running boards blowing whistles, to clear the way, and it was that never-ceasing shrill and piercing sound which seemed more characteristic of the day than anything else. In the afternoon I counted 328 dead lying side by side in the morgue of the clinical hospital, but there were other morgues. It was not possible to count the bodies buried in the wreckage. There could not have been less than 1,300 killed and 2,000 wounded in the eighteen raids. The Government never dared to give out even approximately truthful figures of bombing casualties, lest they should demoralize the populace.

But one does not assess such torture by deaths and wounds alone. Totalitarian bombing is meant to strike terror, to break the morale of the home front, to weaken resistance, because human beings are not built to withstand such horror. It is true that such bombings strike terror, terror that freezes the blood and drives one either hysterical or to the verge of hysteria. But then, too, one would not be human if it all did not cause rage—deep, burning rage. Those Spaniards had to yield to it in the end, because machines are stronger than bodies, but what they felt then must be still corroding within them like poison. Even I, re-creating in my mind those long hours of horror, cannot help feeling again the bitterness and hatred against everything those Fascist bombers stood for, although more than seven years have passed. That was the sort of thing that taught me my politics.

Of course, such bombing is effective. Who can look at the results and not think, "That is what may happen to me next time"? If you had said to those weeping women on March 17 and 18, "Do you want your men to give up and stop this war?"

who can doubt what they would have answered? The strain grew with each succeeding raid. Foreigners were deserting their hotels for the frontier as fast as they could. The Ritz Hotel was hit during the first raid on the 17th, to the satisfaction of those of us in the Majestic who knew the Ritz to be the home of war profiteers and friends of Franco. Certainly, bombing it helped the exodus. The American Consular and Embassy staffs stuck to their posts as they were to do until the end, but they had to move from the Plaza Cataluña to Tibidabo, on the hill. Even that district was bombed, for no part of the city was spared, but it was comparatively safe. We all had a sense of impending disaster. Before we made our rounds the second morning, Delmer, who had a true British contempt for sentiment or weakness, gave Isobel, his wife, some money, "in case something silly happens." The chambermaid said to me hysterically as I went out, "We are all going to be killed, all!" The clerk at the drugstore sighed as he handed over the headache medicine I badly needed. "Oh, for a plane to fly to France!" he said. "I don't want to die."

But life had to go on. After each raid the blood was washed off the streets, the car tracks were repaired, the wreckage was cleared away. Then the people—those who had not fled—waited for the next raid. In the lower quarters of the city they prepared to spend the night in the subways. So many went down that the men had to get out, leaving for the women and children what space there was. Others huddled in their cellars, knowing themselves safe from any but a direct hit.

We did not sleep that night of the 17th. The moon was still strong; the weather clear and windless—and we had three raids. Then three more raids the next day—and at three in the afternoon it ended. No one could ever explain why it ended. The raids were extraordinarily effective; Barcelona was not only terrorized but paralyzed. A continuation might have brought a general hysteria and a mass flight from the city. The Government spared a few precious combat planes from the front, but not enough for any real opposition, and the anti-aircraft fire was pathetically inadequate. The Italians could have continued with impunity. At the time we made two guesses: first, that whatever it did to Barcelona, it was arousing the Catalans as they had not been stirred since Napoleon's time; and secondly, we flattered ourselves that the stories we sent had shocked world opinion to such an extent that the Rebel command decided it was not worth while to continue the bombing. After hearing what the Italians had to say after the war, I believe another reason has to be added, at least as a possibility: Franco refused to countenance the destruction of Barcelona, which he expected to capture in a short while.

Certainly, the Insurgents and the Italian force were making rapid progress toward the coast, with the main axis of attack aimed along the right bank of the Ebro toward Tortosa, which at this time was being slowly pounded to death. But the Loyalist Army had not been destroyed. It had lost much territory and matériel but surprisingly few men, and it had lost neither courage nor morale. Spaniards have a full measure of that rare quality: Not knowing when one is beaten.

On March 22 the Insurgents struck on a new sector, from Saragossa and Huesca toward Lérida. They crossed the Ebro near Piña, with virtually no opposition and in a few days were threatening Bujaraloz, a village which constitutes a landmark in my journalistic career. There is no more difficult or dangerous task in war corresponding than to cover a retreat under modern, motorized conditions of warfare, as I have already stated. Lines are open and everything is coming back at you, with the enemy tanks and cavalry infiltrating the retreat route, while the planes bomb and strafe. Your job is to drive into the teeth of it as far as you can go, see for yourself as well as you can what is happening, and then get out before the next wave catches you. Instinct and experience are helpful, but you need luck, too.

Bujaraloz was a lesson to me. I drove out there on the morning of the 25th with Richard Mowrer of the *Chicago Daily News,* and went well beyond Bujaraloz to the front lines. Everything was quiet; the Loyalists were digging in; morale seemed high; the commanders were confident; reports from other sectors were encouraging. To be sure, the terrain was absolutely flat, **and** perfectly suited to mechanized warfare, not to mention bombing (we escaped a nasty raid along the road). We knew we could have been cut off, and we were uneasy. There is always an impalpable sense of danger brooding over battle lines, but nothing was happening, and things looked good when we started back for Barcelona at one o'clock.

I wrote my story in Barcelona, dating it from Bujaraloz, as I was entitled to do according to accepted journalistic practice, yet before I finished writing the story Bujaraloz had been lost, and by nightfall the Rebels were in Candasnos, twelve miles beyond, on the way to Lérida! As we learned the next day, we were hardly out of earshot when the first wave of bombers came over, and the line broke wide open in the most disgraceful fashion. Had we lingered, it would have been the end of us. I vowed that day never, so long as I live and work at this trade, to dateline a story from any place except where I write it or prepare it for transmission.

Journalistic faking reached great heights in that war, as readers gradually began to realize. There will always be fakers in the profession, and that is why many persons are skeptical of what they read in newspapers. This is the most discouraging of all factors for those of us who have pride in our profession, but it is something which will never be eradicated. The temptation is too great. I do not know and do not care greatly what judgments will be passed on my work when the time comes to write my obituary—save in one respect. No one will ever be able to accuse me of having faked a story or written something which I did not believe to be true.

The issues were perfectly clear to those of us who worked through the Spanish Civil War, and yet I know of no other running story which so confused the average newspaper reader. That was a discouraging aspect of the situation, among many satisfactory ones. I, for instance, somehow never succeeded in making my readers understand that the Government, except in the early months of the war, was encouraging the Catholic clergy and trying to induce them to carry on their religious duties freely. For many months, negotiations went on with the Vatican in an effort to induce the Holy See to sanction the opening of some churches, but permission was always refused. In the United States, those Catholics who had taken it upon themselves to paint everything connected with the Government a solid black, gave the lie to my stories—and yet the proof was overwhelming and was attested by many unbiased witnesses.

The same was true of Russian intervention in the war. Even though an impartial body appointed by the League of Nations filed an official report, at the end of the war, saying that there were no Russian infantrymen in Spain, the belief has undoubtedly persisted to this day. Certainly my stories on the subject were always scoffed at.

Sometimes, matters of opinion and judgment enter into the question. My interpretation of the last part of the war was colored by my personal admiration for Dr. Juan Negrín, then Premier. I see no reason to alter my judgment, although Spaniards are bitterly divided on the subject of Negrín.

There was that desperate period at the end of March, 1938, when the Rebels were driving on Lérida. The situation looked hopeless, but it was saved by Negrín. On the 28th he made an appeal for 100,000 men to volunteer for the army and be ready to go into the lines in ten days (he got about 10,000, at most, from embattled Catalonia). That night he made a stirring appeal over the radio in which the words "resist, resist, resist" were insistently repeated. Negrín was no orator; his voice was bad, his speeches were involved and poorly organized, but he had courage and faith and sincerity, and they more than made up for whatever else was lacking. That Loyalist, Republican, democratic Spain was able to pull itself together and struggle on for another amazing year was due to the determination and faith of that one man. The Catalans hate him for it; the politicians cast him out, but history will give him the credit that is his due.

It all seemed so gloomy and hopeless in those days; and yet we knew the war would go on. The Army was in flight; 100,000 civilians had swept in from Aragon rather than await the Rebels; the rearguard was demoralized; but on April 4 a new government had been formed, without Prieto, and with Negrín in supreme charge. The symbol and the promise came on the 9th, when Colonel Hidalgo de Cisneros gathered all his planes, the old ones and what new ones had come in, and sent them over Barcelona. As squadron after squadron, nearly 100 planes in all, roared over the roofs, the people below went delirious with joy. I have few more thrilling memories in my own life.

So we knew the Insurgents would get down to the coast on that early Good Friday morning, April 15, when Hemingway, Delmer and I left Barcelona for the front, but we knew, too, that it did not mean the end of the war. Tortosa was quiet but as horrible as ever when we went through, wondering as always whether we would be caught by the bombers. It was the final agony of a picturesque and ancient city. Every day, and usually several times daily, it had been bombed during the offensive. On many drives I had seen it intact, during Teruel and before, and I sometimes slept there; to see it gradually destroyed was like watching the agonies of a living thing. Often during the break-through we were in or through Tortosa, and it was always shocking to see the changes in that tragic town. Not a civilian was left on that morning; not a house was intact. Even the trees in the park had been mown down by bombs.

We were a few miles clear of the town when the first planes came over. As we piled out of the car and broke for shelter, the bombs crashed down, well ahead of us, on the Loyalist lines. Just as we decided to start up, the roar of more motors could be heard. They passed overhead, six gleaming white Savoia-Marchettis, and at 9:19 came the first of the day's raids on Tortosa. At one moment we could see the town lying before us, and at the next it had disappeared in a cloud of gray smoke and thunder.

By then the air was charged with tension. One could see it on every face, in the way the cars drove, in the way men scattered wildly under the constant threat of the planes. Motorcycle couriers sped swiftly up and back, many stopping to ask if we knew whether the road was open. That was what we ourselves wanted to know.

At 10:05 we were stopped again. This time there was strafing as well as bombing. Fifteen combat planes circled steadily over

San Rafael, firing, swinging up and around, then turning to
repeat the maneuver. It went on and on. The circles widened
as they bore eastward toward the coast and at the end (there
were thirty-five solid minutes of it) they were bombing and strafing Ulldecona on the coast road.

That gave us the information we wanted, so as soon as the
planes left we sped toward Ulldecona. Officers of a brigade staff
were working over a map, in a garden on the edge of the village,
and we asked them what was happening. It was then 10:45. The
major told us that San Rafael, four miles inland, had just been
taken. The Rebels were using three columns, he said. One was
driving straight toward Ulldecona. Another was coming over
from Chert to Viñaroz. The third was moving up toward Santa
Bárbara, in back of us. They did not know where that unit was,
and had just sent a column up from the village to make contact
with it.

That was just as much a threat to our rear as it was to the
Loyalists, so we hurried back to the far side of Santa Bárbara.
There we stopped in an olive grove to eat lunch. Vincent Sheean
and a few others joined us; later Sheean wrote about it in
Not Peace But a Sword. We studied the road, and, above all,
watched those bombers go over toward Tortosa by threes and
sixes. They flew high, for the anti-aircraft fire kept them up. We
knew there could be only one objective, for the town was a
shambles, without troops or matériel, or anything except automobiles that had to pass through as fast as they could. It was
the bridge they were after, that great, steel bridge which had
withstood repeated bombings and three direct hits.

At first we thought they had little chance, from that height,
but squadron after squadron came over—a dozen, two dozen,
three dozen, and still they came. Six times between 11:40 and
12:30 we saw Tortosa go up in smoke, and most of the time
there was not the thundering roll of bombs dropped successively,
but one, great earth-shaking crash to show that the planes were
dropping their full loads at once and in one spot. Our uneasi-
ness was mounting. As far as we knew, there was only that bridge
by which the Ebro could be crossed. There were the railroad

bridge and a footbridge, but we doubted the car could make either of them.

However, we had first to check up on the road to Valencia, so we drove back to Ulldecona, and at the post of command went over the situation again. The Rebels then were within five miles of Viñaroz. Obviously, it was a matter of a few hours.

We could do no more for the day, and we had our own problem to solve: had the bridge been destroyed? We got the answer as we struck the edge of town, and it set our hearts jumping. A guard ran up to us. "The bridge is down," he shouted; "you can't go that way!" "Can we go by Amposta?" we asked. He shrugged his shoulders. "They are trying to fix the footbridge here," he suggested dubiously.

It had been a half hour since the planes had come over, and they were due again, for doubtless they would want to get that remaining bridge, too. There were trucks piled up helplessly ahead. Still, we had to try it.

The recent evidences of those bombings were fearful to see. By their freshness they gave a new and baleful aspect to the dead city—bomb craters, mounds that had been houses, shattered trees with their fresh spring leaves, newly wrecked automobiles, dust, and smoke. When the car was held up, Hemingway and I ran on ahead to the footbridge and there found a hundred workmen laying down boards in feverish haste to strengthen it, and to cover the holes where two small bombs had hit it a few days previously. They said it was weak, but it would serve. We signaled to Delmer, who was driving the car, to come on, and he edged up alongside of the trucks to the end of the bridge.

Just then an old peasant pulled his heavily laden mule-drawn cart across our path and tried to get on to the bridge. Hemingway and I heaved against it, and with the aid of two soldiers we got it on. It started bumping across, creating havoc with the boards, and an officer shouted that no more carts were to be allowed through.

Still the planes had not come over. Delmer had to wait for some agonizing moments, to give the cart a good start. Then he began coming across at a crawling pace. Hemingway and I walked to lighten the load. At one spot, where a bomb had left a gaping hole through which we could see the water, we held our breath, but nothing happened, and the auto bumped across. A last, nightmarish drive through the inferno of the town, and we were clear. At one point a gasoline truck had been hit and was burning fiercely, in the middle of the street. We had to dash past it, holding our breath for a scorching second or two.

Before dark the Rebels had occupied Ulldecona, Viñaroz and Benicarló. Loyalist Spain had been cut into two zones. But in the uncensored dispatch I wrote that night I was able to say, "The war will go on."

The next day Neville Chamberlain signed the Anglo-Italian "Easter Pact" in Rome, and he and everybody else thought the war was virtually over. That it should have gone on for nearly a year longer is surely one of the more amazing achievements of the human spirit. It was more than a tribute to the fighting qualities of a magnificent race; it was overwhelming evidence of the Spanish people's hatred of Fascism and of the foreign invaders who had come to force it upon Spain. As long as the democracies maintained "Non-Intervention," as long as Germany and Italy continued to pour matériel into Rebel Spain and help it in every other way, the Republicans were doomed to conduct a losing struggle. The Anglo-Italian pact was to be violated in almost every respect but one: Mussolini always made that plain, from the time of the first conversations. Lord Halifax had told the House of Lords on November 3, 1938, that "for reasons known to us all, whether we approve of them or not, he [Mussolini] was not prepared to see General Franco defeated."

The factors which contributed to the resistance were many and complicated, but they would have been valueless without a Government that was ready to take the lead with confidence and full authority. One man embodied the strength, courage, and faith that were needed—Don Juan Negrín. In the light of what happened there are those who say that the price Spain paid for that year of war was too great. For those who love democracy and the liberalism which it embodies; for those who hate Fascism; for those Spaniards and Internationals who were willing to die that Franco and the forces he represented might fail—for all these Dr. Negrín will take a proud place with the great figures of Spanish history.

I often heard him say in those unhappy days, "We are working for history," and in that phrase is the clew to much of what he did and said. He was consistent to the end, for it was he and his supporters who wanted to go on fighting while any hope remained. Azaña, Prieto, Besteiro, Irujo, Aguadé—the politicians and the pacifists—wanted to quit. For Negrín, Del Vayo, Zugazagoitia, Méndez Aspe and others, for the Army and the trade unions, for the Communists, the bulk of the Socialists, the Anarcho-Syndicalists, the true liberals and Republicans, there could be no quitting short of victory or complete defeat. Negrín was not the one to betray his followers or his ideals. So the record is there, clean-cut and all of one piece. Don Juan Negrín is one of those men who believe that to have fought well in a great cause is itself a victory. He has nothing to fear from history.

I made an exciting trip in a police launch from Barcelona to Valencia, June 22, running the Rebel gantlet at night, and for more than a month "covered," with alternating hopes and fears, the determined Rebel efforts to break through to Valencia down that same highway which saw our great days at Teruel. A line had been established in front of Viver and Caudiel, thence swinging eastward to cover Segorbe, and it was wonderful—and terrible—to go out daily to see it take the greatest pounding of the war and still hold. One gun to ten, one plane to four—but it held! Infantry attacks, supported by 500 planes, 150 batteries of four guns each, 100 to 150 tanks, nine Spanish divisions, three Italian divisions—and they never broke through!

Twice I went to Madrid, and was thrilled to see the capital again. For those of us who lived through the war, it is the thought of patient, heroic Madrid which brings the worst heartaches and the keenest nostalgia. What courage, what loyalty, what hopes went down when that city was surrendered! In the second half of the war Madrid was for the most part out of the news. Brunete was the last battle fought in the sector. All of us newspapermen had moved around to Barcelona after the Government went there. So there was no longer anything startling to say about Madrid—just a simple tale of hunger, cold, and disease borne with tranquillity and fortitude. One cannot make daily copy out of that, but one can register it for history. The heroism that led Madrileños to bear that last year and a half was worthy of the great traditions of Spanish sieges.

On July 24 the Insurgents were forced to stop to reorganize, and to bring up new matériel and reinforcements. The next day I could write safely, "The Rebel offensive against Valencia had been halted." It was important that it could have been written as of July 24, because at 1 o'clock on the morning of the 25th the Loyalist Army of Catalonia drove across the Ebro River to set up the bridgehead that it was to take Franco four months to reduce. It ended permanently the drive against Valencia, because the Insurgent command had to shift its spare troops and matériel around to the Ebro.

"The Americans crossed the Ebro like Washington crossed the Delaware." In fact, Captain Leonard Lamb, of the Lincoln-Washingtons, stood up in the boat he was commanding, and struck the classic pose. It was indeed an exquisite revenge for the lads who had been scattered to the winds on April 2 in that same terrain. For them there was no satisfaction like it in the war, and it was to be their last battle.

The Internationals played an important, but by no means vital rôle in the Ebro offensive. It was a well planned attack whose initial impetus was irresistible but which failed of its chief objectives. It could not be exploited for lack of preparation and matériel, and was ultimately thrown back. To hold the bridgehead for four months against seven powerful counter-offensives was surely one of the greatest military feats of the war, but the consequences were the same as at Teruel: it ended with the Loyalist Army exhausted and without matériel, while the Rebel forces had been reinforced with the largest flow of matériel in the conflict and had hardly engaged their Italian divisions.

I went over often to write stories about the bridgehead, and it was always a singularly nasty business. I do not suppose anything in the war was a greater nerve strain. Being in the bridgehead was bad enough, for the bombing and shelling were constant and we had to keep moving around, but the crossings had their own peculiar danger. We usually reduced it by going over before the dawn patrol of Rebel planes made their daily visit, but the trip back was always made in broad daylight, and we had some narrow escapes.

The 15th Brigade, especially the Lincoln-Washington Battalion, was showing that with proper leadership it was as good as the best Internationals had ever been. I went out with Luís Quintanilla, the artist, and Delmer for one last glorious day of action on August 19, on my final visit to the Americans in the line. It was not quite the end of their service to Spain but it was typical of those last days. As an American, I am proud to have that memory of gallant men, holding the line against forces that to me, as well as to them, represented much that has made this world an evil and tragic place to live in. Fate was kind to them, and they were not beaten in Spain as were their Spanish comrades.

The seventh and last offensive against the bridgehead began on October 30. Franco used eleven divisions, or more than 100,-000 men, in that drive, with more matériel than he had ever massed before. The break-through and all the infantry fighting were done by Spaniards and Moors; Italian motorized columns did the exploiting and "harassing" of the withdrawing troops, although they never made contact with them. Against that array the Government used six divisions, with pitifully depleted arms. For the most part they were the same divisions using the same matériel with which they had crossed the Ebro in July. Casualties had not been replaced, and in the middle of the battle the Internationals had been withdrawn.

I had made my last trip to the Ebro on November 5—the one described by Sheean in *Not Peace But a Sword*. Hemingway saved all our lives that day by pulling our rowboat to safety just as it was being carried against the jagged remnants of the destroyed bridge at Mora. The retreat was already in full force but it was hard fought, and the Government managed to save virtually all its men and scanty matériel. The lines were gradually shortened, with the bridge at Flix used as the final escape route. When the last platoon went over, on the night of November 15-16, it needed only the touch of an electric switch to put an end to the Battle of the Ebro.

Lister told me all about it the next day. He roared with laughter over the Rebel communique, which claimed the capture of more matériel than the Government had, and the infliction of more casualties than the number of troops used by the Loyalists in the whole operation. Those communiques were, indeed, amusing at times—except that so many believed them.

The Czech crisis, with the shameful betrayal at Munich, took place when the Ebro battle was fought, and those who selfishly wanted the Government to win at any price were wishing for a European war in which a Loyalist victory would have been a matter of a few months. The French would only have had to send in an army corps and plenty of planes and matériel. With Franco cut off from his German and Italian lines of communication, there would have been no hope for him. He wisely declared his intention to remain neutral. The Loyalists, who had everything to gain by a general war, did the one thing they could do to remove Spain as a cause of international friction and thus make the war less likely. If anyone believed that the spirit of Don Quixote was dead, here was proof to the contrary.

Negrín went before the Assembly of the League of Nations in Geneva on September 21 and calmly announced that the Spanish Government was withdrawing all its foreign volunteers, including those who had become nationalized Spaniards since July 5, 1936. He merely asked that the League appoint an international commission to verify the withdrawal.

"It is not necessary for us to provoke catastrophes to solve our problems," he said. "It would have been sufficient, and it will be sufficient, to recognize our rights and re-establish our international rights that have been violated, to assure a rapid solution of the Spanish problem."

The decision was indeed *muy española* ["very Spanish"], as Negrín himself said in a speech to the Cortes explaining the move and incidentally expressing the "debt of eternal gratitude

that Spain had contracted toward these authentic volunteers."
Those troops were still sorely needed.

Although the Non-Intervention Committee had been doing
everything possible for nearly two years to bring about the withdrawal of authentic and fake volunteers, the British did everything at Geneva that they could to block Negrín's move! They
tried to prevent the League from naming a commission, acting
on the theory that the Non-Intervention Committee should
handle such things. The Spanish Government firmly refused to
permit such a maneuver, that would honor an organization
which they blamed more than any other single factor for the
prolongation of the war. The British reluctantly yielded, and on
September 30 the League Council decided to appoint and dispatch to Spain "an international commission to note the measures taken by the Spanish Government for the withdrawal of
non-Spanish combatants."

A truly impartial group was formed, wisely chosen from high
and conservative military circles in ten countries. One of the four
members of the Secretariat, who was lent by the League, was an
American, Noel H. Field. To his sympathy and interest the
American volunteers were indebted for the relative speed of their
evacuation. They were a "die-hard" bunch, on the whole, just as
the Government wanted them to be, for the stricter they were
the more clearly Barcelona's good faith would be demonstrated.

At the Munich conference Mussolini advised Chamberlain
that he was going to withdraw 10,000 "volunteers" from Spain.
This he did in October, and it permitted the British Government to say that "both sides were withdrawing volunteers." In
the House of Commons on November 2, 1938, Chamberlain declared, "When I visited Munich, Signor Mussolini volunteered
the information that he intended to withdraw 10,000 men, or
about half the Italian infantry forces, from Spain." He said this
despite the fact that official Italian sources had given the total
as 40,000. The truth of the matter was that the withdrawal of
10,000 Italian Legionaries made little difference in the war.
Franco did not need Italian troops, at least not in large numbers;
he needed Italian matériel, specialists, technicians, and staff
officers, and the numbers of all these were being greatly increased

at the time the troops were withdrawn. I was able to give, in my dispatches of October 27 and November 21, some of the details. They were details drawn from official Government sources and were true as far as they went, but, as events proved, they were dwarfed by the actual totals. The stories were not believed in New York and were scoffed at by my Cable Editor, but at least they were printed, and are there for the historical record.

And so, in the middle of the Ebro battle, when the Internationals were so desperately needed, they were withdrawn. There was a last parade in Barcelona on October 28—a proud occasion and a triumphal march. The Internationals, at least, went out of Spain undefeated, and if the next to march along that same Diagonal were the Italians, the Germans, the Moors, the Falangists, the Carlists and the Foreign Legionaries, their steps could not drown out the tread of those free men who had come from the far corners of the world to fight Fascism. The Internationals did not march like automatons; there was no goose step or Roman step. Those men had learned to fight before they had learned to parade. They were not clad in spick-and-span uniforms; their garb was nondescript; they had no arms, and they could not seem to keep in step or in line. But everyone who saw them—and above all those who fought with them—knew that these were true soldiers.

The first and main batch of the Americans, 327 of them, went out on December 2. They were, appropriately, led by their last and best commander, Major Milton Wolff. By January 1, 1939, those who had left numbered 548, leaving only some scattered hospital cases and a small group in the Madrid zone. The casualty figures were never properly kept and so will never be known. My own guess was that at least 500 and perhaps as many as 650 were killed and 1,200 or 1,400 wounded or taken prisoner, out of a total of 3,200 who went to Spain.

The main body of the British (306 men) got out on December 6, but the Canadian Government refused to repatriate its nationals, and they had to stay on in Ripoll until a few days before Barcelona fell. At the end there were 110 Canadians left.

The smallness of these figures may surprise many readers, but they are the official totals of the International Military Commission. The "Provisional Report" made to the League Council on January 16, 1939, after an exhaustive and impartial investigation stretching over three months, cannot be questioned. It is an unassailable historical record, which not only upheld those of us who had been writing about the Internationals throughout the war; in my own case it demonstrated that the figures I gave were actually exaggerated. The Commission not only found that there were no Russian infantrymen, but that there were not even any pilots or technicians. There was just a handful of Russian advisers, whom the Commission could not touch because the Government had exempted them in advance. I do not believe there were more than a half dozen of them and forthcoming events were to prove how useless they were.

The Commission's report came too late to do any good as far as the war was concerned, but, like so many other things, it helped to keep the Government's record clean. It certified that there were only six International Brigades, belonging to two divisions. All told, the investigators found 12,673 foreigners in all Loyalist services, plus 488 prisoners. Of that number only 4,640 had left the Catalan zone by January 14, but the Commission acknowledged this was "owing solely to the length of the diplomatic negotiations and consular formalities," with the French making the greatest difficulties.

I have gone into these facts partly as a matter of personal revenge, because during the war my dispatches on the Internationals were a constant subject of derision and incredulity. In Spain I learned a lot about journalism, and one of the lessons was that one cannot expect the truth to be believed if readers do not want to believe it or if there is enough lying on the opposite side to confuse the issues. At that time I was sore and bewildered by this condition, and this was naive of me. I have since become philosophical (and, I suppose, more sensible), for the war also taught me that the truth will prevail in the long run. Journalism may seem to fail in its daily task of providing the material for history, but history will never fail so long as the newspaperman writes the truth.

Retreat in Catalonia

B**UT IF** truth is bound to prevail in the long run, one cannot say this of goodness or righteousness or justice or virtue in general. That is a lesson I did not have to go to Spain to learn. And if the triumph of evil is a common occurrence in this sinful world, to see it happen is always a bitter business, and in Spain it was made more bitter by the inability of so many to recognize the evil that Franco stood for. At the turn of the year 1938-1939 I endured the experience of seeing the wrong side win, and that was a lesson I shall never forget.

The first three weeks of December were a period of anxious and feverish preparations for the great offensive which everyone knew Franco was going to launch. I have already mentioned the Italian matériel that was being sent in. It is only necessary to emphasize the fact that it exceeded in quantity anything conceived by the Government's worst pessimists. Added to the new German matériel, it provided the Generalissimo with the wherewithal to launch a drive on the scale of any of the World War I offensives.

To us in Barcelona it was extraordinary that Franco should have weakened his southern front to such an extent. He was like a man fighting two adversaries who faces one and deliberately turns his unprotected back on the other. Naturally, we thought that the Madrid zone would save the day. Miaja, by that time, was approaching a breakdown, from accounts I received afterwards. He was drinking too much and had lost what nerve he had once possessed. The picture of the loyal, dogged, courageous defender of the Republic—a picture built up from the first days of the siege of Madrid—was a myth. He was weak, unintelligent, unprincipled, and, in that period, his courage could seriously be questioned. However, the real evil genius of that time was Colonel Sigismundo Casado, once professor in the Escuela Superior de Guerra in Barcelona, which taught the officers of the General Staff. He was a traitor. On the Barcelona side there was a terrible shortage of men and matériel but, as it proved, there was enough to hold the Rebels for two weeks. Had the Madrid zone done its part, the war would not have ended then, at least.

In the three weeks before the offensive began, I made frequent trips to the various sectors, to familiarize myself with the terrain and to become acquainted with the commanders. Lieutenant Colonel Hans Kahle, commander of the now disarmed German 11th International Brigade and after that commander of the Spanish 45th Division, had nothing better to do at the time, and we used to go together. Hans (no one ever knew him as anything else during the war, for he had relatives in Germany) had been in the fight from the first days of the siege of Madrid and was one of the last to go. He was a fine and brave man, of whose friendship I shall always be proud. There were two things which made an especially striking impression on both of us. One was the splendid fortifications and morale of Galán's 11th Corps, covering Artesa de Segre and Pons. Francisco ("Paco") Galán was a brother of the hero of the Jaca uprising, a Communist and an ardent Republican. The sector held by Vega's 12th Army Corps was another matter. The part around Lérida was splendidly fortified, but from there south to the Ebro the fortifications were light and without depth. In fact, we were appalled to see that the sector north of the Rebels' Seros bridgehead, nearly to Lérida, was almost unfortified. That was where the Italian corps broke through, with virtually no opposition.

At dawn on December 23, 1938, Insurgent batteries all along the line from the Seros bridgehead north to Tremp opened up against the Loyalist positions, and the last great offensive was on. The catastrophe occurred near the Seros bridgehead. A combined artillery and air barrage that lasted fully seven hours was laid down along the left bank of the Segre, from Seros to the hydro-electric plant opposite Aytona. Due to a shortage of troops, the Loyalists were spread out thinly, but, to give the soldiers credit, they held their positions gamely all through the barrage. At the end of it a number of their officers, including the staffs, got into their automobiles and drove away! In the circumstances, it is hard to blame the soldiers who thereupon turned and ran. The Italian corps was able to send troops across, build a pontoon bridge, and then drive a wedge six miles through to Sierra Grosa, where for the first time they met with resistance, and darkness stopped them.

Lister's 5th Army Corps had to be thrown in almost immediately, and on Christmas Day he began his great stand before Borjas Blancas by jarring the Italians and Navarrese back on their heels. Tagüeña's 15th Corps, the only other reserve the Government had, also was forced to go in on the eastern side of the Seros bridgehead. The Italians were to fight on doggedly and well for ten days, but it was the Navarrese on their right, in what was probably the greatest stretch of fighting in the war, who smashed Tagüeña slowly back, steadily flanking Lister, and thus deciding the battle. Galán, as had been expected, held firm.

I spent some hours on the 26th with Lister in a command post which was a suitable setting for that great soldier. More than any other man he carried on the glorious tradition of the Spanish guerrilla leader. He was never a man to establish his headquarters far back of the lines, in a safe spot. His leadership was personal, and he wanted to be with his troops. I found him standing in front of a deep cave on a ridge in front of Borjas Blancas, looking out toward the lines. He was a powerful figure of a man, nearly six feet tall and well over 200 pounds in weight, with heavy features, thick, black eyebrows and a great shock of black hair. Brutal and tough he certainly was, and the iron discipline he imposed was partly achieved through the fact that he would execute without mercy any men or officers who showed cowardice or neglect of duty. But his troops worshiped and trusted him, and to those who fought well he was a loyal and comradely friend. To me, too, he was a good friend and a charming host, and I always knew that wherever I found him and whatever the situation, I could count on a hearty welcome and a frank explanation of what was happening.

Every day during that desperate month which ended with the fall of Barcelona I went to one sector or another of the front, and I wish I had space here to tell you about it, for no one else had that opportunity, and the stories I sent, although many could not be published in full at the time, were, I believe, a unique contribution to the history of the war. But this is not a history of the war, and I want here to give you only enough of the highlights to explain how and why the Loyalists were driven out of Catalonia—and I with them.

Within a week there were eight divisions in the Seros bridgehead alone, four Spanish and four Italian, and their concentration of artillery gave them an average of one gun every ten yards. Captain J. R. Kennedy, in *This, Our Army*, writing of the first World War said, "One field gun per 35 yards of front was looked upon as a minimum requirement." Already the Loyalist forces were outnumbered about two to one, and by January 3 Franco was using twenty-eight divisions, nearly 300,000 men, counting his tactical reserve. He was able to throw in fresh troops every forty-eight hours in those first crucial weeks, while the same Republican troops fought on day after day for seven weeks. And yet people were to wonder why the Republican Army finally collapsed! The really remarkable thing was that they fought on so stubbornly for those first two weeks until Borjas Blancas and Artesa de Segre fell.

It was on December 29 that the Loyalists lost Granadella, a village in the center of the Seros bridgehead on a dirt road that went back toward the Tarragona highway. At the time this did not seem important, but it was the blow which broke the back of the Loyalist resistance in that whole sector. The Republicans, with the exception of the disgraceful 43rd Division on the extreme left, were fighting superbly. It was their last great stand of the war. The 14th Brigade (which used to be the Franco-Belge but was now wholly Spanish) withstood seventeen attacks made by the Italians against a hill near Albages, and it was lost in a bayonet charge only when the Brigade had been virtually wiped out. The Italians were fighting well, too, for the first time in the war, and were inching steadily toward Borjas Blancas. Their newspapers had made the error of claiming the taking of the place in the second day of the battle, but despite the overwhelming superiority of the Italians in matériel, and their hard fighting, it was to take them thirteen days. And it was in vain that Ciano wrote in his account of the war, "As always, the Legionaries had in front of them, as direct antagonists, the International Brigades and conquered them with brilliant tactics." The Internationals had been withdrawn three months before, and the Italians were facing their old indomitable enemy, Lister.

New Year's Eve brought "sorrow and mourning to Barcelona," in the words of Negrín, who referred to a terrible bombing of the capital that occurred just before he made a broadcast to America. He called it, and perhaps with justice, "the cruelest bombardment of the war," for it was aimed at the heart of the city—and, after all, it was New Year's Eve. I was with him at the time, for he had asked me to correct the English of his speech, and I had never seen him so moved. The bombs fell around the Plaza de Cataluña, and were small ones aimed for the streets, particularly the Calle Cortes. Exactly two years before, at midnight, I had seen the Rebels send twelve shells into the Puerta del Sol, in Madrid, to replace the traditional twelve grapes eaten as the clock strikes. "Perhaps," said one of the men who were with us in Negrín's Presidencia (I think it was Vayo), "this is 'Happy New Year' in the Italian language." Forty-four civilians were killed and ninety-two wounded.

Late in the evening of January 4, after a covering action to permit the troops to fall back to previously prepared positions, Borjas Blancas and Artesa de Segre were lost, and with them Catalonia, Loyalist Spain, and the Second Spanish Republic. The resistance had been glorious, but the Government had no reserves of men and matériel, and human endurance has its limits. Those two towns had been symbols for the Loyalists—something for which the men fought with superhuman strength—and when they were gone there was an inevitable let-down. Some desperate fighting was still to be done, and hope was never abandoned, but we know as we look back now that the night of January 4-5 was the tragic climax of the Spanish Civil War.

It had been disheartening for the Loyalists to find the Italians fighting well, after their consistently poor performances of the two previous years. They had a new commander, General Gastone Gambara, their only good one of the war, and a genuine Fascist. At the time we all thought the Italians were fighting so well because of a supreme appeal from the Duce, who wanted to have the war virtually settled when Chamberlain made his visit to Rome on January 11. For that reason everyone in Loyalist Spain was calling the Rebel drive "Chamberlain's offensive."

All hopes were in vain, of course, but the next day they soared to the skies when the Republican troops in the southern zone launched what appeared to be a great offensive in Extremadura, and there came the text of Roosevelt's message to Congress, with its attack on aggressors and its clear acknowledgment that the American embargo on arms had harmed the Spanish Government and favored the Rebels. The offensive was to prove a miserable failure, for it was not seriously meant, and the President's timid overtures were to be quickly smothered by effective Catholic action.

Again, on the afternoon of January 13, Barcelona heard the electrifying news that the Government had smashed through the Rebel lines in the Brunete sector, west of Madrid, and that another drive was on, to relieve pressure in Catalonia. The news flew around the front to hearten the soldiers in their weary fight. But that night the war communiqué said nothing about it, and we began to wonder. Nor was it ever mentioned again, and only after the war did I learn from Negrín that Casado, under peremptory orders, had really made an attack in the Brunete sector —but it had lasted exactly one hour! To have called it half-hearted would have been to exaggerate its strength. And that was the last heard of the Madrid region during Catalonia's death struggle.

The Madrid zone could so easily have saved the day for the Government, but, as we learned too late, treachery, sabotage and defeatism had undermined the Southern Army. So far as Casado, Matallana, and perhaps even Miaja were concerned, the two attacks were not even meant to succeed.

In the northern zone the lines had broken wide open. Lister fell back toward the Tarrega-Montblanch road and Tagüeña toward Reus, with a huge gap between them that left the road open to Vinaixa, Vimbodí and Montblanch for a whole day. The Rebels could have marched down the highway without opposition and taken Tarragona a week before they did, had they only known it. I myself drove unwittingly straight through the gap beyond Vinaixa on that day, little realizing that I was nearer to the Insurgent Army than were the Republican troops. Indeed, the next three weeks were to be exceptionally dangerous for those of us who were trying to cover the fronts, for there were no longer to be any fixed lines. It was absolutely open warfare, with isolated points of resistance, and a swift, motorized enemy coming forward unpredictably in constant flanking movements. That "great fortified line" about which all of us wrote in the early days of the offensive turned out to be non-existent.

On January 8 I went up to see Tagüeña in the Sierra de Montsant. His troops were making a courageous, fighting retreat, but were gradually being pushed back. As we had luncheon together, the tall, thin, bespectacled young teacher, whom fate had brought to the command of an army corps, resignedly revealed his appalling lack of matériel and men. That morning he had sent for a battery group, normally twenty-four guns. The group arrived with enough officers and men for twelve guns—but they had only one! His brigades, reduced to 1,600 to 1,800 men, had an average of 250 rifles fit for front-line service.

And so the tragedy continued, day after heart-breaking day. The Rebels were gradually closing in on Tarragona, which, in its fashion, was an excellent symbol of that war. Was this not, indeed, one of the really curious ironies of history? There was the great city that once held a million inhabitants when Rome was in its heyday—the city where the Scipios, Octavius Augustus, Galba, and Adrian, prefects and consuls, great merchants and artists, had built a civilization which still today makes Tarragona the most Roman of all Spanish cities. Yet that was the city which was three quarters destroyed by the Romans of today in well over 100 bombing raids! Certainly, no more than one sixth of the bombs fell in the port, which was the only military objective there. I went through Tarragona dozens of times and was caught in many of the raids, and I know the truth of what I am saying. The civilian population and its houses were the victims of five out of every six bombs.

The inhabitants stuck it out to the end, and proved that with adequate refuges and enough of them, casualties could have been almost avoided. Tarragona had more than seventy shelters of various kinds, and others were still being built when the war ended. The irony caught up with you there again, for, in digging through the ground, many relics of Roman civilization were found, such as statuary, pottery, coins, and utensils. They were all put in the museum, where, I suppose, one can see them now. It was saddening to walk through the streets and think that those heaps of stones, which had been houses before the Italian bombers came, were Roman stones. They were actually the material, remaining from Roman times, with which nearly all the houses of Tarragona were built, save the newest. What Rome made, Rome destroyed.

The weather was especially beautiful on the day Tarragona fell. Trees were beginning to blossom along the coast, and when we stopped to eat luncheon outside the city I was even bitten by mosquitoes—and it was only January 15! The natural beauty of the scenery accentuated the horror and pathos of what was happening to it. Three factors were constant: aviation, artillery fire, and that unending and infinitely unhappy stream of refugees. There was never a stretch of road, however short, without its slow-moving carts piled high with belongings that no dealer in second-hand goods would handle but which to these poor people made up the sum total of their worldly possessions.

That, too was an exodus, a going into exile that had assumed the character and proportions of a Biblical tragedy. Babies, lambs, and kids were born along those roads. Old men and women and worn-out animals died before reaching their haven.

Planes came over, bombing and strafing the roads many times daily, bringing their quota of violent deaths or wounds, or destruction to carts and belongings. The same roads were used by all. It was just another way in which the civilian was caught up in a machine that others had set in motion.

And, with all those ingredients—fatigue, hunger, terror, death—there was no complaining. To meet the smiles, courtesy, and friendliness of all those poor people was to see the tragedy heightened.

"If somebody would put matériel in our hands right now," Tagüeña said to some of us that morning, "the Rebels still would not get to Tarragona." But Chamberlain was then in Rome, making concessions to Fascism, not to democracy.

Tagüeña was talking to Henry Buckley, of the London *Daily Telegraph,* O'Dowd Gallagher of the London *Daily Express,* Frank Smothers of the Chicago *Daily News* and me. There was a mad scramble of troops and matériel coming back up the road from Tarragona. It was one-way traffic with a vengeance, and we made the only exception as we bucked the stream in an effort to "establish" something, since that is what newspapermen are supposed to do.

For that brief period of time, between dawn and late afternoon, the coastal highway between Tarragona and Vendrell, a matter of only 18 miles, was an inferno. No one needed orders to keep going and to go fast, for the Rebel planes were at it all day. There was no escaping them, and we had to get it like everyone else. Just before we reached Vendrell, fifteen bombers went down the coast, while three more came in from the sea. We waited nearly an hour while they bombed and strafed the roads, and when they went away we did some reconnoitering—up the Valls highway, on the side roads, and, finally, back to Vendrell and down toward Tarragona. The wreckage of the bombing we had witnessed kept cropping up with its grim warnings. Not far from Vendrell were two carts whose four mules had been killed. An old man was lying dead by the side of the road. All the belongings in the carts had been destroyed or scattered; rabbits and fowl lay dead or wounded in their crates. Parts of the belongings, and much more horrible things than that, had been blown into the telephone wires and the branches of nearby trees. A handcart and everything in it had been picked off the road and thrown over a wall.

As we stopped to take in this appalling little scene, a peasant woman came over from a side road, and we could see that other women and some children were waiting up there. She was very dignified, and the shock and grief had not even made her hysterical. She was worried about her children only, and how to get all of them away from that road of terror. They had come from Salomó, which they had left only two days before, to get away from the shelling and bombing. Everything of value that was movable had been taken—above all, those four precious animals and food for a month. Now the animals were dead, the food was destroyed, the home was lost. She asked us what she should do; we told her to stop an empty truck and go down to Vendrell. The old man, whose body had been covered with his cloak, was from the same village, and had been traveling with them. His wife had been killed somewhere else along the way; they had no children, so the woman thought perhaps it was a mercy after all.

We went on against a rising tide of terror and danger. Two dead soldiers, then another dead peasant, dead animals, overturned carts and automobiles, the cut-up road, broken trees, dangling telephone wires, and against us this unending, swift-moving stream. Although there was really no panic, the speed and tenseness of it all were so contagious that every instinct in us cried out to turn and go back with them. Still, we had to establish something, and we kept going nearly to the edge of Tarragona, where—for whatever it was worth—we proved that at 1:45 on the afternoon of January 15, 1939, Tarragona was still in government hands. Actually, Italians and Navarrese were already on the southern and western edges of the city, so we turned back just in time.

And then, of course, it was too late to escape the bombers. They caught us ten minutes later, and for eighteen minutes we four correspondents and our chauffeur, as well as everyone else in the region, lived through the sort of hell that modern war brings to all and sundry. Five Savoia-Marchettis came in from the sea with the sun behind them, and bombed the road. Then four more bombers, and then they all turned and came back with machine guns wide open, spraying bullets, like garden sprinklers, in all directions. Six other bombers came down the road, right after them, strafing relentlessly.

Nothing hit any of us, so we went on to Sitges, and then more bombers came. They spared the town and bombed the roads. We flattened ourselves along the wall of a railroad bridge, where three mothers with their children had also taken refuge. One young mother had a great deal of trouble trying to make her two-year-old baby keep his mouth open so that if there were a bad concussion his ear drums would not burst or his lungs collapse.

"Viva la civilización!" said a Spaniard standing next to me.

The fall of Tarragona made hopeless an already desperate situation, although that was clearer outside of Spain than in. With wars, as with individuals, while there is life there is hope, and it is not the part of war correspondents in the one case and doctors in the other to pronounce the patient dead while the heart is still beating. To those armchair strategists, editorial and otherwise, who are inclined to confident prognostications, let me quote from someone who knew as much about war as anyone else:

"We see, therefore," writes Von Clausewitz, "how, from the commencement, the absolute, the mathematical, as it is called, nowhere finds any sure basis in the calculations in the art of war; and that from the outset there is a play of possibilities, probabilities, good and bad luck, which spreads about with all the coarse and fine threads of its web, and makes war, of all branches of human activity, the most like a gambling game."

The Loyalist Army was still in existence; the morale of the better units had not been broken; the determination of leaders like Negrín, Modesto, and Lister was unshaken. But underneath there was much decay. The regular army men yielded to their professional knowledge, and decided the game was up. Negrín was surrounded by panic and disorganization. The Catalans were not responding to the mobilization orders or even to the commands to go out and help to build fortifications. Anarchist organizations were already sabotaging industry. President Luís Companys and other Catalan leaders were still playing regional politics. Azaña was a frightened, trembling old man who insisted on leaving Barcelona long before the danger to the capital had become acute. He refused flatly to go to Madrid, as did all other members of the Government except Vayo, Uribe and Méndez Aspe, none of whom could be spared by Negrín. Thus the burden of the war, to the very end, rested on the popular commanders, the People's Army, the Communist Party, the Socialists, and Republicans, who never lost faith or courage.

General Sarabia was optimistic to the last. It was his nature to be so, and he simply could not help it. Looking back after the war, I regretted keenly that I had relied on him so much, but after all, he was the commander-in-chief of the Catalan army. Anyway, if I a mere chronicler felt that, what must Negrín and the others have felt, who were relying on his reports for the making of vital decisions?

There was a few days' lull on the coast, which aroused vain hopes that the Insurgents were exhausted and the worst was over, but activity was resumed on the 18th with an attack against Altafull, six miles up the highway from Tarragona. On that day, too, Pons was lost, and a long retreat began up the road toward Seo de Urgel and Puigcerdá on the French frontier.

I recall that day as the last quiet one I was to spend in Spain. For eight hours I had been in the territory that stretches from Sitges to Igualada and had seen no airplanes, heard no artillery fire, and found the roads normal. I had a superb lunch with Lister, my last with the commander of the 5th Army Corps. He had a chef (it would have been an injustice to call him a cook) who could turn out, even under the most trying conditions, meals that would have graced the board of any wealthy household, while his pastry cook had worked at the Ritz in Barcelona. Lister knew how to live, as well as fight.

That was the last breathing spell of the war for me. Before darkness descended, the attack had been resumed all along the

line, and it was never to let up until the beaten Loyalists
streamed across the French frontier. It was on the same day
(January 18, 1939) that Alvarez del Vayo made his noble speech
before a singularly ignoble Council of the League of Nations.
He spoke of the report of the International Commission, made
on the 16th, which had vouched for the fact that the Loyalist
Army was 100 per cent Spanish, and contrasted that with Mussolini's statement to Chamberlain that the Italians would remain
in Spain until the final triumph of Franco. He called attention
to the reports of the British Commission, testifying to the fact
that the Rebels consistently bombed open cities, which the Government did not.

"The Council knows my aversion to boastfulness," he concluded, "but if there has been a single time in which I felt fully
the pride of representing the Spanish people, this is it. I feel, at
this moment, all the grandeur of their resistance—a resistance
which neither the direct aggression of the attackers, nor the indirect aggression of those who for three years have consented to
such monstrous transgressions of international law and morals,
can ever convert into submission while there are invaders on the
territory of Spain."

Alas! they were not to yield, but they were to be driven out of
their country, to the everlasting shame of England, France, and
the United States. At that very moment, when fresh men and
more rifles were so desperately needed, two ships bearing all the
Internationals from the central zone—2,830 of them, including
about 125 Americans—were on their way from Valencia to Barcelona. Could anything have been more Spanish than this gesture,
which spared the lives of many foreigners and long periods of
imprisonment for others among them?

That was the period when the last attempt was made in the
United States to lift the arms embargo. It had almost been done
the previous spring, but strong pressure from the British and the
American Catholic lobby in Washington had overcome the wishes
of a majority of the American people. All the polls taken by the
American Institute of Public Opinion (the so-called Gallup Poll)
proved that public sympathy was with the Loyalists, and it was

increasingly so as the war drew toward a close. The last poll taken on the question, in December, 1938, showed that 76 per cent of Americans favored the Government and only 24 per cent voted for Franco.

The testimonies from American public figures were striking. It was well known that President Roosevelt's personal sympathies were with the Loyalists, although he never allowed his feelings in the matter to interfere with his political acumen. Public figures like Mrs. Eleanor Roosevelt and Dorothy Thompson were speaking and writing truths that should have been drummed into the American public for months, or even a few years before. One of the most respected voices in American public life, that of Henry L. Stimson, former Secretary of State and later Secretary of War, was raised on behalf of the Spanish Government, in a letter to *The New York Times* printed on January 24, 1939. It was a calm, scholarly, cogent analysis of international law and practice, especially as regards the United States, applied to the question of the arms embargo, which was called "a complete abandonment of a code of practice which the international world had adopted through preceding ages as the best hope of achieving the same purpose and minimizing the spread of disorder."

"If the Loyalist Government is overthrown," Mr. Stimson concluded, "it is evident now that its defeat will be solely due to the fact that it has been deprived of its right to buy from us and other friendly nations the munitions necessary for its defense. I cannot believe that our Government or our country would wish to assume such a responsibility."

We have that responsibility now, before history, and one can only regret that Stimson, Sumner Welles, Winston Churchill, and so many other sincere partisans of international right and justice, should have waited so long to make their voices heard. Now that the democracies have fought a world war, against great odds for three years, we can see the price that had to be paid for countenancing and helping the Fascist and Nazi triumphs in Spain and Czechoslovakia. It is well to have this on record, although the injustice that was approaching its climax when the

Rebels resumed their drive toward Barcelona, on January 18, 1939, can never be righted.

Because we know now that events were moving inexorably to their tragic conclusion, it may seem incredible that people in Barcelona itself could still retain hope. It was partly that we could not "see the forest for the trees"—just as those fighting in the hopeless defense of Warsaw, not many months later, could not know as well as the most ignorant newspaper reader that there could be but one conclusion. But it was also the knowledge that Barcelona could be defended; it was technically possible, and the leaders were striving desperately to make it a reality. Those were the people who made themselves heard; the saboteurs, the cowards and the weaklings simply kept quiet without lifting a finger—and they won. No force could overcome the terrible inertia that had descended on Catalonia. In Madrid a people aroused and desperate had saved a similar situation. The hope was that Barcelona, too, would rise and defend itself, and that hope died only when the Rebels entered the city.

The beginning of the end was 9:30 on the morning of January 21, when a group of Italian bombers from Majorca attacked the port of Barcelona. From then until the capital fell five days later there was to be no rest from the bombers. Sometimes a few hours separated the raids; sometimes only fifteen minutes, but always they came, hammering away at the port, driving deep into the city to frighten the inhabitants, swinging back to the port and dropping their bombs.

All hope disappeared that day with the loss of Villafranca del Panadés, the last possible place to make a long stand before the capital. Barcelona's million and a half inhabitants went about their business as calmly as if nothing unusual were happening. Nothing could have helped Franco more effectively than their inertia. No "fifth column" was necessary. The poorer people in the port district were, as always, the bravest and most determined. I felt it, on a visit to a house hit during one of the raids. The bomb had torn a huge gap in the side of the building and, as always, had splintered whatever windows were still standing in the immediate vicinity. Seven bodies had just been taken from the wreckage, and thirteen people sent to the hospital. Neighbors were trying to comfort one another. "Now that your windows are broken," one woman said, "you won't have to wash them."

I remember a gesture of courtesy in those days that was typically Spanish. It was in that same district, after one of the bombings. I stopped a passerby, obviously a poor workman, to ask for details, which he gave me patiently and politely. At the end I offered him a cigarette, and we said good-bye.

"I wish I could invite you to my house," he said, "but I have no house. It was bombed a few days ago."

The American Consul, Douglas Flood, sent out the first warning that day, urging Americans to leave. Many Internationals were still waiting to be sent out of Spain, and they were becoming desperate, but the French Government held firm. The Italians and the Germans were in an especially unhappy situation, for it was easy to imagine what would have happened to them if they were captured. Negrín had put the Government's largest and best merchant vessel at their disposal. She had been sent to Bordeaux, and arangements had been made with Mexico to receive about 2,000 men from such countries as Italy, Germany, Austria, and Hungary. The men were put on the train and sent to Puigcerdá—and then the French refused passage from Bourg-Madame to Bordeaux! French courts permitted the Rebels to put a lien on the ship, and in every way the French Government did its utmost to win the good graces of Franco.

The slow, relentless grip of the Rebels on Barcelona was tightening steadily, but the Loyalists went on fighting their hardest, generally without panic, and even counterattacking feebly whenever they could. Lister had taken up positions before Martorell, where his men were to make the last effective stand of any of the Loyalist units. He held it for three days only, but that was something of a miracle, in the circumstances. He had taken up headquarters in the central buildings of Catalonia's greatest wine producers, between Martorell and Masquefa. There were literally several million bottles of white wine and Catalan champagne in the huge cellars dug into the hill. One could hardly imagine a more pleasant or better refuge against bombing and we did, indeed, spend about half an hour inside while the Rebels bombed the lines. Some of the soldiers were getting so hilarious about it that they prayed for the bombers to keep coming over. Lister was the soul of courtesy and camaraderie, as always, and invited us into his office for a glass of wine, while he showed us the positions on the map. He was just as cheerful, just as brave, just as tough as ever. I never offered a more fervent toast than the one I drank to his luck that afternoon of January 22. The next time I was to see him, he was in Perpignan, France.

The Government was still in Barcelona, but preparations were being made to send ministry staffs and documents up to Figueras. Vayo was in Paris, being rudely treated by the French Government. Every time he telephoned Negrín, it was to hear assurances that the capital would hold out. He left Paris only on the 23rd for Barcelona, to find two days later that he could get no further than Figueras.

Barcelona's agony was an unpleasant thing to watch. We had eleven raids before midnight on the 22nd, in addition to the eight attacks of the day before. It was cruel, relentless work and the constant pounding was getting on all our nerves. A subtle change was noticeable in the attitude of the hotel staff and some of the censors. We, too, had become "Reds," and they knew we would have to flee. Some things were stolen from my room, and I had to keep everything under lock and key. Shops were closing all over the city, and everyone asked anxiously if there were a "fifth column" and when it might begin operating. Wild rumors flew about, and more than once Negrín had to reassure the people that the Government was still there, for the Rebel radio, and the foreign newspapermen who were beginning their "death watch" at Perpignan, found it easier to spread such reports than to discover the truth. The constant raids kept the city in almost perpetual darkness, and sleep could come only from sheer nervous exhaustion. The dawn was like a physical release or an awakening from a nightmare.

The port had been thoroughly wrecked before the last series of raids; it was now a shambles, a sort of live horror that gave one the shudders to see. Five British ships were sunk or damaged in three days, much to our pleasure. We wished only that there had been more there to sink, along with a few French ones. The death toll must have been fearfully high, although there was a sort of mass exodus to the upper part of the city or down into the refuges and subways.

Only the Communist Party maintained its determination, loyalty, and courage, but the Communists were becoming desperate. So much so that on the 23rd, in a moment of aberration, they decided to call back the Communists of the International Brigades, who appeared doomed anyway. Fortunately, calmer counsels prevailed. It was pointed out that nothing could harm the Government more, and anyway, the I.B. leaders refused to permit it. The Rebels later cleverly gave out stories of how they were fighting against Internationals in upper Catalonia, but, luckily, the League Commission stuck to its task in Perpignan, verified the fact that the Internationals were where they belonged, and checked them as they came over the frontier. So the Government's record, in the most Spanish of all gestures, remained clean.

But the Spanish Communists at least did resolve to fight on to the end. No Party member was allowed to leave town until the last day. Fortification groups were formed, and were sent out daily until the 25th. On that day a large group of young women Communists went out to dig trenches on the left bank of the Llobregat and were never heard of again. The Moors came in on that side.

In Barcelona the bombers were coming over so often that we all lost count. There was raid after raid, all night, all day, and then all night again. The port and the surrounding districts were a continual inferno. The whole city seemed to shrink into itself. People hardly dared to move out of their houses, while many, many thousands clung grimly to the refuges and subway, panting in the fetid air, without food, water, or light, but they were safe, at least. Other thousands were fleeing from the city, and the streets were gradually clearing of automobiles. The electric lights went out, and we ate and worked by candlelight. Even the water went off for part of the day.

The rumors were maddening, and it took all our resolution not get panicked. I had had no chance to contact headquarters on January 23, for I went to the American Embassy at Caldetas to check on plans for the Americans. Chargé d'Affaires Thurston and Consuls Flood and Jernegan did a brave and cheerful job for Americans, in those unhappy days.

Meanwhile, the city was amazingly calm and orderly, although the tension could almost be cut with a knife. The silence between raids was eerie and almost horrible. If one had only known what was happening it would have been easier to endure those low hours when darkness worked its primitive spell.

The telephones, as well as Radio Española, remained open, so we went on filing stories that were duly, if lightly, censored by two Catalans who were preparing to stay on and greet the Rebels with relief. They were shifty-eyed those nights, and I should have known better than to be turning in last letters to be mailed, with some burning words on Fascism and what I thought of it. Those letters never left the office, and are now, doubtless, a part of my Spanish dossier.

The bombers never seemed to let up that night of January 23-24, but we finally became so sleepy that our nervous systems stopped reacting to the danger, and drowsiness persisted through the booming of bombs and anti-aircraft fire and the almost more terrifying sound of the sirens. About six weeks before, the Government had managed to purchase a few large anti-aircraft guns which made a terrific noise, but never shot anything down, and at the end could not be evacuated. There was one gun, not far from the Majestic Hotel, which made more noise than the bombs.

With the dawn, the windows rattled to artillery fire, which brought memories of Madrid. Indeed, Barcelona seemed strong and almost gay in the brightness of the morning. The city slowly began to shake off its horror, as if it had awakened from a nightmare. It had seemed dead, but now it came to life, with all the cheery, normal sounds that nobody notices ordinarily—automobiles, motorcycles, people talking loudly in the streets, news vendors hawking papers (they all came out that morning), shutters being pulled up, windows opening. It was enough to make anyone recover his courage. Those who read the newspapers saw brave headlines, calling on the inhabitants to defend the city, to go to the fortifications, to erect barricades. Only the Communists responded, and they needed no urging.

Out in the street it was hard to think about anything but the bombers. They were arriving at irregular intervals, sometimes of only a half hour, sometimes of more than an hour. They flew in low over the city, disdaining the feeble anti-aircraft fire, up the Ramblas to Tibidabo, then back to the port district where they let their bombs go. Nine airplanes came at a time, and they looked to us like Dorniers, although the Italians usually reserved for themselves the pleasure of bombing the undefended city.

I spent all morning on top of Tibidabo Hill, on the northern edge of the capital. There was a magnificent bird's-eye view down the coast to Castelldefels, thence across to the Pass of Ordal, then to Montserrat and finally around to Tarrasa, Sabadell, and the northern coast. We could see that there were no Rebel troops on our side of the Llobregat, or between us and Manresa, so it was possible to go back to the Majestic for a tranquil if unappetizing lunch. There were few persons left, but otherwise we might almost have deluded ourselves into believing that things were normal. The barber, with steady hand, was industriously shaving a client, while bombers raided the city; the mailman brought me a letter from a collector who wanted Spanish stamps; the waiters served us with the same good-natured inefficiency.

After lunch, we drove out to Tibidabo again, and this time continued on to Modesto's headquarters, which had been established in a big house between Sardanyola and Ripollet. It was my last visit to that remarkable young commander, a carpenter in civil life but trained to arms in Russia. The staff confirmed our guess that the left bank of the Llobregat was still clear and Manresa had not fallen. Had we gone there a few hours later, the story would have been different.

Early in the evening, Georges Soria, of the Paris Communist

newspaper, *Humanite,* went out to see Modesto. He promised to
return with the latest information. After all, our own safety was
very much at stake. I had arranged to take out William Forrest,
of the *London News Chronicle,* O'Dowd Gallagher, of the *London Daily Express* and Robert Capa, the photographer, in "Old
Minnie," my huge Belgian Minerva. Soria did not return until
late. We heard that considerable ground had been lost, but had
no details, and shortly after midnight I radioed the last dispatch
that was to go out of Republican Barcelona. I thought then that
the capital would go down fighting, for I knew that was the plan.
Someone calculated that there had been forty-seven air raids
since the morning of January 21, and I sent that figure, although
it seemed low to me.

The telephones were not working, and the censors told us
that they would not be on the job the next day, so, whether we
stayed or not, no dispatches could be sent. Since the best story
in the world is worth nothing to a newspaperman unless he can
get it into his paper, we decided to leave in the morning, after
a few hours' sleep. The Government, including Negrín, had
gone to Figueras some time during the evening, and our place,
anyway, was there.

About one o'clock, Soria came back with an alarming story.
The Rebels had crossed the Llobregat about five in the afternoon, south of Olesa de Montserrat, and were moving on Sabadell.
Lister's bridgehead at Martorell, which had covered the retreat,
was gone, and he was falling back through Rubí toward Tibidabo. All along the Llobregat down to the sea, except for a
pathetically weak bridgehead at Prat de Llobregat, on the delta,
the Rebels were either up to the river or there were no troops
opposing them. They were trying to get around to the northern
side of Barcelona, to cut it off, and if they continued to meet no
resistance they would be there by dawn. Modesto's friendly and
firm advice to us was to leave as soon as we could, and, at least,
place ourselves somewhere north of Barcelona. He had asked
Lister to take up positions based on Tibidabo to make a last
stand for Barcelona; 3,000 Assault Guards whom Negrín had
ordered to defend the city were still there; 10,000 Valencianos,

recently brought up by ship, were still fresh; Tagüeña would try
to hold the southern approaches. A fight would be made, Modesto said, but clearly a hopeless one.

We returned to the Majestic to pack, pay our bills and go
through other motions of civilized existence, as if the world had
not been turned upside down. The city had the unreality of a
nightmare. Virtually all cars had gone. Hundreds of thousands
of inhabitants were huddled in refuges, cellars, and subways, for
the bombers kept up their maddening round, hour after hour.
The Plaza Cataluña subway station was an extraordinary scene
of misery and pathos when I went to send my last radio—men,
women and children lying in a fetid atmosphere, with nothing
to eat, nothing to do but wait, and by waiting save their lives.
They somehow knew that it would not be long, and there would
be no more bombardments, once the waiting time was past. But
meanwhile the pounding continued.

The exodus from the city had thinned out by that time. Automobiles were scarce in Loyalist Spain, and without one, escape
was impossible. Indeed, lack of gasoline or a few punctures might
cost one's life. I had prepared a reserve supply of gasoline, and
had groomed "Old Minnie" like a faithful battle-horse. I had not
let her out of my sight for days, and now that the time had come
she was ready.

Barcelona was clearly a dying city, but one in which the
atmosphere was peculiarly tense. Water was scarce, because the
electric pumps which brought it to the reservoir could rarely
work, on account of the bombings. One of the main reservoirs,
that on the Llobregat, was already in the hands of the Rebels,
and they were approaching the second main supply, on the
Besos. The food supply had not been replenished for several days,
and the city was drawing on its meager reserves. It was good-bye
to Catalan Barcelona, even to its language and culture, since
Franco had announced he would have no separatism.

To relieve congestion, outgoing cars were routed by the road
to Granollers, while incoming traffic used the coast highway. As
we were going only to Caldetas, twenty miles away, I cut over
to the coast road. Hundreds of trucks were coming in, all empty,

so that they could be sent away laden. Driving was reckless, for the nerve strain was contagious, and we saw a great many accidents all that day. One man had been killed at the Badalona crossroads, and his body still lay in the road.

It was after three when we arrived at the American Embassy in Caldetas. The house was dark, and we lacked the nerve to disturb Thurston at that time of night, so we spent four bitterly cold hours trying vainly to sleep on the ground or in the car. We were roundly berated for that by the Chargé d'Affaires when he discovered us, but it did not prevent him from giving us a heavenly breakfast of fruit, bread and butter and much steaming coffee. The Americans who were to go out on the cruiser *Omaha* had all gathered there.

Our job was to find out, if we could, what had happened to Barcelona, so we drove back toward the capital, first to Mataró, then up to Granollers, and then back to the coast to within ten miles of the city. We checked with drivers, officers, and military commanders, and always got the same story. Barcelona had not fallen, but they knew nothing of the situation outside. Clearly, we could have gone into the capital, but it seemed no use. Noon had come, and we had to get back at least to Figueras and probably to Perpignan before we could send a story.

There had been at least ten more bombing raids, from what we could gather, and, in fact, the bombers and strafers were at it all the time we were in the neighborhood. We just missed a nasty bombing of Granollers. The traffic meanwhile had become extraordinarily heavy, and it seemed insane to be bucking it the wrong way as we were doing. Soldiers were straggling back, and I remember remarking contemptuously at Mataró the healthy, almost spick-and-span condition of a large column of Assault Guards, all armed with carbines, walking leisurely in the wrong direction. It was only later that I learned from Negrín these were the 3,000 Guards whom he had ordered the Minister of the Interior to place in Barcelona to defend the city. That night Gómez, in clear disobedience of his orders, had sent them out of the capital.

We returned to Caldetas just in time to find Thurston preparing to go aboard the *Omaha*. The refugees had been soundly bombed at Arenys del Mar, and some had lost their baggage, but fortunately none had been hit. As Thurston was driving away from the Embassy, Insurgent planes bombed Granollers, just over the hill. It was a thunderous farewell to one who had served the United States well through stormy times.

The drive to Figueras was a nightmare, particularly as I was becoming progressively more exhausted, and none of the others could handle the ponderous car. We overtook thousands and thousands of refugees, in carts, on mules, afoot, begging rides in trucks and cars, and always wearily struggling forward to that inhospitable frontier which still remained grimly closed to them. Already the vanguard had reached Figueras and would soon be pressing against the border. Those in the rear were to be overtaken, and many were to be killed and wounded in the incessant bombing and strafing of the roads.

Figueras was in a state of appalling chaos when we arrived late in the afternoon. The abandonment of Barcelona had come so suddenly that nothing had been prepared, even for the Government. Vayo and his wife had just arrived from Paris. Negrín, dead tired and discouraged, but as grim and determined as ever, was in the castle on the hill.

"All his convictions, instincts, and desires are urging him to keep on fighting to the end," I wrote that night, "for he is convinced that the Loyalist cause is just and that the world must recognize it sooner or later. But the Army appears to be shattered, and those men cannot fight any more. . . . The problem is whether there is enough new matériel and men to put up a stronger resistance while the Armies of the Ebro and the East are rested, reorganized and reinforced with the new recruits. The failure of the Madrid zone to help relieve pressure has been fatal. No one understands why it should have been such a weak effort, but there seems to be little hope for Loyalist Spain if that is the best that Miaja can do. Until last week the morale of the troops was amazingly good, but they are mad with fatigue and bewildered at being asked to make such hopeless efforts. Some units are still fighting hard and well—particularly Lister's—but the majority are through. All this discouragement may prove temporary. The Loyalists performed the miracle of Madrid, and perhaps they can perform another one."

We spent nearly an hour in Figueras, during which I sat back exhausted in my car and let the others scout around. Capa decided to stay, but the rest of us had to go, for there were no facilities for sending stories. Vincent Sheean came up and cheerfully announced that he was going down to Barcelona. I knew he was not, but did not have the energy to argue. I cannot remember the rest of the journey to Perpignan, but I am sure we went through all the usual customs and passport formalities, at La Junquera.

The hotel in Perpignan was full to bursting. Its plump, mean, pompous proprietor, who used to be polite enough when he needed customers, was now as nasty and officious as only a member of the French petty bourgeoisie can be. He had developed a horror of "Reds," for, after all, had they not lost? It enraged us to think that the "Reds" had been fighting for the likes of him for nearly three years.

I had been on the go since two the night before, and had had no sleep in thirty-six hours, driving almost all the time—and the story still to be written. Harold Peters of the United Press came to my rescue and offered me his room, and somehow I batted out 2,000 words that made sense, too tired and headachy to think that it was the unhappiest story I had ever written.

It was the next day, January 26, that Barcelona fell, and without being defended! I could hardly believe the news when it first came through, knowing the preparations that had been made, and I never learned when or why the decision was made not to put up some sort of fight. There were to be shame and regret later, and no one cared to talk about it, although, to be sure, there were good and plausible reasons for it.

After we had left the neighborhood at noon the day before, the bombings had continued steadily, reaching the astounding total of sixty-two raids in those last five days. The Rebels had advanced faster than had been expected. Anyway, Lister's orders had been changed, and he was told to fall back on Granollers.

To Tagüeña's 15th Corps, which had to retreat through Barcelona anyway, was given the task of falling back slowly so that no men or transportable matériel would be lost.

The Moors entered from the coast side, the Navarrese from the Esplugas road, and the Italians from the Tibidabo side, and, of course, were greeted by the populace with Fascist salutes and cheers. Such is human nature. Then came the "clean-up."

In Rome scores of thousands, herded with customary skill by the indefatigable Secretary of the Fascist Party, Achille Starace, gathered in the Piazza Venezia. Mussolini came out on the balcony.

"Your shout of exultation, which is fully justified, blends with that rising in all the cities of Spain, which are now completely liberated from the Reds' infamies, and with the shout of joy from all anti-Bolshevists the world over," he cried. "General Franco's magnificent troops and our fearless Legionaries have not only beaten Negrín's Government, but many others of our enemies are now biting the dust."

For the sake of the republicanism and democracy which had been so well defended, Barcelona should have been fought for. Of course, there was not enough food for a siege; the people did not respond; there were hardly any machine guns, and without them streets could not be defended. Above all, the Rebels were soon to cut off Barcelona from the north. So there were good reasons for the fall of the city—and yet one must regret that the Catalans, unlike the Castilians of Madrid, the Poles of Warsaw, the Russians of Stalingrad, did not write a heroic page for history to record.

The Spanish Course Ends

THE LAST period of the Catalan offensive, which centered around Figueras and which I covered by daily trips from Perpignan, was one of the most baffling and significant of my career. I often think about it and wonder whether I made a fool of myself, and to what extent I harmed my reputation. After it was over my publisher reproached me with having misled readers of *The New York Times* into believing that the situation was consistently better than it proved to be. From the professional point of view, I had to acknowledge the justice of the reproof. And yet . . .

Negrín's idea to move straight from Barcelona to Madrid, rather than Figueras, was more feasible and nobler, but the other members of the Government, with a few exceptions, were made of weaker stuff. Figueras was the only other possibility, after it became obvious that Gerona would soon be on the battle front. But there had been too much delay, too little preparation in Figueras, and a complete disorganization in all the services, with those thousands of refugees acting as an incubus that could not be shaken off.

Yet there were moments when it seemed as though Negrín could handle the matter, at least to the extent of restoring order and hanging on for a month or so. The two weeks that elapsed before the Rebels cleaned up Catalonia and reached the French frontier seem brief in retrospect—as, indeed, any two weeks must be in the life of a nation—but to those who lived through them day after day they were interminable. There was a great deal of Spanish—and, for that matter, European—history packed into those days, and the session of the Cortes which was held in the

Castle of Figueras on February 1, 1939, will be a symbol as glorious in its way as that of Cadiz in 1811, when Napoleon's Army had overrun the Peninsula. Those are the pages of a nation's history which never fade. Figueras was not the last agony of an ancient order. A live and enduring force was evoked there, something essentially and eternally Spanish, and it will rise again.

That was an instance in which those outside could not see the trees for the forest. Being there, writing about it every day, trying to catch the spirit, the alternating hopes and despair, the humiliations and the glories, was a bewildering and, I suppose, hopeless task. It all seemed ridiculous from the outside. But what I was catching, almost unconsciously, were the last struggles of a people who did not want to die, who could not believe that they would be allowed to die, who still had life and courage and ideals, and even hope. All those things were cut down, and people denied that they had been there, but I saw them, and they still make the elements of history.

Negrín was, as always, the rallying point for whatever strength there was in the resistance. I saw him in the Castle of Figueras on January 27. The Castle had been a fortress, prison, barracks, but never in its long history had it been the seat of government. It was built on a hill dominating the town—a huge, rambling structure, with outer and inner walls, a drawbridge and deep cellars. Safe and powerful it certainly was, but completely devoid of any facilities for being the seat of government. Pieces of paper had been pasted up on various doors: *"Ministerio de Estado," "Presidencia de Consejo,"* and the like, and inside were bare rooms with plain tables and chairs. In contrast with the luxurious buildings in Barcelona, nothing could have been more depressing.

Indeed, every physical aspect of the whole situation was depressing. Figueras was a madhouse of bewildered officials and soldiers, struggling desperately, not only with their own work, but with those thousands of swarming refugees who filled every house and doorway and covered almost every inch of the streets where men, women and children slept through the bitterly cold nights with almost no food, and certainly no place to go.

The inevitable drift was toward the frontier, and there the refugees found the French *Gardes Mobiles*. My guess that day was that there were no fewer than 250,000 unfortunates strung out all along the road and in every village from Mataró to the frontier. That proved approximately right, but I never thought that virtually all of them would end up in French concentration camps. Great efforts were being made to evacuate them from Figueras and Gerona, since those towns were obviously going to be bombed. Indeed, Gerona received a fearful bombing that day, and although we could not know the details, the results must have been sickening. Figueras was raided while I was there, but fortunately on the edge of town. It was terrible to think that the bombers could easily have killed hundreds of persons and wrecked dozens of houses if they had wanted to do so.

But, in spite of everything, there was that high, indomitable resolve which somehow gave a feeling of hope, despite the evidence of one's eyes. Negrín was so positive about it, and I knew the man too well to think that he was bluffing.

"The war will continue; the Army is establishing new lines; the rearguard is being reorganized," he told me. "This is where we stay as long as we can, and we hope it will be indeed long—that is, until we can get back to Barcelona and Madrid."

Foolish words, you might say, but the spirit that prompted them was the same as that which had saved Spain before. You cannot speak with contempt of people who do not know when they are beaten. At worst, they had the foolhardiness of Don Quixote.

I saw Vayo there, too, with Companys, some high staff officers, a few deputies, and many other officials whom I knew from Barcelona, and every one of them was working his head off to get things going again. The problem, fully realized by Negrín, was not so much the Army as the rearguard. The Army would go on fighting as long as the soldiers could stand or had any bullets to shoot, but the rearguard had been completely demoralized by the loss of Barcelona and the presence of the refugees.

However, there was no loss of authority, except in so far as the difficulties of communication hindered the transmission of orders.

There were no mutinies or rioting or usurpations of power. The chaos did not come from that. The customs and police authorities were doing their duties as usual. The Army was taking orders from the Government. There was still plenty of money available. A recovery seemed possible, but only on one condition—and this everyone realized—that new matériel be allowed in. For a few days the Spaniards nourished the hope, despite all previous disappointments, that France would relent.

"The Spanish Government therefore faces an extraordinary difficult task," I wrote on that night of January 27, the day after Barcelona fell, "yet it was made obvious to me today that there was no other solution as they all saw it. Peace or mediation would be a betrayal of those who have been most loyal, who have fought hardest and most bravely, who remain convinced that 'Fascism imposed by a foreign army' is worse than anything that can happen to Spain through their continuing to struggle, and above all of those who still feel the battle can be won."

That was the way I felt in Figueras, talking to the people upon whom the decision lay, and seeing what they were doing or trying to do. Twenty-four hours in the gloom and defeatism of Perpignan gave things an entirely different aspect—one which events were to justify. If the hopes were dashed, if the result sought was more than human beings could accomplish, that does not nullify the historical fact that those hopes and those efforts existed.

When I went back to Figueras the hopes rose again. There had been a lull at the front and a line—a very weak one, but still a line—had been established, with the troops actually counterattacking in some places. Communications, although still bad, had improved. To Figueras had been given a new life, and one with genuine order. Traffic was being routed through with reasonable speed; the refugees were being cleared out slowly but steadily, and those who remained were being fed free at the popular restaurants, where they received one dish per meal, of rice or beans and meat.

The optimism and the confidence were astounding. I succumbed to them to the extent of predicting that Catalonia could hold out for a month or longer if there were not another collapse. It was all over in two weeks, but my friends in Figueras considered me a pessimist.

A reorganization of the Army staff had taken place. Sarabia had been removed and General Jurado named to succeed him. The stories we heard in Perpignan of wholesale desertions or the flight of the Army were false. There had been some desertions, but relatively few in the circumstances, and I saw more soldiers returning toward their units than straggling toward the frontier.

Above all, there was the fact that the Cortes were to meet the following day, February 1. For those who had fought so hard and so vainly, that was somehow a symbol of hope and promise. It meant that the Second Spanish Republic still existed—against Franco and the whole world. The constitution was to be obeyed; the framework of democratic government, however weakened, was to be supported once more. A gesture was to be made, as truly Spanish as any ever made in the tragic and glorious history of the country of Don Quixote.

To go through Junquera alone was a matter of a full hour in a car, crawling by inches through swarming humanity, and often having to stop because of jammed traffic. Fires were springing up all alongside the road, in the fields and back in the hills. The scene was an unending gypsy camp, as those thousands of pathetic individuals, who had nothing to do with that war except to suffer in it, settled down for another cold night.

We were back in Figueras early the next morning, for the meeting of the Cortes. No time had been set, because the Government did not want to send an invitation to the Rebels to bomb them. It was a day of tension, because everyone expected Figueras to be badly bombed. As we drove in, the trucks bearing the artistic treasures of Spain which the Government had so carefully packed and preserved throughout the war were lined up along the road, ready to be driven to safety. The weather was springlike, and the Government's protecting planes, working in relays from the airfield near Vilajuiga, were able to keep up a fairly constant patrol. That doubtless helped to save the town for there were some alarms during the day, but no bombing.

At about four or five in the afternoon there was a parade of Assault Guards through the streets. It seemed like a brave show and we were all duly thrilled—but those happened to be the same Assault Guards who had deserted Barcelona at the critical moment.

From hour to hour we were getting a different time for the meeting of the Cortes, but finally, late in the afternoon, it was definitely announced that the session would begin at ten o'clock in the Castle of Figueras.

Not even at Cadiz had the Cortes been held in so strange and picturesque a setting—down in the dungeon-like vaults of the old castle on the hill. At one time the place had been used for stables, and the stalls were still there, on one side of the low-ceilinged hall. The night was chilly, and some of the ministers and deputies kept their overcoats on throughout the session. The twelve ministers were squeezed together on a plain bench too short for them. Other benches and chairs had been placed facing them, and at right angles on their right, while on the left a dais and a rude tribune had been fixed up for Martínez Barrio, the President of the Cortes. We newspapermen had a place of honor next to the tribune, for we were the chroniclers who were to describe the meeting for posterity. Everyone was conscious of the fact that an unforgettable page of history was being written that night, and those who spoke, particularly Negrín, addressed us more than they did their fellow deputies, because through us they were addressing the world.

Azaña, to his eternal disgrace, had refused to take the risk of being present. Some others, like La Pasionaria, were in Madrid, and could not get there; others, like Portela Valladares, who had rallied to the Government when it seemed likely to win, had thought better of their loyalty; still others, like Caballero and Araquistain, were nursing their bitterness in other places. In all, there were present less than seventy of the full Cortes of 473 deputies.

It was in this setting, with the Republican flag displayed for the last time at a Cortes of the Second Republic, with its tribune covered with red brocade, with cheap carpets on the stone floor and plain wooden seats, that Martínez Barrio tapped his gavel at 10:25 on the night of February 1, 1939, and the session began.

"You are meeting in difficult circumstances," he said. "You are the legitimate and authentic representation of the people. Keep your passions in check. This session will probably be historic in the life of Spain. You are writing a page of honor for the future of the Spanish fatherland."

Negrín was the first speaker, and the only one who mattered. Those of us who knew his state of physical exhaustion and discouragement wondered whether he would be able to keep on talking. Several times he had to stop to pull himself together, and sometimes he seemed almost too dazed to express his thoughts coherently, especially after his notes gave out when he was half way through, and he had to speak extemporaneously. I do not believe any text of his speech has ever been published, and I only have my disjointed notes to go by.

He spoke of the "severe atmosphere of war" through which they were passing, but said that now "spirits were tranquilized and fears calmed." There could have been "a definite disaster," but it had been avoided. For a while "a wave of panic had almost asphyxiated the rearguard, paralyzed the Army, destroyed the Republic." There had been "a lack of communication between the Government and its people, and an exploitation of that panic by the enemy, but there had been no rising against the Government. In fact, the contrary was true."

He then went on to explain why there had been a panic. There were "too many people in Loyalist Spain. Millions had fled before the Fascists, and that is the best proof of the feeling of our people. The massacre of Santa Coloma de Queralt demoralized the rearguard. So did the Rebel aviation; so did the constant retreats. It was no surprise, and the Government was prepared. After the fall of Tarragona it had asked the French Government to accept 100,000 to 120,000 old people, women and children, but had been refused.

"Public order has been maintained by public will, and not by force. The Government's energy is national. In three days it had solved the refugee problem, thanks to the French Government."

Again he spoke of the panic, which had affected many soldiers as well as civilians. They were taking "strong measures," but "the morale of the Army was good." There had been "a panic organized by provocateurs, by lies, which undermined morale. Those were our worst enemies, and we could not combat them for lack of means. There are few examples of an army that fought so long against such odds. Many were without arms, waiting for their comrades to die so that they could pick up their rifles. The lack was not their fault, nor the Government's." (This was the only time in his speech that he showed emotion, and for a moment it seemed as though he would break down.)

Then he gave an account of the military situation, explaining how the Army had been reorganized after the break-through to the coast the previous spring, and described the offensives, particularly that of the Ebro.

"Our terrible and tremendous problem," he continued, "has always been the lack of arms. We, a legitimate Government, had to buy arms clandestinely, as contraband, even in Germany and Italy! We managed to make some, and scrape along."

Fixing his eyes steadily on us of the foreign press, he told of the Government's loyalty and how it had kept all its promises, hoping thereby that the democracies would change their attitude and give the Government a chance. With deep bitterness the Premier spoke next of "the farce of 'Non-Intervention' and 'the Italian withdrawal, [of 10,000 men] followed by new shipments of men and matériel.'"

Before the last offensive he had said that "we would lose ground, but must save the Army, so that if matériel came through we could thus save the situation. We could have brought matériel in if we had kept our nerves, if the rearguard had conserved its unity."

"The Army has reformed," he claimed. "If we can hold on to a part of Catalonia, it would mean the prolongation of the war, with all its consequences."

Negrín's only attack on the British followed. He picked a little thing, the treatment of the Government destroyer *José Luis Díez* at Gibraltar, but from the significant way in which he looked at us, it was clear that he wanted the major point to be driven home. He told how the repairs in Gibraltar harbor were made by the Government at its own expense; how the British had announced the date of departure; how the Rebels were allowed to attack the *José Luis Díez* in British waters, damaging it badly. Finally, he told how the crew was arrested by the British authorities who, ignoring the Government's protests, asked each member separately whether he wanted to go back to Loyalist Spain or into Franco Spain. Every man voted to return to the Government side.

In this protest against a relatively unimportant injustice, Negrín was diplomatically but clearly condemning the whole British system of favoring the Rebels against the Loyalists.

"We are fighting for the independence of our country," he went on, "and also for democracy. This is a struggle of two civilizations, of Christianity against Hellenism. We are defending other countries—which are not only not helping us, but are causing us our greatest difficulties.

"To save the peace of Europe they let Austria go, and cut up Czechoslovakia. If the time came when Spain would provide one more sacrifice, would they be in a stronger position to meet the aggressors, to defend themselves? Here is where the answer will come to the question of whether a few totalitarian powers will control the world, or whether it will continue divided. Hitler and Mussolini are wrong in placing their support behind Franco, because the people are not with him, and because the fruits of victory will never be gained."

The Premier then offered three points which would be accepted by the Loyalists as conditions of a just peace: First, a guarantee of the independence of the country; second, a guarantee that the Spanish people would decide on its regime and its destiny; third, that when the war was over all persecutions and reprisals would end.

"We will fight to save Catalonia," he concluded, "and if we lose it we will continue to fight in the central zone. Countries do not live only by victories, but by the examples which their people have known how to give in tragic times."

It was on that noble theme that the long speech ended. No one could call it an oratorical masterpiece; it was disjointed, and badly delivered, by a man so exhausted that he could hardly stand, yet it should take its place with the great documents of Spanish history.

Representatives of each of the major parties then followed, with brief addresses. Martínez Barrio asked for an explicit vote of confidence in the Government, which was passed unanimously, by acclamation. Then the order of the day was submitted.

"The Cortes of the nation ratify the legitimate right of Spain to carry out its destiny, and, whatever happens, to remain united." It ended with a "salute to the Army, Navy and Air Force."

This time the deputies were asked to stand up one by one and give their vote, "Sí" or "No." Sixty-two voted "Yes," and, in addition, some absentees had sent in their adherence. A few deputies did not vote; none stood up and said "No."

So ended the last Cortes of the Second Spanish Republic. Now that ancient and traditional governmental body of Spain is being reconstituted in exile, and there will come a time when Spain again has her Cortes. When that time arrives, the session of Figueras will be recognized as one of the most glorious in the long struggle for Spanish democracy.

In passing, let us note what Negrín said about Czechoslovakia and Spain. Few persons realize what an opportunity was lost in September, 1938. The democracies would have had Czechoslovakia and Russia on their side. A little help to Loyalist Spain, and Franco with his German and Italian allies would have been swept into the sea, and Republican Spain would have been an active ally of the democracies throughout the war. Italy would have been exhausted and *hors de combat*. The year that was lost was utilized with far greater effect, for increasing armaments, by Germany than by Great Britain and France. Russia joined Germany, not the democracies. Almost nothing was gained by delay and much was lost, including morality and decency. "What is past is prologue. Study the past." Czechoslovakia, and especially Spain, formed the prologue for the Second World War.

It almost seemed as though the Republican Army and people had gathered their last ounce of strength to make the Cortes possible in a brief period of cohesion and resistance. A last lease on life had been taken, a final blaze of glory, and then came death. The Rebels struck again in all sectors, and the thin, weakened line could not hold. In a dispatch written the next day I could give the Government only ten days or two weeks to hold out in Catalonia, and even that estimate was too sanguine.

Whether or not the Spaniards were in a panic, the French were certainly becoming panicky. They had tried from the beginning to wash their hands of the war; now it was coming toward them in the form of 250,000 civilian refugees and about 150,000 soldiers, and much as the French wanted to keep the Spaniards out, it was being realized gradually that the only way to do so would be to line up the French Army along the frontier and shoot the Spaniards down as they tried to come over—which was unthinkable even to the Frenchmen who were handling the situation. In spite of all warnings, no preparations had been made to care for the huge mass of men, women, and children. The French at first wanted none of them; then they thought they would take the women and children. Next, they saw that the wounded would have to be let in, and, finally, that the border would have to be thrown open to all. When that happened, the results were appalling—for the refugees.

The Loyalist soldiers were fighting now only with the primitive instinct of protecting their women and children, their wounded and the old people who were trekking desperately toward the inhospitable frontier while Rebel planes swept along the roads in raid after raid of bombing and strafing. The soldiers had but one task left—to "cover" the refugees until they could get to safety—and then to go down fighting to the end. No other action of the Loyalists did them more honor than that last despairing stand of men so fatigued they could scarcely hold their rifles, with virtually no ammunition, and still facing fearful odds.

As we drove into Spain on the morning of February 4, about 300 Loyalist soldiers and able-bodied civilians were being herded back by the *Gardes Mobiles*. There was no longer a place for them, because even Figueras, only 15 miles from the border, was being evacuated when we arrived.

During the night the Government had gone to the village of La Bajol, just inside the frontier opposite Las Illas. We could not even find them that day, because nobody at Figueras seemed to know where they were. We tried Agullana, which was very near, and actually saw Rebel planes bombing La Bajol without realizing why they were doing it.

The evacuation had been forced by the long-expected destruction of Figueras from the air. Gerona had been bombed sixteen times the day before and an equal number of times on the 2nd. The bombing of Figueras never stopped for five hours on the afternoon of February 3. No one knew why the Rebels did it, since they were advancing as fast as they could go, and it made little difference whether the Government left there on the 3rd or a day or two later. Perhaps it was merely an automatic reaction of the military mind.

Figueras was half deserted when we arrived, and trucks were taking out what civilians remained. Up in the Castle, preparations were under way to clear everything out. Huge piles of documents were being burned. We asked a high staff officer whether we could drive on to Gerona, and he quickly disabused us of the idea. At the end he made a bitter remark which I had heard only a few times during the war: "If we had only fought as the totalitarian powers did, bombing, killing, working on the rearguard as they have on ours, treating prisoners as they did ours, we would not be in this fix."

The town was too unhealthful a place to stay in, and we were lucky to escape a bombing in the two hours we spent there. The important event of the day was a meeting in La Bajol of Azaña, Vicente Rojo and Negrín. Azaña, querulous and frightened, announced that he was through, that he had always said there was no hope, and that the war should have been stopped long before. Rojo said the army could fight no longer, that he had done his best, and that he, too, refused to go to the Madrid zone. Azaña said: "I told you so!" Negrín listened, looked at them as if they were talking a language he could not understand, then rose, and, without saying a word, walked out of the room.

The next morning a report got about that Figueras had fallen. Who spread it, or why, will never be known, but the effect was electrical. For the French it meant that the Loyalist Army was almost on the border, and they could no longer postpone the decision they should have made, for humanitarian reasons, many days before. The frontier was thrown wide open from Cerbère to Bourg-Madame, and the refugees—men, women, children, and soldiers—were allowed to stream into France with all their belongings. For a while the peasants were permitted to take in their carts and mules, even their goats and sheep, but a few days later all that was stopped, and everything was confiscated to be given to Franco. All war matériel was sequestered in fields near the frontier; soldiers were disarmed, and not only that, but their binoculars, cameras, pocket-knives and other personal belongings were ruthlessly taken away and dumped in a common heap. We learned of cases where even cigarettes were taken by *Gardes Mobiles.* Much of it was their plunder, and at least one Guard retired and bought a cafe in Bordeaux with the proceeds. It was all done with a brutality that sickened those of us who had to watch the process day after day.

The order was given in the afternoon, and it was at four-thirty that the first batch of 4,500 soldiers was allowed to come over at Le Perthus. Women and children, trucks by dozens and dozens —even artillery—passed up the road and through the village. Azaña fled to Paris, with Companys. Negrín, Vayo, and a few others stayed in La Bajol to see the thing through.

By reading the Perpignan *Eclair* for the following day one can guess at the welcome the Loyalists received.

"Exhausted chauffeurs slept at their wheels," the newspaper wrote, "awaiting orders to go into the interior of France, which is so hospitable to the Marxist cowards. In one limousine a blonde and outrageously made-up woman could be seen, drinking avidly. . . .

"The number of Anarchist refugees in Perpignan has grown in an alarming manner. Certain of these bandits are circulating insolently. . . . Some of them submitted with bad grace to the search at the border. . . . It is truly scandalous that gasoline trucks have been allowed to come in which, at any instant, might provoke a catastrophe. Everything is permitted to Marxism. . . .

"One comes across police officers of the Russian Cheka, an organization well known under the initials S.I.M. . . .

"Perpignan is now infested with Spanish bandits. . . ."

And so it went. The Loyalists had thought they were incidentally defending France in their long and hopeless struggle, but they were now learning their mistake.

The situation had become intolerable for the Government, whatever the military outcome may have been. If it were only because of the loss of dignity entailed in the treatment of their representatives, the Government would have had to move to the central zone. There was no question of mediation among those who still held what power remained. Vayo had been in and out of Perpignan every day, setting up a temporary organization to handle matters until Catalonia was cleaned up.

The League Commission, at least, was still dealing with the Government and receiving every facility for checking on the Internationals and getting them out. They were all up near the frontier by that time. All the art treasures were out, as I noticed on my trip to La Junquera. I found that village and its surroundings in a state of high tension, bordering on panic. It would have taken very little to set those people on a mad stampede for the border, if it were not for the fact that the Carabinero Corps was still maintaining order and keeping the roads open. They provided, in those critical days, an example of devotion to duty which did much to reduce criticism of their much less effective work at the front. An agreement had been reached between the French Government and the Rebel command not to bomb the border zone, which was fortunate, considering that the results would have been horrible beyond imagination.

The French, much to their surprise, found that the "Marxist horde" gave them no trouble whatever as they came into France. A few dozen New York traffic policemen, stationed between Le Perthus and the concentration camps would have sufficed as well as the huge military forces assigned to the task. The Loyalists simply wanted to know what to do and where to go.

The troops who came over acted like the disciplined soldiers they were. Two files of them crossed the frontier bridge at Le Perthus, one on each side of the road, while down the middle were driven automobiles and trucks, bearing the women, children, wounded and all others who had a right to be there. At the French end they were quickly and brusquely "frisked." Then they continued out of the village and along the road. A few places had been set aside between Le Perthus and Le Boulou as temporary camps, but most of the refugees were directed up the road toward Argelès. The good humor of the crowd would have been remarkable if one did not know Spaniards.

The British Minister, Stevenson, who was at Amélie-les-Bains, was making great efforts to induce the Negrín Government to sue for peace. Jules Henry, the French Ambassador, was likewise doing his best. The British had already begun arranging for the surrender of Minorca to the Rebels—an unnecessary bit of treachery, in the circumstances. It had not yet been learned that "peace at any price" is the equivalent of national suicide if continued long enough. Actually, there was no basis for negotiation. Franco demanded unconditional surrender, and it was obvious that the Government had to yield or fight. They chose to fight, although they knew it would be a lone, hopeless struggle.

To be sure, with the best will in the world, the French Government could not have coped with that sudden and overwhelming flood. On February 6 alone, some 40,000 came over at Le Perthus and about 25,000 at Cerbere, without counting the minor passes. Then there were all the vehicles and all the matériel. One must blame the French, however, for the lack of preparation, and the heartlessness and bad grace with which the thing was done when it had to be done. By "the French" I mean the Government and Army, not the French people, who were kindly and considerate when they came into contact with the refugees. The thousands of women and children who were distributed throughout the villages of southern France received a genuine hospitality that was just as indicative of the true French character as was the callousness of its officialdom.

There was one last, great day—February 7—for which those who believe in Spanish Republicanism must be forever grateful. The stream of refugees, Carabineros, Assault Guards and deserters had flowed steadily across the frontier all the previous night, but by morning it had begun to dwindle, and soon became no more than a trickle. Then the French and the world discovered that they had made a gigantic mistake. Figueras had not fallen! The Army was still fighting twelve miles south of Figueras, fighting in good tactical order, with its artillery and other services functioning smoothly, with not only its General Staff, but its Government, inside Catalonia.

The panic was in the rearguard, not in the Army, and it had been caused by the false report that Figueras had fallen. That report came from very high Spanish sources, and there were ugly tales about it, but the important thing was that the French believed it; the refugees believed it; the panic began, and the French threw open the frontiers because they thought all was over. It was just as well that they thought so, for it permitted the Army to protect their women, children and old folks, and left their rear free for a last, orderly retreat instead of a stampede. The French guessed wrong by only forty-eight hours, but that made all the difference.

And when everyone stood at the bridge in Le Perthus, looking anxiously down the road for the first signs of the fleeing army, what they saw was not a routed force, but a group of Internationals on parade, withdrawing with discipline and pride from Loyalist Spain—flags flying, songs on their lips, and fists raised in the Popular Front salute. Never had they been such a symbol of the ideals for which they fought as when they marched up, four abreast, to be reviewed by André Marty, Luigi Gallo, and Pietro Nenni, while the French officers looked on with respect and the Spaniards present cheered, and wept to see them go.

There were about 750, and more were to come. The Garibaldinis came singing the *Bandiera Rossa,* in a group of about 300. Then another group of some 170 Americans, Canadians, and British marched smartly by, singing the *International,* in which the last contingent of more than 250 Czechs, Hungarians, and men from the Balkans joined.

Marty, whose head was bandaged from a slight wound received

in a recent bombing of Figueras, issued some crisp orders. "Remember that from now on you will be the guests of France," he said, "and you are in no way to cause any trouble. You must maintain your discipline. There is to be no more fist-raising, no more singing of the *International,* no demonstrations. You must not even talk to anyone until the ranks are broken in the camp at Argelès."

Not even the members of the League Commission were permitted to talk to them, for the French authorities said that until the camp was properly organized the Internationals could not be visited. A few of us drove ahead and saw the camp, after which it was easy to understand why the French would prefer not to have League officials see it, and why the Spaniards felt so much humiliation and resentment.

The camp was several miles outside Argelès on sandy ground near the sea. Miles of barbed wire, in three concentric fences, had been strung around, with openings in four or five places, all strongly guarded by Senegalese and *Gardes Mobiles.* Senegalese soldiers were placed as guards at hundred-yard intervals, facing in toward the camp. That Senegalese should have been used was the crowning humiliation for Spaniards who had fought the Moors for more than two years and a half, and indeed, had a centuries-old tradition of fear and hatred of their African enemies.

Men, some women and children, civilians and soldiers, the wounded, the ill and the well, were all marched in, willy-nilly, and that was all. An attempt had been made to put up some flimsy barracks, but few were finished, and they did not hold more than a hundred of the refugees. Once inside, everyone fended for himself, although the wounded and ill got some elementary care from a first-aid station, which was as yet very inadequate.

Everyone slept on the ground, most of the men digging for themselves a slight depression for protection against the night winds. They could not dig more than a foot or so down because water would be struck quickly. That brackish water, incidentally, was the only water available in the camp, for either washing or drinking, and a plague of dysentery spread. There was not a single latrine for those 25,000 persons.

I could go on for pages, with the sickening details. At the time it was impossible to publish them in full, because the French in Washington protested, and some of us got reproaches from our editors. Since editors and readers were not there in France to see for themselves, we could do nothing to prove the truth of what we were writing. In time the facts became known, and are now beyond dispute. Like all neutral observers there at the time, I was hot with rage and helplessness. I suppose one could not expect newspapers to print details so utterly damaging to a friendly country whose diplomatic representatives were making violent, if unjustified, complaints. What we knew was so bad that when the story got around that the Spahis (French Moroccan cavalrymen) were using whips to herd the Spaniards into the concentration camps, we believed it. Certainly Spahis were used because I saw them, and that they should have been employed against proud, sensitive, and courageous people was little short of criminal. The degradation was not theirs, but of the French, who could treat the most courteous and hospitable of races with such utter meanness.

It is well that history should record at least a part of what happened, but that much having been placed on record, it must be said that conditions were gradually improved, until the German invasion.

But let us return to the main story: By the afternoon of February 7 it could be said truly that the Army had performed its primary task of saving its women, children, and useless units. That alone was a great accomplishment, but what thrilled all Spaniards on that day, and restored some of the pride and courage which the panic had taken from them, was the realization that the Army had not broken or fled in disorder. The idealism, the dignity, the traditions of Spanish soldiery, the reputation of the Popular Army—all these had never been lost. That screen of humanity had merely hidden the truth, giving full play to false rumor.

The beginning of the end came the next day, when the Rebels

broke through to Llers, three miles northwest of Figueras, and the final orders were given to retreat into France. To Galán's 12th Corps was given the task of falling back through La Junquera, while Lister's 5th and Tagüeña's 15th, both under Modesto's command, withdrew toward Port Bou. The Government's last refuge of La Bajol was terribly bombed—raid following raid—until it was obvious that no one could stay there, so Negrín reluctantly departed, with Vayo, Méndez Aspe, Uribe, and Rojo.

Meanwhile, two Government promises were kept. As we drove into Le Perthus at ten in the morning, a ragged, bearded, wan-looking column of men marched sadly in. They were 2,000 prisoners of the Government, released to spare them the needless danger of being caught in the firing lines. It was a pity that the gesture, which was typical of the Government's policy, should have been more than wiped out by the murder of the Bishop of Teruel on that same day by some Anarchists who had been ordered to lead him, with other prisoners, into France. Something of the sort was bound to happen in those last bitter, confused days, and it would perhaps be more a matter of justice to wonder that there was so little of that sort of thing at the end of the war, compared to the beginning.

The other promise was kept when two more contingents of Internationals, 1,200 in all, paraded into France. I watched the first group of 800 Hungarians, Poles, Germans, and Austrians of the 11th and 13th Brigades come marching in, with songs on their lips, and flags flying. As they filed onto the frontier bridge they shouted *"Viva la República Española!"* They were "frisked" roughly by the *Gardes Mobiles,* and relieved not of arms, for they had none, but of cameras, field-glasses and type-writers. It was "Chapaieff," the commander of the 13th who had fought all through the war, who led them into France. Gustav Regler, German author and first Commissar of the Thaelmann Battalion, was in Le Perthus to greet his old comrades as they came over. Ludwig Renn was too ill to march, but not too ill to be put into a concentration camp by the French when he was carried out.

On that day there were still about 1,500 Internationals un-accounted for, but they came through during the next few days, over the mountain passes and through Port Bou.

At one o'clock there was a tremendous explosion down the line, and a huge cloud of smoke rose on the horizon. A few days later Lister and others told me that it had been at the Castle of Figueras. The Loyalists had put all their remaining ammuni-tion and explosives in it, something like 1,100 tons, and a mil-lion liters of gasoline. We had felt the concussion at Le Perthus, 15 miles away.

High officers of the Loyalist Army began coming over, and I saw the commander of the Air Force, General Ignacio Hidalgo de Cisneros for the last time there, until we met in Mexico City in 1944. At three o'clock word came through that the Government's cortège was near. The commander of the *Gardes Mobiles* formed his troops, and as the cars drove up arms were presented and a personal greeting was extended by the commander. This was the last official courtesy extended to the Government of the Second Spanish Republic. Negrín and the other members of the cabinet, with Rojo, went into a three-story house on the Spanish-owned side of the street, between the bridge and the customs building in Le Perthus.

Walking back into Spain at about four o'clock I ran into "Paco" Galán, as cool and courteous as ever. "Can you hold for the night?" I asked. "Unhappily, no," he answered. "You know, we have an army with a big head and no body. It has nothing to function with. The men now have rifles, and we got some new American machine guns two days ago, but what can we do with them now except fight the last rearguard action?"

I wondered where those American machine guns had come from. But they had arrived too late.

At dusk one could feel the tension rising, because the trucks which were bringing back soldiers and matériel were piling up at the bridge. The French insisted on searching every one for arms, and that slowed things. Meanwhile, the traffic jam went far back, out of sight, and pleas for urgency began coming from the Spanish staffs down the line. This was something they had not counted upon. At Cerbère the stream of men and matériel never let up. There was only one railroad engine left, and the jam at the tunnel was such that the trains could not get up, so the Government's only new group of Skoda guns had to be left behind. They had never reached the front.

I went back to Le Perthus at one in the morning, at which time the 12th Corps was withdrawing in good order. Bridges were being blown up for we could hear the dull explosions, and someone coming back said the bridge at Pont de Molins had gone.

And that was the end. Twelve hours later the Rebels had reached Le Perthus. Lister was still covering Port Bou, but it was only a question of hours there and at Puigcerdá. The British were turning over Minorca to Franco. Only the central zone remained, and there was so much demoralization around Negrín and Vayo that despite their courage and optimism they were almost overwhelmed. It was only when they, and a few faithful supporters, who were later followed by Modesto, Lister, Galán, and other loyal officers, had shaken off the mire that surrounded them and flown to the Madrid zone, that one could feel sure the war was not over.

The duty to go on, as Negrín and the others saw it, was the necessity for protecting the lives of those whose very loyalty, patience and courage on the Government's behalf made their chances of escaping death or imprisonment very slight. As long as they fought on, there was always hope that a European war might come along and save them. It almost did.

There was a surprisingly quick and quiet end at Le Perthus. The Loyalists had planned to try to hold out through another night, but in the end they found the troops could be evacuated much sooner, as far as Le Perthus was concerned. However, not enough time had been allowed to get out all the trucks with matériel. This was partly the fault of the French, who kept searching every auto and finally closed the frontier to the vehicles, but since the matériel all went back to Franco anyway it made no difference. One of the ironies of that whole situation was, indeed, the great sacrifices made and the pains to which the Loyalists went, in order to save their matériel. They never dreamed that the French were going to turn it all over to their enemies. Had they known that, they would have destroyed it all in Spain.

Some machine gun units of Lister's 5th Corps fought the last rearguard action, just south of La Junquera. Their tradition and history called for that gesture, but there was no need for opposition, and the Rebels encountered very little of it from the time they left Figueras at six that morning until the first small groups from the 5th Navarrese Division strolled quietly up to the frontier bridge.

The end came as an anti-climax. Both sides had promised the French not to indulge in any fighting near the frontier bridge. In fact, a group of Loyalist anti-aircraft men actually walked into France a hundred yards ahead of the first Rebels, both bodies of men being unarmed. Some chauffeurs and stragglers were fooled by the casualness of it all, and before they knew what was going on, they were prisoners.

The formal occupation of the frontier post could be set at 2:10, when Major Rafael Pombo led a detachment of Navarrese up the Spanish side of the street in Le Perthus, tore down the Republican flag and hung out the red and gold banner of the Monarchists.

Negrín, Rojo, and members of the various staffs stayed until 12:20, driving away as the Rebels approached the bridge. The streets of Le Perthus gradually cleared of Spanish vehicles and refugees. Soon the road became less crowded, and by evening one could drive to Perpignan at almost normal speed. There Loyalist generals and colonels changed into mufti, some to await new orders, others to abandon the lost cause.

Over at Port Bou, Modesto, mounted on a horse, delivered a last, moving farewell to his troops, and then returned to the headquarters where Lister remained, fulfilling his last duty as courageously and loyally as he had done everything since the war began.

They, too, came over into France the next day, February 10, 1939. The Rebels reached Port Bou at 1:15 in the afternoon, and

Bourg-Madame at 2:40, thus virtually completing their conquest of Catalonia. Isolated units of Loyalists held out in the mountain passes until February 13, when the Col d'Arès was occupied. The last Republicans who came over fought to the end, and the French could hear machine gun and cannon fire almost to the last minute. The Loyalists actually brought all their matériel over with them! Surely no army could have fought better, under such heart-breaking conditions!

At Port Bou, as everywhere else, the troops came back fighting as they had sworn they would, up to the last yard which could be defended without coming too close to the frontier and creating difficulties for the French. They came over singing—none being left behind except for the casualties suffered in the final combat. A machine gun battalion made the last action about five miles south of the frontier, blowing up the final bridges, so that although the last Loyalist troops sauntered across to Port Bou at eight in the morning, the Insurgents had to take a roundabout route and arrived hours later.

All the great figures of the Popular Army got out safely. I saw them all in the Spanish Consulate at Perpignan, and I was almost ashamed to go up and speak to them. They had been betrayed, and they had nothing to be ashamed of. Whatever soldiers could do they had done. Merino expressed their sentiments best, perhaps, when he said to me:

"We know the bitterness that awaits us here, but we also know that no human beings could have done more than we. Our resistance through these last weeks, when we never abandoned the struggle despite the hopelessness and odds against us, will surely do much to bolster the worldwide struggle against Fascism. You yourself have seen that the troops never lost courage or morale. They always did what we asked of them, and no army has ever been asked to do more than ours—to fight seven weeks, without matériel, without rest, without hope. And we fought! History must give us that credit."

That evening, at the hotel, a group of Nazi aviators, who had been prisoners of the Loyalists, but were set free so as to spare their lives, celebrated boisterously with a feast. They put a swastika flag in the center of the table, to which the fat little proprietor raised no objection, but one of the waiters remonstrated: "You must remember, this is still France!"

I was sick at heart that night when I wrote my last dispatch on the Spanish Civil War, but at least I, in a humble way, felt vindicated. "Countries do not live by victories only," Negrín had said, "but by the examples which their people have known how to give, in tragic times." The Spanish people had, indeed, given a glorious example, and that night in Perpignan, exhausted and discouraged as I was, I knew that the fight had not been in vain.

But what of my reputation as a journalist? The hopes that I had so confidently expressed had been belied by the swift pace of events. The story that I told—of bravery, of tenacity, of discipline and constant decency, of optimism that came from courage and high ideals—had been scoffed at by many. The dispatches describing the callousness of the French and the cynicism of the British had been objected to and denied.

I, too, was beaten and sick at heart and somewhat shell-shocked, as any person must be under the nerve strain of seven weeks of incessant danger, coming at the end of two years' campaigning. For a few years afterwards I suffered from a form of claustrophobia, brought on by being caught, as in a vise, in a refuge in Tarragona during one of the last bombings. So I was depressed, physically and mentally and morally. I felt as if I were crawling home to New York and to my wife and children, a little of a stranger to my family and a little of a failure to my newspaper.

But the lessons I had learned! They seemed worth a great deal. Even then, heartsick and discouraged as I was, something sang inside of me. I, like the Spaniards, had fought my war and lost, but I could not be persuaded that I had set too bad an example.

"Open thy arms," cried Sancho Pança, "and receive thy son Don Quixote too, who, though he got the worst on't with another, he ne'ertheless got the better of himself, and that's the best kind of Victory one can wish for."

Italian

Course

Advanced Course in Totalitarianism

I was to spend the next three years—April, 1939, to June, 1942—getting a close-up of Fascism as Mussolini and his country went down the toboggan slide to catastrophe. As a lesson in politics nothing could have been more instructive, and I set it down, for those who are interested, in my book, *The Fruits of Fascism*. The fruits, needless to say, were bitter—so obviously bitter that no book was needed to demonstrate the fact; but what was needed was a study of the formulation of the Fascist system of government and way of life, because Fascism is, I am convinced, a permanent feature of the twentieth century.

But that is an argument which carries me ahead of my story. What I was feeling during my vacation at home in the late winter of 1939 was a soreness and a bewilderment, a sort of brooding wrath directed as much against the democratic appeasers who had made the defeat of Spain inevitable as against the Fascists and Nazis who were the nefarious instruments of Franco's victory. I had achieved a vague and instinctive liberalism which was, in the long run, to give me faith in the triumph of the democratic ideal, and which was to keep my feet steadily on a path of anti-Fascism, but in those few months I was still too close to what had happened to want to take the long view. I could only feel, and meanwhile wait for my skin to toughen again, for I have never been so abnormal as to hold that the woes of the world are more important than the business of living and bringing up children. Being an American, that was permissible luxury, and I should never dream of apologizing for making the most of it. Poor Ernst Toller committed suicide in New York in that period because he could not bear the tragedy which Spain meant. I went on a vacation to the Bahamas with Nancie, and it was a lovely vacation. And meanwhile Spain was having its last agony.

The end of the war was a peculiarly sickening business. All the ugly things came out—treachery, desertion, internal strife, toadying for the favor of the victors. The rats deserted the sinking ship; the passengers naturally followed suit. After all, civil wars are fought by the extreme wings. The percentage of people willing to die for a cause is bound to be relatively small at best, and when it is a lost cause the instinct of self-preservation leaves the few desperate loyal ones isolated and hunted.

The people were sick of the war, of course. In Madrid they were dying of starvation after two and a half years of siege. The cases of rickets among children and of pellagra among adults were fearful in number and severity. It was the third winter of war, without heat, adequate clothing, or enough food for bodily warmth. Despair, discouragement, hopelessness—these were the ingredients upon which the traitors worked, and the result was never in doubt. Though the end was sordid, one cannot take any glory away from that heroic siege. No people could have done more, and they would surely have fought on to the end had they been asked.

Negrín knew they would, and he had gone there to ask one last sacrifice. There were more than sixty divisions in the central zone, 800 cannons, a few tanks and airplanes, and, above all, an excellent system of fortifications. There was fully a quarter of Spain in which to maneuver, and enough food for scraping along. Don Juan was sure they could hold out until September or October, and if an honorable peace was not won by then, perhaps the international situation would save the Loyalist cause. Who can say he was wrong? The second World War began on September 1, 1939.

There were many thousands ready and willing to fight to the end, and to die. The heroism was there, and it could have sustained the structure for a while, if it had not been beaten down from behind. A handful of traitors was able to accomplish in a few weeks what it would have taken Franco months to do.

The dominating force among them was Colonel Sigismundo Casado. Although justly kept in a subordinate position throughout the war, he had managed in the final months to gain ascendancy. The best that could be said of him up to that time is that he was a defeatist, convinced that the game was up, and desirous of doing his part to end it as quickly as possible. However, one had now to add that he was a traitor, who wanted to see Franco win and who was dealing with the Generalissimo at a time when he was professing his loyalty to Negrín and the Government. The psychology behind his motives was subtle and complex, for he himself gained nothing but infamy.

There is no place in this book, which is primarily a personal account, for a detailed history of the collapse of the Spanish central zone. I am only sketching in some of the outstanding features, in order to maintain a continuity of outline of the events of the years I am describing, and to give the reasons why those events made me feel as I did. The educational process did not halt merely because I, myself, did not happen to be on the scene.

The diabolical cleverness of Casado's treachery was that he made his revolt appear a defense against a Communist uprising. Newspapers throughout the world were thoroughly deceived, and even the best informed readers must have been so confused that they never learned the simple truth. The few journalists there had either to send Casado's version or none at all.

This was the lie: "The 'Reds' have risen against the Republic!" When it is considered that Casado, and those who supported him, were working for precisely that, the overthrowing of the Republic and the turning over to Franco of what was left of Republican Spain, the enormity of the lie becomes evident. The "Reds" were the genuine defenders of the Republic, those whose loyalty and courage led them to struggle on to the end. They were not even exclusively Communist, by any means. It was true that all the Communists remained loyal, but so did many Socialists, Republicans and even Anarchists. To complete his picture, Casado painted Negrín as a "Red" who had sold his country to Moscow. That was the greatest lie of all.

On Sunday night, March 4, the Casado forces instigated their revolt in Madrid and Cartagena. In the latter city it took only two days for the new rebels to get the upper hand. The fleet mutinied and sailed for Bizerte, Tunisia. In Madrid the signal for the uprising was a series of raids by Casado's men, among whom were many Anarchists, on the headquarters and homes of prominent Communists. Those captured were jailed, and some were even court-martialed and executed, beginning an internecine strife that was to make the end of the war especially horrible. Lieutenant Colonel Mera, himself an Anarchist and commander of the predominantly Anarchist 4th Army Corps, stationed at Guadalajara, supported Casado from the beginning, lending him troops and matériel. Colonel Juan Barceló, Communist divisional commander, took over leadership of the loyal elements, but the confusion was too great to permit the organization of an effective resistance.

As far as the Government was concerned, the game was quickly up. Negrín, who had set up headquarters at Caudete, between Valencia and Madrid, had planes with trusted pilots ready for an emergency in a little field outside Caudete, but he did not want to leave until he had done everything he could. All his efforts in those two days had been hopeless, and when at two in the afternoon on March 6, he learned that Alicante had fallen to the new rebels, it was obvious that he and his followers could do no more. They all took off at about 4 o'clock, the cabinet in one large Douglas passenger plane; Modesto, Lister, and other Army leaders in another. For Negrín it was the beginning of a long exile in France and England; for the Communist leaders it was the first stage of a journey to Moscow and further military commands in the Red Army.

The arrival of Mera's Anarchist troops in Madrid on March 9 decided the issue in favor of Casado and Franco. By Monday evening, March 11, Casado was in complete control. A slaughter of prisoners followed, in the next few days, which was more revolting than anything that had previously happened in the war.

On March 14 Casado announced that "the revolt was smashed."

Some of the principal Communist leaders had managed to escape before the end. They were too valuable for the Party to lose, and would not have been allowed to stay if they wanted. Among them were La Pasionaria, Jesús Hernández, the Minister of Education, Vicente Uribe, the Minister of Agriculture, Colonel Martínez Cartón, commander of the 8th Army Corps, and Pedro Checa. They, with "Paco" Galán, who had been carried off to Bizerte by the mutinous navy, sailed from Oran May 11 for Marseilles and Russia.

On March 18, while the Casado junta was broadcasting an abject appeal to Franco for peace negotiations, the "Central Committee of the Communist Party of Spain" issued its last manifesto of the war—a pathetic, but dignified and even noble document.

"We have fought, and will be fighting for the Republic," it said in conclusion, "for a system of liberty and democracy which will allow the Spanish people to solve their problems in peace, to solve their economic as well as political problems, to solve the land question, to reorganize the national economy of Spain, the emancipation and the liberation of the working class.

"Our banner is the banner of unity, of democracy, of peace. Our banner is the banner of the Popular Front. For this struggle we will continue our fight under new conditions. And we will win, because we have faith in the working class of Spain."

It was the one sincere Socialist and Republican of the lot, Julián Besteiro, who did what little negotiating there was. On the 19th the Rebels insisted on a "victorious peace," and a few days later it was arranged that a mission should pass from Madrid into the Insurgent lines to find out what was meant. They quickly learned, what they must have known in advance, which was that it meant unconditional surrender. It was impossible to accept this openly, but arrangements were made so that by combined pressure from Franco on the outside and Casado from within, the capital could be taken over as if it had not surrendered. Thus Franco needed to show no mercy whatever, and thus the diabolical quality which the whole last stage of the war possessed was maintained to the end.

The Casado mission returned to Madrid on the 24th, and after a day of theoretical discussions, Franco launched his last "offensive." Characteristically enough, the chief work was done by Italian motorized columns which were in a position to strike swiftly in all directions, and give the slight push necessary at each point down to the coast. There was no opposition.

"Once again," wrote Count Ciano in his article on the Italian Legionaries, "the volunteer troops had the honor of participating, moving to the attack from the bridgehead of Toledo. In a few days they occupied Aranjuez, Tarancón and thence Guadalajara, Albacete, Alicante, where the victorious Legionaries could at last take their merited repose."

In view of what happened during the great war, it is interesting to see how he ended this well known article:

"The war in Spain, which had ended with the complete defeat of those who had so often declared their certainty of conquering Fascism, signalized the collapse of the Bolshevik movement in Europe. It consecrated the solidarity of the Axis powers, and demonstrated how they represented a sure guarantee of order and peace in the world."

The full measure of the uselessness of Italy's exhausting effort in Spain is to be found in the falsity of those predictions.

The symbolic end of all the noble sentiments, ideals and courage which made the siege of Madrid a glorious episode in Spanish history came shortly before 1 o'clock on March 29, 1939, when two Savoia-Marchetti bombers flew low over the Puerta del Sol—and the crowds cheered! Automobiles, displaying "blood and gold" flags, soon entered the plaza. Drapes appeared as if by magic on all balconies and windows. Cheering mobs paraded through the streets, and the soldiers who entered were embraced and decorated with flowers. The Spanish Civil War was over.

The vengeance wreaked upon those who had supported the Republican cause was brutal and terrible in the first days, systematic and hardly more merciful in the succeeding weeks, months, and years. In the United States a strong campaign was initiated to induce President Roosevelt not to recognize the Franco Government unless some assurances were received that amnesty would be granted to those whose "crime" was merely to have supported the Republic. On the other hand, the powerful American Catholic element, which was then the best organized and most militant in the world, was using all its influence to bring about recognition of Franco. Those business interests which had helped him and wanted to see a resumption of trade with Spain, were, naturally, eager to see the new Government recognized. Unfortunately for the Republicans, Ambassador Fernando de los Ríos, in Washington, did not have the energy, courage, or desire to stick by Negrín. On March 31 he yielded his Embassy and Consulate into the custody of Colombia and Cuba, thus making it easy for the pro-Franco element in the State Department of the United States to win Roosevelt's consent to recognition.

Our Ambassador to Spain, Claude G. Bowers, who was in New York at the time, was not even notified of the impending move; indeed, he was led to believe that it was not imminent. Throughout the war his dispatches, which while friendly to the Republican Government were accurate and well informed, were ignored at the State Department, and, what was worse, were on many occasions kept from the President. Bowers actually found it necessary throughout the greater part of the conflict to send two copies, one to the State Department and another to Roosevelt.

The President went away from Washington for that weekend of March 31-April 3, apparently washing his hands of the whole matter. All the documents were prepared and signed, but the understanding was that they were not to be issued without asking his consent. That may or may not have been true, but the fact is that on April 1 the United States accorded formal diplomatic recognition to the Franco Government. Roosevelt's historical record, therefore, remains a complete one of personal sympathy for the Republican Government, but of public action which favored the Rebels.

No appeal was made to Franco for leniency toward political prisoners.

On that same day, April 1, 1939, Pope Pius XII sent a telegram to the Generalissimo which read:

"Lifting up our heart to the Lord, we give sincere thanks with Your Excellency for Spain's desired Catholic victory. We express our vow that your most beloved country, with peace attained, may undertake with new vigor the ancient Christian traditions which made her great. With affectionate sentiments we send Your Excellency and the most noble Spanish people our Apostolic blessing."

The Second Spanish Republic thus passed into history, but it left a heritage which Franco, his generals, and the aristocrats, priests, monarchists, and Fascists can never destroy. In spite of them all, it made Spain a better country.

In Italy, where I arrived on April 16, 1939, I felt some personal satisfaction in seeing the extent to which the effort of helping Franco had bankrupted the country without bringing any positive results whatever. The smugness with which the victory was accepted by nearly all Italians, the gloating of the Fascisti and their press, the ignorance of what had happened and what it all meant which extended even to the most decent anti-Fascists, were bitter pills to swallow. I even had the painful duty of covering for my newspaper the triumphant return of the Legionaries. I wrote mechanically, but with burning thoughts.

My attitude toward Fascism was now definitive, and it can never change. I had learned the hard way, in a slow, blundering fashion, but it was a real "experience," in an almost religious sense of the word, and I felt from then on that I had earned the right to be anti-Fascist. Originally I had said that if the Italians wanted Fascism, that was their business. Like Goethe in his old age (Thomas Mann somewhere quotes him to that effect), "it was never my way to rail at institutions. It always seemed like presumption, and it may be that I learned courtesy too early." Nothing else pleases me so much as to be let alone, and such an attitude, applied to politics, brings a "live and let live" philosophy. That, I suppose, is an instinctive form of liberalism, but one of the many things I had learned in Spain was that Fascism and Nazism were not going to "let live."

Anyway, I was no longer as young as in the days when the mock heroics of Italian Fascism had vaguely appealed to me. "In the morning of our days," wrote Edmund Burke, "when the senses are unworn and tender, when the whole man is awake in every part, and the glass of novelty fresh upon all objects that surround us, how lively at that time are our sensations, but how false and inaccurate the judgments we form of things!"

As I have said before, when Fascism became an "article for export" I fought it, just as I would fight a Russian version of Communism for the same reason, if such opposition became necessary. My reason was a crude and simple one, but I have since added a much more important and subtle reason that I will not anticipate here, but which is concerned with the spread of feelings and beliefs that have the same philosophical and political bases as Fascism, and are linked with the totalitarian way of life.

I had seen international Fascism in Spain, and with a new vision I was now to see Italian Fascism in its home. The world, as well as I, had changed a great deal since I had last been in Italy in 1936, immediately after the triumphant end of the Abyssinian War. Japan and China had already been at war for several years. The progression of events was so clear that in my book, *Two Wars and More to Come,* written in 1937, I had called attention to the similarity of the Japanese and the Nazi-Fascist aggressions, and had made the obvious prediction that the lines would meet. "The youth of the world is going to war—one in Africa, one in Europe, one in Asia," I wrote, "and who shall say there are not more to come? You who stroll along the 'Great White Way,' thinking complacently how far away it all is from peaceful America—you, too, will feel a tap on your shoulder one of these days, and will hear the call."

So, in Italy in the spring of 1939, after the Fascist Regime had "conquered" Albania, it was already clear that the outbreak of another war was only a matter of time. The Fascisti boasted of it and of the great part they were supposedly going to play; the people never believed it possible, and certainly did not want it. I could see immediately that Fascism was now unpopular, although Mussolini retained a good deal of his popularity. Italian complacency, indifference, and ignorance disgusted me, but I always retained a feeling for and a faith in an Italy that was at that time a sort of separate identity to me, apart from Fascism. The divorce was a specious one, since Fascism was not an accident in Italy, but I regarded it as a loathsome disease or a temporary madness that had overcome a dear friend. However, I have always upheld the thesis that Italy as a whole deserves the blame for Fascism and must accept full responsibility for its crimes. No one who saw the passive, cynical way in which the nation accepted everything that Mussolini did, including the "stab in the back" of France, could come to any other conclusion.

In my book, *The Fruits of Fascism,* I described the dizzy course of Mussolini's chariot of Phaëthon, and there is no need to repeat it here. I learned more about politics in those three years, 1939-1942, than in all the former years of my life put together, but the course was an advanced one which revealed no new truths that I could see about Fascism, Nazism, and "appeasement" by the democracies.

The most valuable lesson, by far, was the Russo-German Pact of August 22, 1939, which gave Hitler the "go-ahead" signal, and, in a sense, made World War II possible. At the time, I missed the larger point completely. It was a shock to me, because I had retained from Spain a good measure of belief in the consistency and determination of Russian anti-Fascism. I had not, at that time, made the study which I later did of the course of Soviet foreign policy from Lenin onwards, with its steady urge toward an alliance with Germany. Not being a Communist, I could not go through a dialectical process of saying to myself: "Communism is a great ideal; this reversal of policy will help Communism to reach its goal; therefore it is a valid move which must be accepted." I could see only the cold, calculating, brutally "realistic" policy that was willing to sacrifice countries and millions of lives to a nationalistic and imperialistic policy which I, being neither Communist nor Russian, could not consider justified.

I thought of it then as a betrayal of all those idealists who had come from the four corners of the world to fight in the International Brigade in Spain. I felt it to be, also, a betrayal of that Spain which was prostrate, thanks largely to the Hitler with whom Stalin now made his alliance. However, in the light of what has happened since, and in view of the fact that all the men involved seem willing to accept and understand and consider satisfactory in 1945 what the Russians did in 1939, it is not for me to complain on their behalf. For my part, I went on feeling bitter about the matter.

I was at the British Military Attaché's home on the evening of the day on which the Russians invaded Poland and began to seize the Baltic states, and I remember remarking naively, "Well, I suppose you will now declare war on Russia." The officer looked embarrassed, as well he might, for he knew only too well that England had more than her hands full with Germany alone, without taking on the U.S.S.R. The British were not going to let their proclaimed ideals interfere with their hopes of survival and of seeing Germany and Russia embroiled with each other in the course of time. In effect, the choice which was to bring Communist Russia into her strange alliance with the democracies was made then, and so far as winning this war was concerned it was the wise and even unavoidable decision.

Nothing is inevitable in politics or war, and to argue that the Nazis and Communists were bound to quarrel in the long run is to display cheap wisdom after the event. It is hard to believe that Stalin would have attacked Germany, while Hitler's move against Russia is generally considered the greatest blunder of his career. One may hope that enemies will make mistakes, but they are not to be counted upon. The simple truth of the matter was, at the time of which I am writing, that Great Britain was too weak to embroil herself with the Soviet Union.

I could recognize that fact, and it made me all the more furious with the appeasers who had brought a once mighty Empire to that pass. Emotionally I was stirred, as was everyone else, when the course of the war went from bad to worse. The appeasers still in control in England and France made it certain that catastrophe would come, but that was no consolation when it did come. The moral decay of France, with its Army and Navy undermined by leaders like Pétain and Darlan, already linked for two years to the Cagoulard terrorists and Fascists; the helplessness of Britain, under Chamberlain, still not aroused to the greatness that was to come; the "phony" war of that winter of 1939-1940, coming after the real tragedy of Poland, were enough to keep one's mind and feelings in a state of commotion, and to induce discouragement, cynicism, and even disgust. However, I am glad to say that I was illogical enough to feel sure, at all times, that the Axis would be defeated in the long run—a case, no doubt, of the wish being father to the thought. But looking back now, we can realize how close to disaster the democracies came.

In the case of the Russo-German Pact, I could see afterwards the extent to which I misjudged the move, and it started me on an effort to understand Soviet foreign policy, an effort which may or may not prove successful but which, at least, provides material as a basis for judgment.

In that connection, anyway, the years have been strengthening in me an innate tendency to accept inevitabilities and try to make the best of them. That may not be a policy of courage or idealism, but perhaps it is a step toward wisdom. The gravitation of Russia and Germany toward each other is a development which has deep roots and a degree of naturalness that must be accepted. Insofar as it proves a danger to the sort of world that I want to live in, I will oppose it. It is my privilege to defend my liberal attitude in whatever way it needs defense, but at the same time one must accept facts which have taken on the inevitability of a vast historic movement. I want to make the best of them, not the worst. I had learned long before August, 1939, the falsity of viewing things as black or white. When Russia joined hands with Nazi Germany she was looking out for herself and her hopes of world Communism. She did the same when she defended herself so superbly against that same Germany of Hitler, and she is doing the same now in the hours of victory. That is her right and her privilege, and I can understand it. On balance, and up to the present time, the democracies have benefited by Soviet policy in the prosecution of the war. That is no reason for gratitude to Russia, since she did what she had to do when Hitler turned on Stalin—any more than Italy, for instance, has reason to be grateful for its "liberation" by the Anglo-Americans. In the long run we may all regret the development of Soviet policy, but there will be time to consider that.

Italy was in some respects a good grandstand from which to observe the European tragedy. She had one foot in the war, and one out. The cost of participation in the Spanish Civil War had been so great that Ciano was constrained to tell Ribbentrop that for three years Italy would not be again in a position to fight. That is one of the debts which Europe owes to the Spanish Republicans. It was not until Mussolini convinced himself that the European conflict was almost finished that he dared to enter.

There was a peculiarly distressing quality in the sufferings which we Americans in Rome endured during that terrible spring of 1940. Misery loves company, but there in Italy we could only read the gloatings of the Fascist press, see the tremendously effective German newsreels every time we went to the cinema, and note the cynical indifference of the average Italian, who no doubt regretted what was happening but who accepted the worst and thought Mussolini clever to have chosen the winning side.

On the afternoon of June 10, 1940, Mussolini came out on his balcony and announced the declaration of war against France and England, amidst the indifference of all but a few hundred organized applauders, mostly students, on the Piazza Venezia. I can recall few moments of more intense bitterness in my life, not only for the defeat that it symbolized, but because Italy meant so much to me. Fortunately, the Italians we knew—the decent, honorable, loyal Italians—were even more deeply shocked than we, since it was their shame. They were the Italians who made it possible to retain some faith and affection in the country that I had then known for fifteen years. That is why I am mentioning the subject here, because it was in its way a lesson in politics, the simple one of separating a people and its country from complete complicity in the wickedness of a small group of its leaders. One could not, and cannot before history, absolve Italy and Italians from the crimes committed by Fascism, but one can recognize mitigating circumstances, and degrees of guilt. The average Italian was a passive and unthinking actor in the disgusting drama which his country played, and for that he deserves blame and punishment, but there was a difference between his attitude and the active criminality of the Fascist leaders.

Of course, the war did not end in three months, nor, for that matter, in three years, and Italy as well as Fascism paid the price for Mussolini's miscalculation. For a year and a half I watched the course of the war from the inside. For Germany it was a triumphant period, and Hitler was able to carry his accomplice Mussolini through the disgrace of the Greek campaign, which was fundamentally a defeat for the Italians, and to let him share in the spoils of the Balkan victory.

In recalling that period I can see now that I was making the great mistake of considering the weakness of Italy and Italians as a weakness of Fascism. That belief was to lead me temporarily to the false conclusion that the collapse of Italy was *per se* the collapse of Fascism, which it was not. I did not then appreciate the depth of the roots of Fascism, or totalitarianism, in its various forms, its insidious and complicated hold on twentieth-century mentality, and its widespread, hydra-headed quality. Those were things that I learned in the long months of our "liberation" of Italy, but in 1940 and 1941 I was living in a fool's paradise of complacency and optimism.

During almost all of the latter year, it was obvious that sooner or later the United States would be involved in the war, and that we Americans in Italy would find ourselves enemies in a friendly country. The friendliness was so palpable, and the unpopularity of the war and the Fascist Regime was so great, that when the blow was struck at Pearl Harbor it almost seemed possible that Mussolini would stall again. I suppose he would have done so, if he had had any choice in the matter, but although he stood at the helm the ship of state was at the mercy of a storm far beyond his power to ride.

A few anxious days, and on December 11, 1941, at three in the afternoon, I stood under the famous balcony in the Piazza Venezia and listened to Mussolini declaring war on the United States. It was not Italy which declared war, not the Italians, but Il Duce and a handful of his followers. I knew that, and it injected an element of sad consolation into the bitterness and anger of the moment. The cheering of the few was false; the indifference of the many was typical, and beneath it was much genuine sorrow.

That was one of the crucial moments of Fascism, with its criminal recklessness, its immorality, its inherent weakness, its violence and tragic urge toward disaster. But it was also a critical moment in the history of the Italian people. They accepted—and in that lay their crime. They accepted cynically, weakly, foolishly, just as they had accepted many years of what they knew was wrong and wicked. Theologically there is a hell for such people, but there are practical hells, too, and the Italians are living in one in 1945 because there was a just price to pay.

In my life, that moment was singularly outstanding for more than its historic content, for a few hours later I found myself in Regina Coeli jail, and crowded into a small, dark, very dirty and very cold cell with two of my newspaper colleagues. It was a bad experience for one with more than a normal amount of sensitivity and with a decided tendency toward claustrophobia, yet even at its worst I was philosophical enough to realize that it was doing me a certain amount of good. I believe in having experiences, for that is the only way by which one can know and feel how the world is going. In this unhappy time, millions have suffered imprisonment, in various forms, not for criminality but for political reasons, and that is doubtless going to continue for years. If I tell you who read this that some day you, too, may be looking through prison bars or the barbed wire of a concentration camp, no doubt it will amuse you. But do not laugh too heartily. Keep a wholesome respect for Nemesis. Most of those who suffered imprisonment would themselves have laughed ten years ago.

I know now what it means to lose one's physical liberty, and I account it one of the most valuable lessons of my life. I can feel, now, the suffering that it means to unhappy millions, and it makes me want to fight a world where such things happen. I was fortunate in learning my lesson without having to pay a high price—or any price, in the long run. Three days after we were thrown into jail we were out, in a cheap boarding house on the Corso Umberto with detectives sitting outside our doors. After ten days of that, we newspapermen were transferred to Siena, where we stayed nearly five months in a mild sort of internment. If I had had the choice of any place in Italy for internment, I would have picked that lovely, medieval town, which the world has passed by for centuries. I came to know and love every stone of it. I bicycled every morning up and down the Tuscan hills, and as a "natural" experience I have known nothing more thrilling in my life than watching those lovely hills pass from the snows of winter to the fresh green of spring. I worked every day preparing the material for my book on Fascism, and it was typical of that easygoing country that no one disturbed me at my work or showed any interest in it. It was fruitful and healthy, but very boring, and the time was very far from happy. We could not know when our internment would end, and there is no happiness for a man who is not free and who does not know how long it will be before he sees his wife and children. I have had more than my share of separation in these past ten years, so it did not need this war to teach me what millions have been learning since. Exile can take many forms.

> *Tu lascerai ogni cosa diletta*
> *più caramente; e questo è quello strale*
> *che l'arco de lo esilio prìa saetta.*

We Americans, though, are the fortunate people of this earth. Our country is free, our citizenship is recognized and respected throughout the world, and even the exile knows that some day he will return. It seems so trite to say such things, but for those of us who have seen what it means to others to have their country overrun by hated foreigners, to lose their citizenship and their hope of returning home, these sentiments are not trite, and they should never lead us to accept lightly or without sympathy any movement to help the refugees of this world.

For me, at the end of five months, there came release in an exchange of American journalists for Italian, and I returned home. It was not to be for long; never in ten troubled years has it been for long. This time I was under orders to go to India, a completely new world to me. I almost had to look it up on the map to see exactly where it was. The Cripps Plan was the sensation of that period, and like those of most Americans my sympathies were completely with the Indians and against the British. However, I was by then too old a hand to make up my mind in advance. I had no knowledge, and no axes to grind and I had no intention of letting my bias interfere with a complete presentation of the facts as I saw them.

There certainly was no lack of indoctrination, to begin with. The case which was presented to me seemed plausible, and I believed it, partly perhaps because I wanted to believe it. Those in the United States who called themselves liberals were 100 per cent for the Indians, with that intolerance which has been behind their attitude toward all international problems since the Abyssinian War. The underdog is always right; the imperialists, the capitalists, the Fascists, and the British are always wrong. But a poor newspaperman can only judge by what he sees and hears. India is today the most complicated problem of its sort in the world. The eleven months I spent there were among the richest in experience of my life, but I think the main lessons taught to me were curiously negative: the necessity for humility in the face of such stupendous problems, the value of reserving judgment, the recognition that both sides can have much of right and much of wrong in their attitudes, and that there is such a thing, in a given situation, as an insoluble problem. It was still possible to pass judgment, but not without reserve.

So the process I went through was bewildering and not highly satisfactory, but I had a fascinating and instructive time and it was impossible not to be deeply moved by a degree of human misery unequaled in the world. That, too, called for humility.

To have started from zero was an advantage. India was a sort of "dark continent" so far as the knowledge of Americans was concerned. For me, and for most readers of *The New York Times* and its affiliated newspapers, this was the discovery of India.

Indian

Course

The Discovery of India

EVERYONE is his own Columbus when he goes to India. The experience is like discovering a new world, one that in childhood and youth seemed something romantic, incredibly far away, full of Gunga Dins, cobras, and naked, bearded men who stuck pins into themselves. The mere facts that it was a country of high civilization in the millennia before white men even found America, and that it has a fifth of the world's population, did not cut much ice. It was not part of our world, and we just did not care about it.

Romance, like faith, has to be in things unseen, and yet reality can bring its compensations. India's teeming life, her color, her aspirations toward freedom, her combination of gentleness and brutality, her fabulous wealth and her abysmal poverty, all go to make up as moving and poignant a picture as the world can show us. One can think of it as a pawn in a great game which nations are playing, or one can look at it as a purely human problem—four hundred millions who are trying to live their own lives in a world that will no longer let anyone mind his own business.

I flew into Karachi on August 24, 1942, and was immediately caught between two fires, British and Indian. Both sides presented their cases with such complete conviction and intransigeance that I began with a bewilderment which I never quite overcame. From the beginning I was given a choice between black or white, between take it and leave it. Less than two weeks later I radioed to my newspaper a despairing piece which struck a keynote that was not to be abandoned in the next eleven months.

"It does not take a newcomer long to discover that India is just about the hardest nut to crack that any foreign correspondent, however seasoned, can have wished upon him. It would seem well to put this on record at the beginning of what threatens to be a long and intricate quest for truth on an encyclopedic subject.

"The trouble with expert opinion on India, your correspondent quickly discovered, is that everybody you meet is quite certain he knows all about it and the other fellow is all wrong. I have never in twenty years' career encountered such complete assurance on the part of all individuals and such equally complete differences of opinion. I have never found a situation where the argument gets down so quickly 'ad hominem.'

" 'Gandhi is a sincere, honest idealist,' one man says.

" 'Gandhi is a dishonest politician,' says the next man. 'You can't trust him.'

" 'We don't believe the British. They have betrayed us so often,' many Indians told me.

" 'The Indian never says what he thinks,' many Britishers tell me.

"Yet if nobody is going to believe anybody else, what is a poor foreigner supposed to think? One man tells him that the Indians are in a state of revolt, another that the situation is well in hand. One says that Congress is deliberately playing the Japanese game, another that Congressites hate the Japanese. Indians say they want the British to leave; the British say that the Indians as a whole do not give a hoot. Indians accused the British of creating communal trouble; the British say that communal trouble was indigenous, that it is at the heart of everything and they regret it sincerely.

"You go to see one of the high Indian officials and he says: 'I'll give you a correct picture of the Indian situation'—and he is quite sincere, but it is unlike any picture other high Indian officials have given you. You go to see a British official and he tells you he has been in India thirty-four years and still does not understand the Indian mind—which you are quite willing to believe after he gives you his idea of the situation.

"But, then, who does know? What is the situation? What, indeed, is India?

"Time, perhaps, may tell, but it is going to take a long time and a lot of traveling and a lot of listening and seeing. At the end your correspondent may feel sure he knows all about India, but the question will be whether anybody else will agree with him."

It was not so much the magnitude of the problems involved which dismayed me as the absence of a middle ground from which I could calmly survey the countryside.

There surely is no other place in the world where the journalistic and human temptation to simplify facts and draw confident conclusions and tell everybody just what it is all about, is less excusable than in India. At the same time, there is also no excuse for falling into the other pit and saying that because the situation is so complicated it is impossible ever to understand it. I found a tendency on the part of some British officials, who had spent decades in India, to take the line that an outsider was wasting his time in trying to get the correct picture, and that in the long run he would only mislead his readers. However, because the Indian picture puzzle is made up of hundreds of pieces does not mean that it cannot be fitted together well enough to afford a clear idea of its outlines.

It is customary for foreigners going to India to discover that it is not a country, that it is a continent, that it has many races, religions, and languages. To write about India as a unit would be about the same as writing about Europe as one nation. Actually, that is a specious difficulty which could be overcome with enough time, patience, and energy (although, perhaps, more than a man would have at his disposal in a lifetime).

The real trouble is the all-too-human one of various people looking at the same things and arriving at opposite conclusions. It is a case of distrust and misunderstanding, of good intentions paving the way to hell, of sordid interests being rationalized into pious convictions, of struggles for political power and patronage being disguised as patriotism. Shot through it all is a good deal of honesty, sincerity, courage, and patience, under desperately trying conditions. What is most lacking is a spirit of compromise and goodwill; the realization that all the wrong is not on the other side and that there are motes in one's own eyes as well as beams in the other fellow's, and that when the house is afire the inheritors would do well to put the fire out instead of fighting to see who is going to get the house.

The practical effect of all this has been to tie India into a Gordian knot. There are so many good intentions on all sides that no one can understand why you do not see the matter from his particular viewpoint. British officials were surprised, during my stay, that Americans arriving in India were more inclined to sympathize with the Indians than with them—as I did, for that matter. At the same time, Indians were convinced that Americans did not understand them, and that we were all duped by British propaganda.

It is a case of the old dictum, "if you ain't for us you're agin us." It would certainly simplify matters if one could take a particular point of view and interpret everything in India from it. That is what a British official does, or an Indian Congress follower or a Moslem Leaguer. To them it is all as clear as crystal —granting their premises.

The British say: "We came here at a period when conquest was the natural order of things. We put our genius, our soldiery, our commercial and administrative experience, at the service of India and Britain. We brought peace, administrative unity, and the benefits of Western civilization, and it was we who taught Indians what democracy and freedom mean. We are willing to go now, and we have promised to do so, but first we have got to win this war and be assured that our vast interests are protected and India will not be torn by internal strife."

The Congress follower says: "The British are conquerors, usurpers, and tyrants. They have exploited India for their own selfish ends, and have deliberately kept the people in ignorance and poverty. India is a potentially rich country, and yet her masses are the most wretched in the world because the British would not develop our own industries or intensify our agriculture. The world has gone beyond the age of imperialism, as

Sumner Welles said, and each nation has a right to independence and self-government. Let the British stay here and win this war. If they give us our own civil government we will help them, but why should we fight for one tyrant against another? All Indians want the British to go, and once they do go we shall quickly reach a friendly agreement with the Mussulmans."

The Moslem Leaguer is not so sure of that. He, too, says, "We want the British to go," but he adds that he sees little advantage in exchanging the British Raj for the Hindu Raj. "Your two years and seven months' rule in the provinces, from September, 1937, to December, 1939," he tells the Congressite, "taught us that you intend to keep us in subjection. Therefore, the only solution is for you to give us the same self-determination that you demand, and permit us to set up our own nation of Pakistan. Then Hindus and Muslims will live side by side in complete understanding and friendliness, and we will get rid of the British quickly after that."

The Britisher addresses himself to the world; the Congressite to the Britisher, and the Moslem Leaguer to the Hindu, and nothing for years has seemed so beyond the realm of possibility as that the three should get together and talk to one another.

As a matter of fact, the true complications of the situation lie in the reasons for this irreconcilability, in such questions as these —why a handful of Britishers can dominate India, why so many Indians distrust the British, why the Hindus and Muslims cannot solve the communal problem. There is so much that cannot be settled by logic and reason, so much that is emotional, so many settlements that will work hardship to one side or the other, whatever they may be! Each side has right and wrong, justice and injustice, in its attitude.

So, it was, indeed, a test in journalism, and in detachment and impartiality. I feel no need for too much modesty, since ignorance or knowledge is a relative matter. As Samuel Johnson said, "He that knows which way to direct his view sees much in a little time." Indians labor under two delusions about their country: first, that no foreigner can be expected to know as much about India as they know, and, secondly, that because they are

Indians they do know all about India. Actually, the average educated Madrasi knows as little of Bengal, the average Bengali as little of the Punjab, and the average Sindhi as little of Madras, as the average Frenchman knows of England. And few of them know anything about the Princely States.

The individual Britishers, however long they stay, get to know only a very small part of India—the district or province in which they do their work out in the countryside, and then New Delhi, where they end their career. However, I must say I have found among the Britishers more willingness to admit ignorance than one finds among Indians.

One trouble is that there is no such thing as a typical place in India, and as for typical Indians—there are 400,000,000 of them, speaking dozens of languages and hundreds of dialects. When Gandhi wanted to select his home and settle down, he chose the geographical center of India—Sevagram, just outside Wardha— for in no other way could he get a place symbolical of India as a whole.

That struggle to find out what India is, to grasp its essential oneness, to find the unity in its bewildering diversity, is as difficult a proposition as one can hope to solve. The geographic limits are there, neatly sealed off by oceans, the mighty Himalayas, and historic passes. Politically and administratively, also, you can neatly divide the continent into British India and Princely India, although when you look at the map you find that the Princely States are scattered as haphazardly as pieces in a patchwork quilt. And beyond that, you get into complications which glib generalizations do not help to unravel.

"In India today no one, whatever his political views or religious persuasions, thinks in terms other than those of national unity," wrote Jawaharlal Nehru not many years ago. Nothing could be wider of the mark. The negotiations between Gandhi and Jinnah in September, 1944, broke down over that very issue.

"We maintain that Moslems and Hindus are two major nations by any definition or test of a nation," said Jinnah. "We have our own distinctive outlook on life and of life. By all canons of international law, we are a nation."

"I can find no parallel in history of a body of converts and their descendants claiming to be a nation apart from the parent stock," tartly replied the mahatma. "If India was one nation before the advent of Islam, it must remain one, in spite of a change of the faith of a very large body of her children."

Diogenes searching for truth had nothing on a poor American correspondent trying to find out what India was, or to find something, some place or some people typically Indian. Certainly, New Delhi, where we and the government worked, is not India, nor is Bombay, Calcutta, or Madras. There one met politicians and rich industrialists, civil servants, and those educated Indians who have something to do with governmental and political questions. They are the ones who will some day run India, and a strong case could be made for the thesis that they truly represent the majority of their countrymen, however inarticulate or apolitical those millions may be. They could also argue that they are typical Indians, but they certainly are a tiny minority in the sea of humanity that makes up India.

India is an agricultural country. More than nine of ten Indians are cultivators, and, with rare exceptions, humble, illiterate, poverty-stricken people. If they could argue at all or had any ideas on politics, which they have not or have only very superficially, they would say, "We are the typical Indians."

However, that is simplifying the question, and, as I have said before, nothing is so fatal, in trying to understand India, as simplification. Because the question arises, "Who is the typical cultivator? Is he a Bengali or a Pathan from the Northwest Frontier? Is he a Madrasi or a Punjabi? Is he a man from the United Provinces who knows Gandhi and what he stands for, or is he a peasant from a backward Rajputana state who never heard of Congress and who does not even know there is a war on?

Even Gandhi's choice of the geographical center of India as a home is valid only as long as India remains united, which she will not do if Jinnah has his way and forms the separate "nation" of Pakistan. One becomes so dizzy in thinking about such things that it almost seems logical to be like the farmer who looked at a giraffe in the circus and solemnly announced: "There ain't no such animal." Indeed, some thirty years ago Sir John Strachey wrote that "the first and most essential fact that could be learned about India is that there is no such country."

It would be comforting, to be sure, if we could only say, "There is no India," but it so happens that there is, very definitely, such a thing—at least, common sense would seem to indicate as much, despite appearances to the contrary.

On my first trip to the Punjab, at the end of October, 1942, in talking with Moslem villagers I found them referring vaguely to "Hindustan," meaning the country of the Hindus beyond the Jumna River, while to express India in our sense they used the English phrase, "All India," which is the prefix to the names of some political organizations such as Congress and the Moslem League. The late Sikander Hyat Khan, then premier of Punjab Province, frankly admitted that he considered a Bengal Moslem as foreign as a Chinese. After ten days in the Punjab I made a note, "Nobody knows India; there are only degrees of knowledge or ignorance." Nothing I saw or heard in the months that followed made me change that opinion.

At Christmastime, in the state of Cooch Behar, which is in Assam not far from Burma, I could find no villager who knew where Madras was, and few indeed who even knew that the Central Government was seated in New Delhi. The Tamil and the Telugu peasants in Madras Province were no wiser.

So, then, was I to say with Strachey, "There is no such country"? It was tempting to do so, but not satisfactory, even though the bewilderment grew.

My first trip out of New Delhi took me to Jaipur and Bundi, both typical Rajput States in their respective ways. Bundi was where I got my first shock of doubts about what I had been told in New York. It is a good example of that old, unhappy India which the Congress wants to reform or abolish, but which meanwhile was going through a slow, painful process of modernization, thanks to a young, energetic, English Dewan, Mortimer Robertson. There was evidence both of the good which the presence of Englishmen can do in India and of the haphazard way in which it is done, for the ruler of Bundi might well have had a less efficient servant. Bundi needed a new Dewan in 1936, and the Maharao Raja, Ishwari Singh, accepted Robertson and gave him a free hand. The new Dewan happened to be a first-class executive and one of those English civil servants (not at all rare in Indian history) who love India and work for her good.

Americans think of maharajas as rolling in wealth. The ruler of Bundi gets $32,000 a year, and that is a good income for an Indian prince. He apparently means well by his people, but until he engaged Robertson he did nothing to show his good will. Probably alone among all the 550 princes, he does not speak English. He is not cruel, vicious, or lustful as are so many maharajas in the movies, and as a few real ones have been whose names are infamous by-words like the late Maharaja of Alwar. Bundi's Prince is merely a henpecked husband whose two wives—they are sisters—give him much less peace than he would like to have.

He lives in "such a palace as men built for themselves in uneasy dreams—the work of goblins, rather than of men," as Kipling wrote. It hangs in tier upon tier on the steep side of a hill above the town of Bundi—fantastic and charming, but not particularly comfortable. There he spends nine tenths of his time, going out now and then to shoot the tigers and panthers which abound in his country. Until Robertson took office the Maharajah did not let the cultivators kill the wild pigs which ruined their crops, because tigers ate pigs and became sleek and fat, and hence more satisfactory to shoot. The Dewan insisted that the peasants be allowed to protect their crops and the Maharao Raja good-naturedly agreed. This seems like a little thing, but, actually, much of Bundi's fertile land was lying fallow because cultivators would not use it for the benefit of the wild pigs.

In short, things have been stirred up in Bundi, but the problem is to keep them stirred up. As Kipling wrote, "it is a beautifully lazy city, doing everything in a real, true, original, native way." That is its charm—but the wretched peasants whom I visited do not appreciate charm. For foreigners it is nice to learn that the gates of the city close at midnight, to see narrow, unpaved bazaars, to hear the palace musicians playing at the famed

Elephant Gate. A state guest is carried up a steep path to the palace, in an ancient conveyance borne by six men whose ancestors before them for centuries followed the same profession. As one enters, a tall guard armed with a scimitar and dressed in an orange robe with a red sash and a red turban, touchès his forehead and then bows to touch the ground before you. It is just like the movies, except that the guard's robe is not long enough to hide the bandaged ankle which shows that he has guinea worm from drinking the polluted water which comes from the famous and beautiful "baori" or step well. There is no outside water supply in Bundi.

"This is old India—beautiful, but unhealthy and unhappy," I wrote in a dispatch. It was there that I learned to my surprise that Gandhi could be unheard of in the heart of India, and that it could be laughable to talk of the Indian villager as politically conscious, or knowing even vaguely what independence means, or wanting the British to quit India. That experience was repeated so often, in so many parts of India, that what I then thought was an unfair test later proved to be applicable to the greater part of the vast continent.

After all, India is overwhelmingly agricultural, and if there is anything or anybody representative of the true India, it is the village and its peasants. Congress claims that it has reached deeply into the villages. It has in a few regions, such as Bombay Province and the United Provinces, but in general it has only scratched the surface—in itself a great feat in a country as diverse, teeming, ignorant and poverty-stricken as India. But the record has to be kept straight.

Bundi was the first place in which I resented the propaganda which had been foisted upon me. As the months passed, I was to do harm to the Congress cause in the United States by continually harping upon the contrast between reality and the picture which I and others received. I regret it, and perhaps it was not charitable. But it was, in a sense, a duty, and the blame should surely go in part to those who drew false pictures and thus made it necessary for a foreign observer to correct them.

The chief falsity, as I quickly discovered, was the assertion that Congress was India. Perhaps, at the height of Gandhi's influence in the 1920's it could have been considered so, but those days were past. Congress had done great things to arouse and reform India. It had, and still has, brilliant, patriotic, self-sacrificing leaders, whose sincerity cannot be questioned. It is still the strongest political party or organization in India, and today it would sweep any elections in provinces where Hindus have a majority. It does represent the vast majority of politically conscious Hindus in British India (not Princely India). These are great claims to respect and admiration and had the picture been so drawn I would have been the first to recognize them, and my work would have been, from the viewpoint of Congress, a positive instead of a negative one. It is a good example of the boomerang quality of propaganda.

I learned very quickly that the Moslem League under Mohammed Ali Jinnah was far, far stronger than anybody in the United States had realized. In fact, as time passed I was to find that Jinnah and his organization could speak for as vast a majority of the politically conscious Moslems of India as Gandhi and the Congress could for the Hindus.

I began soon to realize that the British were not so black as they had been painted. I found them getting along very well, indeed, with the villagers, even at a time when the country was in the throes of a great unrest (I had arrived in India just after the arrest of Gandhi, Nehru, and the other Congress leaders, in August, 1942, which was followed by the civil disobedience campaign that the Mahatma rightly called "open rebellion"). I found evidence of the good as well as the bad which the British had done and were still doing. I learned to appreciate the extraordinary difficulties and complications of their task.

The Punjab was a real eye-opener in that respect, and naturally so, for it has rightly been called "the last refuge of the British raj." The stories I wrote from the Punjab aroused dismay in pro-Congress circles in the United States, and the reports elicited that mixture of anger and commiseration which much of my work was to arouse from then on in certain circles. Their answer had to be that I was being misled and taken in by the

British. It was easy to fall back on the consolation that I was a foreigner, knowing none of the Indian languages and forced to rely upon British or Indian officials for much of my interpreting! It is true that the Indian villager inevitably connected me with authority, and therefore was careful or sly in what he said. When C. R. Rajagopalachari, whom I came to know and admire more than any other of the Hindu politicians, told me so in Madras, I respected his opinion.

But an experienced newspaperman is not to be fooled so easily. The limitations are there, and I called attention to them as frequently and honestly as I could. Many truths are self-evident, and others are to be found with patience and digging, and above all by a simple quantitative process of addition and comparison. If an ignorant villager in the Punjab tells me something and I hear it repeated by equally ignorant villagers, speaking different languages in the United and Central Provinces, the Northwest Frontier and Madras, and if other factors bear it out, I can feel fairly sure of my ground. Moreover, for the most part, the very Indians who complained knew less of India in the years 1942 and 1943 than I got to know. That assertion may seem presumptuous, but it is true. Very few Indians have the opportunity to go about India as I did, seeing such a variety of people and places, and very few, indeed, see as much of India in a lifetime as I saw in those eleven months. There are exceptions, and I respected their knowledge if I could not always trust their judgment, but on the whole I would agree with F. Yeats-Brown, who wrote in *Indian Pageant:* "I must enter a protest against the idea that only the Indian-born know India. Many Indians of high attainments know next to nothing of the people in other provinces, for in addition to the formidable barriers of caste there are those of tongue and temperament."

For the Westerner, India must either be shut out, as most Britishers do, living their lives as nearly as possible to life in England, or it must be fought, almost physically. You must fight through its horrors of climate and disease, of ignorance and filth, its swarming people whom you can never understand and who can never understand you. Your intelligence tells you that at the core of things is much that is fine and patient and wise—only you must search for it, and to a Westerner the search is only too often a weary, bewildering task. I made such a struggle for eleven months, and I do not believe anyone questioned the sincerity of the effort. That I failed in many respects is neither here nor there, since the failure was a foregone conclusion. No mind can grasp or convey the whole truth about India, and mixed with my professional presumption was a great deal of humility.

"The East is a university in which the scholar never takes his degree," Lord Curzon once wrote. "It is a temple where the suppliant adores but never catches sight of the object of his devotion. It is a journey the goal of which is always in sight but is never attained. There we are always learners, always worshipers, always pilgrims."

I may be wrong, but I felt nearer to the heart of India and the Hindus in the little Rajput State of Dholpur—talking hour after hour, day after day, with its remarkable ruler, and keeping my eyes open—than I did in New Delhi, Bombay, Calcutta, Lucknow, and Allahabad, with their Indian officials and lawyers, business men and politicians. The one was typical of old India; the others of the new order. Mind you, I am not saying that one was better than the other; I am merely saying that I felt in one place that I was in Indian India, and in the others in British India.

I went to school and took my lessons from a wise and good teacher, the Maharaj Rana of Dholpur, Sir Udaibhan Singh Lokindra Bahadur; but I do not claim that he taught me everything, by any means, or that everything he taught me was wisdom.

I had met him first in Dholpur House in New Delhi, when, through some mutual friends, Sir Evelyn and Lady Wrench, he invited me to lunch. At first I was as aghast over the things he said as was Edgar Snow, who had a similar experience and wrote in *People on Our Side* about his "incredible conversation" with the Maharaj Rana.

"The solution of India's problems can only be a return to personal, autocratic rulers," His Highness said over our luncheon table. "The monarch is divinely chosen, and the people of India recognize such a relationship. Therefore, if the British want to settle the Indian question within a few months, all they have to do is to place power for a direct settlement in the hands of the British Crown. Let the king take direct command, make his own appointments, and take a personal interest in India. Indians would understand that, and the various factions would soon compose their differences. There is no feeling for democracy in India, but there are complete understanding and acceptance of and desire for personal rule.

"Religion is at the core of Indian thoughts, feelings and daily life, and it is the key to everything."

Respect for religion, he continued, made him and Gandhi close friends, although they were far apart in other ways. He spoke with the greatest respect and friendship of Lord Halifax, who preceded Lord Linlithgow as Viceroy of India. "When a man is religious he is close to the Indians, and Halifax, when he was Viceroy, understood us."

Nothing could have seemed more "anachronistic," to use Snow's word, but I was willing to admit that "this was the voice of Old India which is very much present today." It so happened that I was to visit Dholpur several times and see its ruler on other occasions, and I corresponded with him regularly, so I could not rest on a mere feeling of anachronism. I never believed in revealed political truths or in the universal application of any political doctrine. If countless millions of Indians felt that a certain way of life was natural and desirable I could pity them for their ignorance, but I could not deny that they felt the way they did. This is not a plea for either *laisser faire* or for the Princely States as such. I am merely making the point that autocratic rule is not necessarily bad rule, and that India is not the United States, nor is it Russia, nor even China. I visited a dozen or more typical Princely States, and I saw in them much that was good as well as much that was bad. In any circumstances they are not to be waved haughtily aside as if they have no place in India and were as black as Congress likes to paint them.

Let me tell you something about Dholpur, for it will give you

—as it did me—much insight into one important part of the Indian picture.

Five thousand years of history have passed lightly over that little corner of the eastern Rajputana on the edge of the United Provinces, so that there today you really do find eternal India, with her autocratic ruler, her worshiping people, her faith in the transmigration of souls, horoscopes and the influence of gems on human lives. This is life as the mysterious East has always known it and always will know it. A simple, innocent, logical foreigner like myself walks into Dholpur State on his feet, but he comes out wondering whether he or the extraordinary man who rules it is standing on his head.

The three days that I spent there on my first visit might as well have been lived in another world. Nothing matters there but Dholpur, and Dholpur is what it always has been. War, progress as we know it, the rights of man—all such things are unknown there, but that does not mean the people are ground down by tyranny, heavy taxation, or cruel laws. On the contrary, they are ruled with extraordinary kindness, sympathy, and understanding. Their taxes are lower than those of British India, and the laws are so elastic that any subject can appeal personally to his ruler for justice—and he appeals to a ruler who believes that God has sent him to dispense absolute justice.

The Maharaj Rana was then forty-nine—a small, thin man who dresses unostentatiously and talks with friendly courtesy to the lowest of his subjects. He is famous among other things for his blameless private life, which is unusual for a maharaja, but above all for his deep religiosity, whose sincerity none ever has or can question. Upon it his philosophy and system of government are based.

After lunch the first day, sitting in the blue and gold living room of one of his five palaces—a rambling Victorian affair—he spoke of religion and of the wild animals he tends and loves. It is a question of kindness, he said, and all animals, including man, will respond to it.

Lord Halifax, during a duck shoot near Simla, once asked him how it is that the Hindus worship so many gods? (Dholpur, incidentally, holds the Indian record for a day's shooting—403 ducks, picked up.) He answered that they do not worship many gods, but only one, and to explain his point in the simplest way, said to the then Lord Irwin:

"Now, here in the car, you are one man, a friend, talking to a friend. When you meet your secretaries and aides at Simla, you will be their boss. When you drive through Simla and greet people, you will be the Viceroy. At home a woman will be waiting for you, to whom you will be a husband only, just like millions of other husbands. In the playroom will be three children, to whom you will be merely a father. Tomorrow you will ride in your robes of state and medals to the Legislative Assembly to open the session. If you, a mere flea in the universe, so to speak, can in twenty-four hours be so many men, how much more is that true of the Almighty?"

He went on to say that the Hindu religion tries above all to avoid the godless man, whereas in the West a man either believes in God, or is an atheist. Here, if one manifestation of the Godhead does not satisfy a man, there is another, and another, until he finds one that responds to his feelings. Yet it all rises, at the end, like the longitudinal lines of a sphere, to the same point. I asked what manifestation of God pleased him most, and he replied Rama, or Ram, the Ruler.

On another day he came back to that accusation of idol worship, about which he is sensitive. He told of the catechism to which a child is put. For instance, he is asked by his teacher, "What are we doing?"

"We are sitting here talking."

"Tell me, which is you and which is I?" The pupil reaches over and grasps his hand.

"This is you."

"No, this is only my hand." So the pupil grasps his shoulder, and gets a similar answer. At last, he embraces the teacher.

"Now," he says, "I have you."

"No, this is only my body."

And so the child learns that in knowing and, in a sense, worshiping his teacher, he is worshiping the image only of the real teacher. So it is with the images of the Hindu gods, which are all merely the outer expression of the one Godhead.

"Some people might say to you," continued the Maharaj Rana, " 'I prefer you in a dinner jacket.' Others might say, in uniform, others, in a blue suit, and so forth, and if they prefer you one way or another, why should you deny them that pleasure, or feel that they are liking someone else every time you change your clothes?"

(I was to learn in the course of time that this is, truly, the Hindu teaching, but only the well educated are capable of reaching such heights.)

Like all other Hindus, the Maharaj Rana believes in the transmigration of souls and the caste system.

"Transmigration," he says, "solves logically all the problems of inequality and divine justice. Man has three primary temptations: money, power, and position. In a democracy men strive for these things and are corrupted by them, but chosen souls, born as rulers, are freed of these temptations. Few men in a democracy will be able to dispense absolute, conscious justice.

"If you live a good life you are bound to go upward in your next incarnation. If my stewardship satisfies the Creator, I may be granted a bigger state, with more people. Or perhaps He will say: 'This man is tired of ruling,' and give me some less material reward."

So the Maharaj Rana, naturally, takes the adoration of his subjects as a matter of course. As he drives his car along roads and through villages men drop what they are doing, put the palms of their hands together, in that charming Hindu gesture, touch their foreheads, and bend low. In the crowded, bazaar-lined streets of the towns as we passed through, the men and children all cried, "Sri Maharaj!" which means roughly, "God bless the Maharaja!"

Any maharaja gets that respect, as I was to discover in all the States, and even the unworthy ones, but there was no mistaking the affection and trust with which the people crowded around our car to speak to their ruler. His state is only 1,200 square miles, and since he has ruled it for thirty-three years he knows every inch of it and every personage above the ordinary.

Once, as we drove through the village of Bari, an agitated, middle-aged Hindu stopped our car and spoke imploringly to the Maharaj Rana. It was a wealthy landowner, who said that his son had been ill for eight days with fever, and the local doctor could not seem to cure him. He obviously considered it only natural and right that the Prince should do something about it. The Maharaja, in fact, said that he would send a physician down from the main hospital in Dholpur town, and told the Hindu to advise him what the doctor said. A few days later the Hindu notified him that by the time the doctor arrived his son's fever had gone down, and he was sure that the intervention of the Maharaj Rana had, in itself, been enough to effect the cure.

One morning I drove through Dholpur town with the ruler's aid-de-camp, who told me that it takes His Highness at least an hour to get through, because dozens of his subjects importune him and he always carries medicines and money, and even, in winter, warm clothes and blankets, to meet their demands.

"They ask only to be treated kindly," said the ADC, who was a relative of the Maharaja. "As long as they have enough to keep alive, that is all they ask. See how contented they look!"

I had to take that statement for what it was worth, since I could not question them, but it was true that they seemed contented, and their masters were willing to believe that contentment was enough, whatever the level at which it was enjoyed. They were not educated, for education is neglected in Dholpur and is not considered important, least of all for girls. The Maharaja is said, indeed, to spend less on education, proportionately, than any of the other rulers. Theoretically, there is compulsory education for boys up to the age of 12, but His Highness admitted that "many parents do not like to send their boys to school," and presumably they are not forced to. Girls should go, too, but the Maharaja clearly does not believe in education for them. Their parents want them to learn cooking and housewifery, he said. Their place is not only in the home, but in *purdah*. About matrimony he feels firmly that the woman should look to the man as the subject to the ruler—a representative of the Godhead. "And you will be surprised how many happy marriages there are in India," he added, "millions and millions of them."

He feels that nothing else counts so much as land and its produce, and Indians should occupy themselves in agriculture. So he does not encourage manufacturing, but spends most of the available state money on irrigation. His taxes are very light, with no income tax, only small license fees for shopkeepers, a nominal water tax where there is irrigation, and small excise taxes on goods entering and leaving the state. I wondered where his annual income of $54,000 came from, until I learned that he has extensive landholdings in the United Provinces.

So long as he rules the way he does, the Maharaj Rana of Dholpur has nothing to fear from British interference. The "Paramount Power" intervenes only in cases of the gravest abuses extending over a good deal of time. So His Highness is accountable to no one but his Creator, for either his expenditures or his rule. He is his own Dewan, or Premier, and although he has councilors, they are considered more or less nonentities. Every morning he is up long before dawn, for his spiritual exercises, and by 7 o'clock he is out in a little automobile, which he drives alone through the villages and along the roads, stopping whenever anyone indicates that he wants the Prince to speak to him. He takes with him no officials or witnesses, so that the poorest people can approach him, knowing that their headman or petty official or police officer, if they wish to complain about him, will not know they have gone directly to the ruler.

Now and then the Maharaja goes among them like Haroun al Raschid among his people. A few years ago there were complaints about a frontier constable who was accused of taking bribes, among other things. So one evening the Maharaja disguised himself with a big mustache and beard, and put on the garb of a Hindu shopkeeper. Then he went to the frontier post, bribed the constable himself, and went on toward Agra. Once out of sight he took off his disguise, and returned as Maharaja.

Then he accused the constable of bribery. The man denied it vehemently, but this time without avail.

"Word flew around the state," said His Highness, "and for years afterward people with anything on their consciences would see me like a ghost walking toward them at dusk."

There is capital punishment in the state, but the ruler had hanged only man in thirty-one years, and then for an especially cold-blooded murder. When cases are important enough, he makes it a point of judging them himself, and his sentence is above any law or court. He says he always talks to the accused alone, asking about the crime and why he did it, "because I want to study human nature."

Some years ago a case came to him of a 72-year-old man who had admitted beating a money-lender to death. The case had been cut and dried from the beginning. The man had gone to the police and had confessed, and at each appeal of his lawyers, in each succeeding court, he had repeated his confession, so there was never any question about the sentence. The man came of a good and well-to-do family, and the case became a celebrated one, in the three and a half years it dragged through the courts. His Highness told me he called the man to him, who repeated his confession and would not deviate from it, but the Maharaja felt intuitively that such a man (the ruler basing his judgment on his ability to gauge character) could not have committed a brutal murder, so he postponed the hanging for a further, personal investigation. He put his own secret police to work on the case, and they quickly discovered the truth. The murder had been done, in a fit of anger, by the great-nephew of this man. The lad was only fifteen, and the last remaining male of an important local family. The old man had been in Agra when the crime was committed, and the family had called a hasty conference, to which he returned. The members of the family could not bear the idea of losing their last male and, as the old man told the Maharaja later, he was old and tired and had lived his life, so the next morning he went to the police and gave himself up—incidentally bribing them with a large sum of money not to do any more investigating.

In view of the boy's youth, the Maharaja kept him in jail only five or six years. On one of the Prince's visits to the jail a few years later, the boy went to him, prostrated himself, and wept. The ruler asked what he was weeping about and what he wanted, but the boy said he wanted nothing; he was happy that the truth had come out. When I visited Dholpur he was a wealthy and respected landowner, married and with children.

Such is justice in Old India, and I found in my wanderings that that was the sort of justice which Indians understood and wanted, not the machine-like, formal, rigid justice by law which the British misguidedly took to India as if they were bearing a revealed truth or the Ten Commandments.

For the Maharaj Rana, Lord Hardinge was the best Viceroy of this century, and when Halifax asked him why he thought so, he replied, "because he was so unconstitutional."

The political beliefs of this ruler naturally fitted into his general philosophy of life. He was continually harping upon the necessity for the British to do something.

"They cannot keep 400,000,000 people under their thumb forever," he said. "They must do something, and preferably along monarchical lines, something the Indians will understand, something human that will appeal to the minds, hearts, and imaginations of the people. Bring the King-Emperor out in other ways than as an effigy on coins and stamps.

"Some day there will be a terrible eruption if the British don't act. I have no sympathy for Congress, although I have the highest regard and friendship for Gandhi as a religious man, but I told my British friends that if it were right for them to close that door, they should open another. We are a sentimental and emotional people, and our response is to human understanding. So long as the British administration remains a machine, it will never win the hearts of the Indian people."

He once told me about the efforts of Congress to proselytize in that part of his state bordering on Agra, during a very lean year. He heard of it, and called all the important *zamindars,* or landowners, to his office and saw them one by one, saying: "I know everything that has been happening and just how you have been approached. I know that you listened to the Congress agitators with some benevolence, but that you all refused to do what Congress asked, or, at any event, that you have done nothing to date. This has been a lean year, and if you had refused to pay taxes, as they suggested, it would have been very hard for the state. I appreciate your attitude, and since what you have done is of benefit to the state, you may be sure that if you get into trouble or need help, the state will come to your aid." To each one of them was given the traditional ceremonial robe as a gift and, said His Highness, "they went away happy." Certainly, he has had no trouble from Congress, although the adjoining United Provinces are one of the strongholds of the organization.

This unusual ruler considers the wild animals in his state his subjects, as are the human beings, and he treats them with equal kindness. It was an extraordinary experience—and I was to enjoy it on a number of occasions—to go around feeding his special pets. The first afternoon I was there, we drove out to one of his palaces stuck on the top of a hill in a jungle section of the state. On the way we stopped at a place where every afternoon the Maharaja goes to feed his samburs (a species of elk) and his peacocks. The samburs are one of the shyest of wild animals, with extra-keen senses of smell and hearing, but they came up and ate out of our hands, begging for the special food he has prepared for them, a sort of rich bread, more nourishing than the *chapatis* which men eat, and also grain for the peacocks and partridges. He had greens, too, for the samburs that day, and told of one which had had a goiter which he treated and cured with iodine.

Later we drove to a rendezvous with a group of jackals. They are too shy to eat from the hand, so we stayed in the car, but they came up, quite close, and one of them was expert at catching chunks of bread. There was one little gray fox which came right up to the car every day to get his tidbits, but when he went away I noticed that he had a wary eye for the jackals, and scampered off. His Highness knew all the jackals, and had given them names. He said their faces varied as do those of human beings, when one got to know them.

As we drove along, more samburs came up and we stopped to feed them. There was a covey of partridges which waited trustingly on the road for their grain.

At dusk we drove up to a lake on the edge of which was a palace such as one dreams of—long and low, of dull-red sandstone built by the Emperor Shahjahan and restored by the Maharaj Rana. He showed me his apartment, with the old architecture intact, but with electric lights and plumbing, and modern furniture. I was to spend a few happy days there the following year.

Each time I visited the state we spent one delightful afternoon cruising on a big lake, and along its tributaries, in the Maharaja's launch, with him at the wheel. We wound along banks where trees and high grass came down to the water, watching samburs and crocodiles, and one day we spotted two huge tigers at the edge of the water. They stalked back into the jungle as we came up, but returning fifteen minutes later we found one of them crouched in the grass, with his great head lifted. He stared at us as we cruised around in circles looking at him.

At 5:30 sharp another launch came up and tied itself to ours. On it was a table covered with tea and good things to eat, with a butler and two waiters, not to mention three boatmen. His Highness cut his motor and the other boat chugged gently along, taking us with it as we ate and drank. Then we went off for a last ride around in the fast disappearing light, the half moon growing stronger and stronger until it bathed us and the lake in its glow. We made for the lights of the boathouse, where the butler was waiting with a flask of whisky, while another waiter stood by with a bottle of soda. Sometimes journalism has its compensations.

Staying in one of the Maharaja's villas during my first visit was a *sadhu,* or holy man, Swami Nirmalaland, who claimed to be a disciple of the great Swami Vivekanada. It was a charming little house on the shore of a pond—a sort of Petit Trianon—and the morning I went out there I found the Prince feeding his cows. For him, as for all Hindus, animals have souls as human beings have, and are, in fact, going through the same endless cycle of reincarnation and Karma, banished now to a lower order, for sins committed in past lives.

The *sadhu* was dressed in the customary saffron robe, and had shaved his head. In the course of thirty years' wanderings he had been in every corner of India and through the Himalayas, staying a short while at each place. He had been in Dholpur for three months, and said it was the longest he ever stayed anywhere, but I could see the reason, for in the Maharaja he had a host who was made to order for *sadhus*. He said he had lost his wife in youth and was heartbroken, and had given up everything for his wandering life. I thought him a charlatan, but it was not for me to judge.

The holy man claimed that on a visit to a wise man in Tibet, a Chinese, "who is 500 years old," he had asked the recluse what he should do. The reply came in English, "Cease thinking!" It reminded me of Boswell's decision: "After much speculation and various reasonings, I acknowledge myself convinced of the truth of Voltaire's conclusion, '*Après tout, c'est un monde passable.*' But we must not think too deeply. . . ."

His Highness spoke of *sadhus* whom he had met, one 120 years old and the other 200. It was Shangri La all over again! In introducing me to Swami Nirmalaland, the Maharaj Rana remarked that as a Hindu he, of course, believed implicitly in transmigration. He did not know how I felt about it, but he was certain from the first moment he saw me that we had met somewhere in a previous incarnation. He had had the same feeling, he said, with Lord Halifax and "my dear little Edward," meaning the present Duke of Windsor, who was then the Prince of Wales.

The swami began with what seemed to me like sheer quackery a system of horoscopes worked out by him, and based on certain types and related to the planets. I was number 5, Mars, he said, and the character description was largely the opposite of what I am. The Maharaja interrupted him to tell a story about himself which he said was on record.

"I was the second son in our family, which meant that my older brother, who was born ten years earlier, would inherit the throne. When I was four hours old, my father's astrologer completed his preliminary horoscope. As you know, the court physician waits with a stop-watch to get the exact minute of the child's birth, because even a minute out of the way could make all the difference in the world. This astrologer predicted that in my eighteenth year I would inherit the throne and would marry. My father thought there must be a mistake, but he died some years later and my brother became Maharaj Rana; but in my eighteenth year he died and I ascended the throne. That same year I married."

His Highness has several court astrologers, who inherited their posts, and he will do nothing important, such as starting a journey, commencing a new irrigation canal, or holding a council meeting, unless they tell him that the day and the hour are auspicious. This, I discovered, was true of virtually all maharajas, and I cannot overemphasize the fact that anyone who does not realize the part such beliefs still play in every phase of life cannot understand India. There is probably not a villager among her teeming millions who does not believe firmly in horoscopes. In every ten peasants there will be one who can work out crude horoscopes. Skeptical western minds like Jawaharlal Nehru's, are very rare.

In Dholpur all clocks are run on sun time, because the ruler does not want to confuse the simple, popular astrologers who would go all wrong if their reckoning were incorrect by one hour. Some years ago there was a *sadhu* at court who, I was told, read dreams, but, as the Maharaja's ADC said, "that is an extremely difficult art and we have no one here now who can do it." His Highness does not place too much stock in palmistry, he told me, because he has found that the lines of the hands change, "probably in conjunction with the stars."

The Maharaj Rana carries always a gold cigarette case inset with the nine stones of the *nau rathan,* corresponding to the nine planets. The nine stones are blue sapphire, coral, pearl, diamond, ruby, catseye, emerald, white sapphire, and garnet. I never was able to find any agreement on which stones were related to which planets, but the use of the *nau rathan* is universal in India. By wearing them one is supposed to be able to neutralize the effects of the planets. Swami Nirmalaland wore the stones in six rings, three on each hand.

"Sapphires and catseyes have an especially powerful influence," the Maharaja said. "Whenever I am interested in one of those stones I keep it for a week to see what luck I have, and if it is bad, I give the gem back to the jeweler."

Does this seem as strange to you as it did to me? It is not strange in India, and you must keep that in mind. Let me tell you one other story that the Maharaj Rana related to me the last time I visited Dholpur. I had had it previously from another source, and knew it to be true.

"Suttee, in the olden days," said His Highness, "was purely voluntary. There never was any question of forcing women on to the funeral pyre, as happened later. The real suttee is still practiced quietly, hundreds of times, in India.

"Remember that for us the ideal relationship between man and wife is that the wife should worship God in the form of her husband. He and she almost make one soul, and we believe that if the husband dies and the wife commits suttee she will join him in the next incarnation, since the last wish of a virtuous soul is what determines its destiny more than anything else, and she commits suttee because she wishes to remain with her husband.

"When my father died I was six years and a half old. My own mother had died when I was a baby, but my stepmother had been as devoted and loving as a real mother could be. She showed no grief over the death of her husband, and everybody wondered why, for they knew she had been faithful and loving. She called my brother, who was ten years older than I, and gave him the keys to the strong-boxes and other locked places, telling him that he would be head of the family now. 'But,' he said, 'you will be here always. Why don't you keep them?' She insisted gently, and sent him away.

"Then she called the male servants to her. She had always observed strict purdah, but that day, for the first time, she unveiled herself before them. She told them that they had been good servants, and she wanted them always to remain in the family and to serve the children faithfully. Then she gave each one a present, and dismissed them.

"I was with her all this time, and was dimly beginning to understand. There was a sister, six years older than I, and she was the last one my stepmother called in. When I heard her say to my sister, 'Now, you must be like a mother to this little boy,' taking my hand and putting it in the hand of my sister, I realized what she planned to do. So I ran up to her, clasping her knees, weeping, and cried: 'Mother, stay with us.' For two seconds her woman's heart softened and I thought she would yield, but then a wave of hardness seemed to rise over her body and face, and she gently pushed me away. Turning to my sister, she asked her to acknowledge that she had always been a faithful mother and wife. My sister was crying, and couldn't say anything, at first, but our stepmother insisted.

"'Please hurry,' she said. 'You know that I never kept your father waiting.'

"All through this she had been perfectly calm, and it was as if she were already dead. She was like someone who was being awaited in an automobile. The driver was holding the door open, and she was impatient to get in and drive away.

"My father's body was lying on a bed in the room where all this was happening, for he had just died. The end came when I saw my stepmother drink the contents of a little flask. Later I learned it held cyanide of potassium. Then she lay down beside her husband, and in a short while was dead."

It was at the end of my first trip to Dholpur that the Maharaj Rana, in bidding me good-bye, said: "You have listened patiently to all this old-fashioned talk of mine in this little, backward, pre-historic state. It must all sound strange and foolish to you, but, believe me, these are living forces in India. They are old ideas, but they will never change so long as India is India."

I felt the strangeness of them so much that it seemed desirable to me to end with a warning the stories that I wrote about my first visit to Dholpur: "Lest anyone ascribe the beliefs related here to mere ignorance, it should be stated that the Maharaj Rana of Dholpur is a highly cultured man, truly learned in religious matters, and that he has done a fair amount of traveling abroad. He speaks English perfectly, and he keeps in touch with political developments all over the world."

What I have told you here, but with much less detail, was the picture I drew for *The New York Times'* readers after three days in Dholpur with Ben Robertson as a fellow guest—Ben, who was later to give his life in a plane crash, leaving the memory of his humor and courage and goodness. We both enjoyed the experience hugely and we were glad, among other things, to convince each other that we were not dreaming. It amused him to hear me keep saying, "Imagine getting paid to do this!"

But we were not dreaming. We had been taken to another world, and neither of us felt inclined to say that because it was like the other side of our looking-glass it must be all wrong and distinctly bad. No other experience in my life has been so chastening as my sojourn in India. It is the place to learn that there are more things in heaven and earth than are dreamed of in our Western philosophy. I was not being merely curious. The simple truth is that one cannot understand India without appreciating the strangeness of the world in which Indians—and especially Hindus—live.

It was only after my return to the United States that I learned, to my astonishment, that critics of the "liberal," pro-Congress school said that I had misled my readers and had exaggerated greatly. In truth, there was as little exaggeration in my dispatches as there is in the statement that Americans chew gum and as a matter of fact only a portion of the American people chew gum, whereas virtually all Hindus and a large part of the Moslems in India believe as the Maharaj Rana of Dholpur does. Skeptical Westerners may believe what they please about such things, but trying to understand India would be waste of time if one did not realize the part they play in every-day life—and that includes politics, too. You cannot govern people as they want to be governed if you foist upon them a way of life which does not conform to their profound beliefs—at least, you cannot do so unless you educate them out of those beliefs, and this the British certainly have not been able to do. When India achieves independence and men like Nehru and Jinnah, with their Western ideas, take power, that process of education will doubtless begin, but it will take generations. Meanwhile, the contrast remains between Old India and the Western, democratic ideas of Congress and the Moslem League, and between that same ancient civilization and its British conquerors.

I could write a number of chapters on all that I saw and heard about astrology and horoscopes, but they would only belabor a point already made and expatiate on what I learned in Dholpur. I had my own horoscope drawn up (in Sanskrit, of course) by the court astrologer of Cooch Behar—and I wish I believed in horoscopes, because, on the whole, mine was a good one, even if a reading of one of my stars indicated that I would be "fierce, stubborn, irritable, reddish-brown in color, and seeking after other women."

I do not assert that sophisticated, foreign-educated princes, politicians, or business men take horoscopes too seriously if they do not conform to their desires, but even rulers who do not believe have to abide by the findings of their astrologers, since their people expect them to. The same astrologer who drew up my horoscope had also made the horoscope for the marriage of the sister of the Maharaja of Cooch Behar to the Maharaja of Jaipur. I was told that in important cases of proposed marriages the court astrologers can find that the horoscopes of the young man and woman match beautifully, if some minister of state greases the astrologer's palm. However, the unworldly creature who made that particular forecast (a man who would have done perfectly in the role of Romeo's apothecary) pronounced the judgment that the match would not be good, only tolerable. No mother who is about to make an excellent match for her daughter can be easily discouraged, and the dowager Maharani of Cooch Behar, a famed beauty in her day and worldly-wise, simply ignored her court astrologer. "They are fifty per cent wrong anyway, most of the time," she confided to me. The marriage took place and so far it has been a happy one.

But astrology is only one of many beliefs, some of which we Westerners once had but have abandoned, which play their part on the Indian scene. When I was in India, four men were sentenced to death and three to life imprisonment, in a trial in Jubbulpore, Central Provinces, for killing a "witch." There had been a cholera epidemic in their village of Gudi, and the cultivators had decided that a woman named Mussamat Rahim had cast an evil spell upon the inhabitants. Responsible men of the village got together, and one night took the "witch" to the village tank, ducked her, and then beat and trampled her to death.

"The law does not recognize witchcraft," said the Indian judge in pronouncing sentence, "and he who kills a 'witch' commits murder. Still, in the case of the superstitious rustic the court may view his feelings with some leniency in awarding punishment for murder as his feelings may be due to relics of barbarism and animism. In the present case, however, the village is a fairly large one and the people concerned with the crime do not belong to the backward classes. A doctor had visited the village during the epidemic and explained to the leading men of the village, including all the accused except one, the causes of cholera and how to combat the disease."

No doctor trained in Western medicine was going to convince the Indian villagers that there are no witches. There have been "witches," so to speak, in India for 5,000 years, and Western medicine is, at most, a century or two old there. "But faith is very old and science is new," wrote Gaetano Mosca. India is very old, too, and the Indian villager, who has not been educated at Oxford or Cambridge, makes up 90 per cent of her population. What he knows has been handed down to him through hundreds of generations. What is one man's superstition is another man's wisdom or religion. They have used systems of medicine—the Ayurveda of the Hindus and the Unani of the Moslems, the latter derived from the ancient Greeks—for thousands of years, and they believe in them.

In Calcutta there is an open shop run by a Sikh called Kavinaj Babacharan Singh, who proudly displays a certificate from the "State Faculty of Ayurvedic Medicine." It is a horrendous shop, with greasy remnants of snakes, lizards, scorpions, alligators, storks, and the bones and brewed flesh of many other animals.

Hundreds of skulls are piled on each other—human, monkey, bear, tiger, rhinoceros, alligator, deer, and many others. Some seemed prehistoric, but they were heads picked up in jungles or along rivers. Sometimes a man drowns, and his body floats downstream. Water buffaloes will eat the body and leave the head. Sometimes, as with the Naga hillsmen, the head is kept when a person dies, and now and then it reaches the market. "Those skulls," said Babacharan Singh, "are excellent for casting spells."

There were shells, bones, and horns, of many kinds, with herbs, roots, leaves and poisonous thistles, and trays full of charms and amulets. And seated deep inside was Babacharan Singh, his eye-rims blacked for beauty and his knowledge available to passersby at a price. He compounds medicines for whatever ails one, grinding skulls into medicinal powders, boiling down snakes or lizards into nauseating liquids that will soothe any hurt from a cut to a tumor and cost only 4 annas (8 cents). From roots and herbs he will make panaceas, aphrodisiacs, or potions guaranteed to make women fertile. If your child has a cough he chops up feathers finely, burns them and mixes them with honey. The root of a certain poisonous thistle, boiled, mixed with peppercorns and used in homeopathic doses, is a sure remedy for venereal diseases of all kinds. Shells, when burned into ashes and ground into a powder, are sovereign for asthma. Monkey skulls burned down and ground finely are excellent for tumors and cancers. For female disorders, pulverized beehives are prescribed. Oil boiled down from peacocks' feet relieves earaches, and snake oil cures ingrown hairs. The powder made from certain roots will cure leprosy.

When I asked what European medicines he used, Babacharan Singh shook his head disapprovingly. There was nothing so simple or newfangled in his pharmacopeia.

Two owls stood in a cage next to him, and hissed at me continuously.

"What are they for?" I asked.

"For witchcraft," he said.

I, myself, like Cleopatra, swallowed pearls. That was in

Hyderabad, in the fine, new, modern hospital which the Nizam built for the practice of the Moslem Unani system of medicine, in which he is a firm believer. The peculiarity of the Unani system is that it uses oxidized jewels, which are mixed with Indian herbs of an extraordinary variety, dried fruits, and, invariably, honey and sugar, which make all medicines pleasant to the taste. Ashes of pearls are considered the best form of calcium, and a sovereign tonic. The medicine given to me was delicious.

Unani practitioners claim that jewels provide chemicals in their purest form, and have some virtues beyond their chemical composition. When oxidized they all turn to a white or slightly brownish powder—and, needless to say, they are costly. Emeralds are the best medicine for the liver and kidneys, I was told. Rubies are for the heart, coral for asthma and brain trouble, and diamonds for external salves. Gold oxide is prescribed for tuberculosis and sexual impotency, silver oxide for heart diseases.

The hospital would stand comparison with any in the West. It is modern and spotless, and elaborate records of the patients are kept. And in diet and regime the latest discoveries in calories and vitamins are used. So one must guard against thinking that Indian medical practices are purely the fruits of ignorance.

Here in the West a man who believes in metempsychosis, the transmigration of souls, is considered queer or superstitious, but for the Hindu such belief is, perforce, simple knowledge. In the Princely State of Mysore, the superintendent of the government house, a Brahmin named Ganghadara Ayer, who took me around, said he does not like dogs and cannot stand their odor, but he loves cows. In India dogs are considered vile creatures, and only the very low-caste *syces* will take care of them, while cows are sacred. He showed me, with pride, the reservation set aside on the edge of Mysore city in which old cows end their days in peace—and suffering. When I said that it seemed to me more charitable to put them out of their misery, he asked, "Would you put human beings to death when they get old?" At the factory where silk parachutes were being made, he said of the silkworms, in a sort of wistful voice as if trying to convince himself,

"Perhaps they are fulfilling their mission and were sent on earth to save humanity by their death."

Here we are, wandering, you might think, in a misty world of make-believe, or, if it be real, what, you may ask, has this to do with the "beer and skittles" of modern politics and the desperate game of world affairs in which India must play so great a role? But be patient a while, and let us travel further into the land on the other side of the looking glass.

Through the Looking Glass

So EVERY American soldier arriving in India got off the gang-plank of his troopship or out of his transport plane and found that, like Alice, he had stepped through the looking glass. This was not at all the world he knew, with its simple, matter-of-fact life, its bacon and eggs for breakfast, its newspapers, radios and sports, its people who wore the same clothes, thought like him and spoke his own language—which was not Oxford English, either.

India to him had been some far-off, romantic country, vaguely connected with the Arabian Nights, full of maharajas, Kohinoor diamonds, tigers, elephants, cobras and nautch girls. It was the home, he knew, of a strange old man, toothless and hairless, wearing only a loin-cloth, who spent most of his time fasting to annoy the British.

If he had been interested at all in radical or liberal politics, India, to him, would have been the land of an oppressed people, seeking their independence from the British imperialists, just as Americans did more than a century and a half ago. His sympathies would naturally be with the Indians, particularly as he would always enjoy that good old American pastime of "twisting the Lion's tail."

Very few would go beyond that point, but some had to. For instance, officers and engineers who built our airfields quickly found themselves in collision with that most characteristically Hindu of all institutions, the caste system. Americans have some vague ideas about castes and outcastes and they think of the Pariahs, or "Untouchables"—the real damned-to-hell on earth— as outcasts—which they are not. They are merely very low caste, and they have many subdivisions whose members look down on other Untouchables. "There is no being so poor and so contemptible, who does not think there is somebody still poorer, and still more contemptible," as Johnson said to Boswell.

The English call the Untouchables the "Scheduled Castes," and Gandhi, who has done much for them, gave them the old name of "Harijans," meaning "God's Men." (All God's chilluns got wings.) In so far as they are organized they follow and worship Gandhi, although their outstanding member, a Columbia University graduate, Dr. B. R. Ambedkar, is a bitter enemy of the Mahatma, whom he accuses of using the Untouchables for selfish political ends.

One of the first questions asked by a foreigner in India is, "How do you know when a man or a woman is an Untouchable?" The answer I received was the rather cruel one, "You will know, all right, without having to ask." And it is true that the unhappy fate of these people has made them squalid, dirty, and hangdog, while breeding has given them especially dark skins. They are supposed to number some sixty millions.

Castes are one of the things that you must know about if you want to know India. They are little social worlds in themselves, set in the greater world of Hindu society as a whole. There are strict rules of social precedence in the classes of castes, which run as high as 200 to each of the many linguistic divisions in India. The Brahmin is always at the head of the hierarchy, and he still plays an important role in the Congress organization although Gandhi comes from a much lower caste, the *bania* or commercial group, once a part of the Vaishya order.

There are food and very strict marriage taboos, between castes, and there are many occupational restrictions. Untouchables alone can be street-cleaners or handle ordure. There are *chamars* (shoemakers), *syces* (grooms), *dhobis* (laundrymen), *kahars* (servants), *bhangis* (sweepers), and innumerable other subcastes whose restrictions are breaking down very slowly, but are still strong enough to cripple the economic structure of the country—even if there were no other factors to do so. Caste is one of the fundamental causes for India's poverty, in that it is a great factor in limiting production. For instance, certain castes among the cultivators may not touch plow or digging tools, while others may not manure their fields.

It was the Maharaj Rana of Dholpur who first gave me the ideal basis for the caste system, although he claimed that a monarch in India should have no religious or caste prejudices. All men are brothers, but they have different functions and shapes. He pointed to the electric fan, the electric light, the electric stove, and so forth, all different in the roles they performed in the house, but all receiving their energy and life from the same source of power.

"Inequality among men," he went on, "is explained perfectly by transmigration. You are what you are because of your actions in former lives. There are four great orders of castes, derived from the fact that a man must have a wise brain, a strong arm, a good digestion, and strong legs, and a nation must have wise counselors, a strong army, flourishing trade, and willing labor."

The original four orders he mentioned are the Brahmin, Kshattrya, Vaishya, and Sudra, and, according to Dr. G. S. Ghurye, in *Caste and Race in India,* the names are said to have come from the mouth, arms, thighs, and feet of the Creator. The old literature called them the four *varnas.* The first three *varnas* are called "twice-born" because they have to go through the initiation ceremony which is symbolic of rebirth. The privilege is denied to the Sudra, who is therefore called "once-born."

Gandhi, incidentally, is the chief exponent in India today of the four old orders, although he has never made it clear just how he proposes to reinstate them. However, the Mahatma lays great stress on birth and heredity, and subscribes to the view, "once born a Brahmin, always a Brahmin," although he would undoubtedly propose some respectable status for the Untouchable. It must be remembered that Gandhi considers himself an "orthodox Hindu."

To an outsider, however, the four-*varna* theory does not make much sense, since he sees not four but hundreds of castes, with only the Brahmin remaining of the ancient orders.

As a matter of fact, Americans found they could get Indian

workers to do almost anything, whatever their caste, but there was a good reason for that. "Where there is no eye, there is no caste," runs an old saying. In the villages, under the watchful eye of the priests or of malicious neighbors, caste taboos are respected. In the cities, where the use of buses, hotels, and restaurants makes many caste restrictions impossible, a man will ignore them, but not in his home village. There one finds a holy fear of caste justice, and a villager does not perjure himself as he freely does in an ordinary court. When he is tried by the caste *panchayat* there is usually genuine justice, and the worst thing that can happen to him—worse than death—is to be out-casted.

This progression into an intricate and baffling subject is made because it is vital to any understanding of Indian society, its politics and its economics. Caste is an overshadowing phenomenon which leads one inevitably into the mysteries of transmigration, and thence to fatalism, which is at the root of the Indian's outlook on life.

Life is an illusion, a dream within an unending cycle of dreams, all of them imprisoned and dominated by Karma. Every action is determined by countless acts in former incarnations, and it in turn determines the future, and thus into eternity.

"When one considers the doctrine in all its implications," wrote Lord Ronaldshay in *India: A Bird's-Eye View*, "one realizes in what a terrible and remorseless net those who held it found themselves enmeshed. For if the doctrine were indeed true, human existence must be eternal. There could, apparently, be no escape. Man was constrained by inexorable fate to pass through a never-ending succession of births and deaths, fulfilling the effects of former causes and simultaneously creating new causes which must lead to subsequent effects. He was the impotent victim of an inflexible and automatic system."

The singleness of all reality, Ronaldshay wrote in another book, is "the great central idea of Indian speculative thought." The individual man is God, an absolute, abstract, ideal God. But, Swami Vivekananda wrote, since Brahman, the Absolute, is "too much of an abstraction to be loved and worshiped, the *bhakta* [devotee] chooses the relative aspect of Brahman, that is,

Ishvara, the Supreme Ruler," who is also the personal god. And, no doubt, from then on we go down to all the hundreds of thousands of gods which the masses worship.

So the Hindu, as you see, takes an attitude toward life that is quite different from ours. He flees from the world, looks inward, and wants, above all things, to escape from life into nothingness. Or, if he cannot think in philosophical terms, he can suffer as an animal suffers, dumbly and patiently—and so it will be, until Congress, or its equivalent, teaches him that life can mean other and richer things than he has known.

I found it fascinating, and very enlightening, in going about India, to visit some of the famous *ashrams* where those who had temporarily or permanently abandoned the world spent their days as disciples of great "saints." For thousands of years Indians have worshiped their Godhead in the persons of such seers who had an "experience" which lifted them above the common herd and brought them, it is believed, close to the Godhead. Hence, others seeking spiritual uplift gather around them in a sort of colony or *ashram,* generally abandoning the world and living an inner life that seeks to suppress or overcome emotions and longings for material, earthly things.

Every Indian has that instinct to escape from the world. Where a Westerner, when he withdraws from the world, has to tear himself away from it to the spirit, or renunciation, the Hindu starts with the instinct for renunciation and has to tear himself away from it to join the world. The instinct is especially strong as the man grows older.

I went to Sri Aurobindo's *ashram* in Pondicherry, where I saw Margaret Wilson, daughter of Woodrow Wilson, not many months before she died. At Tiruvannamalai, near Madras, I watched and learned about Sri Maharsi, whom Paul Brunton made famous to mystics throughout the world. On the sacred soil of Mount Abu, in the Rajputana, I talked to a famous Jain *guru,* or religious teacher.

In Madras I spent many hours drawing out Rajagopalachari, Brahmin of Brahmins, on religion, which he said he knew, not as a student, but "just as the mango tree knows the earth in which it has its roots." And everywhere I went—in Delhi or Calcutta, Benares or Bombay—I, too, sought for some of that age-old wisdom of the East, and many were the books I read on it, not for knowledge's sake or because it fascinated me, which it did, but because I saw in religion one of the keys to the Indian enigma. It explained Gandhi and non-violence and a great deal more about Congress and India, better than any interviews or direct approaches could have done.

Others infinitely more competent have written on India's religions. I will merely describe to you here one experience, to show the influence that a "holy man" can have in India. It is the story of the Jain *guru* at Mount Abu.

Maharajas and industrial magnates, Brahmins and low-caste Hindus, go in a steady stream to that spot, which is one of the holiest in India. Since prehistoric days there have been temples there, and the hillsides are dotted with stone huts or caves where *sadhus* taught their disciples.

Now men were going from the North and South, from Afghanistan and Ceylon, to seek comfort from an illiterate shepherd who was, I was told, the outstanding *guru* of Western India. Millionaire textile-mill owners from nearby Ahmedabad and from Bombay, further south, went to that teacher for advice on their big deals. He knows nothing about business and cares nothing for money, but they trust in his foresight, which they consider supernatural.

For the British he is a tower of strength, because he will have nothing to do with politics but will use his immense influence in worthy causes such as raising money for hospitals or aiding Red Cross drives. Congressites were then contributing large sums to the war effort, only because he had asked them. He can get things done in that part of India which no amount of police or governmental authority can command.

This man is one of those extraordinary religious characters who rise from the lowest levels of society through sheer force of personality and goodness. His teachings are simple. I went out to the *ashram* in which he was living, a seven-mile walk along a mountain road to Achalgarh, where temples and holy men existed long before historic records were kept.

The *guru* sat cross-legged on his bed in a cell-like room while I sat Hindu fashion on the floor below him, and we talked for an hour through an interpreter. He speaks a local mixture of Marwari and Gujerati, which he learned during his boyhood as a shepherd. He had just shaved his beard, as Jains must at least twice yearly, and he appeared hollow-cheeked, with the blazing eyes of a fanatic, tempered by kindliness and humor.

His undoubted virtuousness had not removed a certain, child-like vanity which made him spend the first quarter hour showing me books in which he had been mentioned, and the names of foreigners who had come to see him. He is proud of the title which his English devotees have given him, "His Holiness," and the card he had had printed began that way, followed by a long list of Sanskrit titles. Here is a free translation:

"His Holiness, World Preceptor, Worthy Initiator, Greatest Blessed, Head of Yogis and Jain Saints, Mighty as Indra [King of Gods], Revered Victor of Peace and Lord Amongst Holy Men."

When his disciples write or telegraph to him they insert the phrase: "Sri 108," which means worshipful or honorable to the 108th degree—and that, I was told, is tops in honorific titles.

He is proud of this adoration, and patently jealous of such rivals as Gandhi, of whom he has the lowest opinion since the *guru* does not believe in mingling politics and religion. I saw him just after Gandhi's ill-fated fast of February, 1943, and he referred to the Mahatma as "a political charlatan." The summer before he had predicted that Congress would suffer a great set-back during the succeeding months—and it did.

The sum total of what he teaches is comprised in the words, "Universal love and peace," which does not differ from what all religions have taught. Those four words seemed to comprise his entire stock of English, for he used them repeatedly during our conversation. His only parable was the ancient story of the five blind men and the elephant. At the end the *guru* takes them all around the elephant so that they can see what his shape really is. So when one knows all, there will be love and peace.

To that idea he adds the ancient Vedic creed of the all-pervading soul of God. When I asked if he had any message for Americans he could only repeat the same simple precepts.

So, there was nothing new in what he teaches. What was new and strange to a Westerner was his belief (in which his host of followers share) that his individual soul is a channel for God's will, and that God will some day bring universal peace and love through his soul force. That personal quality is typical of Indian religiosity. During my stay at the *ashram* I heard many tales of his "miracles" related in all sincerity. He gave me a sandalwood rosary, and blessed me in the obviously complete conviction that he was bestowing something precious and divine. Some dozen pilgrims outside his door looked at me, as I went out, as though I were a mortal favored by the gods.

The wheel of Indian life turns on that hub of religion, which explains a great deal that is otherwise puzzling or incomprehensible to the Westerner. You can see, from Mount Abu, the simple progression from religion to business and politics. You can see why magnates like G. D. Birla, R. K. Seth Dalmia, Walchand Hirachand, Sir Purshottamdas Thakurdas, and even Parsis like J. R. D. Tata and Jains like Sir Hukumchand Swarupchand, support Gandhi and Congress for sincerely religious, as well as practical reasons. Religion and business are one in India, and so are religion and politics, and without realizing that, you can understand nothing that has happened and is happening in India. For a Westerner it is rather horrifying, or, at least, it makes one uneasy. It is not a case of the politician or business man being religious, which he can be in any country. There it is the use of religion for business and political reasons that horrified one. Gandhi, for instance, frankly admitted it when he spoke of "the religious use of politics" in his activities.

The Maharaj Rana of Dholpur told me that religion was the key to everything in India, and I found it to be true. It is not at first obvious in the villages or cities, and that puzzled me until Rajagopalachari pointed out to me that thousands of years of village life with the same beliefs had, so to speak, compressed feelings so that religion was "like finding the carbon in the diamond." He admitted, though (and many others confirmed it) that religion is weakening in India and especially among the younger, politically conscious elements; but those who pull the strings of politics and economics, and the immense, inert masses, are still steeped in religious feeling. Even when, like Jinnah, they are skeptics, they must conform in public, or lose their following. Jinnah's newspaper, *Dawn,* on April 13, 1943, had an article saying that "to Moslems, religion and politics are wholly intertwined, interdependent, inseparable,"—and they are, although less so than with the Hindus.

Let us consider one very important aspect of religion, because it leads us straight into politics and modern Indian history. Gandhi calls it by the old name *ahimsa,* non-violence, or, in its political form, passive disobedience or non-co-operation, which is linked to the endless cycle of transmigration and Karma, to the renunciation of life, and to fatalism.

Practical, hard-headed, clear-thinking Hindus like Rajagopalachari, whose book learning far exceeds Gandhi's, will tell you that non-violence is foreign to the true Hindu religion and thought, but the Mahatma often strikes deeper than mere book learning. There seems to be something fundamental in the Hindu character which leads to that extraordinary process which I sometimes called "biting off one's nose to spite the other fellow's face."

An American missionary, with whom I rode on a train to Gulbarga, in Hyderabad State, told me how in a village inhabited primarily by folk of the so-called "criminal tribes," who are ignorant outcastes on the lowest level of society, non-violence was practiced in the normal course of things. There was an old woman who felt she had been wronged by a *bania* (moneylender), so she took a rock and went to his house. If this were an American story, the sequel would be that she heaved it at him, or through the window, which we would say was the normal thing to do. But she was an Indian. She plunked herself down in front of his doorstep and beat herself into unconsciousness. Now, if

the man had been an American—or a Britisher, for that matter—
he might well have said, "Serves the old crack-pot right!" or, if
he were more charitably inclined, he might have called an ambulance and said, "Take this poor woman away; she's mad."
However, being a Hindu, with innumerable incarnations ahead
of him and his *izzat*, or "face," to be kept up in the village, he
was undoubtedly very much distressed and chagrined.

It was not uncommon, this missionary told me, for offended
persons to throw themselves into the village well in order to
punish those who had done them wrong. We would say that the
ones who committed suicide came off worse. That would be our
way of saying that 2 and 2 make 4, but a Hindu thinks along
other lines. This life of his is only one of countless lives, and
a man dies only to be born again. Your enemy will suffer in
his next, and perhaps for many incarnations, from the stain you
have placed upon his character, and in this world his neighbors
will feel that he is a man accursed.

To be sure, one must perform non-violence against someone
who believes in it. V. D. Savarkar, former terrorist and head of
the militant Hindu Mahasabha, reduced Gandhi's fast of 1943
to the absurd by asking what would happen if Churchill fasted
in order to make Hitler stop the war? What Gandhi did could
have been effective only if the British cared, and in this case
they did not.

There were other cases. In Guntakal, the railway staff declined
to draw their salaries from November 5, 1942, as a protest against
the rejection of their representations for a larger dearness allow-
ance. It did not work. The Koli tribes in Bhavnagar State, according to the newspapers, worked out a drastic form of pressure
against the Indian government during the civil-disobedience
campaign. "The Koli community," said a dispatch, "has decided
to suspend all marriages for a year" as a protest against the
arrest of the Congress leaders. That must have resulted in a
great many marriages without benefit of clergy, but the Congress
leaders were not released. A month before, in Sind Province, the
young men and women in a village also agreed and vowed that

they would not marry until India received her independence. The threat has not been enough.

A British district commissioner told me of an English police officer who was riding through a town in the Punjab with some of his inspectors, when a few brickbats were thrown at them by a group of students. The Englishman and his men rounded up the boys, and, there being a pond nearby, ducked them in it in good, Anglo-Saxon style. That might seem a sensible way to treat youngsters who misbehave. However, these were Hindu boys, not Anglo-Saxons. The local student body met and decided it was an outrage which had to be avenged in drastic fashion. So the students formed a procession, marched solemnly through the streets of the town, and into the pond! Three of them were drowned.

Does that make sense to you? Not if you start from Western premises. After Gandhi's fast, a Hindu doctor solemnly assured me that it could not have been a failure, for the Mahatma had set soul-forces in motion which would not only affect the individual lives of his opponents, such as Churchill and Lord Linlithgow, but might alter the course of the war. He told me about his own experience with fasting, some ten years before. For two years he had been having hallucinations, and his practice was being ruined by certain men, he said. Life was not worth living, so he decided to commit suicide. Although a doctor, with access to all kinds of quick poisons, his mind inclined him to a more subtle, and typically Hindu, method of death. He went on a fast. On the thirty-eighth day there was what he called a "revelation," and when it was repeated on the forty-fifth day he understood it to mean that the purpose of his fast had been accomplished, and he could end it on the fiftieth day, which he did. Nothing seemed to have happened, except to himself, but then, he said, "Two people shortly paid with their lives, and others are still paying."

I told that to Professor J. P. Bhansali, fanatical follower of Gandhi, who was himself then recovering from a sixty-three-day fast of protest against the government. We were sitting in the main room of Gandhi's *ashram* in Sevagram. Bhansali shook his head disapprovingly. "You cannot do evil with a fast," he said; "you can do good only. A man with a pure soul, sitting in the Himalayas, can affect the whole world."

Bhansali carries non-violence so far that years ago (he is now 49) when a girl with whom he had fallen in love rejected him, he went off to a Himalayan retreat and sewed his lips together lest in his pain and anger he would say something unkind about the girl. It was fitting to find such a man in Gandhi's *ashram*.

As you see, there are forces in Hindudom which do not exist in our world. Gandhi once said to his English friend and biographer, C. F. Andrews, "India is a country of nonsense." That was apropos of *swadeshi,* the Mahatma's campaign to turn the clock back many hundreds of years and make every Indian village into a self-contained unit. It was economic nonsense, as Gandhi knew, but he felt it would work in India. Anything seems possible in that country.

If Lewis Carroll and Edwin Lear had been newspapermen they might have felt at home in India, but they weren't. Rudyard Kipling was very much of a journalist, but he has Lord Dufferin say to his successor, Lord Lansdowne, in "One Viceroy Resigns":

> "You'll never plumb the Oriental mind,
> And if you did it isn't worth the toil."

That did not stop Kipling from trying all his life, with varying success, but let us remember that he was the one who said, "Oh, East is East, and West is West, and never the twain shall meet."

In good American parlance, Kipling "said a mouthful." Trying to explain the Indian—and particularly the Hindu—mind in terms of Western thought is often like attempting to describe the fourth dimension. All one can do is postulate it, as mathematicians and philosophers sometimes do with the fourth dimension.

Often I have sat in hotels, or train compartments or clubs, talking to Indian graduates of Oxford, Cambridge, or Harvard, and been lulled into the belief that these people talk my language, wear the same clothes, play better tennis than I do, read the same books, and therefore they must think as I do. But they do not, at all, and they never will. I might add that there is no reason why they should. This is in no sense an effort to demonstrate that Indians think crookedly and we think straight, or that our standards are moral and those of the Indians are immoral. I am only attempting to point out why "the twain"— British and Indian—have never met. The same goes for an American, of course, and for the thousands of American soldiers now in India. It is not our world.

All the arguments that centered around Gandhi's fast were proof that after two hundred years of rule, the British and the Indians do not understand each other. Gandhi and Lord Linlithgow, the Viceroy, exchanged a long series of letters without either discovering what the other was driving at. "I have failed to find your meaning," writes the Mahatma. "I am still, I fear, rather in the dark," answers the Viceroy. They both used the King's English, but it was worse than if Gandhi had used Sanskrit. At least, one could have the Sanskrit translated, but if one knew only Euclidean mathematics and a man argued that 2 and 2 equaled 5, the temptation would be to say like the Viceroy, "You are just a blackmailer, and I am not going to pay." But perhaps the man is not a blackmailer; perhaps in his system of mathematical thought 2 and 2 do equal 5.

For the British the answer is simple. They say: "Our world has always been run on the principle that 2 and 2 equal 4, that certain effects will follow logically from given causes, that justice, logic, and government are sciences, and that the world itself is a real, material, practical world. We cannot conceive of any other world, and, since we are running India, you must conform."

But remember that the instinct of the Indian is to consider the outer, material world as unreal. And politics in India is not the specialized system that we in the West deem it to be, or try to make it. There it is an inextricable part of the social and religious life—that life which has its roots 5,000 or 10,000 years deep. Gandhi's roots go down to ancient India; Nehru's do not—

and that, in a nutshell, explains why the Mahatma has an immense mass following and Nehru speaks for only a relatively small, enlightened, politically conscious element of the Hindu community.

It also, in part, explains why the hard-headed, practical British have no roots in India. They work—for the most part honestly and sincerely, and self-sacrificingly in many cases—and then they go home and live on their pensions. They never become a part of India. They never live like Indians; their Indian friends are found among those who follow, or are willing to accept, the Western style of living, and who speak English to boot. In his work the British will talk Hindustani or Urdu or the local language, but the language of society must be English.

Between Indian and Englishman is a misty no-man's land that never can be crossed. So often the Britisher has said: "See what fine citizens my system of education has developed! See how well our parliamentary government has worked! See how incorruptible and fair our justice is! We will give to the Indians the benefits of these systems of education, government, and justice." So, for 150 or 200 years the British have earnestly worked to apply their principles to India. And even now, so few of them are willing to admit that what is food for Englishmen is poison for Indians!

Let us look at the system of administering justice, for instance. What the British want, and have tried to establish, is a precise body of law, carefully written down, and administered by incorruptible judges who will decide each case strictly in accordance with the letter of the law, regardless of any ulterior factors or the standing of the parties involved. British judges in India dispense justice in exactly that fashion. "The law defines what is right and what is wrong, what is a crime and what is not. Obey the law!"

But that is not the sort of justice Indians want or have known in the past. If incorruptibility means decisions in their favor, they want it, of course, but that is a question of particular cases or individuals, and I am arguing—or they are arguing—in general. On all communal questions, of course, only the British can render impartial justice at the moment. Also, with the present set-up, the poverty-stricken peasant is more likely to get justice from the Britisher than from his own people working through the British-made system of justice. However, the cultivator does get justice of a sort within his caste, and in many of the Princely States he will get it from the ruler—just that sort of personal, human justice which he understands and wants.

And there we have touched the heart of the question, not only in the judicial system, but throughout the whole structure of life and government in British India and the States. The Indian wants justice to be rendered loosely, according to the merits of the individual case, not according to the strict reading of the law. It always infuriates Indians to say so, but it is true that they have different standards of honesty and morality from ours. That is natural for races which have entirely different outlooks upon life, and it is not a reproach to say it. There you have one of the subtle but profoundly important ways in which Indianization of the government would permit more suitable and satisfactory rule in India, more understanding and elasticity, more adaptability to the people.

"India is being ruled by a complicated machine," Rabindranath Tagore wrote in 1930. "The mechanics who drive it have a long training in power, but no tradition of human sympathy, which is superfluous in a workshop. They are incapable of understanding the living India, owing to the natural mentality of bureaucracy, which simplifies its task and manages an alien race from a distance through various switches and handles and wheels and hardly ever through human touch."

That is one of the chief complaints which Indians have against the British, and it is all tied up with the unbridgeable gap between East and West. Indians with experience in statesmanship and government have no illusions about it. They do not claim that if or when the British quit India, the government which follows will be more efficient; they know, in fact, that it will be less so, but it will be nearer to the heart's desire of the Indian people—and, after all, that is a good test for any government.

It is a commonplace to say that these people were highly

civilized at a time when the British—and all of us, for that matter—were savages in forests and caves. The British set their modern machines of administration, industry, and society upon this immense accumulation of past millennia and, in a fashion, they work. But they do not *belong,* and they do not really set all that accumulation into motion. It exists beneath and apart from them in a world of its own which the British can never touch and only dimly understand.

How can a Britisher (or an American) understand the sacredness of the cow, the influence of gems, transmigration, astrology, "the religious use of politics" (to cite Gandhi)? Yet these are fundamentals in the daily life of every Hindu.

Consider that extraordinary institution, the sacred cow. Try to tell your children that the placid creature which once jumped over the moon and now gives them fresh milk should be worshiped. But we all have that background, so far as the cow is concerned—a most inelegant animal, somewhat ridiculous, useful and good. But sacred!

"The cow is a poem of pity," says Gandhi; "cow protection to me is one of the most wonderful phenomena in all human evolution." Dogs are considered vile. No one will kill them, because of the religious prohibition of taking life, but the Indians will maltreat them and let them become mangy or starve to death. It appears that they have earned that fate from sins committed in previous incarnations.

I told you about the Brahmin in Mysore who was surprised when I suggested that it would be more merciful to put cows out of their misery when they grew old than to keep them on a reservation. "Would you put human beings to death when they become old?" he asked. Grant his premise, and he is both logical and right. Grant mine, which is that there is a world of difference between a human being and a cow, and therefore the analogy is incorrect—and he is both wrong and illogical. But that happened to be India, not the United States, so I was wrong.

Jains will tenderly care for the vermin on their bodies, for it is against their religion to take any life whatever. Sir Hukumchand Swarupchand, merchant prince of Indore and a devout

Jain, built himself a fabulous palace and in it he placed a fabulous bed, yards and yards in size, for his Buddha-like body. Every night a servant lies down on the bed for a half hour or more, so that he may attract to himself any insects that may be there, or, if it be fated, kill them in rolling from side to side. Then Sir Hukumchand gets into bed; his mosquito nets are carefully tucked around him, and he goes peacefully to sleep in the knowledge that for one night, at least, he will not take a life.

It is all very touching, but let us look further into the matter. Gandhi admits, "I do not know that the condition of the cattle in any other part of the world is so bad as in unhappy India." This is putting it mildly. Dr. Sam Higginbottom, American Presbyterian missionary and founder of the model American Agricultural Institute in Allahabad, who is our idea of a mahatma, or great soul, said to me that forty years of observation had convinced him that Indians are, of all the world's peoples, the most cruel to animals. Once, in Calcutta, he took the trouble to count the bullocks that passed during a certain period of the day. Ninety-eight per cent of them had their tails disjointed, for the owners twist the tails, with the delicate and concentrated nerve centers, in order to make the bullocks obey them.

If I, or anyone else, could explain the logical process which leads the Hindu to believe that animals have souls and the cow, among other animals, is sacred, and at the same time leads him to maltreat those animals, we would have the key to the Indian mind, and we would not have to say that East and West can never meet.

The ability of educated Indians to accept contradictions and inconsistencies is extraordinary. The most consistent characteristic of the Hindu, Dr. Higginbottom once remarked, is his inconsistency. Even Lord Ronaldshay (now Lord Zetland) former Governor of Bengal, lover of India and profound student of its philosophy and life, had to write of "a certain inconsistency or something which is better described, perhaps, as an immense capacity for remaining unaffected by inconsistency of thought and action—a characteristic which, it may be observed incidentally, has proved a constant source of bewilderment and embarrassment to those engaged in the task of administration in India."

This characteristic runs through every phase of life. There is non-violence, on the one hand, a natural trait of the Hindu, but undoubtedly more murders are committed in India than in any other country, even on a percentage, per capita basis. If one wants to commit a murder and get away with it, India is the place. By no means all the murders, let me say in passing, get into the official statistics, so let no one quote them against me, although they are bad enough. I visited many country districts throughout India, and I could write a chapter as long as this, entirely about crime. It would give the false impression, however, that the Indian is a criminal, which of course he is not. Katherine Mayo's book, *Mother India*, made a similar mistake.

Here, what I am driving at is simply that nothing could be further from the truth than to think of the Indian as a mild, inoffensive creature. You go to a village in the Punjab, or the Central Provinces, or eastern United Provinces, and it appears peaceful, almost idyllic. Then you inquire into conditions there; you talk to police officials; look up the records, listen—even though at second hand—to their complaints and worries; and you realize that mixed with many splendid features is a residue of hatred, fear, rivalry, and the oppression of the Untouchables and other low-castes by the Brahmins and *bania*—moneylenders or merchants. Sex "rears its ugly head" with a violence that is often startling.

I can give you a brief example of what I mean by the clash of Eastern and Western logic in the villages:

Mrs. Higginbottom, whose work among the villagers around Allahabad, and especially among the lepers, is one of the purest pages of mission work in India, told me how she had a simple, model house built in a village, and set about trying to persuade the villagers to copy it. They replied that it cost too much and that it was a better investment to buy jewelry for their wives. As they have no vaults or locks on their houses, this jewelry has to be worn. One day, as Mrs. Higginbottom came to the village, she found the inhabitants in a turmoil. A woman had

had her throat cut, and 175 rupees' worth of silver anklets and bracelets torn off her body.

"Why do you put your money in these jewels?" Mrs. Higginbottom asked the men. "You see what it leads to."

"Our wives will run away if we don't," they answered.

"Don't they sometimes run away with the jewels?" Mrs. Higginbottom asked.

"Yes, they do."

"Well, they couldn't run away with a model house such as this."

To me that was good, sound logic. But did the villagers spend their money on model houses? The answer is No. For thousands of years they and their ancestors had bought jewelry for their wives and had lived in filthy, disease-ridden houses. Here is a form of logic, too, the sort of logic that Indians understand. It may be less sensible, but it is human.

When Gandhi gets one of his inspirations and does something like his famous fast to "capacity" in February, 1943, the Hindu nods his head wisely. "Of course, mahatmas always get these intuitive flashes from the eternal, all-pervading soul of Brahman. We understand perfectly."

But Lord Linlithgow, and the rest of us, can only throw up our hands in defeat, and say with good old Samuel Johnson, who was expatiating on the "inward light":

"If a man pretends to a principle of action of which I can know nothing, how can I tell what that person may be prompted to do? When a person professes to be governed by a written, ascertained law, I can then know where to find him."

The trouble is that Indians do not "profess to be governed by a written, ascertained law." Moreover, they do not want to be. And why should they, if they do not want to be? India is India, not England or the United States as I remarked before. India for the Indians. The East for the East. Our wisdom lies in recognizing that "never the twain shall meet."

However, we must avoid the temptation to "shake well and throw out the window." You cannot get rid of India so easily as that—even the British cannot. Kipling was thinking of the personal equation, and viewing it from that angle, he was right. The Occidental and the Oriental will never understand each other, never feel alike, or think alike about the same things. The West can never play Jonathan to the East's David, for there will always be a no-man's land in the realm of the spirit.

But there is another aspect of the problem, which can be summed up in the word "Westernization." As the world becomes smaller, and global wars turn it into a ball of fire, East and West are thrown together. It is like mixing oil and water, you can never get a proper emulsion, but you keep shaking them hard enough and they do mix, after a fashion.

Anyway, there is no longer any choice. Isolation is a figment of some American Congressmen's imaginations. What it amounts to is that the East has not been able to keep the West out, so it has had, after a fashion, to learn to work and fight as we do, to co-operate or go under. Japan dimly realized something of the sort a century ago, but she drew from the West only lessons of materialism that have proved like dangerous toys in the hands of a vicious child. However, we of the West who invented Fascism and Nazism are not, at least collectively, in a position to throw stones, but it is a perversion of Westernization to think that all it means is industrialization and modern armaments.

In India, at the turn of the century and later, Indians were taught by scholars and holy men like Swami Vivekananda that their own cultural heritage was superior to that of the West, and that it was for the materialistic West to learn from the spiritual East. It would be hard to find a more seductive or mis-leading generalization, but it is one still current in India, and it plays its part in hampering the meeting of East and West. Gandhi himself is, in fact, an outstanding example of the Indian who feels that almost everything Western is materialistic and bad for India, which must turn back to its simple, ancient customs and its Hindu culture. Yet Gandhi himself owes much to Western education and thought, and the Congress movement headed by him stands for a form of Western democratization and nationalism which is foreign to Indian culture and traditions.

It is a typical case of mixing oil and water, but such attempts are now inevitable, and arguments about the relative merits of Eastern and Western culture are beside the point. And if Western culture seems materialistic to Orientals, it is simply because they know it only in terms of industrialization, railways, commerce, and political systems which are utilitarian and not religious in basis. That is what they mean by Westernization, and it is true that such are the bases on which West and East are meeting.

Modern transportation, industrialization, nationalism, trade unionism, freedom of the press and speech—these are more or less valued gifts of the West to India.

Democracy as we understand it is another importation from the West, although it does not follow that because it is the best political system for England it is necessarily suitable or desirable for India. Indeed, Pandit Motilal Nehru, Jawaharlal's father, once said in the Legislative Assembly that he did not want "a system that is not native to India." He did not say which system he would like, but one could be malicious and point out that the only one which has been native to India is the autocratic ruler.

The Indians would like to have their own national language, but it is more than ever obvious, now that communalism has divided the country so sharply, that the only *lingua franca* is English. When a Punjabi talks to a Madrasi, or a Bombay merchant to a Calcutta client, he must talk in English. Some day it may be different, and it should be different, for no educator will deny that one of the fundamental errors of Indian education in the past hundred years has been its use of English and the English school system, even though the Indians themselves demanded it. The modern literature and philosophy of India have a strong British tinge, and one wonders if it will ever disappear.

However, Western-educated India (Lord Zetland called it "Indo-Anglia") is a tiny minority in a vast population whose literacy, even in Indian languages, is only 12.17 per cent. It is customary for Indian nationalists to blame the British for this, but no student of India, thinking objectively, can escape the conclusion that whether India is run by the British or by Indians, it is going to take generations and colossal sums of money to bring literacy to the villages. The magnitude and the complications of the problem, involved as it is with caste, religion, poverty, lack of teachers, and staggering cost, are such as to doom the Indian masses to a large degree of illiteracy, for many years. The very advanced State of Mysore, which is far ahead of the average of British India in social and governmental affairs, spends 13 per cent of its budget on education, yet literacy is only slightly above 10 per cent.

In considering India's problems, one must acquire some of the patience of the East. And, above all, let us not be "superior." In that lies another, and an ugly reason why the twain never meet. British "superiority" is something to be reckoned with anywhere in the world, since they exercise it against all and sundry, including Americans. As between white men it is not to be taken seriously, since it is a mixture of reserve, aloofness, shyness, insularism, abrupt and impersonal manners. It is a surface phenomenon, a defense mechanism which is not fundamental, and is easy to break down. But toward the Indian one often finds the same attitude that a Southerner in the United States takes toward the Negro. For instance, in New Delhi, it is *infra dig* to ride in buses and streetcars, because Indians use them. Sometimes, as with our Southerners, this means treating the Indians with understanding, kindliness—and condescension.

There is no feeling of equality. However, it is curious to think that the Indian, who minutely classifies his own people into inferior and superior grades, and even places some 60,000,000 of them beyond the pale, should be so militantly sensitive about what he feels to be the attitude of superiority of the Westerner.

He has a genuine grievance, but there are motes in his eyes as well as beams in the British. If many of the diehard Britishers have to get over their feeling of superiority, it is equally true that Indians must outgrow their feeling of inferiority. Americans going to India without any idea of superiority over Indians are constantly embarrassed by the subservient attitude they meet with. Hindus, especially, often assume that feeling of inferiority against the wishes of the white man. Many, many times in India I was irritated and even disgusted by Indians whom I wanted to feel—as I felt they were—my equals in every respect; but it was they who were subservient, although, for all I know, they may have complained of my air of superiority.

Lord Linlithgow, Viceroy while I was there, evidently had an unhappy faculty of making Indians feel that he was condescending and looking down on them. Knowing the man as I came to know him, I feel sure it was unintentional and, more than anything else, an inability to assume a kindly and gracious air. Still, he often irritated the Indians with whom he came in contact, partly, no doubt, just by being British, and partly by his complete assurance, which left no room for bargaining or the subtleties of argument. I remember seeing, on two different occasions, important Indian officials immediately after they had come from the Viceroy's office, and both times they were furious.

To be sure, viceroyalty in India is a very grand thing. When Edward, then Prince of Wales, visited India in 1921 and lived for a little while in the Viceroy's House, he is supposed to have said, "At last I have seen how royalty lives!"

The ceremony and the wealth of some of the maharajas, also, are proverbial, so just as a corrective and a relief from more serious affairs, come with me to Hyderabad where the richest and strangest man in the world rules over a State as large as Italy with a population of more than 14,000,000. It is a genuinely feudal survival, with a large element of that Moslem aristocracy who are descendants of the Mogul conquerors. The noblemen own one third of the land and are not taxed, while the Nizam's vast holdings are also tax free. It is one of those States where one finds extremes of opulence and poverty, but since 87 per cent of the population is Hindu of a passive, fatalistic type there is much misery but no active discontent.

No miser in history has ever been so favored by destiny as the Nizam. He is the fulfillment of the dream of all misers since the world began. Yet, the curse being what it is, even his mountains of jewels and gold leave the craving unsatisfied.

He received me in his small, dilapidated house in the center of Hyderabad City, and apologized for keeping me waiting for only a minute or two. As we sat down I looked at him eagerly, having heard many stories of the untidy way in which he dressed. His clothes were, indeed, very ordinary and badly rumpled, his fez was worn and soiled around the rim, but his shoes were a bright, shiny new yellow. Afterward I was told that he must have put them on in my honor, and the word went around the salons of Hyderabad. As a matter of fact, no one could remember when the Nizam had given an interview to a newspaper correspondent, but I had the impression, after he questioned me, that he did not realize who I was or what he was doing. My office, incidentally, which did not realize what a journalistic rarity it had, hacked the piece in two, and put it at the end of a dull story about Hyderabad State.

His Exalted Highness Nawab Sir Mir Osman Ali Khan Bahadur Asaf Jah VII, Nizam of Hyderabad and Berar, possesses something like $1,200,000,000 worth of jewels, but he did not wear even a ring on the day that I saw him. Nevertheless, it was impossible, as we talked of Hyderabad State and the future of India, not to be conscious that before me was one of the most extraordinary men in the world, a man whose power, riches, and eccentricities will be remembered throughout India's history.

As a boy, he and his brother used to play with three big bags of marbles, just as boys have always done, but their marbles were of emeralds, rubies, and uncut diamonds. The paperweight on his father's desk was the largest uncut diamond in the world. These jewels were an infinitesimal part of a collection which has been accumulating since the days of the Mogul emperors. Part of it is loot from Mysore. The Nizam, in recent years, has been adding dozens and dozens of the finest pearls, emeralds, and diamonds to be found in India. The estimate of value which I gave is not exaggerated, but it is arbitrary, for there are unique and world-famous items which are literally priceless, such as the Jacob diamond, the third or fourth largest in the world, a cup of a single flawless blue sapphire, and a snuff box whose cover is a huge, perfect emerald.

The Nizam takes only 50,000 rupees (the rupee is worth about three to the American dollar) from the State budget, but his privy purse from his vast landholdings amounts to at least 15,-000,000 rupees. He has spent very little of this, for he lives in extremely modest style, so it goes into jewels and great heaps of gold. When it is considered that he inherited great wealth and has been on the *gadi* for thirty-three years, it is easy to see why Indians laugh when Americans list him only third or fourth among the richest men in the world. There probably never has been such an accumulation of wealth in the hands of one man since the beginning of time.

It was all around us as we talked, in the cellars and rooms of the villa which he calls "King Kothi." The house was given to him by his father, and it was once the home of a private citizen. The owner had defaulted on his taxes, so the villa was expropriated and the late Nizam gave it to his son, then a young man. The owner's initials were "K.K.," and all the linens and silverware were so marked, so the future Nizam asked his tutor what they should call the place. The tutor, an Englishman, as a joke said: "King Kothi" (*kothi* means "house" in Urdu), and the name stuck. The Nizam, of course, has a number of really magnificent palaces, but he uses them only on state occasions. In the same way he has Rolls-Royces and similar automobiles, but he himself uses one ordinary car until it nearly falls apart like the one horse shay. At first he had a Model-T Ford, which became legendary as the years passed. When I was there he was using the third of the line, a three-year-old Humber, which had followed a Chevrolet.

Thousands of his subjects have more pretentious houses than "King Kothi," but pretentiousness is the last vice of which the Nizam of Hyderabad can be accused. He sat in front of me almost timidly (at least, he gave me that impression), a little, old man, with a droopy, stained mustache and black, broken teeth. He is said to suffer terribly from pyorrhea, but will have no other treatment than his Unani doctors give him, the Moslem system of medicine I have described. Probably because of his teeth, it was hard to understand him, especially as he is not one of the English-educated rulers and speaks English with a little difficulty and a slight accent.

I was warned not to refer in any way to his riches. Few persons have ever seen any of his jewels, and he never wears any, even on state occasions. They are his private property, to see, handle and enjoy, and it has nothing to do, so to speak, with the Nizam, ruler of the largest State in India, the last surviving vestige of the vast Mogul empire.

In this ruler one finds a shrewd, intelligent, hard-working prince, keenly interested in everything that is happening and well informed on world affairs.

"Thank God the tide of war has changed," he said, and it must have been genuine fervor, for Hyderabad contributed much to the war effort and maintained its close, cordial links to the British paramount power. Whenever I brought up the question of the future of India and the States, the Nizam returned to that aspect of paramountcy. The British are responsible for his state, direct his policies, and will settle the destiny of India, he said. Like the Maharaja of Mysore, whom I had seen a few weeks before, he was pessimistic and worried about the future, seeing a grave danger of chaos and civil war.

Being a Moslem, and the ruler of an overwhelmingly Hindu State, I asked him what he thought of Pakistan, Jinnah's scheme for a separate Muslim nation. "We are outside of that current," he replied. "It does not really concern us. We go our own way. Haven't you talked to Jinnah about it?" I told him I had, often, and that Jinnah proposed three Indias—Moslem, Hindu and Indian India. He nodded in emphatic approval, but said, "Not Indian India, Princely India." For this little, bedraggled old man is really very much the prince and very conscious of his position as India's first and most important ruler, who alone among princes bears the title, "His Exalted Highness." His mountains of jewels and gold, like the poems he writes in Persian and Urdu, are something apart, something that makes him as typically Indian as Gandhi, who incidentally started his 21-day fast to capacity on the day I saw the Nizam, February 10, 1943.

The interview ended in a fashion characteristic of the extraordinary man who granted it. It was he, the Nizam of Hyderabad and Berar, who said to me, nodding his head toward his office in the next room, "May I take my leave now?"

The State, which is larger than England and Scotland together, was a good object lesson in the importance and detachment of the Princely States, which occupy about two fifths of the territory and have more than a quarter of the population of India. Nobody cared there whether Gandhi fasted or not. Gandhi and the Congress, Jinnah and the Moslem League primarily concern British India—and it will be that way as long as the British remain the paramount power.

Hyderabad is a meeting place of virtually all the races, languages, religions, and cultures of India, situated as it is almost in the center of the continent. But it is still a feudal State, with its Mohammedan noblemen and its ruler who is a direct descendant of a Mogul Emperor's Viceroy. As feudal lords, the aristocrats even have retainers.

The population, as I said before, is nearly nine tenths Hindu, which means that there cannot be any representative government without a revolution. At the same time, the Nizam is careful not to antagonize and arouse his Hindu subjects, and so has one of the lightest taxation systems in the world. That means a ridiculously small budget of 110,000,000 rupees, and this, in turn, means little money for education, hospitals, roads, and irrigation. By not educating his subjects, the Nizam indirectly sees to it that they do not acquire political consciousness, which could be dangerous for him.

So it is a backward state, and, like so many others, it is lax, inefficient, burdened by the weight of inertia, privilege and conservativeness. Life moves slowly in old, Princely India. There are no less than 165 holidays annually in Hyderabad, including Queen Victoria's birthday.

The situation seemed ideal for Congress agitation, and the Party did its best. During the period of Congress rule in the provinces, from 1937 to 1939, they sent in thousands of agitators and financed the *Arya Samajists,* a Hindu communal organization seeking a Hindu *raj*, but they failed to do anything except gradually to force the opening of more administrative posts to Hindus. What they did do there, as in many, if not most states, was to frighten the ruling classes to such an extent that any hope of achieving the federation planned by the Act of 1935 has been put off indefinitely, if not permanently. As things stand at the time of writing, no one seems to want it. All the rulers I questioned about it were opposed to federation, while the extreme Congress stand is to abolish the States altogether. Jinnah cagily says that the Princely States do not interest him.

As far as Hyderabad is concerned, the British are keeping a firm grip. Britishers hold a number of key positions in the State, and Sir Arthur Lothian, the Resident, wields more power than the resident in any of the other States I visited. Hyderabad is geographically vulnerable, for it has politically agitated Bombay and Central Provinces on its borders, but it seems destined to carry on.

Many people are, rather ghoulishly, waiting for the old Nizam to die so they can see the extraordinary display that is expected to be made of his incredible wealth. Miserliness is not hereditary in the family. The Prince of Berar knows how to spend money, but he and his brother are kept on small allowances by their father. They are both married to beautiful Turkish princesses— the Prince of Berar to the daughter of the last Caliph, an intelligent and charming woman.

There are innumerable other children, but they do not count, as they are not in line for the throne. I use the word "innumerable" advisedly. That delightful personage, the Maharani of Cooch Behar, told me once of going to dinner at the Nizam's palace in New Delhi, and of her host asking to see the ring she was wearing. As a connoisseur he appreciated it, asked how much it cost, and passed it around for others to admire. Then he said, "You should not spend your money on such trinkets."

"I have only two children," the Maharani replied, "and money to spare. How many children have you, Your Exalted Highness?"

The Nizam thought for a while, shook his head dubiously, and replied, "I can't say exactly, but I will find out and let you know tomorrow."

"But don't you see your children?" she asked.

"Oh, yes, I see them running around the grounds. I knew how many there were a few months ago, but I cannot say how many there are now."

The next morning he told her the correct total—apparently several dozen.

"Well, you see, Your Exalted Highness," she said, "I have only two."

"You are right," the Nizam replied; "there is something in that."

On May 10, 1943, the newspapers carried an item telling of the birth of another son to one of the Nizam's wives. As a Moslem he is entitled to four wives, although his children need not be limited to the four.

I once heard, from an exalted source, a story, about the present Nizam's grandfather, which would indicate that an eye for women runs in the family. He was leading a ceremonial procession through the streets of Hyderabad on his richly panoplied elephant, with other State elephants trailing behind and hundreds of officials and subjects on foot. In a window he saw a gleaming eye and a pretty hand, so he stopped his elephant, climbed down and entered the house. It was late morning. Lunchtime passed, the afternoon, dinner time, the evening, then the night. At ten o'clock the next morning the Nizam walked out of the house, climbed up on his elephant, and the procession continued. He did not say a word, and neither did anyone else.

Such, I may also say, is life in Old India.

The Gordian Knot

I AM, of course, picking and choosing the things I am writing about India. Otherwise there would be a whole book on India, but it is also because I want you to know those factors and features of the Indian scene which shaped my ideas on that formidable subject, just as I feel they should contribute to shaping yours. I had preconceived ideas, and even hopes, about India which were reshaped by investigations on the scene. It was not my attitude toward the fundamentals of liberalism and democracy that changed; it was simply that the facts did not fit the ideas or, especially, the practical, common-sense necessities of any working conception of freedom and democracy as I knew them.

I am a firm believer in the doctrine of the possible in politics and international affairs. I believe, for instance, that any nation of 400,000,000 souls, possessing a sincere, capable, patriotic ruling class (and India has that) is entitled to freedom, but I cannot jump from that premise to the apparently logical conclusion that freedom should be granted immediately to Indians. There are too many other factors which enter the picture—undesirable factors which temporarily counterbalance and even overwhelm the good, and which must be taken into account.

Do not think that I am now espousing the British viewpoint in its entirety, for the British go much too far in the other direction and have been derelict in their duty of preparing and providing India with the possibilities of achieving independence.

I have already told you how quickly I discovered the contradictions, the incompatibilities, the amazing complications of the Indian story. You will never get from me any simplification. Actually, my Indian sojourn was, in effect, a gradual progression from the simple ideas held in so-called liberal circles in America to a greater and greater complexity.

It does not follow that one should have no opinions, or that there are not innumerable facets of the Indian gem which are quite clear. For example, the political situation, which is all-important, is capable of a good deal of understanding.

When I arrived in Karachi on August 23, 1942, my simplicity was still complete. I saw Sir Hugh Dow, the Governor of the Province of Sind, and when he told me that Congress was of no importance in Sind, that Gandhi was an opportunist, that Nehru had no solution for the crisis, that the British would soon suppress the agitation, which was then at its height following the arrest of the Congress leaders, I discounted everything he said. I preferred, instead, to believe what the Congressite premier, Khan Bahadur Allah Bakhsh and other Congress followers in Karachi told me—which was exactly what I had been told in New York.

In Delhi it was the same. Sir Reginald Maxwell, Home Member and Vice-President of the Viceroy's Council, was the first to tell me that it was wrong to think (as Americans did) that Congress was synonymous with India. Most Indians did not care who ruled them so long as they were left in peace, he said. I felt certain he was quite wrong. To be sure, he told me other things, such as that Congress rule in the provinces from September, 1937, to December, 1939, was "appalling," which proved to be misinformation, but in those days I could not have any opinions based on knowledge of my own.

One of the first things I learned was that the Indians, on the whole, did not trust the British, and did not for a moment believe their pledges to grant dominion status to India after the war. This still remains one of the permanently crippling factors of the Indian situation. The feeling worked both ways, of course, for the British did not trust the Indians who would have taken power. The British said: "Help us win the war, and then we will grant you independence." The Indians said: "Grant us independence, and we will help you win the war." Gandhi said to Jinnah: "Let us drive the British out, and then we will settle our communal problem." Jinnah replied: "First settle our communal problem by giving us Pakistan, and then together we shall drive the British out."

There never seemed to be any middle ground. Partisanship, one-sidedness, distrust, were all-absorbing. Everyone seemed to have blinkers on, and a poor outsider was torn in all directions, especially a poor American who was continually being told by Indians that the United States must intervene to force the British to grant independence, and by the British to mind our own business because we did not know what we were talking about. Both the Viceroy, Lord Linlithgow, and Marshal Wavell, then commander of the Allies' forces in India, now Viceroy, said as much to me, in no uncertain terms, in my first week in New Delhi.

I realized later that I was being very naive with various responses that I thought were logical. One of my early talks on politics was with Dr. Shyamaprasad Mookerjee, Working President of the Hindu *Mahasabha,* the intransigent Hindu political party which is the counterpart of the Moslem League. He referred to one variation of a vicious circle. Hindus say, "We cannot settle the communal problem unless you go." The British say, "We cannot go unless you settle the Moslem problem." I said: "Since you feel that the British are deliberately profiting by the communal problem, you can be sure they will do nothing about it. Then, if you are all agreed that you want the British to go, why can't you be patriotic enough to reach an agreement somehow, at least until the British do go?"

That was an example of over-simplification, among other things, as well as an instance of preaching conciliation in a situation which admitted no possibility of it. Being a moderate, I was continually critical of the fact that there was no moderation in India, which was a different attitude from the one I took in Spain. There I felt the nobility and necessity of intransigeance in a great cause; here I believed it was misguided and harmful to the Indian cause—and, as I keep repeating, I feel that political activity must be keyed to the possible and practical.

It seemed to me a tragedy that India's great moderates—and

they were some of the finest characters in the country, men like C. R. Rajagopalachari, Sir Tej Bahadur Sapru, M. S. Aney, Sir Mirza Ismail, Sir C. P. Ramaswami Ayyer, the late Sikander Hyat Khan—should have been ignored or abused while extremists alone could obtain a hearing and a following. Sometimes a situation demands a clean-cut, all-or-nothing solution, as in Spain. But sometimes it is the part of wisdom to accept 50 per cent when you cannot get 100 per cent, and India, it seems to me, has been in that situation for some years. I have no doubt whatever that if Gandhi had not continually insisted on 100 per cent; if he had taken what he could get, given the Muslims a share of government in the provinces during Congress rule, accepted the Cripps plan, permitted men like Jawaharlal Nehru to help the war effort, India would now have 75 per cent of her independence, and the communal problem would be much less acute. Intransigeance has merely stiffened the British attitude and played into the hands of Jinnah.

Of course, this, too, is a form of *naïveté*. It is asking Gandhi not to be Gandhi, the Hindu not to be a Hindu, or the Moslem a Moslem. Gandhi was responding to all the irresistible impulses of the Hindu character. He can no more understand the British than they can him. To help the war effort runs contrary to his deeply felt pacifism. To grant places to anti-Congress Muslims does not fit into a scheme of autocracy and patronage which is oriental at heart, although it touches our Western totalitarianism. Patronage is as deep-rooted as anything in India, for its basis is the family, which is the heart of social life. When an Indian gets into the Civil Service he is expected to support his whole family and get jobs for them. In a Hindu business it is rare to find Moslems, and vice versa. If a Brahmin is appointed to an office, he will hire Brahmins to work with him. It is inevitable that this profound tradition should spill over into politics.

It was the same with the 100-per cent "Quit India" policy of Gandhi. Logically and practically, it made no sense, since the British could not and would not quit India in the midst of a war, but if you recall that the Indians do not trust the British and, I might add, do not understand them, if you take into account the gulf between East and West, Gandhi's attitude is at least explicable, even if unwise and impractical.

I criticized the attitude—and still do—not only because it was impractical but because it was based on a falsehood. I had heard it again and again before going to India, and it was dinned in my ears innumerable times during my sojourn. Sir Sultan Ahmad, Law Member of the Viceroy's Council, and one of the first men to whom I talked in New Delhi, put it this way: "The Hindu people, down to the lowest villagers, are absolutely for ousting the British. It is not true that they do not care. They may not know anything about politics, but that is one thing which Gandhi and the Congress have put over."

That was a gross exaggeration, to say the least, as I discovered at first hand. I not only saw British and Indians living and working together harmoniously in villages in all parts of India, as they did in most places even during the disturbances of 1942, but also I found, among the villagers a complete indifference and ignorance regarding independence. It could not be any different, if one stopped to think. The villager is ground down to a very limited and miserable existence. He is illiterate, has no political consciousness (even Rajagopalachari admitted that to me), has no knowledge of India beyond his village, and is in no position to feel the oppression of British rule—so why should he be supposed to be anxious for the British to "quit India"?

Here, again, I must make it plain that this is no plea for the British to remain, and no attempt to excuse the ignorance and misery which makes the Indian villager apolitical. I am merely setting straight a record which ought never to have been falsified.

Is it not enough to say that virtually every politically conscious Indian wants independence? And that when Indians are made to feel the meaning of freedom, however dimly, they will then sincerely shout, "Quit India!"? There is a powerful case for Indian independence—after the war—yet it is rare to find Indians making it. They prefer, instead, such exaggerations as the claim that all Indians want the British to leave immediately, or that they all hate the British, are ardent followers of Congress or the

Moslem League, are capable of electing their political leaders by due democratic process.

The claims are made. Then an unbiased observer with the duty of describing what he sees goes to India and is forced, in the interests of truth, to shoot the picture full of holes. The result is that the Indian cause is harmed and (what matters infinitely less) the observer is accused of selling out to the British or, at best, is told that it was naive to expect anything different. And "look at Russia, where the ignorance was once as great and the politically conscious class as small as in India!"—which is begging the question, and an analogy more specious than accurate.

My idea of sense is what a Sikh villager in the Punjab said to me when I asked what he thought about freedom: "A belly filled with good food and a safe job. Otherwise we don't care who runs the government." To be sure, an Italian can—and does—say the same thing right now, which is simply a case of putting first things first, from the viewpoint of the man in the street. If an Indian can be made to feel that freedom will bring him those things, and a new dignity and pride as well, it would be different, but education has not reached that point in India.

Sometimes I would be told by a Moslem peasant that independence means "freedom from the Hindu raj"—or the opposite for that matter by Hindus in a Moslem province. In the jungles of the Central Provinces a Gondi tribesman showed me his ragged *dhoti*. "I paid 3 rupees for this two years ago," he said. "Now it would cost 8 or 10 rupees, which means that when this goes I shall have no clothes to wear." Many, many millions of Indians are saying the same thing now, and you can draw two conclusions for political argument. The British can say: "You see these people do not want independence. They want only food and clothing." But Indians can and do say: "You see how miserable these people are after 200 years of British rule. If India were free, we would see to it that they had enough to eat and wear."

Whether the British or any other government could do so is highly doubtful, to say the least, given the reasons for and the immensity of Indian poverty—but the argument is a good one and, naturally, it brings votes.

Learning about elections in India provided one of my disillusionments. Congress deserved to win in the 1937 elections because it was the legitimate representative of a majority of the Indians in British India (that part of the country exclusive of the Princely States) but the fact remains that it won because of good organization, plenty of money, Gandhi and his magic name, and shrewd, often misleading pledges.

When Congress was campaigning in the Tamil villages near Madras, the leaders promised an era of plenty to follow, with less taxation. S. Satyamurthi, member of the Madras legislature, made a speech to the cultivators in which he promised more rain, good crops, and no disease if they would vote for Congress— which they naturally did, since that was what they wanted. In Bilaspur and Raipur, Congress workers went around threatening the people with cholera if they did not vote for Gandhi and the "Yellow Box" in which they deposited their votes. That well-earned title of "mahatma," which means "great soul" or "saint," was enough in itself to swing the votes of the religious-minded peasants.

All of which was fair enough. It does not alter the fact that Congress deserved to win, but when one talks of elections and democracy in India, these are things to be kept in mind. Even in a Muslim province like the Northwest Frontier, whose politically conscious elements are now overwhelmingly Moslem League, Congress might still win because of its organization and money, and that result would be the reverse of democratic. On the whole, though, I would agree with what Rajagopalachari once told me, that many millions of villagers do know and trust Congress, and while they do not know what the concept of independence means nor can they conceive of India as a nation, they have faith if Congress tells them that they will be better off when the British leave India and they are free.

Hazlitt somewhere writes that "Defoe says that there were 100,000 stout country-fellows in his town ready to fight to the death against popery, without knowing whether popery was a man or a horse." All the same, things are often worth fighting for even if you do not know what they are, and independence is definitely one of those things.

On that basis, the Indians have all my sympathy, but when men like Nehru mislead me and others with statements about the desires of every villager for independence, it gives me a pain. I presume that Nehru, for one, fools himself, since I would be the last to deny the uprightness, sincerity, and patriotism of one of the greatest men modern India has produced, but that does not alter the fact that his picture of Congress in many respects fails to depict the reality. Perhaps one explanation lies in what I wrote previously about the inability of anyone to know India as a whole. Nehru knows really well only the United Provinces and Bihar Province, where he has lived and worked, and where Congress is strong.

Naturally, I spent much of my time trying to obtain a picture that would fit into whatever of the truth I could find. It was a great handicap not to have personal contacts with Gandhi, Nehru, and other important Congress leaders, all of whom were in jail when I arrived and who remained there *incomunicado*. However, there was no lack of unjailed spokesmen for Congress, and very important ones. I talked to many of Gandhi's close associates, and, among others, to the two sisters of Nehru. Throughout India men and women presented the Congress case authoritatively. And in addition there were the writings and speeches of Gandhi and Nehru, which I studied. Both are men of great and persuasive charm, and I am sure the appeal to my emotions would have been considerable had I met them, but I am not sure that the picture would have been made clearer by them than it was, let us say, after many earnest hours with Rajagopalachari, Aney, Birla, Devadas Gandhi (the Mahatma's son), Sapru, and Jayakar. I would, no doubt, have felt the Congress case more deeply and hence, perhaps, understood the Indian viewpoint a little better—emotionally if not rationally or logically—if I had talked with Gandhi and Nehru. But I think I was able to collect enough elements for judgment, despite the handicaps.

One of those handicaps was the ideas I brought to India. The first thing I learned on reaching Karachi was that Congress was very weak in Sind. Then I discovered that it was completely out of the picture in most of the Princely States, and not strong in any. As time passed, I learned from observation that it amounted to little or nothing in the Punjab, and that its hold on the Northwest Frontier Province had been precarious.

There were other elements which kept weakening the colors of the Congress picture, such as the knowledge that the enormous majority of Indian villagers, who constitute more than nine tenths of the population, was not at all interested in politics. One of the greatest revelations was the strength of Jinnah and the Moslem League, of which I had no inkling from the things I had heard and read in the United States.

And so it went, with this new knowledge naturally disappointing and annoying me since no one cares to be fooled. Fortunately, there was the incentive to refute some unfair British and Moslem League claims, which helped to keep the record straight.

On one subject I spent much time and patience, for it was of crucial importance—the period of so-called "Congress rule" in eight of the eleven provinces of British India from September, 1937, to December, 1939. It was on the basis of that period that Jinnah built most of his political following among Muslims and his effective propaganda among the masses. The story that he told is one of misrule, terrorism, oppression of the Mussulmans and interference with their religious observances. All that is pure nonsense, and likewise are the British charges of misrule and corruption.

With the possible exception of the Central Provinces, Congress rule was efficient and honest, firm and fair with the masses, and genuine efforts were made to better the conditions of the workers and the peasants. The organization tried terribly hard to make good, and put in some of their best men. Rajagopalachari's job as Premier of Madras Province was outstandingly meritorious.

But—and it is a very big "but"—Congress did run the show on purely totalitarian, one-party lines. It refused to form coalition governments, even in a region like the United Provinces, where the Mussulmans were politically and economically powerful. In fact, no Muslim got an official position unless he joined the Congress party. Gandhi sat back in Sevagram and pulled all the strings, and when the British took India into the war without consulting the Indians he ordered the provincial governments to resign, which they did on December 22, 1939. Whereupon the clever Jinnah proclaimed a "Deliverance Day" for the Moslems and made, from then on, wonderful political capital of it all.

That "one-party" aspect of Congress (and the Moslem League, for that matter) is one of the unpleasant features of Indian politics and one which bodes ill for the future. An attempt was made during those thirty-one months to make Congress the only political party in the country, and Congress showed it was not prepared to share power with minorities. Since then, the attitude has been corrected to conform to the reality and to face the inevitable, but the damage has been done.

As Guy Wint rightly pointed out, Congress is not so much a political party in our sense of the words, as it is a political mass movement. Loyalty goes to the organization, not to a parliament or legislative assembly such as the provinces had. The ministers were directed by "zonal dictators" who, in turn, were under the Congress Working Committee and that was controlled by Gandhi. When they resigned they still had their duly elected majorities, and the electorate did not ask, and presumably did not want them to resign.

Whatever can be said about Congress in this regard is equally true of the Moslem League under Jinnah, who got his political training as a loyal Congressite. That, too, is a totalitarian structure, and we must remember what Leopold von Ranke called "the tendency to despotic autocracy which Islam so peculiarly favors."

The reasons for this are deep and complicated, and they need no elaboration here. I mention the fact partly for clarification and partly to explain the disappointment that any liberal must feel on learning such facts.

I never, myself, felt any repugnance over learning that Congress was financed by the big *bania,* or Hindu industrialist elements. It surprised me, to be sure, as this is not one of the things which Congress propagandists or sympathizers could be expected to mention. But for a man from a country like ours, where big business men regularly contribute to the Democratic and the Republican campaign funds without our fearing any disastrous control from the donors, it is not logical to criticize India. Because the support of men like G. D. Birla, the great textile magnate, is not entirely disinterested does not necessarily mean lack of sincerity or patriotism on their part. I saw a good deal of Birla, and always felt that he was sincere. Moreover, those *banias* and *marwaris* were not favored during the period of Congress rule, and they have no guarantee that it would be any different in an independent, Congress-ruled India.

It is significant that the real Congress stronghold is Bombay, where industry is dominated by the Indians. That great city always provided an excellent antidote for the belief that the Congress movement had been forgotten or seriously undermined because the Government suppressed the civil-disobedience campaign and arrested the Congress leaders. Bombay Province is overwhelmingly Congress, as even highly placed Britishers have always admitted.

In Madras I found Congress dominated by the Brahmins, with the Tamil and Telugu villagers almost forgetting that they had voted for "Gandhi and the Yellow Box" in 1937. And in Delhi, Allahabad, and some other cities I felt uneasy about the virtual monopoly which lawyers had over the movement. In fact, lawyers dominate the Moslem League also, and politics in general, to a much greater extent than in the United States. Of them, one who suffered for eleven months can say, with heartfelt emotion—and with a few honorable exceptions—that they conform to Jefferson's description of their (and his) profession: "To question everything, yield nothing, and talk by the hour."

But Bombay is genuinely impressive—politically conscious, aggressive and competent, and its sentiment is overwhelmingly Congress. No one can escape from one central fact, that (as a high British authority put it to me) "every Hindu is at heart with Congress." It represents the vast majority of politically conscious Hindus in British India, and when the lid is lifted it will again lead and dominate that element in India.

So when Congress, under Gandhi's direction, began to line up against support of the war effort and in favor of immediate independence, the necessity for the British to move quickly and effectively was obvious—to all but the Hindus, who appear to have been caught by surprise. From the viewpoint of the war, it is hard to see how anyone could blame the British, but, as a matter of fact, Congress sympathizers took the line that the best way to line up India behind the United Nations was to grant the Congress demands.

Nothing which has happened since the civil-disobedience campaign began in August, 1942, bears out that contention. I myself was deluded for a long while, and felt very dubious when leaders like Wavell said they were getting all the soldiers they could possibly use and that war production (after the first flurry of strikes and sabotage) was satisfactory. However, investigation on my many trips, and above all the events themselves, proved the British were right. They gambled on the Japanese not attacking India during the crucial period of unrest, and they won that gamble. Gandhi thought that the British would lose the war, but he guessed wrongly—as Mussolini did upon another occasion.

Parts of India still remain ignorant of the fact that there has been a World War, even though it has affected their lives in the prices of food and cloth. Other parts, like the Punjab, contributed heavily in men to the war effort and were keenly war-conscious. On the whole, India made a very great contribution, for which she deserves reward. Unfortunately, as Mrs. Vijaya Lakshmi Pandi (Jawaharlal Nehru's sister) ruefully admitted to me, the British can say that Congress hindered the war effort and hence has no right to demand a part in the peace, much less any reward. The Moslem League is not much better off, since Jinnah always refused to call for support of the war effort; but he never obstructed it, and the Muslim community did much in support of it.

The Sikhs proved, on the whole, a disappointment to the British in the war. Certainly they have lost a good deal of their martial spirit, which is not a natural one, so to speak, but a traditional one fostered by training, fighting, and education. Moreover, as I saw in their villages and in cities like Lahore and Amritsar, they are now very anti-British.

Wavell once angrily remarked that the soldiers are "as representative of India as the politicians who are causing this trouble," and they will have a right to help to run the country. They not only kept out of the civil-disobedience campaign, but sometimes helped to quell it.

That whole "open rebellion" of 1942, as Gandhi called it, really was a fiasco, although for a few months it proved very serious. What mattered in the long run was the fact that it turned out to be restricted to certain localities—primarily Bihar and the eastern part of the United Provinces, as well as the cities of Bombay and Ahmedabad—and, above all, that it never really gained mass support. In some places the peasants were aroused by agitators, but as soon as they saw that the British *raj* was not going to be overthrown and was, instead, hitting back with formidable power, they returned to their usual friendly apathy.

All that is obvious now, but it took much work and traveling to discover it in 1942 and 1943, and it was another feature which did not fit into the picture drawn by Congress sympathizers. The Moslems kept out of it at all times and the Hindus respected their feelings, but it greatly weakened the campaign. The Indian police, the constabulary, remained "true to their salt," as Sir Richard Tottenham, the British official primarily in charge of internal security, put it to me. The constables were, in a sense, the key to the whole British plan of repression. Had they sided with Congress, the situation would have been as desperate as in the Mutiny of 1857, but it has always proved true that the Indians will not unite against the British or any other invaders, and that is another reason why a handful of Britishers can rule four hundred millions.

The conclusion I reached was that the rebellion was never spontaneous. It was a case of partial organization at the top, and blind, mob violence at the bottom, responding to issues that were only dimly recognized. The students, especially in Benares but also in other cities, played a great part in starting the violence, as did some minor Congressmen. The important leaders, with a few exceptions, undoubtedly wanted the uprising to remain non-violent, but it quickly got out of hand, as it had to, considering the inflammable material which was being ignited.

Moreover, sabotage was considered "non-violence," although some of the train wrecks led to loss of life. Definitions of non-violence became rather loose. Mrs. Aruna Asaf Ali, Congress leader who "went underground," said, "short of taking life, everything is permissible." But many lives were taken on both sides, and the term non-violence became something of a mockery. Churchill, in speaking to an M.P. at the time, said: "It is plural and it bounces." What the Prime Minister would always think about *ahimsa* is quite obvious. Sir George Schuster tells of Churchill walking up to an M.P. just after he had made a non-violence pacifist speech and saying: "Jimmy, whenever I hear you speak, I think of Belloc's lines,

"Pale Ebenezer thought it wrong to fight,
  But ruddy Bill, who killed him, thought it right."

Yet there is no question of the reality of the feeling for non-violence in almost all Hindus. As a political instrument it will die with Gandhi, for the younger and left-wing elements of Congress will not stand for it, but nothing will ever change the Hindu instinct to rely upon renunciation rather than action, for it is, as Lord Ronaldshay wrote, "an Indian belief of immemorial antiquity."

The sincerity with which that very extraordinary man, Mohandas K. Gandhi, embraced *ahimsa* is not to be doubted, and I never felt any inclination, either, to doubt his intention and belief that his last call to civil disobedience in August, 1942, would be non-violent. His belief was naive almost beyond words, given the situation—but then, from our viewpoint, Gandhi's life has been a queer mixture of goodness and illogicality.

I never had a chance to meet him, so I do not plan ever to make up my mind about him—at least, not in print. I never met Hitler, and I do have very decided opinions about him, and ditto for Franco, but in Gandhi there is no such clear-cut case, nor are there criteria of Western thought and ethics by which to measure him, so far as I am concerned.

I saw and studied the effects of his actions in politics, and there I have the definite opinion that of late years he has done his people and country more harm than good, and has made inexcusable errors. My work led me inevitably to explode the Congress myth that he was known and adored in every village in India. There, as in other cases, the really impressive truth that many millions of ignorant villagers did worship and follow him was obscured by the exaggeration of propaganda.

No one could ever doubt his political importance, and the British never underrated him. Sir Gilbert Laithwaite, Lord Linlithgow's astute secretary, used the analogy of chess in talking to me once. Gandhi is always a queen. Even if he be a pawn one day, he is capable of moving into the opponent's last line and becoming a queen whenever he wishes to do so. Rajagopalachari, however, disagreed with the British thesis that Gandhi is an astute politician. "He never was that," Rajaji said to me one day. "Sometimes he has been shrewd and has acted in a way to give the impression that he is a clever politician, but his mind doesn't work along political lines."

I culled so many confusing opinions on Gandhi that it was impossible to make up my mind. It was natural that the praise and adoration of the Hindus should have left no impression on me. Nor did the oft-heard British opinion that he was a charlatan and political opportunist. It did impress me, however, to hear Ambedkar's bitter tirades, and most of all a regretful, reasoned criticism from Dr. Higginbottom, the missionary, who has known Gandhi very well since the first World War and once worked closely with the Mahatma. Gandhi asked him to deliver the opening address of the National Conference of Congress before the "Salt March," and he offered to put Dr. Higginbottom in charge of Congress agricultural work, with unlimited resources.

"In the past three or four years I have lost my faith in Gandhi," Dr. Higginbotton told me in 1943. "I believe that, after all, he is a politician—and not of the statesmanlike kind.

He does and has done nothing without an eye to votes. At the time of the Untouchability work, Gandhi adopted legally an Untouchable girl, which was much advertised and praised. However, none of his biographers and admirers has noted that soon afterwards, not liking something which she did, Gandhi sent her away. I reproached him for it, but he would not listen. Gandhi has given up the ownership of wealth, but not the use. He is an individualist of the strongest sort. I, as a missionary, must say that I consider him the greatest anti-Christian force in India today."

My chief task regarding Gandhi was to follow his fast of February, 1943, and write about it daily—with a growing lack of sympathy. It was not a good introduction to the life of Gandhi, but at least it was an important event in his career, and rereading now what I wrote then I can see no reason to change anything I said. The fast was one "to capacity," which Gandhi had rightly gauged at twenty-one days. It followed an exchange of correspondence with the Viceroy which I have already mentioned as evidence of the inability of East and West to meet.

It was obvious as early as the fifth day that the move was going to misfire politically. It had stirred many elements of the Hindu community but it did not arouse the country, nor did it induce the British to weaken in the slightest. The Moslem community washed its hands of the whole affair. Everybody but the Hindus was mystified. "What does he want?" Jinnah asked me, rhetorically, after the second week. "I have questioned everybody who has come to see me, including Gandhi's friends, but not one of them could tell me." Liaqat Ali Khan, Secretary General of the Moslem League, said the Mussulmans "do not approve of or believe in spiritualized politics."

For the British—and quite genuinely—it was "blackmail," and, as Maxwell put it, "repugnant to Western ideas of decency." But for a Hindu member of the Legislative Assembly, L. K. Maitra, it was "vicarious atonement." The idea of the fast unto death is an ancient one, developed at first by the Jains in their effort to escape from the pitiless cycle of Karma by abstaining from action. Suicide by starvation was one good way of abstaining.

Other Hindu speakers in that same Assembly debate of February 14, 1942 (the fast began on February 10) all made a similar argument: "Gandhi is a great world figure and is revered by all Indians. His fast is making him suffer, and he may die. If he does there will be a terrible reaction. Therefore he should be released immediately and unconditionally." The appeal was to sympathy, humanity, and good will. Practical, moral, and ethical principles were ignored.

As Gandhi's condition weakened and it seemed he would die, three members of the Viceroy's Council resigned. A great meeting of two hundred of the most important figures in Hindu India was held in New Delhi, where Rajagopalachari made a typically subtle Hindu plea.

"It is a struggle between a positive force and the force of public opinion," he said. "Everyone in the country, whatever his political or racial opinions, would agree now that his heart would be gladdened if by any means Mahatmaji were released now and his fast terminated."

In other words, the Viceroy and his Government were keeping Gandhi against the wishes of 400,000,000 Indians, according to that argument, and therefore it must be a bad government and wrong. Rajaji also made much of the fact that Gandhi was being detained without trial and asked only: "An opportunity to plead for his freedom, review his opinion, and give his advice to the country as a free man. Not getting his rightful claim to a trial before a court of law, he has applied for a habeas corpus to the judgment seat above."

The argument, of course, overlooked the fact that the British Empire was at war, and during war there is, in many circumstances, the equivalent of martial law. The chief point, though, is the one I have made before. Indians cannot think in terms of machine-like, legalistic government. During their long history, government has been personal, elastic, with subtle adaptations to the psychology of their people. Good government, to them, is paternal, sympathetic, and human. In this case, it was enough to them to say: "We love Gandhiji. We all want him to be released. If you do not release him there will be a lot of trouble throughout the country. Therefore, it is to your advantage to release him." The British, on the other hand, said: "Gandhi has done wrong. Therefore he must be punished, and he has no right to consideration different from that accorded to any other Congressite."

By Western standards of logic and justice, Gandhi was wrong. One can argue about political expediency, about mercy, sympathy, or other qualities of mind, but, granting the strictly legal premises upon which the British rule India, there was no escaping the conclusion that the Mahatma had no right to demand his unconditional release. And so one returns to that hopeless, misty no-man's land where East and West can never meet. The British can say, with genuine conviction, that the Indians are wrong because they do not see the plain logic of a situation like that, but the Indians say the logic is wrong.

Maitra, whom I mentioned above, said during a debate at the time of the fast that "there is no greater criticism of British rule than that a man like Gandhi has no other place than in prison." You have to think twice before you see that there are many "undistributed middle" terms in Maitra's ratiocination, which make his statement and the deductions one is supposed to draw at least highly debatable. It is typical of the subtlety of the Hindu mind and also of the way it functions.

Hindus feel genuinely that Gandhi is not like other people and should not be treated as if he were. Maitra, at another point, said, "Gandhi has a different code from ours." Another assembly member, J. M. Joshi, added, "We cannot judge Gandhi by our standards."

That is doubtless true, but to the British it does not excuse Gandhi's conduct in any way; to Hindus it does. They humor him as though he were a child, admit his idiosyncrasies, and love him the more for them. Gandhi is a law unto himself in their eyes, and they felt that the Viceroy, in being coldly logical about the Mahatma's fast, was unjust. It all comes back to that constant demand in India for understanding and sympathy, not for machine-like justice or efficiency. Those people did not blame Gandhi for being Gandhi; they blamed the Viceroy for not being, as they saw it, human enough to accept Gandhi for what he was.

For once, Gandhi was up against a will and a belief in right-eousness that were as strong as his. Linlithgow was adamant, and even the certainty of Gandhi's death would not have moved him. Never in the history of Gandhi or the Congress had such firmness been displayed. From the beginning, a stand was taken based upon rigid principles of justice, logic, and right as the Britisher saw them. Gandhi was not treated as Gandhi, that unique, unfathomable, incomprehensible creature who for twenty-five years had been a law unto himself, who had fought the political game with religious weapons and had constantly dismayed the British by his sway over the Indian masses. Never before had the British been willing to face a showdown with him, but now in Linlithgow he met an opponent as indomitable and as stubborn as himself.

Later, Britishers said that "Gandhi's bluff had been called," and that his fast was a fraud. Because he survived, and, indeed, took a sudden turn for the better just after the Viceroy's final refusal to release him, it was argued that his life was never in danger. These accusations were unfair. The Government had two doctors of its own in constant attendance on Gandhi, and they, too, thought at one time that he was dying. Gandhi always made it clear he did not intend to starve to death, but only "fast to capacity"; he knew his own capacity, and he did really fast.

In short, though, my ideas on Gandhi were not highly complimentary, after the fast. I tried to be fair in an article summing up what I thought of the Mahatma, which I wrote for *The New York Times* Sunday Magazine Section when I was at Mount Abu the month after his fast.

"Is Gandhi a saint or a charlatan, a patriot of pure ideals or a party politician?" I asked. "This article could be written from one or the other viewpoint with a wealth of quotations, facts and authoritative opinions to support whatever thesis pleased the writer. It has been done innumerable times in the past thirty years by sincere, truth-seeking men and women.

"But suppose you are an outsider who has never come under the sway of Gandhi's extraordinary personality? Suppose that the biased pictures drawn by British and Hindus alike do not impress or convince you? Suppose you merely try to weigh the evidence fairly, impartially, unemotionally? Let us see what the results are:

"One of the first things that strikes you here in India is the way arguments are always fought out *ad hominem*. A disputant will give you his idea of the personality of some leading figure—Gandhi, Jinnah, Linlithgow, whoever it might be—and from that premise he will deduce motives for their actions. Gandhi's fast was interpreted according to the individual's opinion of the Mahatma's character. To most Hindus, Gandhi was a tormented spiritual leader seeking truth, justice and 'soul force'; to most Britishers he was a shrewd, dangerous politician seeking to gain his way by a particularly low form of blackmail.

"You do not know any more about Gandhi's character in the end than you did at the beginning, but at least you know what Hindus and Britishers think, and that is what counts."

I went on to point out that in a village near Nagpur, on a day when Gandhi's condition was very critical, an old *sadhu* lay dying. His last act was to dictate a letter saying that Gandhi would not die for he, the holy man, was transferring his remaining share of life to the Mahatma. That story appeared in the press after Gandhi's fast ended, and it was true to Hindu feelings and beliefs. Whatever one thinks of Gandhi, there is no denying that he has an extraordinary hold over those Hindus who have seen him or know about him or have heard that he is a saint. That is the important thing. It is religion and the force of a great religious personality that sway the Indian masses.

Gandhi's secret has been to use religion as a political instrument, in a country where religion is the most powerful factor in a man's life. "Politics divorced from religion has absolutely no meaning," Gandhi once wrote. He has often referred frankly to what he called "the religious use of politics." To a Westerner it seems sacrilegious. Britishers are always shocked and irritated by it, and sometimes embarrassed. They feel it is not a fair weapon. Certainly it is one, like fasting, that cannot be used against Gandhi, and it is powerful.

Gandhi's mass following does not arise from his political successes, but from his religiosity. Hindus adore him because they think he is a saint, not because he has done more than any other man to give national consciousness to India and lead her on the path toward independence. I have remarked on my failure to find Gandhi followers in many villages I visited in various parts of India, but that mass following could have been created—and genuinely so—in a few hours. It would have been necessary only for Gandhi to have gone there and for the peasants to be told that he is a "mahatma," which means "great soul," and they would have prostrated themselves and worshiped him, or they would have risen and done what he told them to do—civil disobedience, non-violence, home spinning, or whatever it might be.

But, then, Gandhi would go away. India is a vast country, and there are many places to visit. The years pass. Other holy men come. The people will vaguely remember Gandhi; they will grieve if they hear he is dying; they will worship him if he is dead, but the things he taught are gradually forgotten. They never meant much in themselves. They were something personal, exhortations from a great *guru* to which the people responded gladly, but blindly. Only if the Congress organization stepped in and kept the flame alive would the teachings be remembered. Congressmen go to jail, and the flame dies down; they come out, and it flares up again. This is politics in India.

It is the personal element that counts, and in that personality it is saintliness which the Indian seeks. Gandhi has it, among other qualities. He is profoundly religious. His private life is utterly simple and blameless. There is a genuine, natural kindliness and humor about him which endears him to children and adults alike.

During the first World War, when influenza swept over India and hundreds of bodies polluted the sacred River Ganges at Benares, Gandhi personally organized and took part in burial parties, which was something unheard of in India, where to touch dead bodies of low-caste Hindus or Untouchables is pollution. His belief in the sacredness of all life is religious. So is his shrinking from violence.

These and other qualities cannot be denied him. In one sense his life has been a long struggle on behalf of India's poverty-stricken millions and, above all, against that horrible institution of Untouchability which few others in Indian history have fought so courageously to destroy. Once he said, "If I have to be reborn, I should wish to be born an Untouchable, so that I may share their sorrows, sufferings and the affronts leveled at them, in order that I may endeavor to free myself and them from that miserable condition." In 1932 he fasted to prevent the British from establishing electorates for Depressed Classes, thus separating them politically from the Hindu community.

But now we are getting into politics again, and politics is not saintly. Dr. B. R. Ambedkar, himself a member of the "Scheduled Castes," and one of their leaders, is a bitter opponent of Gandhi. He and others accuse the Mahatma of obstructing the emancipation of the Untouchables in order to keep the Hindu majority intact.

The same thing happened in the matter of Hindu-Moslem unity. It is one of Gandhi's dearest, and doubtless sincerest, wishes to see such unity, and in 1924 he fasted twenty-one days to bring about an end to communal strife. But both intransigent Hindus and Muslims accuse him of seeking communal unity only on his own terms—terms favorable to the Congress movement.

It is the same way with non-violence. The Hindus say, "But Christ taught the same creed!" The British answer, "Yes, but not for political reasons." They point to what Gandhi's pacifism meant in 1942. Once he told the Chinese people, "It is unbecoming for a nation of four hundred millions, a nation as cultured as China, to repel Japanese aggression by resorting to Japan's own methods." When Gandhi sought leave to visit China, ten years ago, to address meetings, the Chinese refused to let him enter the country. In 1939, during an interview with a *New York Times* correspondent, Gandhi recommended unilateral disarmament by the democratic powers. "I am certain," he said, "that this would open Hitler's eyes and disarm him." That may be saintliness, but it is not practical wisdom.

All through, one encounters baffling paradoxes. "The central fact of Hinduism," he once wrote, "is cow protection. Cow protection to me is one of the most wonderful phenomena in all human evolution, for it takes the human being beyond his species. . . . The cow is a poem of pity. She is the mother of millions of Indian mankind. Protection of the cow means protection of the whole dumb creation of God." On the very next page, as I have said, he related how cruelly the Indians treat cows. But Gandhi was not being sentimental or hypocritical. He is utterly sincere about cow protection. He does not say, "something is wrong with a system that still works so miserably after thousands of years." Instead, he says, "I will make Indians, and through Indians the whole world, realize why the cow is sacred and why it must be protected."

So he preaches to villagers, and they listen and try to satisfy him. Then he goes away, and they forget. The effort is noble, even saintly, but it is aimed at turning the clock back, and is therefore impractical and illogical.

So much of Gandhi's life has been like the attempt of King Canute to stop the tide from coming in; so much of it is overestimation of his power to move India and the world. Great reformers and religious teachers always have been like that, and only in the course of years or centuries can one measure their contribution to human progress. Meanwhile, one cannot quarrel with them, on moral grounds, unless conviction of power becomes pride, or the power, itself, is used for worldly ends.

And here, again, we return to the thin ice of politics. The Mahatma's lifelong friend and biographer, the late C. F. Andrews, wrote of "the gentle dictatorship of a saint," but there are many who do not look at it so charitably. Jamnadas Mehta, head of the Railway Workers' Federation, and an important Hindu politician, told me that Gandhi "allows his followers complete liberty of speech and complete paralysis of action. Nobody without Gandhi's support could be elected or appointed to a high post in Congress or the provincial governments during the Congress party's rule. So, naturally, those seeking political power took orders from him. I am doubtful whether Gandhi is a good force in India today. He has enslaved the souls of four hundred millions."

When Gandhi makes a move he is always so convinced of the righteousness of his cause that his followers have had to move heaven and earth what few occasions they opposed him. During the fast of 1943 no one dreamed of trying to persuade Gandhi to abandon it. They knew such effort would be hopeless. He is especially adamant when he feels that he has had an inspiration from on high. He accepts his inner convictions as truth, and his followers agree implicitly. His opponents question both his inspiration and his sincerity. I met many Britishers who said, and obviously believe, that Gandhi is a complete fraud, a cunning, vain, hypocritical showman, using his hold over the masses to glorify himself and the Congress party. It is an opinion very hard to swallow, but so is the Hindu thesis that Gandhi is an unadulterated saint. Nevertheless, both opinions are held in India, and because Gandhi is still the most important Indian political figure, those opinions affect the situation profoundly.

The truth generally has a habit of lying between extremes. Gandhi is a human being with human failings—and we can leave it at that. On history's judgment day there will be some undoubted vices to weigh in the balance against some genuine and very great virtues.

For the present, what is important to recognize is that Gandhi is a despot—kindly, paternal, high-minded, or anything else you please, but despotic he certainly is. He is dictator of the Congress movement and party. Because of him, Jawaharlal Nehru, whose great abilities, idealism, patriotism, and common sense even his British opponents do not deny, has been frustrated and prevented from serving India as he could have done. He was kept in jail throughout the war because he followed Gandhi, and not because of his reasoned beliefs. With rare exceptions, when anyone has had to change his mind it has been the other fellow, not Gandhi. He and his immediate followers developed Congress into a one-party organization as disciplined as the Fascist or the Nazi Party. Just as the Italians taught that "Mussolini is always right," so Congressmen had to believe or persuade themselves. that Gandhi is always right.

The younger men in the movement have been fighting that trend. I heard many Congress sympathizers say privately that Gandhi has been India's misfortune in the past seven years, that he has outlived his usefulness and greatness, and that until he dies India will be "enslaved" by his well-intentioned but misguided despotism.

The circle of this argument is now turning back on itself. Gandhi can be a despot because he has an immense mass following, and he has that following because he is a great religious leader. His roots lie deep in the soil of India, in those villages which are India, and in those peasants whom ten thousand years of history have changed so little. He feels as they feel. He understands them, knows what they need, and expresses their longings, in simple ideas. Let us look at those ideas briefly, since they give the measure of the man.

The key to Gandhi's economics is the food and raiment of the poor. Just as he mixes politics and religion, so he mixes economics and ethics. In a letter to Rabindranath Tagore, written more than twenty years ago, he said: "Economics that hurt the moral well being of the individual or nation are immoral and therefore sinful."

For Gandhi, the only moral way of life is the peasant's life—that simple, ancient way of life which Indian peasants lived before modern civilization came with the British invaders. "The rude plough of perhaps five thousand years ago is the plough of the husbandman today. Therein lies salvation," he wrote in his *Confession of Faith* in 1909.

And so he evolved *swadeshi*, that "spirit within us which restricts us to the use and service of our immediate surroundings to the exclusion of remoter things. . . . If not a single article of commerce had been brought from outside of India she would today be a land flowing with milk and honey. . . . I think of *swadeshi* as a religious principle to be followed by all."

Then there is that key principle of *ahimsa*, non-violence. *Swaraj*, the independence of India, is another and all-absorbing feature of Gandhi's teachings. There is the fight against Untouchability. There is also his struggle for the equality of the sexes, with its campaigns against child marriages and *purdah*. He has fought for the prohibition of alcohol and drugs, for Hindu-Moslem unity, for the use of native languages instead of English. Allied to non-violence is that sister principle of *satyagraha*, which means truth force or soul force, and which turns into civil disobedience or resistance.

But here we are, back at that mixture of religion and politics. You cannot get away from it. Politics, someone said, is a dirty business. Religion is not. If a saint becomes a politician, is he not like the Biblical image with its feet of clay?

Perhaps we have, at last, struck upon the true analogy. Had Gandhi, like the simple *guru* on Mount Abu, held to that guiding star of "orthodox, conservative Hinduism," as he called it, there would be no quarrels about him. But then, he would not be Gandhi and we would lose ourselves in an absurdity. Let us take him as he is—enigma, paradox, saint with clay feet. Call him what you please; you cannot deny he is a great man who has profoundly affected the course of contemporary Indian history and who will be worshiped by Hindus in their countless reincarnations.

For my own part, I still think that (in the political balance) Gandhi has been weighed and found wanting. His act in withdrawing the Provincial Governments in 1939 and his rejection of the Cripps Plan were major political errors which most Indians now privately admit. Guy Wint was not too unfair when he had a mythical Indian "count the cost of the Mahatma's methods."

"He has introduced into Indian politics the adulation of the leader and the habit of blind obedience which is the essence of Fascism," Wint writes. "As the test for fitness for public life he has put the willingness to suffer imprisonment in the place of intellectual ability; and has exalted the amateur and dilettante at the expense of the expert and the efficient. By reviving and painting in rosy colors the older ideas of Hinduism he has encouraged India to look behind instead of forward. . . . The economic ideas which he preaches are opposed to all the compelling forces of the age and have set India on a false course. . . . His campaigns of civil disobedience have brought the law into contempt and have fostered the habits of revolt. It is difficult to see how any man with a normal sense of responsibility could have risked these consequences, least of all in India, the curse of whose history has been lawlessness and violence."

I think one should add to Gandhi's political sins his paralyzing effect on Jawaharlal Nehru. Gandhi has been a genuine "Old Man of the Mountains" astride Nehru's shoulders, and whenever the latter's friends and relatives take their hair down they admit it. However, as even Nehru's sister, Mrs. Pandit, said to me, Jawaharlal cannot command a mass following and Gandhi can. Nehru himself admitted it in an article he wrote early in 1939.

"In trying to analyze the various elements in the Congress," said he, "the dominating position of Gandhiji must always be remembered. He dominates to some extent the Congress, but far more so he dominates the masses. . . . It makes little difference whether he is formally connected with the Congress or not. The Congress today is of his making and he is essentially of it. . . . In any policy that might be framed he cannot be ignored. In any national struggle his full association and guidance are essential. India cannot do without him."

Nehru's skeptical, Western mind is far removed from Gandhi's. Writing about Gandhism once, he said, "There is little stress on the mind in it or on the processes of the mind, and too much on an intuitive and authoritarian interpretation." Nehru is not "authoritarian." On the contrary, he has displayed an unwillingness or inability to stand up for his own ideas, and this can only be characterized as weakness.

"I have been an individual in this great organization, and that is always a difficult task," he at one time said plaintively. "Often I have felt that I am a square peg in a round hole. . . . I have been and am a convinced socialist and a believer in democracy, and have at the same time accepted wholeheartedly the peaceful technique of non-violent action which Gandhiji has practiced so successfully during the past twenty years. . . . I am convinced that strength can only come to us from the masses."

One hears among Indian radicals divergent opinions regarding Nehru. Some call him a "parlor pink," and point to the fact that he never openly helped the Communists or even the Socialist wing of Congress, despite his Socialist preachings, but he is recognized generally as the only Working Committee member who sympathizes with the radicals and supports them in debates behind the scenes. They appreciate his intense patriotism. P. C. Joshi, of Bombay, the young Communist Party leader, told me that Nehru is "a sincere liberal," and the Communists respect him as such and feel he never willingly supports the Congress opposition to Communism. They, like so many other Indians, deplore Nehru's all-absorbing loyalty to the Congress Party and his insistence on party discipline at all costs, but that is something which a Communist can understand better than anybody else.

As far as the future of India is concerned, one can hope that this sincere, self-sacrificing, cultured man will play the great role to which he is entitled—but that role will not be one of replacing Gandhi. The unity of the Congress Party will not long survive the Mahatma. Already it has been weakened by the rebelliousness of the younger, radical elements who are going to scrap non-violence and other antiquated political theories as soon as they can.

And the greatest source of weakness of all, from the Congress viewpoint, is the defection of almost the entire politically conscious Moslem element, who now follow Jinnah and his fantastic scheme of Pakistan.

Communalism is, perhaps, the outstanding feature of the Indian political scene today, and that is another thing you must know about if you want to have any understanding of what is happening in India. I went into the involutions and convolutions of that knotty subject as deeply as I could, since it was obvious that neither I nor the readers of *The New York Times* could form any judgment on India without knowing something about the communal problem.

According to the 1941 census, the population of India is divided thus: Hindus 66 per cent, Muslims 24, tribes 6, Indian Christians 1½, miscellaneous 2½ per cent. So one starts with the central fact that the Hindu represents a goodly majority of the Indians, about 260,000,000 to the Moslems' 90 to 95,000,000. On a basis of the right of the majority to rule, the Hindus should rule India. But a minority of 95,000,000 means more people than there are in England and Italy combined, and if they or their political leaders do not want to live under a Hindu *raj,* as they call it, then the situation becomes complicated.

Until World War I ended there was no great problem, because both Hindus and Moslems were united against a common enemy, the British, and were working harmoniously together on the political plane. However, the approach of dominion status was like an apple of discord thrown into their midst. In the background is the constant danger of disorder, like a volcano that may and does occasionally erupt.

Lord Ronaldshay put the matter astutely when he wrote: "By a peculiar misfortune, Islam, like Hinduism, was less a religion than an entire civilization; and two ways of life more antipathetic it would have been hard to conceive. Indeed, had it been attempted deliberately to frame a culture point by point the opposite of Hinduism, no better results could have been achieved than the system of Mohammed. In theological ideas, in legal conceptions, in philosophy of life, in the family organization, in food, social customs, language, even in clothes, Hindus and Moslems found themselves opposed. . . . Bitter though the communal feeling would have been in any circumstances, it was exacerbated by the caste system, which of all the institutions of Hinduism was the one most fatal in consequences. . . . Because of caste the Hindus were unapproachable and unaccommodating; instinctively applying caste categories, they saw the entire Moslem community as a caste subordinate, unclean, and untouchable. . . . Under the Hindu social system men are graded minutely and segregated in an infinite number of watertight compartments: under Islam all men are equal. Hinduism is es-

sentially aristocratic: Mohammedanism is emphatically democratic."

And so it goes. Just think that no Hindu in all of India can
be related by marriage or blood to a Moslem! The Mussulmans
dearly love to sacrifice cows, for it gives them great virtue—let
us say, in numerical terms, eight points to one for a goat. Yet
for the Hindu, the cow is sacred. The Sikh religion, a derivation
of Hinduism, seems even more deliberately designed to antagonize the Muslim. For instance, the Sikh loves pigs, which are
anathema to the Mohammedan.

The history of communal disorders in India is a bloody and
terrible one. Often outbreaks started from the most trivial incidents. The District Commissioner of Attock, in the western Punjab, told me of some typical trouble which he had encountered.
It started on an Id day in Rawalpindi. In the early morning
some Hindus tossed the head of a pig over the wall into a
mosque, and it took a great deal to hold the Muslims down.
Three weeks later, on a Hindu festival, the Muslims cut a cow
in three and put the pieces in three Hindu temples. In general,
it took him a year to settle the question of religious processions,
for the Hindus deliberately insisted on going past mosques, halting and making as much noise as possible in front of them, and
the Moslems did similar things.

Yet I did convince myself, and I still believe, that under
normal conditions Hindus and Moslems get along well together
in the villages—which means in nine tenths of India. In regions
which are overwhelmingly Hindu or Muslim, it is natural that
the minority element should not look for trouble. In other
places, there is the normal tendency of neighbors dependent on
each other and knowing each other, to accommodate themselves
harmoniously to conditions. After all, communal trouble is a
relatively new feature in Indian history, following on centuries
of peaceful life together.

However, conditions are not normal now. Indian nationalists
blame the British for fostering communal dissension. They base
their assertion primarily on the fact that the British profit by
Indian disunity, which gives them one of their best reasons to

remain in India. The nationalists thus deduce that the British are therefore causing the dissension. I could find no proof of this contention. British officials, of course, get black marks if there are communal disorders in their districts, and no ruling power enjoys having civil disturbances.

The accusation that the British back Jinnah and encourage him is another matter, and one not so easy to dismiss. To be fair, however, one must point out that communal trouble in India is fundamentally political. It began in serious fashion after World War I, only when Indians saw or thought that freedom was approaching. That started a scramble for political power and patronage which is the immediate basis of communalism in India. Jinnah and the Moslem League are political, as well as religious and racial phenomena. Except for a small element of descendants of Persian and Afghan tribes in western and north-western India who migrated with the Mogul conquerors, Muslims are of the same racial stock as the Hindus. One should not, however, confuse racial stock with national sentiment, as we in America can testify. No one can tell us that we are not Americans because we are of English, German, Scandinavian or other blood, and no one can tell an Indian Moslem that he is really a Hindu if he would only stop to think about it. Jinnah turns the argument the other way about, and claims—as he did to some of us—that "we have five hundred times more guts than the Hindus"—which is not true, either.

It is true that one can provide some plausible arguments for Jinnah's contention, and some convincing evidences of the great differences in temperament and capacities of the Hindus and the Moslems. The latter have none of the religious and social traditions of renunciation and non-violence of the Hindus. Hence, although there are fine fighting stocks among the Hindus like the Rajputs, Dogras and Marathas, the general run do not make as good soldiers as do the Moslems. On the other hand, it is universally agreed in India, and proved by all tests, that the Hindu is a much brighter, more intelligent, quicker and sharper mind than the Moslem. The reasons are again, social and traditional, rather than racial or fundamental, but the differences are there and are a great embarrassment to the rulers, who must apportion posts according to communal representation and not ability. The Muslims never adopted British education, as the Hindus did; they remained attached to and steeped in their Islamic traditions. Lord Zetland ascribes to that fact the backwardness of the Moslem, compared to the Hindu. "Pride of race, a memory of by-gone superiority, religious fears, and a not unnatural attachment to the learning of Islam" are the factors which he cites.

The two main Indian universities, that of the Hindus in Benares and of the Muslims at Aligarh, deliberately foster communal sentiments among their students. They teach them to be good Hindus and good Moslems, not good Indians.

So, to return to the original proposition that the British created and are maintaining communal dissension, one can see that there are many factors involved. Nothing, as I have often remarked, is simple in India.

When, on December 17, 1942, Lord Linlithgow, in a speech in Calcutta, stressed the importance of unity, there was a furor among the Moslems, since unity is the Hindu thesis. A point which the British are continually making is that the Moslems appeal to them for support, not they to the Moslems. Jinnah has never hidden his desire that the British remain in India until he acquires his Pakistan or its equivalent. He and his followers fear that if the British go, the Moslems will be at the mercy of the numerically superior, richer, better educated, and better organized Hindus. This is a natural fear, and it was not created by the British. It derives, in its latest and strongest form, from the period of Congress rule in the provinces about which I wrote. Both communities, in fact, want the British to take sides, since the game would obviously be three quarters won by whichever element the British backed.

In general, to be sure, British sentiments and predilections lean toward the Moslems. Lieutenant Governor Bampfylde Fuller of Bengal said to a reporter of the Calcutta *Amrita* (off the record, the Lieutenant Governor thought) that the British in India were like a man with two wives, one Hindu and one

Muslim, and he added that the latter appeared to be the favorite.

The reasons for this feeling should be obvious. The Moslem is much nearer to the Westerner in religion, thought, and social customs. One does not feel, with the educated Mohammedans, that degree of strangeness which I have described. The Moslems did not join the civil-disobedience campaign in 1942; they supported the war effort loyally, and the political elements do not want the British to quit India immediately.

Jinnah, in playing his own game, has incidentally played into the hands of the British, so why should they hinder him? Of course, the whole business of communal dissension plays right into the hands of the British. Penderel Moon, in his remarkably acute little book, *Strangers in India,* has his character, Lightfoot, say:

"I have only twice met a viceroy, but on each occasion he made the same remark, 'I've never known communal feeling worse than it is now. Have you?' This may be just a stock remark which viceroys make to district officers to keep up their spirits. But its tacit implication is quite clear. If communal feeling is worse than ever, then the barometer is 'Set Fair' for a continuance of British rule—a reflection comforting to the viceroy if not to the district officer. This attitude of mind affects policy. I don't suggest that it causes us wantonly to aggravate the communal problem, but it does diminish our readiness to perceive or devise ways of solving it. It encourages us to lie back and leave Hindus and Muslims to their sterile negations. That is why I say that subconsciously we make use of their divisions."

The first thing that Lord Linlithgow said to me in my first talk with him was precisely this—that the communal problem was "all-important, very deep-seated, the overruling passion of the people, the thing they think of above everything else." Much to my surprise, I came eventually to the same opinion. When I arrived in India I believed the Congress thesis that communalism was a creation of the British, and that once the British left, the two communities would settle their differences quickly and amicably. I found no basis for that contention. My first real study of the problem was in the Punjab, and the "lead" of my main story on my experiences was this: "Deep in the heart of the Punjab, where no automobile can go, where life is as simple and natural as it is in ninety per cent of India, everything revolves around the distrust and antipathy between Muslims and Hindus."

It was a genuine discovery for me to learn of Jinnah's importance and the fact that the Moslem League commanded the support of the vast majority of politically conscious Mussulmans in British India. (As always, the Princely States are out of the political current. Neither the Moslem League nor the Congress has any appreciable following in the States, and there is no communal violence—another proof that the basis of the trouble is the struggle for political power.)

I wrote a good deal about that astute and rather unpleasant character, Mohammed Ali Jinnah. The Moslems have no figure with the color, the charm, the articulateness, the flare for publicity of Gandhi and Nehru, and that has been a great handicap to them in foreign countries. Americans know the Congress viewpoint only too well, thanks to Gandhi and to books like Nehru's brilliant *Autobiography*.

However, I did find that out of the throes of India's travail a new figure had arisen who held in his hands more power for good or evil than any other Indian politician. He was that tall, thin, supercilious, exasperatingly deliberate man who seemed to be taking a diabolical pleasure in keeping the world guessing—Mohammed Ali Jinnah. In his delicate, old hands lay the answer to the riddle: Can the Hindus and Moslems agree? From one viewpoint, it seemed fortunate that so complicated a situation should have been that much clarified on the political plane, but it was something like trying to solve the riddle of the sphinx. If the sphinx refused to answer, all the simplification in the world was not going to help—and Jinnah, even in the spring of 1945, was giving an excellent imitation of a sphinx.

To give him credit, it is true that even if the Hindus and Moslems reached a settlement, it would not necessarily follow that the British would pack up their bags and go. In fact, there are the best of reasons to believe the contrary. But if the British were faced with a communal understanding and a united demand for a national government, they would be in a very awkward position if they tried to maintain their present attitude. Their best excuse for failing to make political concessions would be removed, and that is why Jinnah (and, to be fair, let us say Gandhi also) bears so heavy a responsibility. Neither man yielded on fundamentals in their fruitless conversations of September, 1944, but it is true that if Jinnah had been ready to compromise at any time in the past three years India would have won a large degree of political unity. That is why the British keep their eyes so anxiously on Jinnah. What he thinks about, God (or Allah) only knows. His strength lies more in not making decisions than in making them, in avoiding power than accepting it. He is waiting for the mountain to come to Mohammed Ali Jinnah.

The Moslems admire Jinnah's probity and the fact that he has never accepted anything from the British, nor has he supported or praised them on any public occasion. In fact, he has often criticized them roundly. He made his money as a lawyer, and he never accepted office or any other honors. Jinnah, unlike Gandhi, is not a religious figure. No one could be less religious, and therein lies his greatest weakness as a mass leader. While Hindus revere Gandhi as a saint on earth, no Moslem who knows anything about Jinnah can have such feelings about him. He does not say his prayers, other Moslems have told me. He does not fast on fast days. He likes bacon and eggs for breakfast. And he married a Parsi. However, the Mohammedan masses do not know these things and, anyway, they do not follow Jinnah; they follow his goal of Pakistan, which they are assured will be a realm in which all their economic, political and religious ills will be cured. Pakistan is the rallying cry of the Moslem League, and Jinnah is the powerful and only boss of the League and he exercises iron discipline; those who disagree with him must go, and that ends their political importance. His tongue and pen are exceedingly sharp, and when he is crossed he minces no words.

As things are now, in 1945, he is the kingpin of Indian politics, and the vast majority of his followers are convinced he will do the right thing for the Moslems when the right time comes. Meanwhile, he is doing the right thing for Jinnah. He is like a card player with a perfect poker face. His opponents will not know whether he is bluffing until he is forced to put his cards on the table. Meanwhile, he is playing as though he has four aces. Everyone keeps asking whether Jinnah is sincere, but no one knows. His speeches are as bafflingly simple as Hitler's were during his rise to power, and Jinnah undoubtedly studied the Fuehrer's technique. He hammers away at a few simple ideas, using the same formulas in speech after speech, "Pakistan; self-determination; we are a nation; our birthright." These are words and phrases never missing from any of Jinnah's addresses. Some think his Pakistan is a bargaining card, and that when the showdown comes he will compromise. Perhaps that was the case once, but, to change the simile, it has become more like a Frankenstein's monster which Jinnah created and now cannot escape from, even if he wanted to.

No doubt you have been wondering just what is this Pakistan? You may well wonder, so to speak. The general idea is clear enough, but when it comes to details and practical features, you have nothing to grasp, for the reason that Jinnah will not give you any rope with which to hang him.

Pakistan would be an Indian nation with a vast Moslem majority. Therefore, it would include all, or a large part, of those regions of India which fit that requirement—the Northwest Frontier Province, Baluchistan, the Sind, the Punjab, Bengal. However, when you look at the map you see that one part of the mythical Pakistan is separated from the other by a great stretch of India. Once, in talking to me, Jinnah said, blithely, "There could be a corridor between the two"—a corridor that would make the Polish one seem simple and natural! Jinnah will not define the precise or even approximate geographical frontiers which he wants for Pakistan. They will be settled in negotiations with the Hindus, he says.

Pakistan would have a hard time of it in economic affairs, since the most fertile parts of India and the great industrial cities (except, perhaps, Calcutta) would be in Hindustan. However, Jinnah once said to me: "Why do the Hindus worry about us so much? Let us stew in our own juice if we are willing. Afghanistan is a poor country but she gets along, and so does Iraq, and they have only a small fraction of the 70,000,000 people we would have. If we are willing to live simply and poorly, as long as we have freedom, why should the Hindus object? They would be getting rid of the poorest parts of India, so they ought to be glad. The economy will take care of itself, in time."

Others claim, although without yet providing statistical proof, that Pakistan would work economically as well as politically. Some very distinguished Indians—notably Rajagopalachari and Ambedkar—believe in its feasibility.

The Hindus assert that it was Sir Stafford Cripps who put Pakistan into the political arena to stay—but that is one of those over-simplifications, as well as a statement incapable of proof. According to Jinnah, "while Cripps virtually conceded Congress demands for a Hindu majority, he merely recognized the possibility of Pakistan." Everything, during the Cripps visit, provided an atmosphere favorable to Jinnah's machinations, and the Hindus obliged by playing into his hands.

Jinnah and his followers started from the thesis that Congress wanted to establish a Hindu *raj*, opposing the Moslem right to self-determination. Firoz Khan Noon, Defense Member of the Viceroy's Council, in a press interview with us, said: "Rather than submit to a Hindu *raj* in Delhi, I would join hands with any foreigners from the West, and every Mohammedan feels the same way. Every one of them would be a Fifth Columnist."

The most famous utterance on Pakistan made while I was in India came from Zafar Ali, Moslem League member of the Legislative Assembly, who said during a debate: "Pakistan is our goal, and we will fight for it with our backs to the ground." His imagery was distorted, but his emotion was real. The Muslim slogan is, "Pakistan or bust."

Jinnah angrily denies that he is playing the British game. "I assure Gandhi," he told me, "that the Mussulmans of India depend upon their own inherent strength." However, few observers would disagree with the Mahatma. Nehru, during an exchange of letters with Jinnah, in a vain search for a Congress-League accord early in the war, concluded, "I am compelled to think that the real difficulty is a difference of political outlook and objectives."

In my final article from India I wrote: "Your correspondent's studies in every part of India, where he went into the question of communal tension, convinced him that at least nine out of ten politically conscious Moslems in British India are with the Moslem League. A corollary to that is the overwhelming importance of communal dissension, which, in the writer's considered opinion, is the most important factor of the Indian situation today. It lies at the basis of the whole political structure, providing an apparently insuperable cause of disunity. The idea of Pakistan, with all its weaknesses, has gained the Moslem League a tremendous following, and it is hard to see how it can be abandoned now, even if Jinnah wanted to. Indeed, India is full of centrifugal forces—Hindus against Moslems, Brahmins against non-Brahmins, Indians of British India against Indians of Princely India, and, above all, Indians against British."

If India is not a Gordian knot, there has never been one in history. The question is: "Can the British, or anyone else, cut it?"

The White Man's Burden?

I F YOU want to become disheartened about India, re-read Kipling and compare what he wrote back in the 1880's with the situation today. The India of his time is still with us to a startling extent. "How exasperatingly slow history is in moving, at least compared with the brevity of human life," wrote Gaetano Mosca, the Italian sociologist, and it is painfully true of India. There are few literary parallels so amazing as the efforts of a present-day journalist to find out about India and "The Enlightenment of Pagett, M.P." in *Under the Deodars*, by Kipling.

India evolves so slowly—in her social, political and communal problems, her relations with the British, her poverty, disease, and illiteracy. Perhaps we expect too much. Only fifty or sixty years have passed since Kipling wrote about India, and on the positive side there has been much progress. If we think in terms of the immensity of the country, its teeming millions, its complications of races, religions, and languages, and all the other handicaps, perhaps the wonder is that India has gone as far as she has.

You will still find belief in the evil eye, as in "The Recrudescence of Imray," in *Mine Own People*. Metempsychosis is an "old tale" to Grish Chunder in "The Finest Story in the World," and it would be to any Indian today. "I am afraid to be kicked," says Grish Chunder, acutely, "but I am not afraid to die, because I know what I know. *You* are not afraid to be kicked, but you are afraid to die."

You can still buy a girl at a market near Simla, as Holden did in "Without Benefit of Clergy." The "great, gray apes of the hills" still have their god, Hanuman, upon whom Fleete put "The Mark of the Beast." The *banias*, or money lenders of "Gem-

ini" are just as rapacious, just as much hated as they were then.
The chorus could sing again of the villager, as in "The Masque
of Plenty":

> At his heart is his daughter's wedding,
> In his eye foreknowledge of debt.
> He eats and hath indigestion,
> He toils and he may not stop:
> His life is a long-drawn question
> Between a crop and a crop.

This, about the Princely States from "The Man Who Would
Be King," could be written today: "The Native States have a
wholesome horror of English newspapers which may throw light
on their peculiar methods of government and do their best to
choke correspondents with champagne or drive them out of
their mind with four-in-hand barouches. They do not understand
that nobody cares a straw for the internal administration of the
Native States so long as oppression and crime are kept within
decent limits and the ruler is not drugged, drunk or diseased
from one end of the year to the other. The Native States were
created by Providence in order to supply picturesque scenery,
tigers, and tall writing. They are dark places of the earth, full
of unimaginable cruelty, touching railway and telegraph on one
side and on the other the days of Haroun al Raschid."

The British case has never been better stated in terms of the
"white man's burden" than in the short story, "On the City
Wall," from the collection, *In Black and White:*

"Year by year England sends out fresh drafts for the first fight-
ing-line which is officially called the Indian Civil Service. These
die or kill themselves by overwork or are worried to death or
broken in health and hope in order that the land may be protected from death, sickness, famine, war, and may eventually
become capable of standing alone. It will never stand alone, but
the idea is a pretty one and men are willing to die for it, and
the yearly work of pushing and coaxing and scolding and petting
the country into good living goes forward. If an advance is made,
all the credit is given to the native, while the Englishmen stand
back and wipe their foreheads. If failure occurs, the Englishmen

step forward and take the blame. Overmuch tenderness of this kind has bred a strong belief among many natives that the native is capable of administering the country, and many devout Englishmen believe this also, because the theory is stated in beautiful English with all the latest political color."

That, we would say today, is "going rather strong." Let me quote you, as a corrective, a few sentences from *The English People,* by D. W. Brogan, more in line with present-day thought:

"But when all is said and done, it merely means that not the worst has been made of a very bad and almost impossible job. . . .

"Behind all the failures and limited successes of English rule in India lay the fact that it was foreign. . . . But that the English solution was worse than any alternative solution, or that there was any alternative solution for 'India,' is not certain, perhaps not even probable. . . .

"It was Indian weakness, not English strength, that made English paramountcy possible."

Lord Linlithgow once said to me, "The Indians give us credit for more subtlety than we have," and that was very true, indeed. I remember the scientist, Raman, saying to me in Bangalore that the secret of British success in India was a very subtle one, and it was to be found in the "Honours List." To get the title of "Sir," or even to be a "Rai Saheb," the Indian will do anything the British want, he said. And he added that he was sorry he had accepted a knighthood from the British. At the September, 1920, conference of the National Congress, as Professor William Roy Smith wrote in *Nationalism and Reform in India,* two of the things demanded were the boycott of the British courts by lawyers and litigants, and the surrender of all titles and honorary offices. Out of 5,000 titleholders, twenty-one resigned, and "only a few lawyers gave up their practice."

To Professor Raman, the British were being subtle and clever with their "Honours List," but in reality they were being straightforward and crude, as they usually are. The trouble is that the Indian, who has a really subtle mind, is always interpreting British actions and words in tortuous ways. British rule is just as simple as Ralph Waldo Emerson described it when he wrote that the Englishman "sticks to his traditions and usages, and, so help him God! he will force his island by-laws down the throat of great countries like India, China, Canada, Australia."

In an article which I wrote for my newspaper just before I left India, after eleven months in the country, I summed up some of my own opinions on the British:

"One has," I wrote, "for some reason rather sheepishly and apologetically, to admit that the British picture is not nearly so black as it was presented. There is plenty to criticize. There are some Britishers who are as bad as all Britishers are supposed to be. British policy is frankly imperialistic—at least since the tide of war began to change—and as Americans we do not like imperialism.

"They helped to bring about the Indian deadlock and intend to continue it so long as the war lasts. They have done nothing to help the Indians solve their present difficulties and they have, in general, adopted a negative attitude toward Indian aspirations for independence, or even increased political power. They have not, even to an unbiased neutral like the writer, provided convincing evidence that they really intend to grant India self-government at any foreseeable future time.

"However, it is only fair to add that the British are faced in India with problems whose intricacies and difficulties are without parallel in the world. Their past imperial policy has brought them into a situation from which they cannot extricate themselves without something comparable to a major operation on the body politic of the commonwealth. One must grant their responsibility to the war effort, and one must keep in mind the extent to which the Indian problem is a world problem.

"The British record in India, as a whole, has been efficient, honorable and just. The average British administrator is an earnest, hard-working gentleman who sincerely intends to serve the best interests of India and often does so. His compatriots in the business field have less admirable elements among them, but at least they are not now the menace to India that they were up to twenty years ago.

"The British are not villains or tyrants oppressing the poor Indian people. They are men who are ably carrying out the most difficult and complicated administrative job in the world, and if they and their empire profit by it, they are at least rendering some service in exchange, however unwelcome it may be to many Indians, who sincerely feel they can do much better. In any event, such Indians claim the right to run their country as they please and every American must, in theory, grant them that right."

I told of the pessimism and frustration that I found in going around during the spring and early summer of 1943. So my final picture was a somber one, little resembling that brightly colored painting shown to me in New York a year before. India's tragedy was only too clear. It lay in the inability of Indians to get together, in the effort of Congress to get totalitarian control, in communal politics, in the opprobrium cast upon those who walked the middle way.

How few among the thousands of Indians I met were willing or able to say, "I am an Indian, first, last, and always!" Not they! They were Hindus or Moslems or Brahmins or Punjabis or Bengalis. True nationalism was the ideal of Congress, but one that few Congressmen lived up to, and it was rare, indeed, to find an Indian who thought of his country as we in the West think of ours.

India is like a country that has been cursed by some malignant deity, and innumerable millions of Hindus look on life as an unhappy burden imposed by an impersonal, all-absorbing Godhead. It is a country blighted by the weakness of its people, by dreadful poverty, ignorance, and disease, and by religions which are sources of political strife and social oppression.

But these are only a few pieces of the jigsaw puzzle. They are important because they explain so much of India's present unhappiness. There are other pieces that tell of a kindly, tolerant, hardworking people, the heirs to one of the great cultures of history. They tell of soldiers as brave as any in the world, and of refined, cultured men who are suffering uncomplainingly in jail, for ideals and for a leader they believe in. India's land is rich; her industrial potentialities are enormous. She has many enlightened minds who, in spite of every obstacle, are moving forward in politics, administration, and education toward a brighter future.

This race was old and highly civilized when the aborigines were roaming the forests of Britain, but it has not found its place in the modern machine age. Strife, perhaps even chaos, lies ahead. All the elements of trouble are there, and the fires are being fanned by the Indians themselves. The path to nationhood is blocked not only by the British but by those Indians who will not co-operate, who will not seize opportunities when they are offered, who quarrel among themselves while John Bull looks complacently on. He will not have to liquidate his Indian Empire so long as that condition persists.

But how can the Indians get together? How can a nation be made where none ever existed before, where language, race, religion, and culture are as mixed as on the European continent? What form of government has the modern world evolved to suit such a situation?

These questions could go on endlessly, and never be satisfactorily answered. There is no panacea, no simple, happy solution. In India, Britain has a Gordian knot which she has been trying fitfully to untie—but Gordian knots are never untied. You either cut them or you leave them alone. The British must now decide whether they will cut loose or hang on.

Certainly, to change the figure of speech, they are sitting on a lid, rather comfortably since the triumph over the civil-disobedience campaign of 1942, but, still, they have a rather strong brew under them and they may well be blown off if they do nothing. One must take it for granted that, as the British have officially promised, something "no less liberal" than the Cripps Plan will be offered, and that India will receive dominion status or a guarantee of it sooner or later (my own guess being later). It does not seem as though a revolution or another "open rebellion" will have any chance whatever of success at any foreseeable time. However, it is always arguable that even an abortive uprising serves the purpose of bringing pressure on the British and

attracting worldwide attention, and perhaps Indians will feel
it is worth the price.

My thesis, on leaving India, was that the British had no intention of granting Indian independence for a very long time. That
was based largely on what I saw and heard in India, but also on
the clear statements by England's political leaders. I see no reason
to change it.

Churchill's now famous statement had a ring of such heartfelt
sincerity that one can know for certain that nothing drastic will
happen so long as he or others like him hold office. "Let me make
this clear, in case there should be any mistake about it in any
quarter," you will recall he said in the House of Commons on
November 10, 1942: "We mean to hold our own. I have not
become the King's First Minister in order to preside over the
liquidation of the British Empire."

Once before, in another famous speech, in 1930, Churchill said:
"We have no intention of casting away that most truly bright
and precious jewel in the crown of the King, which more than
all our other dominions and dependencies constitutes the glory
and strength of the British Empire."

Two things were clear about the British attitude in the year
1945: First, no move would be made while the war lasted; and,
secondly, that when the time comes, the Indians must form a
national government and show that they are in a position to run
their country peacefully. This is a very great condition, and
that is why I do not believe the British intend to quit India.
Their promises are, no doubt, sincere, but if they first make conditions that are just about impossible of fulfillment in existing
circumstances, then the promises do not mean much.

One cannot doubt that the British will insist on an internal
settlement before they grant anything approximating independence. L. S. Amery, Secretary of State for India, has said in Parliament that there would first have to be "the framing of an agreed
constitution." Lord Samuel, in the India and Burma Bill debate
of October 20, 1942, said that, as a matter of course which he felt
everyone would accept, if, after the war, "no solution [of the
communal problem] has been reached; if then it is found that

both sides are arming one against the other and that there is certainty that a British withdrawal would be chaos, the British Government would be compelled to go back upon their pledge, and to plead that *force majeure* has compelled them to continue the existing situation."

Lord Simon, the Lord Chancellor, said in a debate in the House of Lords on the same bill: "It is only when the people of India find a way of working together that they would create a situation which would be able to produce a constitution in the future. We are bound to take the line that during the war it is impossible to make any fundamental constitutional change. Immediately the war is over, we wish to have the fullest contribution from Indians themselves. All we stipulate is that they really should come together. It is not we who are going to bring them together. They are much more likely to come together by themselves."

The word "stipulate" means "insist upon." But, from the Indian side, as I have remarked, it all looks so hopeless! Congress, officially, still stands on its demand for a united India with a constitution based on "independence and democracy." The Moslem League demands its Pakistan before independence. And there is much loose talk of civil war by elements that cannot conceive of its terrors. Until Indians think of India in terms of their country as a whole, and not of their religious community or political party, there will be no unity. That day seems far off.

And yet there are so many elements which show that Indians can run India. Certainly, an Indian government will be much less efficient than the British—at least to begin with—but Sir Henry Campbell-Bannerman's famous dictum is still valid: "Good government is no substitute for self-government." When Congress ruled the provinces for thirty-one months, in 1937-1939, it did an excellent and honest administrative job. The governments in some of the Princely States, such as Travancore, Cochin, Mysore, Bhopal, and Bikaner, are outstandingly good, and in many respects are better than those in British India. Travancore has not been conquered since the ages before Aryan times, and its Hindu dynasty is now twelve centuries old. Many of those States are strong enough to stand on their own feet without the aid of the British paramount power, but most of them, of course, are kept in existence only because the British are there, and they will be overwhelmed when the lid is lifted—although the British are hardly likely to leave India without some guarantees that the liquidation will be amicable. Lord Linlithgow, a maharaja told me, said to a group of princes when Cripps was in India: "We stand by our pledges and treaties. We will not let you down."

For Congress, of course, as Nehru put it: "The feudal Indian State system, the gilded maharajas and nabobs, and the big land-lord system, are essentially British creations in India. . . . We recognize no such treaties and we shall in no event accept them." Jinnah is willing to let the States alone. For the purposes of this book we can do likewise, since the Indian Princely States are, as the Simon Commission report put it, "without precedent or analogy elsewhere," and it is certainly beyond my knowledge or ability to solve that problem for India.

Autocratic rule has its obvious advantages and disadvantages. When it works in India it is unquestionably the most suitable and the best government for the Indian people at their present level of political consciousness. But—and the "but" is an enormous one—how are the Indian people supposed to be guaranteed that they will have benevolent, efficient rulers? How can the Maharaj Rana of Dholpur, for instance, feel sure that his successor will be as virtuous as he?

However, the Maharaj Rana may well ask, "Is India, then, ripe for democracy?" The answer, of course, is an emphatic "No!" Indian history has no background of democracy in any period. Government has always been arbitrarily imposed by force from above, and it has never sent roots down into the masses from which new plants of democracy could grow. The caste system to a Westerner, would in itself seem to make anything approximating a democracy impossible. Human equality cannot be accepted by those who believe in caste, *Karma,* and reincarnation. One must also say that, judging by Western standards, there is a great lack of civic virtues among the Indian people. Their impulses to contribute and sacrifice go to the family, not to society, state, or nation.

Rajagopalachari once worked it out for me, with typical Hindu subtlety, that India finds her democracy and a real gift for it in her caste system, since within a caste all men are equal, and they learn customs and practices which are genuinely democratic. However, that overlooks the highly aristocratic and hierarchical structure of the caste system as a whole, which is the reverse of democratic. An Indian professor of St. Stephen's College to whom I talked in Allahabad quoted his shoemaker's remarks on education: "What is the use of my son learning to read and write a little? He is a *chamar* [shoemaker] and he must always remain a *chamar*. I want him to be a good shoemaker. That is all that is of value to him. If he goes to school for several years he loses that much time from learning his trade."

One might as well face the fact that throughout their history the Indians have shown little inclination to unite in defense of their political, or what we might call today, their national independence. Some races, such as the Rajputs and Jats, have fought hard, but for themselves, and they are exceptions. India has always been a pushover for a small, determined force of invaders. There have been no popular, peasant leaders, and, until this century, no middle class capable of or willing to seek power. There have only been the rulers and the unorganized, apolitical people. Public opinion, in our sense of the term, hardly existed, and even today it is the monopoly of a small minority of educated, middle-class Indians.

Democracy, as we understand it, is an importation from the West, one that Congress embraced eagerly and hopefully, but so far with little success, although, considering the factors involved, it is extraordinary that India has made the progress toward democracy that she has. "Democracy is an Occidental idea," the Maharaja of Benares said back in the 1880's. "A Hindu cannot comprehend it so long as he is a Hindu. It is against his religious beliefs. So long as Hindus remain in Hindustan you cannot succeed in extending the democratic idea." The Maharaja overlooked the fact that there are kinds and degrees of democracy, but his thesis is arguable. However, this is not by any means so true of the Moslems, whose religion and social customs predispose them better toward the democratic way of life, although until they achieve widespread political consciousness that disposition will not have much practical effect.

As you might suppose, India's inarticulate, illiterate, poverty-stricken masses are in no position to understand ideas like democracy, or to care about them. Their answer to questions about government is simple and understandable: "What is the difference? We want food to eat and cloth to wear; that is all." There is a saying which I heard all over India, but which originated in the south, and it expresses an age-old wisdom of the villager: "Whether Rama rules or Ravana, the same weight is on my head." Rama is an Aryan god, depicted as a hero in the epic of *Ramayana.* Ravana is a Dravidian king, who is supposed to represent evil. So, whether there is a good ruler or a bad ruler, nothing changes for the people, and much of the philosophical acceptance of British rule which one finds among Indian villagers is based on that ancient precept.

It is, indeed, old wisdom that it does not make much difference to the common man who heads his government, and that has been especially true in India. The best answer is the one which Rajagopalachari gave me: "The educated Indian must be trusted to do what is right for his people. As an Indian, he knows what they want and need, even if they cannot express themselves in terms of modern democratic politics." That, surely, is fair enough, as long as one frankly admits the truth about the masses and makes no wild claims, as Congress does, of a responsible, representative government based upon the will of the people expressed by due democratic process in the voting booths. India will come to that when her masses are educated, but, as I said before, education is literally an insuperable task, short of generations of work and colossal sums of money. Meanwhile, it is a contradiction to talk of a democratic system in a country whose average of literacy is 12.17 per cent.

No doubt, one should add that you cannot have a democracy with a people as wretched as the Indians. One in four, or about

100,000,000, get malaria every year, and other diseases are terribly widespread. In general, Indians have a lower nutrition level and a higher incidence of illness than any other people in the world. It has not helped the situation to find Gandhi continually singling out Western medicine for sharp attacks. Hospitals, he wrote in *Indian Home Rule* in 1919, were "institutions for propagating sin," while the medical profession was "injurious to mankind."

One reason for ill-health and poverty is, of course, overpopulation. It is almost incredible but it is true and appalling that in the decade between the 1931 and 1941 censuses India's population increased more than 50,000,000. That increase alone is more than the population of the British Isles. India is now on a level with China and perhaps is passing her, with much less territory. Between them they have two fifths of the population of the globe. There are more Hindus than there are Protestants in the whole world.

In India, the population is bred up to the maximum. When a canal is made, enriching an area by irrigation, the families immediately increase their numbers up to the point that the increased output can stand. Hence, the raising of the standard of living is extremely difficult. The population decreases only when it starves. Birth control is one of the important answers; but only a few in the middle classes use it; there are great religious prejudices against it, especially among the Hindus. In some ways, population is India's problem number one. You could maintain the present level of food production with half the population and have a vastly higher standard of living. Unfortunately, there is little cultivable soil to be taken up, and however much industrialization is pushed it can hardly take up more than a small fraction of an annual increase of five millions.

I once talked to the Maharaj Rana of Dholpur about birth control and the population problem. Needless to say, he was completely unsympathetic. "If the population is too great," he said, "the Almighty, who knows everything, sees everything, takes care of everything, might send an influenza epidemic to restore the balance. We must leave it up to Him. We have no right to destroy souls. It is only God who has that right. Anyway, perhaps the suffering caused by the epidemic would be deserved. There was that time Gandhi destroyed a calf with poison because it was suffering. People then said: 'That calf was ordained to suffer in that incarnation. By cutting short his suffering you make his soul carry that much unfulfilled destiny into the next incarnation, when he will suffer all the more for it.' "

There is no co-operation, in short, by either the masses or their rulers, and the pressure of population in India must be expected to continue until Nature—or the Almighty, as the Maharaj Rana put it—takes a frightful price. The Malthusian theory of population is being borne out in India, as Captain R. G. Wreford demonstrated in his report on Jammu and Kashmir for the 1941 census.

"Malthus affirmed that the power of population to increase is infinitely greater than the power in the earth to produce subsistence for men, and that population, when unchecked, increases in geometrical ratio, while subsistence only increases in arithmetical ratio," he wrote. "The geometrical ratio Malthus had in mind was not *any* ratio but a particular ratio, *i.e.* doubling every twenty-five years, and it was the ratio that would operate not in any population but in an unchecked population. . . . The essence of his teaching is that the tendency of a population to outpace the means of subsistence is, and always has been, constantly operating and is causing dreadful things, misery and vice, here and now, and has always done so. . . .

"The methods of contraception now practiced in Western countries are practically unknown in India except in the cities, and even where these methods are known the facilities for using them are limited and the cost beyond the means of the masses. . . . The conditions in India today in general more closely resemble the conditions in Europe in the time of Malthus than present-day conditions in Europe, and the Malthusian theory applies with full force to our population problems."

And so you have your grinding poverty, due not only to factors beyond human control such as unhealthy climate, rainfall, and uneconomic distribution of natural resources, but to that frightening pressure of population.

"No one can understand India who ignores this degrading, debasing poverty which is one inseparable link in the vicious circle of ignorance, superstition, oppression, ill-health, infant mortality, lack of sanitation and the continued persistence of such epidemic diseases as cholera, dysentery, plague, enteric, malaria, hook-worm, smallpox and other preventable diseases," wrote Dr. Higginbottom in his book, *The Gospel and the Plow.* "It is a poverty which robs manhood, womanhood and childhood of all that is best and most worthwhile in them."

The Simon Commission made the very optimistic estimate that the average annual income of the Indian in 1935 was £8 (then $40). However, even granting that, you must keep in mind that if $40 is the average, many millions are below that figure. The earnings of the villager are lower than those of the urban worker, and the villagers comprise nine out of ten in India. So the real remedy for India's poverty (granting the inability to restrain population) is raising the level of agricultural production. Dr. Higginbottom, who not only is one of the real experts on Indian agriculture but who proved at his 700-acre model farm outside Allahabad just what can be done with the ordinary means and methods at the disposal of any Indian, maintains that the problem of poverty could be solved if the land were made to yield what it is capable of yielding. Religious inhibitions, waste, poor technique, and not enough work are the answers, he says. Because of the Hindu rule against taking life, pests cannot be fought. Parrots and crows eat what they please, and so do insects. Each one of them has a soul, according to Hindu transmigration, and it must go through its cycle. It is only the low-caste Hindu (the *Mali*) who can grow vegetables. The higher caste, who grows wheat, rice, millet, and other grains, will not under any circumstances grow carrots or cauliflowers. If each farmer set aside a little vegetable patch he could grow enough to keep his family in vegetables, and malnutrition would end for millions of Indians. Instead, he has to buy vegetables, or do without them.

According to Dr. Higginbottom, India is, on the whole, the

richest agricultural country in the world. In most of the cultivable lands there are two to four crops a year, with often never a month in the year without crops growing. The depredations of monkeys and other wild animals are tolerated because they must not be killed. The cattle problem is outstanding. "Cow protection," that tragic farce, means the maintenance of far more cattle than is economically desirable. More than 90 per cent of the cattle are an economic loss to the country. India, with one forty-third of the habitable area of the world has one third of the cattle population. There are two head of cattle to every three persons. Indians pay more to keep cows alive than all their taxation put together. The best bullocks are castrated, for draft purposes, and the worst are used for breeding. The poor products cannot be prevented from breeding, in turn, for it is against religion to interfere with the process of procreation.

The Jam Saheb of Nawanager once told me that no ruler could try to reduce the number of cows. His subjects would stage a revolution. Four hundred years ago an ancestor of his who was religiously inclined decreed that cows were not to be taxed, so when he tried to tax them in Nawanagar there was such a protest he had to stop, but he is eliminating goats from his State, by progressively higher taxation.

As the sensible Sam Johnson remarked, "A cow is a very good animal in the field; but we turn her out of the garden."

If the Indians could only eat the cows—but, of course, that is out of the question. Malnutrition is probably worse in India than anywhere else in the world. It can be demonstrated that many millions of Indians are living on less than is required to keep a body alive, for the fact is that they are slowly dying. I watched the Bengal famine of 1943, which took 1,000,000 lives, shaping up from before Christmas of 1942, and it was a terrible experience. Six months before it broke into widespread famine, such as the British thought they had banished from India forever, it was correct to say, "There are reasonable chances to save the country from grave developments." The British failed to do so, and the failure is one of the black marks against their rule in

India, although it is only fair to add that they received no help from those Indians in a position to aid their fellow Indians.

The famine, at any rate, was another proof that the secret of increasing India's well-being lies in raising the level of agricultural production. Gandhi knows that, but he refuses to believe that the increase should be sought in modern, improved methods. His economic program, on the whole, would reduce production. For instance, he wants the Indians to use the plow of five thousand years ago, although newer and equally simple types of plows have been proved better. However, his encouragement of village industries is doubtless sound, and especially so in this period of disrupted communications and high prices of factory-made goods.

I visited Gandhi's All India Cottage Industries Association, which is affiliated with his *ashram* at Sevagram. It sounded the keynote of the Mahatma's economic system, which consists of reviving ancient village handicrafts, in order to employ peasants between crops—a sound idea. The Association was then in a moribund state, with its leaders imprisoned, and all over British India I noticed the extent to which the whole system of village industries, so laboriously but sketchily erected, was collapsing. It was not proving a success, either economically or in arousing mass support, which was regrettable. The economics of it are not conventional. I went through the paper-making factory where a coarse, poor-quality paper was being made by hand with simple, ancient methods. Although many workmen and much labor were involved, the paper was cheaper than the mill-made product, but one had to be patriotic to want to use it. On the other hand, one still finds in India beautiful examples of hand-spinning and weaving (*khaddar,* it is called) and other of India's dying handicrafts which Congress is trying, with good reason, to keep alive.

In general, Gandhi's economic ideas, although capable of sound development along some lines, are a case of fighting against that same industrial revolution through which countries like England went more than a century ago.

It is true that the Indian village seems to have the permanency of mountain tops in the Himalayas. Sir Charles Metcalfe, reporting to the East India company in 1832, said: "The village communities are little republics, having nearly everything that they want within themselves, and almost independent of any foreign relations. They seem to last within themselves where nothing else lasts. Dynasty after dynasty tumbles down; revolution succeeds revolution; Hindu, Pathan, Mogul, Maratha, Sikh, English, are all masters in turn; but the village communities remain the same."

One permanent feature of village life which both the British and the Congress have been trying, with little success, to combat is the system of indebtedness—and it is a veritable system—that oppresses the villager. Nehru, with great assurance and inconsequentiality, makes out the solution to be a simple one. "The most important and urgent problem of the country," he wrote in 1936, "is the appalling poverty, unemployment, and indebtedness of the peasantry, fundamentally due to antiquated and repressive land tenure and revenue systems, and intensified in recent years by the great slump in prices of agricultural produce. [Prices have since risen.] The final solution of this problem inevitably involves the removal of British imperialistic exploitation, a thorough change of the land tenure and revenue systems, and a recognition by the state of its duty to provide work for the rural unemployed masses."

It is true that the British, inadvertently, are to blame for the land system which led to the peasant being enslaved to the money lender—the vicious, blood-sucking *bania* and *marwari* from the Gujerat, Kathiawar, and Rajputana. Penderel Moon, for one, frankly admits it. The British created new classes of landlords whose tenants became virtual serfs, while millions of other peasants received proprietary rights in small landholdings which gave them a source of credit which they did not know how to use wisely. By the time the evil was recognized (following a real *jacquerie* in the Deccan in the 1870's), it was too late. The *bania* is now protected by the British legal system, whereas in the old, easygoing days the money lender, whatever his legal rights, was not allowed to suck the peasant dry. Now, in the Punjab and a few other provinces, laws have been passed to protect the villagers, but the result has merely been to dry up credit without in general relieving the indebtedness of the peasant.

It is not "the antiquated and repressive land tenure and revenue systems" which cause peasant poverty and indebtedness, as Nehru says. He overlooks the fact that in many parts of the country, such as the Punjab, Bombay, and Madras Provinces, the peasant proprietors own most of the land. Moreover, the land revenue, in continuance of the Mogul system, is not oppressive in comparison with those of other countries.

Peasant indebtedness in this twentieth century is, however, an overwhelming fact, whatever the original reasons were, and it is the indebtedness which sets up a vicious circle that contributes greatly toward keeping the villager desperately poor. If he increases his production, the money lender gets the increase. If, through irrigation, his yield is higher, that increases his credit, so (after first arranging to have more children) he immediately borrows more—not, unfortunately, to improve his land, but invariably for such uneconomic purposes as funeral or marriage ceremonies. It is not unusual for a peasant to spend from one to three years' income on the marriage of his daughter, and the money is borrowed from the village *bania*. "Keeping up with the Joneses" is a major Indian vice. There is no race more sensitive about "face"—or *izzat* as they call it. The Hindu would rather submit to violence, theft, or perjury than to loss of *izzat*. To be humiliated is the ultimate insult which he will never forgive.

It is that same *bania* and *marwari* element, plus the Bengali Hindu and the Parsis which dominates the Indian industrial and financial fields. To give them credit, even as village money lenders, they play a role which has its useful side, for in bad years they have to carry the peasants who owe them money. There is an old Punjab saying, "In good times the *bania* eats us; in bad we eat him." Moreover, the usurious rates they charge are partly justified by the high proportion of bad debts and the danger they run from desperate villagers. However, the village money lender is an unattractive creature at best. He improves a good deal when he goes to the cities and becomes an industrialist or banker.

Bombay has been conquered by the Indian industrialist. Where Calcutta is dominated by the great British managing agents, Bombay, the second largest city in India, is under the control of Parsis and Hindus, who have proved that in the stern and bitter struggle for business supremacy Indians can hold their own. Bombay has Indian business leaders like J. R. D. Tata, the young head of a great Parsi firm which controls the highly efficient steel and iron industry of Jamshedpur as well as many other businesses; G. D. Birla and his two brothers, who have immense textile and other interests, and Walchand Hirachand, whose construction works alone employ 100,000 laborers.

Such Indian magnates are looking ahead to the days when the country will be run by their own people. Immense and rosy vistas lie before them, marred only by the danger, which they admit, of chaos or even civil war which might follow the struggle for power when the British withdraw.

"We have all the important material resources except oil," Tata told me, "and we have inexhaustible man-power which has proved that with training it is as good as any. Enormous returns would follow the investment of revenues in roads, sanitation, education, agricultural improvement. The villager has never had a chance, but by raising his standard of living we can create vast purchasing power in our internal market alone. The British need not go, but they have so antagonized us by their die-hard tactics, and have done so much to retard Indian independence, that I am afraid they will find it difficult to carry on. If they had made friends with us, they would have had Indian good will, but they are deluding themselves in counting upon it now. In the future, India's links will be with the United States rather than with Britain."

Birla and Walchand, on various occasions, talked a good deal to me of India's future in international markets. The country will become another Japan in that respect, judging from what they and the Indian business men of Calcutta and Delhi say. "There is no mystery about it," said Walchand. "You in the United States pay your workmen $4 or $5 daily. I pay mine 1 rupee 8 annas [45 cents]." However, he and the others deny the

British charge that they use sweated labor or underpay their workmen. Birla, for instance, claims that his organization treats laborers better than the British, understands what they feel and what their grievances are, and, in general, is more loyal to them. I happen to know, however, that Birla's benevolence toward his workers is a relatively recent matter, for in earlier days his laborers worked under exceedingly bad conditions. Now Birla claims that a study of statistics would show that on the whole his firm pays workers higher wages than do the British firms. He, like other Indian industrialists, asserts that Indians are more efficient than British.

One of the most important accusations against the British is that they retarded industrial development in India and are still doing so. Walchand Hirachand is one of the most vocal Indians on that subject. He is the stormy petrel of Indian industry, fighting tooth and nail to build up shipping, automobile, and aircraft industries in India and, according to him, meeting nothing but obstruction from the British authorities. It would take much space to repeat his detailed account of the obstacles which he says the British have put in his way during the past twenty-five years. It has made him bitterly anti-British, and he resents intensely what he feels to be the British assumption of social superiority and the treatment of Indians as inferiors. Birla also had some bitter things to say regarding his youthful struggles in Calcutta. Whatever justification there may be, there is no doubt that the British have made enemies of these powerful business leaders, and their animosity is playing a part in the political struggle in which the Congress is being financed by these industrialists.

That whole question of the British control of India's economic resources is, of course, fundamental. The British went to India and conquered it—much to their surprise and partly without wishing to do so—on a business venture of the East India Company. The exploitation of India is one of the standard accusations against the British by Indian nationalists and their sympathizers. So let us look dispassionately at the situation.

Calcutta, the city where Clive began the long British tradition, is the place to go, for it is there that those powerful industrial forces which dominated India are making their last stand, backed by the real source of their strength—the City of London.

You begin from the undoubted fact that industry was built up by the British. They started the jute mills, built the ships, exploited the coal mines and the tea plantations. To do so, they created "managing agencies," which are unique. Bird & Co., for instance, correctly advertises that it has "activities in practically every field of Indian industry." That includes jute, coal, canvas, cement, engineering, insurance, lime, minerals, oil, paper, stone, and sugar. McKinnon & MacKenzie dominate the shipping industry and have other important interests.

These agencies resulted from the difficulties of financing, transporting, and marketing Indian products, and now fully half of the country's industries are controlled through such firms, with the Indians adapting the same formula, although the British control a good deal more than do the Indians. Birla Bros., Ltd., for instance, handle cotton, sugar, paper, shipping, insurance, jute, machinery, and other odds and ends.

The managing agency is the channel through which the British dominate so large a part of Indian industry. The agents are about 75 per cent British. You cannot establish a new industry in India except through agents, because the banks will not lend money until a business is already functioning. Hence, the agents must float the company, either through credit or by putting shares on the market with their backing. There is plenty of Indian money invested through these shares, and, theoretically, the shareholders could get together and assert themselves, but practically the managing agents run the whole show.

The system was a natural development, designed to solve the problems of transportation and marketing from remote India. A normal tea garden of, say, 350 acres, could not afford to advertise, ship, and sell its tea in England and elsewhere. An *entrepreneur* handles of dozens of such plantations, which is economical. Hence, it is the group in the managing agency which has the control, and the profits depend upon the efficiency of its management.

The coal, jute, tea, chemicals, and copper industries, for instance, are controlled up to 80 per cent by the British. Indians are strong in the textile, steel, and sugar fields, in which they have, so to speak, beaten the British at their own game. Exchange banking, however, is entirely British (although there are Indian banks for internal financing). This is very important, for it means the British have the grip on imports, exports, and shipping.

These managing agencies are immensely profitable concerns, and, naturally, the British wish to retain them. (Here are some average dividends for 1941, and succeeding years have been at least as profitable: Cotton mills 14.44 per cent, jute mills 18.99, engineering works 13.54, sugar mills 11.58, tea companies 18.79, paper mills 13.19 per cent.) At the same time, it is certainly natural that their Indian rivals should try to divert businesses away from them, and in that struggle much is involved which is political as well as financial.

The British managing agents are largely employees of former founders and partners who have retired, and have gone home with their holdings. They reside in London, and it is to their interest to see that British policy does not result in their firms being put out of India. That is the sound basis for the accusation that the City of London influences the British Government's attitude toward Indian independence. Three lords controlled enormous holdings in India and still do, or, at least, their families do—Lord Inchcape, through McKinnon & MacKenzie and other firms; Lord Catto, through Ewel & Co.; and Lord Cables through Bird & Co. (Cables is dead, and the control now is through Sir Edward Benthall, War Transport Member of the Viceroy's Council, the son-in-law of Cables).

The British business men, of course, are greatly worried by the prospect of Indian freedom. They point to the fact, which I have already mentioned, that big Indian *banias* and *marwaris,* such as the Birla brothers and Walchand Hirachand, finance Congress. Therefore, it is argued, Congress will have a debt to pay to them, and that payment will result in the elimination of the British business interests. B. M. Birla, G. D.'s younger brother, who works in Calcutta, made it clear to me that he is openly determined to oust the British. Moreover, the Indian industrialists I talked to are not afraid that Nehru's socialistic ideas will gain the ascendancy. Even if he should run the show later, there is an evident belief that he will be "sensible," and if he is not he will find both Indian and British industrialists united against him. During the war, indeed, most Indian business men have kept their feet in both British and Congress camps.

Another thing the British fear is that Birla and others want to buy out their interests. B. M. Birla wants to use the recently acquired sterling credits of India to purchase British holdings. The British claim that would be unfair, especially since there is no way of estimating the value of their interests which, they say, consist largely of good-will, training, experience, the ability to run their affairs well, and a reputation for integrity and efficiency. Indian investors and producers trust them, and they claim they are more efficient than the Indians. One British leader said to me that it is like a man seeing someone riding in a Rolls Royce. Naturally, he would like to have that Rolls Royce, but has he the right to it and can he pay for it? The Indian shareholders, the British assert, would be the last to want to see the British go, and they also say that Indian laborers prefer to work for the British because they get better pay and treatment.

The Indians, of course, argue differently. They say that British good will is exaggerated, or even lost, due to political animosities, and that, anyway, the British have been overpaid many times for their good will and everything else, by enormous profits made over generations. Another objection is that the British do not stay in India, nor keep their money or profits there. They work and make fortunes, and then go home. As Sir Badridas Goenka, the most powerful *marwari* of Calcutta, said to me, "It would have been all right if, like the Parsis from Persia, they had become Indians, absorbed in the country's structure, instead of remaining foreigners who exploit the country for Britain's benefit."

R. R. Haddow, President of the Bengal Chamber of Commerce and bursar of McKinnon & MacKenzie, made the point that the Indian threats forced the British business community to go into politics—which is another of those vicious circles. "It is the wish of the British community in India to continue to be of service to the country and to assist in its progress, both in regard to agriculture and industry," he said in a speech while I was in Calcutta. "All they ask is that they receive the same treatment in India as the Indians receive in Britain."

And always there is the charge of the British hampering or even preventing the proper industrialization of India. The British admit that this was true in the past—which it certainly was— but they claim that since the fiscal reforms of the early 1920's that has been changed. They point to the industries now dominated by the Indians, as well as to a certain amount of tariff protection now being granted to Indian industries. Moreover, they say, with justice, that they merely followed in India an economic policy of *laissez-faire* which has been in the British tradition for centuries and was not adopted exclusively for India. That is their answer to the Indian complaint that the British have refused to help industrialize the country, and this is, in fact, the chief grievance of the Indians. Any virgin field such as India, they say, needs tariff protection, subsidies, preferences, and priorities, all of which the British are either withholding or granting in the most niggardly fashion. The textile and the steel industries were established, according to them, against British desires and by fighting at every step against British obstructionism.

When the Indians run India, they say, it will be different. So their patriotism and their financial interests run parallel, leading them to the logical conclusion that the British must quit India.

(Incidentally, I might better have used the word "Scottish" instead of "British," for the Scots dominate the business field in India. Numerically, they are a small minority, but they have most of the top positions. Virtually every tea plantation manager in Assam is a Scot, and so are the most important figures among the British managing agent firms.)

Sir Frederick Stones, who runs Sassoon's great establishment in Bombay, frankly admitted to me that the British industrialists are fighting a losing game in India. For years they have ceased expanding, and there is little desire to invest new money in India. Certainly, one of the outstanding features of the Indian situation is the fact that Indian business men are making good and gradually overpowering those British industrial forces which have played so great a role in the domination of India.

The question of Indian business ethics is one on which I heard many burning words from the British in Calcutta, Bombay, and Madras. To assert that Indian ethics and standards are different from ours is to make a simple statement of fact. It could not be otherwise, given the differences in tradition between Orientals and Occidentals. An important English business man of Madras, dealing with an Indian whom he had known for years, asked him whether he thought he, the Englishman, could be bribed. After some coaxing, the Indian said, "Only a very big bribe." But that Englishman had Indians working for him (and the same was true of other firms) who had powers of attorney and could sign away all the company's money. They trusted them implicitly. Yet those Indians, they asserted, would not trust their fellow Indians.

In Bombay, an American connected with the Sassoon organization told me that it is impossible to get an honest statement of accounts or auditing from Indian firms. The figures must be audited by the British as well, before Indians themselves will trust them. One very high British official claimed that the "chartered accountant" system, which the British introduced into India, is the secret of British success. Indians saw they could trust British accountancy, whereas their own firms had to make 25 per cent profit for the directors before they began passing earnings on to the shareholders.

These charges are angrily denied by Indian industrialists, who claim that the British resent the greater efficiency of the Indians and are trying to discourage them by making false accusations. As is usually the case in India, "You pays your money and you takes your choice."

Not having time to visit a large number of factories, mines, or plantations and to make comparisons, I was in no position to decide whether conditions under the Indians were better or worse than under the British. Both sides made the usual contradictory claims. An International Labor Office report said that conditions of work in India compare favorably with those in many European countries, and Sir George Schuster, an expert in such matters, doubtless put it fairly when he said, "They are probably more advanced than in any other Asiatic country." We can leave it at that.

To be sure, the Communist leader, P. C. Joshi, and other Bombay labor leaders claim that working conditions are extraordinarily bad in the factories and mills. Joshi said to me that there was little to choose between Indian- or British-run concerns, but Indian employers understand their workers better and, in general, laborers prefer to work for them. One often finds individual Indian employers who are quite progressive, he added, but the British keep to a machine-like level which is never better than average.

The labor-union movement in India is pitifully backward, quarrelsome, and corrupt. The difficulty of organizing Indian workers and peasants, even in the best of circumstances, can easily be imagined, but when there is added to that the fact that union leaders oftener than not betray the workers and abscond with their money, one can appreciate how impossible the situation has been. There is a veritable curse over the labor movement. Ahmedabad, where there are great textile mills, is one of the few well-organized trade-union centers, and that for a very Indian reason—Gandhi, himself, did the organizing and is the inspiration of the movement. The workers follow him, and when there are strikes as many as 80 or 90 per cent go out. However, in normal times membership is down to 20 per cent.

Communism has made very little impression on India as yet, but with the prestige, advice, and money of Russia behind it, the movement could become important. As a matter of fact, the best organizers which the party had were British Communists, who took over for a while, some twenty years ago. The active membership now, P. C. Joshi told me (and other leaders confirmed it), was less than 12,000, but there are many more sympathizers, of course. The movement was illegal until Germany attacked Russia, and the Communists expressed their desire to help in the United Nations' war effort.

Congress leaders, and especially Gandhi, always fought the Communists, although Nehru defended them behind the scenes. In view of their avowed espousal of the working-class cause, Congressmen in the past could not very well put the Communists out, but they try always to weaken them, and no Communist has been allowed on the Working Committee, the highest Congress body. The Communist social and economic philosophy and anti-religious doctrines are anathema to Gandhi, not to mention their antipathy to non-violence. Rajagopalachari, however, told me he believed that some form of Communism, "different from Marxism," and on the order of Owenism, could get a hold on the Indian masses. There is a sort of basis for Communism in the family community, which holds together tenaciously, divides its property, and shares its resources, but there are, of course, very great factors opposing it, such as religion, the fact that India is rural and not industrial, the caste system (although you have there a possible variation of the syndicate), the lack of discipline and political consciousness, the intense feeling for private property.

The oft-made analogy between Russia and India appears unwarranted to me. Russia did not have the ancient village system, the joint family, the overpopulation, the communal problem, the States or the paramount power. On the religious side, one cannot conceive of the Moslem tolerating an anti-religious movement although the Hindu, despite his religious feelings, is so tolerant of other religions that he might also be tolerant of none. The Hindu is, on the whole, not good revolutionary material, and he would have less discipline and energy than required. The chief obstacles, clearly, are the communal problem and the Princely States.

At the same time, no one can deny, as Edgar Snow rightly points out, that five- or ten-year economic plans on the Russian order could do great things for India, although there is neither the leadership nor the authority as yet to put them over. More-

over, the Russians are accomplishing exactly what India needs—
a rapid, efficient industrialization and collective or co-operative
agriculture. Certainly, the young Indian intellectual is correct
in looking to Russia for guidance.

One could wish that the signposts in India were set more
toward Communism and Socialism than toward Fascism, but it
would be gullible to think so. I have already pointed to the
one-party tendencies exemplified by Congress and the Moslem
League, by Gandhi and Jinnah. There are other elements that
show a Fascist, not a Communist, trend—big business, high officialdom, the Princes, the Army. It is unfortunate, but true, that
a Fascist structure of government and society is much more easily
possible (I feel almost inclined to say "suitable," if Fascism can
ever be suitable) in India than Communism.

It need hardly be added, India being what it is, that the radical elements, like all others in the political arena, are split into
many factions. Joshi, for instance, calls the Socialists "Trotsky-
ites."

This has taken us somewhat far afield from the question of
the British industrial grip on India. As I said, it is weakening.
Moreover, we have witnessed in these years the extraordinary
shift of India from a debtor to a great creditor nation *vis-à-vis*
England. London spent all its rupee balances, and owes India
something like the equivalent of four or five billion dollars in
sterling credits now that the war has ended. It is one of the
ironies of history that Great Britain, which is accused of being
the great imperialist, and of literally drawing the "wealth of the
Indies" out of her crown colony, should have run more and more
into India's debt. In a sense, it is India which is now exploiting
England.

But the important thing to keep in mind is that India is an
overwhelmingly agricultural country, and no amount of industrialization will greatly affect the living standards of the masses,
for many years.

"For any appreciable advance in the standard of living of the
Indian masses there is only one method, and that is to increase
the productivity of their labor," wrote Sir George Schuster. "If

the whole of the profits of big business in industry were divided equally among the whole of the Indian people, that would only give them an extra 3 annas [the anna is worth about 2 cents] per head per year. If the whole of the peace-time cost of the Army and the whole net annual charge of the Indian national debt were remitted and a corresponding sum divided among the people equally, that would only give them about 1¼ rupees per head per annum. If the value of India's exports were increased by 25 per cent and there were no corresponding rise in the cost of India's imports, the net benefit to the Indian people would only amount to 1 rupee per head per annum. . . . By industrial development alone it will be impossible to lift the whole level of Indian standards adequately and, indeed, there can be no sure foundation for industrial progress itself unless the condition and purchasing power of the agricultural population are concurrently improved."

The Maharaj Rana of Dholpur—and Gandhi, for that matter— are not advocating unsound economics in wanting to concentrate on the betterment of agriculture and village economy. This would be a true Indian way out of the present distress. But industrialization is coming, whether they like it or not, and the Indian themselves will adopt it. That basis for British imperialism is doomed, along with others, although Indians are not willing to admit it.

However, a witty Moslem writer in *Ulus,* Falih Rifki Atay, makes fun of his compatriots by adding a new detail to the famous elephant story, in which the Britisher writes on hunting, the Frenchman on the elephant's love life, the German a scientific monograph in five volumes, the Russian a mystical work on "Does the Elephant Exist?", and the Pole on "The Elephant and the Polish Question." Atay adds that the Indian nationalist writes a book entitled "The Elephant, Another Victim of British Imperialism."

If one yields to the temptation of making a sweeping generalization, it seems safe to say that imperialism, however successful in previous centuries, has been a failure in the twentieth, and its day, as Sumner Welles expressed it, is over. The British are faced in India with one of its evils. Once a great power takes over a lesser country, it is almost impossible to get out or give up peacefully. You become involved; you set up standards, make connections, rouse hopes and promises, develop duties, and, in a sense, become dependent upon your dependency.

It does not follow that Churchill, Linlithgow, Wavell and the others are any the less imperialists. Lord Linlithgow used to talk of being "a servant of His Majesty's Government as well as of the Indian government." At the same time he claimed that everything the British have said and done showed they were gradually getting out of India.

"Money isn't being invested here," he said, "and men won't volunteer for the Indian Civil Service. It is because we are leaving that we have no friends. If we said we were going to stay seventy-five years more, we should have plenty of friends. No one wants to be friends with a side that is losing and disappearing."

I had a number of frank and revealing talks with Lord Linlithgow in India, and since I came to know him fairly well I can no longer allow myself the luxury of painting him as all black or all white. He had both great drawbacks and great gifts as a viceroy. Certainly, he was a servant of His Majesty's Government first, and a servant of India only secondly. That was, so to speak, his job, and the British will doubtless rate him in their histories as one of their great viceroys. He saved India for the British Empire, in a very crucial period.

How much good he did for India is questionable, although he and his admirers can rightly point to the fact that preparation for the war and the conduct of India during the war were his primary tasks and were all-absorbing. I asked him the day before I left New Delhi (which was a few months before the end of his record term of seven and a half years) if he were not discouraged, but he said he had not expected to solve all India's problems. However, I did have the impression that he was somewhat discouraged, sensitive, resentful, and very conscious of the criticisms that had been leveled against him, but at the same time he was utterly sure that he had done the right thing and had taken the only line that could have been taken. He kept harping upon his responsibility, and the total lack of responsibility among his critics and all others who were commenting on the Indian situation.

"That is the key to everything," he said. "When you are grappling with the immense problems of order, administration, and the like, all you can do is work from day to day, handling your daily problems. There is very little scope for looking ahead to long-term policies. Ever since 1938 my policy has had to be dominated by the war, and many things went by the board."

I had the feeling that the Viceroy was very conscious of "the white man's burden," although he never used the words. He did say that we in the United States and they in Britain come out to India with higher standards, ideals, and ideas than the Indians have, and the people cannot rise to them. I pointed out that while the State Department would doubtless not bother him or his successor again during the war, and would not bring pressure as it had in 1942, most Americans felt that something ought to be done or tried, even with the certainty of failure.

"Do you mean long-term or short-term?" he asked.

"After the war," I said. He nodded, and answered that he had the impression that Ambassador William Phillips had gone back to the United States convinced that something could be done during the war, but he, Linlithgow, was certain nothing could.

"I have the responsibility of running the country, and, faced with that, there is nothing that can be tried. I told Mr. Phillips that I was certain of the correctness of my attitude, and that I would not change. I faced up to Gandhi once, and would do so again."

I put forward the possibility of accomplishing little things, such as the complete Indianization of the Viceroy's Council, appointing an Indian chief justice, closing the Indian Civil Service lists to Englishmen, and cited a statement by King George VI assuring India of further self-government after the war.

"I give you full counts on all those points," he said, "but you do not have to run this country. You do not know the intelligence reports. You haven't got the responsibility of seeing that everything connected with the war is properly handled."

So, your judgment of Lord Linlithgow must depend on your point of view. You cannot doubt his sincerity, honesty, or motives, for they were crystal-clear. In working for His Majesty's Government, I am sure he felt he was doing what was best for India. Moreover, he did try to put the 1935 Act into effect, and it was during his term that the Cripps Plan was offered.

"Look at these nearly four years of war!" Sir Gilbert Laithwaite, the Viceroy's Secretary, said to me as I bade him farewell. "We put up target after target, and they just shot them down, with a few on the corners taking angle-shots just to make sure that nothing was left. Then they said, rubbing their hands: 'Well, that's that!' All right, but what have they offered in exchange? Nothing! Sometimes one gets tired of being told all the time, 'It is up to you to settle this for us.' "

That is a legitimate viewpoint, although it leads to that *impasse* I mentioned earlier. The British are telling the Indians: "Settle your political and communal problems, propose a feasible national government to us, demonstrate that you will respect our rights and maintain order, and we will grant you dominion status and quit India." But the Indians cannot do those things, in the circumstances, so they all go round and round the vicious circle, and nothing happens.

It is all right to blame the British, because they deserve blame and, besides, as Laithwaite said to me, "the British don't mind criticism; that's what we are here for." But while we are apportioning blame, we must deal out a fair amount to the Indians.

Congress, as George Bernard Shaw said of Lord Rosebery, "has never missed a chance of losing an opportunity" in recent years. It demanded the impossible, overestimated its own strength, and underestimated that of the British. At the most critical period of the British Empire and the World War, it started an "open rebellion." Meanwhile, the Moslem League took a negative, impossible stand for a mythical Moslem nation. The Cripps Plan was a great step forward, and many Indians told me privately they regretted that it had been turned down—but that is the sort of mistake which is becoming commonplace in India. Is it any wonder that the end of it all is frustration and bitterness? Four hundred millions run by a handful of foreigners just because they cannot get together and throw the foreigners out!

Just stop to think how few Britishers there are in India. According to the 1941 census, there are only 135,000 "Europeans of origin," including the normal army garrison, in India, which is one European to 3,000 Indians. By 1942, Indians already topped the British in the Indian Civil Service by 632 to 573, and the proportion is still higher now. The Provincial Civil Service is entirely Indian in composition. In 1,500,000 government servants, 3,000 are British. In the police services there are 400 British in 200,000, and in the general administrative services the proportion of Indians to British is eight to one. Yet, it is the British who run India, and they run India because the Indians will not unite —and the Indians will not unite for all the complicated reasons I have given in these pages.

And so the wheels within wheels revolve, and the British stand complacently by, strong in their unity of purpose and loyalty, while Moslem and Hindu, Brahmin and non-Brahmin, Khan and non-Khan, Shia and Sunni, Digamber and Savitamber, chase each other round in vicious circles. Is one being sarcastic, or wise, to point to the timelessness of the East?

Time, in India, is often represented as a wheel revolving eternally, swinging up toward evolution and back toward involution, thus ending a period and beginning another. The first revolution is still taking place, according to Jain chronology, and Lord Ronaldshay, in one of his books, gives the revolution of the wheel in that first swing, according to the Jains, as four *crores* of *crores* of *sagaropama*. A *crore* is ten million, and a *sagaropama* is 100,000,000 of *palya*, multiplied by 100,000,000, and the *palya*, itself, consists of countless years. "Even the geologist must feel chastened when confronted with this specimen of time, chipped off from eternity by the meticulously minded Jain," concludes Ronaldshay.

Someone once spoke of the Indians as living in "pathetic contentment." Certainly, there are a patience and a submissiveness worthy of a better reward.

The East bow'd low before the blast,
In patient, deep disdain.
She let the legions thunder past,
And plunged in thought again.

But today the legions will not thunder past. The world is now too small, and India is a world problem. The British rightly ask whether, if there is a civil war, the four major powers will create a *cordon sanitaire* and will wash their hands of the matter, or will one or all establish a protectorate, or will the new United Nations Organization intervene? In view of India's importance, can it be allowed to create a chaos, which might stir the Moslem world all through the Middle East?

It is safe to say that today the chief preoccupation of the British with Indian independence is the fear that if they leave and chaos or civil war occur, the Russians especially, but also the Afghans and perhaps the Chinese, will come in to quell the storms and remain there. The British are certain that these others would not let India stew in her juice—and they are on her frontiers, not half way across the world. If the British get out, the balance of three continents will be upset, and that is something which few people stop to consider, the former Viceroy said to me on two occasions.

I believe the British to be entirely sincere when they say that if, or when, they go there will be many years of civil strife and chaos. All signs, indeed, point that way, and many important Indians admitted as much to me. However, exactly the same thing could have been said—and was said—of the thirteen American colonies—but out of civil strife and chaos the United States was fashioned. It all depends on who is paying the price, and what the rewards are.

The Indians have a right to self-government and they are capable in the long run of governing themselves, but they will not find independence along the roads on which they are now traveling. They will find it only when Hindu and Moslem, Punjabi, Bengali, Madrasi, and Pathan, Prince and villager, can stand up together and say, "We are Indians, and we will all fight together for India."

Recess in Afghanistan

WHEN Alexander the Great, as Samuel Johnson put it, "swept India," he went through what is now Afghanistan, and Darius went before him. If Hitler, who was also seeking new worlds to conquer, had crashed through the Caucasus, as he was expected to do in 1942, he, too, would have gone through Afghanistan. There one finds the roads to India, those ancient caravan trails that men and riches followed millennia before Christ. From Lazul, in Badhakshan, came blue stones, which the ancients called "lapis lazuli," to gladden the heart of pharaohs of Egypt ages before the exodus of the Jews. And still today, in the old bazaar of Lab-i-Darya on the river that runs through Kabul, you buy from venders squatting in their stalls the best lapis lazuli that the world can provide.

The Hinduism of the Aryans and the Zoroastrian teachings of the Parsis began there in the Hindu Kush Mountains and on that plateau of Pamir which is called the "Roof of the World." At Bagram, only forty miles north of Kabul, in the Panjshir Valley up which Alexander went on his campaign to Bactria, one can walk in the fields and pick up relics of great schools of Greek, Indian, and Chinese art. The two-thousand-year-old ivories that have been found there by a French archaeological mission, and which are yet to be written about, are unique— miracles of delicate beauty, and abounding in joyous life. There are vases, of colored or painted glass, as dainty and detailed as anything Venice could produce. Balkh, in ancient Bactria (now northern Afghanistan), was the center of a great civilization long before Alexander reached it.

Wealth, culture, history are not accidents. Those same reasons of strategy and economics which made Central Asia one of the crossroads of the ancient world make Afghanistan important to the world today. Its culture died away; its wealth was scattered to the winds; it withdrew into its mountain fastnesses and tribal strife, and shut out the world in days when the world could be shut out. But those days are gone, and stubborn factors of geography, trade routes, and power politics can no longer be ignored. That still-hated process of Westernization is only another way of getting in tune with the rest of mankind, and the wisdom of accepting the inevitable and profiting by it is being recognized. Afghanistan is emerging from her shell.

We, too, in America are coming out of our shell to join this rapidly contracting world, and in the process we are making new acquaintances. It is time we met Afghanistan, we for whom she was a vague, incredibly remote spot on a map rarely looked at. We must learn a new lesson in geography, history, and current events.

For me, it was one of the most fascinating experiences in a decade that took me into many odd and beautiful places where danger or knowledge lay. Of all the things I have done, it has retained, more than any other, a quality of remoteness and romance, as of something that I dreamed rather than lived. And yet the very fact that I, an American newspaperman, was permitted to visit Afghanistan, which no more than fifty Americans in our history have ever visited, was proof that the ancient barriers were breaking down, that remoteness is a quality which the modern world has eliminated, and that, after all, romance is to be lived and not read about. I have as much right as anyone else to say that it is a small world, after these years, and it has given me some pride to think that my profession of journalism has done much to make it smaller.

Afghanistan was for me a brief and thrilling interlude of only nine days in the early part of May, 1943. Only two or three journalists had ever been allowed in before me, in all Afghanistan's history, and none has gone in since, to my knowledge. I would not dare to write about it had I not been able to pick the brains of experts such as our Minister, Cornelius van H. Engert, and his Military Attaché, Major Gordon Enders, who headed an American colony of fourteen, of whom ten were attached to the Legation. I spoke to a number of high Afghan officials, of course, and an experienced newspaperman, after all, can see much in a little time, as Samuel Johnson would say, and what I want to tell you about, more than anything, is what I saw. There are only two Americans who have traveled extensively in Afghanistan. Enders (the son of an American missionary in India, pilot to Chiang Kai-shek and adviser to the Panchen Lama of Tibet) is one of them, and Albert W. Payne, former teacher in Kabul, is the other. I stayed with Enders and the secretary of the Legation, Charles W. Thayer, and their hospitality was like the green oases of that barren country.

There is no use trying to read books about Afghanistan, for the experts say that the only book to be recommended is the *Life of Abdur Rahman,* which is the autobiography of the famous emir who ruled from 1880 to 1901, and whose work is just as true today as it was a half a century ago—which is an indication of how little the country has changed. It is hopeless to ask for statistics, because there has been no time yet to build up a proper bureaucracy, and statistics are strange things in Central Asia. Moreover, the foreigner is a suspected creature in that land where they are still called *feringi,* which was the name the Turks used to characterize the crusaders, so it is not much use asking questions.

You will find Afghanistan tucked, like a larger Switzerland, between British India, Russian Turkestan, and Iran—a sparsely populated, barren, mountainous country of 12,000,000 persons working the land of green valleys, or trekking as nomads along rough roads. Caracul skins and dried fruits are Afghanistan's chief exports, but she is believed to have great mineral resources waiting to be tapped.

You enter the country from India by that defile redolent with history—the Khyber Pass, whereby, as early as 1500 B.C., Aryans invaded an India whose civilization was even then ancient. Many a bloody battle has been fought for that strategic gateway, and now the British hold it. They left their dead in the barren plain beyond, but the Afghans left many more, and cemetery after cemetery with stone-topped Moslem graves bears witness to the ferocity and courage of the tribal warriors.

The road is symbolic of Afghanistan; it is rough, entirely unpaved, often running for miles along the beds of streams and rivers whose bridges are out of repair. Yet it is one of the most important highways in the country. One drives through the Khyber Pass on a first-rate, macadamized highway, and from the moment you strike Afghan territory, and for eleven or twelve hours on the 200-mile journey to Kabul, you are jolted and bounced unmercifully. And it is the same or worse everywhere in the country. There are a few blocks—perhaps 400 yards—of paved street in Kabul (pronounce it "Cawble," incidentally)—and that is the sum total for the whole of Afghanistan.

It is a beautiful, barren country, with its snow-capped mountains against the bluest of blue skies, and the camel caravans and herds of goats to remind you that wherever the Mussulman has gone with those animals he has made a desert. But the road is, above all, a symbol of that determination, only now relaxing, to keep away the world, the New World with its comforts and education, its social progress, and religious skepticism.

There is a strategic reason, too, for those bad roads. "This poor goat, Afghanistan, is a victim at which a lion on one side and a terrible bear from the other side are staring and ready to swallow at the first opportunity afforded them," wrote the wise and cruel Abdur Rahman. Afghanistan's importance in the past and in the future of the Middle East lies in her geographic position between Russian Turkestan and India. She commands all the important routes into northwestern India. Yet she, herself, is in that unenviable position of being a buffer state, or bastion, between two great powers whose interests, except during the recent war, have always clashed. Both the Russians and the British have military strategists who feel that their "natural" line of defense is the Hindu Kush Mountains.

So Afghanistan will always be a factor in power politics, although her primary desire is to maintain her independence, which she has done with reckless and indomitable courage. The border tribes on the east afford means of offense or defense against the British or the Indians. Hence, it is imperative for the Kabul Government to keep them satisfied. Moreover, the present ruling family was helped to its throne by the Waziris, and therefore owes a debt of gratitude to them and to the border tribes generally.

Those tribes, from ancient times, descended into the plains of India, as warlike hillsmen always do, and their modern tradition, of course, is to fight the British, which they have done for more than a century. Under Amir Amanullah they had a regular war with the British as late as 1919. Part of them had previously lost their independence to British India, and they form that restive element of Pathans, Afridis, and Mohmands on the Northwest Frontier. Others are kept in a sort of no-man's border zone between the Durand Line, established in 1893, and the administrative line of British India. Racially, all those tribes consider themselves Afghans, whichever side of the border they come from. My driver, for instance, was a Mohmand (Mohmands are Pathans from the northern side of the Khyber Pass), but when I asked him what he was his blue eyes flashed as he said, "I am Afghan."

I was told that outside official circles Afghans talk freely of descending on India when the day comes. Karachi is the port they want. One of them said, "We are not going to be like the Swiss," while eastward their *terra irredenta* reaches to the Indus River. Their slogan is "Oxus to Indus," and they can find all the historical precedents they want, by going back to the Mogul emperors or before, or even to the last century, when they lost much territory to the British. Some say, "If there is a Pakistan, we will take it." However, that would not be as simple as it seems. In the first place, the Kabul Government never has a really strong grip on the border tribes, which are unruly, strong, and fiercely independent, and it is not as though the Kabuli could use the Pathans as instruments of policy. Those tribes are more marauders than conquerors, and the inhabitants of the Sind, where they want to go, are on a higher level of civilization and would not bear the yoke of domination passively. Besides all which, the present Government has not the slightest intention of attacking India, so long as it remains in power.

However, the tribes have a long anti-British tradition and the Government needs the support of those tribes, so it cannot very well openly take a pro-British line. That was true as far back as the time of Abdur Rahman, who wrote: "I was unable to show my friendship publicly to the extent that was necessary, because my people were ignorant and fanatical. If I showed any inclination toward the English my people would call me an infidel for joining hands with infidels, and they would proclaim a religious holy war against me." To a warring race like the Afghans, not to fight the British is almost an admission of being pro-British.

The British, on their side, are using silver bullets as well as the threat of real ones. When I was at Peshawar I went out to watch a ceremony where 750 Afridi chieftains gathered to talk things over with Sir George Cunningham, Britain's remarkable Governor of the Northwest Frontier Province who did more than all others, put together, to keep the frontier quiet in the crucial war years. The Afridis were there to collect their annual subsidies of 240,000 rupees, paid ostensibly in lieu of the tolls they used to take from caravans going to and from Afghanistan, but it was a prime element in keeping them quiet. They made a striking picture, sitting before us in tight ranks under bright-colored tenting, with their own khaki-clad police standing guard. Afridis are another branch of the Pathan race—fine, big, bearded men, dignified and outspoken. We were out in their territory, under an old Sikh fort, and looking down on us were those mountains of the Hindu Kush whose history was old when Alexander the Great went through in 327 B.C. with his conquering armies.

But an even greater historic and geographic threat to Afghanistan comes from Russia, and that fear has been accentuated since Russia and the British went into Iran. It has always been part of Afghan foreign policy to desire pledges from the British against the Russians, but that is out of the question, at least for the time being.

In the first World War, Amir Habibullah was careful to maintain neutrality, despite the machinations of the Germans. Had he attacked India he might have had some local, temporary successes, but in the end Afghanistan would have been wiped off the map. In the second World War the country was in the same position, and fortunately acted in the same way. Under pressure from Russia and Britain, the Afghans sent Axis diplomats home from Kabul, which, however, remained a center of intrigue and espionage which would have supplied E. Phillips Oppenheim with a plot per day. There is a true story to be told some day (Enders has it) about Subhas Chandra Bose, the Indian Quisling, and his escape across India into Afghanistan and thence to Berlin which will make fiction seem commonplace.

It was not easy for the Kabul Government to maintain a steady course of neutrality during a period when nothing would have been easier than to stir the troubled waters of the Northwest Frontier, with dire results. One should remember the staggering blows to British prestige early in the war, the apparent crumbling of Russia, the advance of Japan to India's very frontiers. If the British had had to face attacks from both sides, at that period, the situation would have been extremely dangerous. But, on the whole, it is the Afghans who think of being invaded, rather than the other way around.

The canny Abdur Rahman (who is, by the way, the Durani chief of Kipling's "Ballad of the King's Mercy") had no intention of building super-highways for enemies to roll along. "By making the country easily accessible," he wrote, "foreign powers would not find much difficulty in entering and spreading themselves over our country. The greatest safety of Afghanistan lies in its natural impregnable position."

In these days of tanks, jeeps, and airplanes, no country is completely impregnable or inaccessible, but I could appreciate the reasoning of Abdur Rahman as I jolted wildly over the stony plain of Jalalabad from the Khyber Pass and on to Nimla, where the Emperor Akbar built himself a garden of singular beauty. Then the road mounts in steady, sometimes perilous curves to that other famous pass, the Lataband, where Nur Jehan, "Light of the World," was born while her parents were going by caravan from Persia to India. Nur Jehan is a great name in Indian history for she became, in circumstances strangely like those of David's Bathsheba, empress-wife of Jehangir, whose son Shah Jahan built the Taj Mahal in Agra.

In Afghanistan one always thinks of history, and sometimes of the dawn of history. There, history is in many ways, the Arabian Nights and the Bible. The bazaars of Kabul, Kandahar, Berat, and Balkh are the same as Haroun-al-Raschid walked through in disguise; and out in the fields the women glean ears of corn as Ruth did, "and beat out that which they had gleaned." The men use plows of donkey's skulls, and grind their flour in crude stone mills such as Boaz must have used.

Here, and in Iran, Iraq and Palestine you learn what it meant to the Jews of old to "lie down in green pastures." It is no symbol in Afghanistan; it is the poignant reality of every-day life. These nomads, the Khana-Bedush, the "people without homes," who were trekking northward when I went to Afghanistan, through barren miles upon miles and over bare mountains, does it not rejoice their hearts, as it does even a sophisticated city-dwelling foreigner riding in an automobile, to come suddenly upon a hollow or valley as green and lush as any promised land? Is it any wonder that green is the color of Islam?

For this country is the last refuge of fanatical Mohammedanism. Everywhere else—Turkey, Egypt, Arabia, Iran—religious bars have been lowered, and religion has been adapted to the modern world, but here in Afghanistan, *mullahs,* or priests, still hold sway. When King Amanullah tried, among other reforms, to remove the impenetrable and hideous veils behind which women live outside their quarter, the *mullahs* helped to foment a revolution, and he was lucky to escape to Italy. Amanullah built himself a palace in Kabul like a great French chateau, with superb formal gardens. He imported marbles from Italy, machinery from the United States, furniture from France. But his people, and especially the *mullahs,* grumbled that foreign material should be used and that so much money should be spent on luxury. It was another reason to drive him out. He never quite finished the palace, and now it stands just as he left it, with the present royal family not daring to use it—a monument of modernity in a country that has been taught to hate modernity.

So fanatical is religious feeling that it is one of the few countries in the world where Christian missionaries have never been allowed to set foot. Nowhere are women kept so secluded. It is said they are beautiful, but one can only know that from the country-women and nomads who go unveiled and who are, indeed, often beautiful. The priests have tried to keep the women as ignorant as they are secluded, but the bars are breaking down gradually, and the day probably is not far off when, like their sisters in Turkey and Iran, they will put aside forever that ugly, coarse *burka* which veils them from top to toe.

One must not be misled by that seclusion. The history of Central Asia tells of a long line of women rulers and warriors, and the Afghan women of today are made of the same stuff. The last siege of Kabul, in fact, which was against the Amir Abdur Rahman only fifty years ago, was led by a woman. It is a fighting race, and the women are no exception.

When Afghan tribes are not fighting the English they are fighting each other. They have known no other life. Americans can think back to their own history, with their Indians who lived only to hunt and fight. To quote Abdur Rahman again, "Every Afghan prays when he goes to bed that Allah will give him a soldier's death on the battlefield."

Here reigns always ended in revolution or sudden death, and woe to the losing side! Amir Habibullah, son of Abdur Rahman, father of Amanullah, had eighty children. When Amanullah fled, some of his brothers who were left behind were shot from the mouths of cannons.

The fact that the Premier and War Minister are both royal highnesses gives the key to how the country is run. They are brothers of the late Nadir Shah and uncles of the present King Zahir Shah. For this is a patriarchal, tribal country whose only occupations are agriculture and war. The ruling house is as strong as possible in a country where a tribal, primitive, independent, and turbulent people has to be controlled. Heredity is not enough with these fighting races. You have to show that you are the best man, and, ordinarily, the throne is seized by the commander of the Kabul garrison, the equivalent of the Roman Empire's Pretorian Guard. This time was a rare exception and when Nadir Shah was assassinated in 1933 his brother, Shah Mahmud, now Minister of War, had the loyalty and common sense to install Nadir's son on the throne. He was the "king maker," as generals always are in countries where the army is the major instrument of politics.

It is a land of tribes, and the patriarch rules, so the real power in the country is not the King but his uncle, the Prime Minister, brother of the late Nadir Shah. He is the oldest member of the family, and so long as he lives the King would not think of exercising the real authority. This family, indeed, has shown a sense of loyalty and cohesion most unusual in oriental countries, and it has contributed enormously to the stability of the country.

Personality is all-important. The administrative machinery is rudimentary. There is no civil service, no code of procedure, no body of precedents. Everything depends on the attitude of the person in power, who acts in accordance with his personal inclinations. Whatever traditions there are center around tribal and patriarchal loyalties and the intensely religious feelings of the Moslem Sunnis, who constitute all but a small percentage of the population. The country is really a loose confederation of tribes, kept together by an intricate balance of diplomacy, firmness, and money. Internal stability depends on the support of the various tribes and, above all, of the chieftains, to whom must be given a maximum amount of independence consistent with holding the country together and furthering its policies.

The great tribal expert is His Royal Highness Shah Mahmud, Minister of War, who is the equivalent on that side of the frontier of Sir George Cunningham on the Indian side. Between them they performed an exceedingly important and delicate feat in keeping the border tribes quiet during the war.

The Kabul Government has a typically oriental method of helping to keep the tribes in line. The sons of chieftains are invited to Kabul for schooling. If the chieftain refuses, it is a sign of hostility. If, as almost always happens, he agrees, then the

Government has a hostage who is sometimes kept in Kabul for years without being allowed to go home.

These young men are imbued with new ideas, but youth has a hard row to hoe in an ancient, tribal country. Respect and obedience are the qualities most in demand. However, their modernity does not worry the Government, which is anxious to Westernize the country as much as possible. Amanullah lost his throne when he tried to emulate Kemal Pasha and Reza Shah Pahlevi and moved too fast, so the present family must go cautiously. The Government has a weight of ignorance and religious fanaticism to fight against, but, as in all oriental countries, there is a strong trend toward Westernization, and a realization that the world has become a small place and no country can stay out of it. The men who rule Afghanistan are, for the most part, cultured and in some respects worldly-wise, and they want to move with the times—but if, for instance, they passed an order today unveiling women, they would have a revolution tomorrow. Amanullah found that out to his cost.

It is religion that keeps the Afghan women more secluded than any others in the world, but it must not be thought that they are down-trodden or enslaved. Women have played a great role in Central Asian history, and they have a high place in family life.

Their oppressors, and the country's greatest handicap to progress, are the *mullahs,* of whom there are about 20,000. Thanks to the ignorance and fanaticism of the tribal folk, the priests exercise a great, although not supreme, power in the country. They come, generally, from the lower classes, and rise through ability, religious fervor, and shrewdness. They are the product of a primitive, rural world, and they fatten on the ignorance they foster. It is important to keep them in line, which the Government does partly by paying the influential ones well and partly by conforming to their old-fashioned ideas.

They are the dispensers of justice, for there is no civil code. Justice is based on the Hanafi Code of the Shariat (Mohammedan religious law). No punishment is prescribed until the crime is committed, and then it is roughly based on the Mosaic law of an eye for an eye. One of the causes of Amanullah's overthrow was his effort to codify the laws. The Minister of Justice is a *mullah,* and he appoints other *mullahs* as judges.

Education, too, is largely in the hands of the *mullahs,* but the Government has been working hard, and with modest success, to establish modern schools. There are some excellent schools in Kabul, and I saw some in other towns. Half of the budget goes to war expenditures, which does not leave much for education, health, or public works. As a matter of fact, the educational problem is one of the most difficult in the world to solve. The population is not homogeneous; there is no national language; there are few communications and no traditions. The Government is trying to make Pashtu the national language, and it is spoken extensively in the eastern part of the country, as it is in northwestern India. The court and the educated people speak Persian. French is the leading foreign language, because of an excellent school in Kabul, rather than for any other reason. English comes next, for obvious reasons. There is even a girls' school in Kabul and the *mullahs* were so shocked when it was established, in 1938, that it had to be called a midwives' school.

Cultural traditions go far back into history, to a time when Central Asia saw the flourishing civilizations of the Greeks and the Aryans, and the region was so rich that when archaeological excavations really get under way the world of art will have one of the most exciting periods in its history. The Kabul Museum has newly acquired riches which will make that city a Mecca for orientalists and art students—if they are allowed in. At Bagram, there is a great field for archaeologists. And one that I was assured Americans would be welcomed to help develop.

Afghanistan frankly admits that she needs help, and feels with justice that she can repay it. The problem of the democracies is to see that they, and not others, win Afghanistan's friendship. From the United States must come teachers, technicians, and, above all, trade connections. His Royal Highness, Mohammed Hashim Khan, the Prime Minister and one of the outstanding statesmen of the Middle East, told me that Americans are considered by Afghan village folk as "useful"—a high compliment from those simple people who divide foreigners into "useful" and "harmful."

It was only in 1926 that our diplomatic relations with Afghanistan began, when we made a treaty of friendship with Amanullah. Even then, ten years passed before the American Minister to Teheran was also accredited to Kabul, and it has only been since July, 1942, when Minister Engert arrived, that we have had a minister accredited to Kabul alone. Enders arrived in Kabul twelve hours before the attack on Pearl Harbor, and it was he who had to notify the Afghan Government that we were at war with Japan. (It was Engert, his wife and two children whom I found "holding the fort" in Addis Ababa in May, 1936, when I rolled into the Abyssinian capital behind Badoglio.) The Afghans realize that the United States has no political designs in that part of the world, and they are not afraid of us as they are of Great Britain and Russia.

They are a tough, hard people, and they can certainly be cruel, but they are, on the whole, what we call "square-shooters," with a strong if simple sense of justice. When punishment is merited, or when they are beaten in a fair fight, they hold no malice. They do not kill women or children in their family or tribal feuds, and that is why, when driving about the countryside, one sees the women and children dressed in red. From a distance it is hard to tell a man from a woman by the shape of their clothes, so an enemy sighting his rifle on a figure working in the field knows that, according to the code of his country, he must not shoot when he sees red. Sometimes timid men don red clothes, showing that they do not want to fight, but that is the equivalent of showing the yellow streak, and they are ragged unmercifully for it. It is against the rules, also, to shoot an unarmed enemy. The last word, always, goes to the rifle, which is the ultimate in argumentation. Until recent times, that was how a foreigner was greeted. He was an infidel and an intruder, one who had come to take away that most prized of all Afghan possessions, its independence. He was fair game.

The British cannot be expected to feel sportsmanlike about it, so to speak. One of the truly famous shrines in Kabul is a small,

stone monument on the edge of the city, near the British Legation. On that spot in 1936 an Afghan killed the British Military
Attaché. The authorities formally apologized, paid an indemnity,
and hanged the culprit. So far so good. But then they built a
monument to the assassin on the spot where the Britisher was
killed, and it is now a holy place visited by pious pilgrims who
tie strips of cloth to a pole there, in Moslem fashion.

The British viewpoint was given, typically and with a certain
amount of justice, by Lord Ronaldshay in *India, a Bird's-Eye
View*. He wrote that "the distinctive characteristic of the tribes
inhabiting this wild borderland [the Northwest Frontier] are
selfishness, vanity, treachery, vindictiveness, and general lawless-
less. . . . This inter-tribal aggressiveness is only overruled by
religious fanaticism and the fear and hatred excited by the smallest suspicion of foreign interference, so that it is said of the
Afghans of the frontier that they are never at peace except when
they are at war. . . . Their favorite pastime is raiding and
thieving."

That is the British experience of the border tribes, and they
have a reason for their judgment—as long as they use a Western
criterion of ethics. But in Kabul I heard the Afghan described
in more favorable terms. Long before Americans got a colorful
picture of murderous tribesmen waiting behind every rock for
unsuspecting foreigners, there had been a change. There is only
one region of central Afghanistan where it is considered dangerous even for an American to travel, but otherwise one is greeted
with charming courtesy and hospitality. When Afghans meet
you, or thank you for any reason, they put their hands upon
their hearts, in a gracious gesture that is symbolic of a genuinely
hospitable and warm-hearted people. The foreigner is an object
of intense curiosity but of invariable friendliness, especially when
it is learned that he belongs to a faraway country which has
never attacked or fought against the Afghans.

They, themselves, rarely travel, except to neighboring countries that can be reached by caravan, although, of course, as
many as can do so, make the pilgrimage to Mecca. Wherever they
go, they take with them an intense pride in their country and

their race. Shah Mahmud told me of an Afghan who had to cross the seas, but was too poor to pay for his passage, so he shipped as a stoker. But he always refused to tell anybody where he came from or what his race was, for he was ashamed to let the world know that any Afghan could be so poor he would have to do menial work. When official Afghan groups go abroad, as one did on King Amanullah's famous world tour, they are rigidly insistent on precedent and protocol.

Curiously enough, that pride makes the Afghan a poor sportsman. He feels that he must win. There is a guidebook available in Kabul which says: "In sports, as in everything else, he never forgets that he is an Afghan and, according to the traditions of his country, should never lose a contest or fight, whether in his own land or abroad. They play to win against all odds and not for the mere love of the game." So they take their sports seriously, and important wrestling matches, for instance, usually end in free-for-all fights, with spectators as principals. Those who backed the loser get so enraged they do not go for the loser but for the winner and his backers. Afghans, in short, are not good losers and therefore they are not good sportsmen. But what is a vice in sport can be a virtue in a warlike life.

There is a tendency to softness in the Kabuli, which bodes ill in an iron country where the tribesmen are fierce, independent fighters. You can tell a countryman in Kabul's bazaars. You see him stride through crowded streets, big-boned, tall, black-haired, blue-eyed. He is no man's inferior, least of all the white man's. There is none of that cringing which is often so distressing to a foreigner in India. The Afghan tribesman will share the street with you courteously, but it were better not to crowd him.

It is a colorful bazaar, teeming with life and spirit. There you can buy brightly colored vests or golden slippers with upturned toes, rubies from the ancient mines of Jagdalak, carpets from Bokhara, spices and cloth of silver—and, curiously enough, old clothing from the United States, one of the main items of import from America. The cook of the house in which I stayed wore a bellboy's uniform from a well known Chicago hotel, and when you see an American uniform in the Lab-i-Darya Bazaar, it will not have an American inside it.

Over the Kabul River, where the bazaar begins is an ancient bridge which is part of the bazaar, for it has the same sort of shops on both sides. It reminds you of an even more famous bridge in Florence, the Ponte Vecchio, but Kabul's bridge is so old that tradition says it is the prototype of all such bridges in the world. There, donkeys laden with salt rock move like little Juggernauts which turn aside for no man. There, clumsy camels stride haughtily and disdainfully, for they, alone, say Mohammedans, know the hundredth name of Allah.

When you leave the bazaar there is nothing to see but endless streets of dust or mud, and endless walls on each side. You see no houses, only bare walls eight or ten feet high, built partly for protection and partly to screen the women from worldly eyes while they walk in their gardens. It is only outside Kabul that you see women and houses and life. To leave the city is to go back to a still earlier world. In the villages of Kohistan, where I went one day, as a very rare privilege, quail are still hunted with hawks and hooded falcons. Wild ducks are decoyed to ponds, and there stunned by clay pellets shot from bows. In the *caravanserais* you sleep and eat in simplest fashion. Enders and I stopped at one in Charikar for a pilaff of wild rice, lamb, and meat balls, that would gladden the heart and palate of any epicure.

We had gone up the Panjshir Valley, with the Parapanesus Mountains on our left and the Hindu Kush on our right. This was the "Panjshir of the Caucasus" of the ancient Greek chroniclers, which puzzled historians for a long time, since they did not look for the Caucasus so far to the east. But it was the trail of Alexander the Great, and Major Enders and I followed it a few miles afoot up above Ghulbahar (the name means "City of Spring Flowers"), along the steep banks of the Panjshir River where Alexander went with his chariots to conquer Bactria, nearly twenty-three centuries ago. I wondered that chariots could climb over its rough, stony way, and so did Enders.

"I could take a jeep up here easily," the Major remarked.

And so it must have been with the conqueror. "I can take chariots up here easily," he doubtless said, and he did it.

That was a long time ago, but the transition from chariot to jeep is a recent one in Afghanistan. She is being asked to jump overnight from the ancient world into the modern, and that is not easy. In Kabul you go by summertime, as you do in Dholpur, but everything else seems even more topsy-turvy there. Play poker, and three of a kind beat a straight or a flush; on Arbor Day they dig up trees instead of planting them. Someone has even said that in Afghanistan the sun sets in the east.

Every day, as noon approaches, a *mullah* watches the sundial, and when the sun is directly overhead he gets up, goes to the telephone and puts in a call for the station on the top of a neighboring hill where there is a cannon. What few telephones there are in Kabul do not work well, and sometimes it takes five minutes, sometimes more, to get the officer in charge of the cannon. However, sooner or later it is done, and he walks to the cannon, gives the signal, and off it goes! That is noon, and you set your watch by it. Each day noon comes at a different time, by your watch, but, whatever your watch says, noon is when the cannon booms and not before. The *mullahs* will have it that way—but at least they use the telephone, and some day they will set their watches to Greenwich mean time.

When I left, my watch was thirteen minutes faster than the cannon, but I kept it that way, for British India does go by Greenwich mean time. On my way back I could not help thinking of the obvious fact that India and Afghanistan are so closely linked that no peace settlement in the Middle East can ignore Kabul. The racial, social, and economic ties are such that anything which happens in India reacts sympathetically in Afghanistan. Karachi and Bombay are the trade ports of Afghanistan, as Genoa is of Switzerland, for neither country has an outlet to the sea.

I talked to the Afghan officials about India and, in general, they indicated they would like to see an independent and peaceful India, since they dislike the British and do not want to have civil war or chaos on their eastern frontiers. With the British gone, one of the two perennial fears of the Afghans would be removed and their independence would be safe from that side. However, Russia would be the greater menace for that.

On the Indian side there is the problem of keeping the border quiet which Congress writers and leaders never mention or seem to think about. All they did was try to organize the Pathans into "Red Shirts" under Abdul Gaffar Khan and make them non-violent. It was like trying to make the leopard change his spots. The Pathan is not only anti-English; he is anti-Hindu, and, in so far as he is politically conscious, he is now Moslem League. To India's many complications we must add the delicate and costly problem of the Northwest Frontier.

My stay in India was drawing to a close. I have written about it thus far as if there were not in India many thousands of fellow-Americans, suffering its climate and doing a tough job with homesick grace. Yankees in King Arthur's court would have been just as much at home as G.I.'s in India.

Yankees in King Arthur's Court

You would have thought we had gone to India not to fight the Japanese but to free Indians from the British yoke. It was partly our fault, of course, what with the Atlantic Charter, the Four Freedoms, the encouragement given by Colonel Louis Johnson at the time of the Cripps visit, and the generally sympathetic American press. Americans came full of zeal for the underdog and imbued with the traditional joy of twisting the Lion's tail, and that encouraged the Indians, too. From the moment I arrived in Karachi I was asked why the United States did not intervene to solve the Indian problem, and that question was asked of me a thousand times, in all parts of India, until at the end it became a hopeless reproach. We all became a little irritated by it, as I recall, and sometimes told Indians that if they wanted independence they would have to get it from the British in the same way the Americans did—which was neither wise nor generous advice.

The United States did try, in a mild, quiet way, to do something about the matter, with the State Department in the autumn of 1942 bringing enough pressure to bear to make the Viceroy and others resentful and Churchill quite furious when he saw Ambassador Phillips. However, once the British had told us —which they did—that India was none of our business and they knew what they were doing, there was nothing more to be said, and we washed our hands of the matter.

To be sure it was, and it still is, awkward to explain to the Indians why the Atlantic Charter and the Four Freedoms do not apply to them. Also, at a time when Sumner Welles was Assistant Secretary of State, we said that "the age of imperialism is over," but, Indians asked, why not do something about it? It is a fact, however, that our attitude toward imperialism is still a disturbing one to the British Conservatives, who fear that our policy of leaving Asia to the Asiatics is going to reap a whirlwind some day. "You are just storing up trouble for the world by your policy," one high official told me. Rajagopalachari, like all other Indians, was taking the line that we, too, were going imperialistic, and would soon understand and sympathize with the British attitude. "The British Empire exists on certain bases, and India is one of them," Rajaji said. "Without India there would be no Empire"—which is not far from the truth.

"You are letting your hearts get the better of your brains," Wavell told me, bluntly. "It is easy to sit in chairs 12,000 miles away and tell us how to run India. Give us credit for knowing what we are doing. We are out to win this war, and we have taken the only line possible under the circumstances. How could we turn this country over to Gandhi and Nehru, who have shown that the question of defense is, at best, secondary?" And that, too, was not far from the truth.

But we have an obligation to apply the Atlantic Charter and the Four Freedoms everywhere, and now, after the war, if we do not make an effort to do so with regard to India (should it be necessary) we shall be derelict in redeeming our pledges. During the war it was hard to see what could be done about it if the British asked us to keep our hands off. Now we must, in justice, support the legitimate Indian claims, for we have promised to do so.

"We have always believed," Secretary of State Hull said in a speech on July 23, 1942, "and we believe today, that all peoples, without distinction of race, color, or religion, who are prepared and willing to accept the responsibilities of liberty, are entitled to its enjoyment. We have always sought, and we seek today, to encourage and aid all who aspire to freedom to establish their right to it by preparing themselves to assume its obligations. . . . It has been our purpose in the past, and will remain our purpose in the future, to use the full measure of our influence to support attainment of freedom by all peoples who, by their acts, show themselves worthy of it and ready for it."

The conditions he made should be carefully noted, but the promise is, nevertheless, a clear one.

The American soldier never did seem to know what it was all about, or to care very much except for their vague antipathy toward the British and their sympathy for the Indian underdog— a sympathy not unmixed with condescension in many cases, since our first airforce out there was largely composed of Texans, to whom Indians were pretty much like colored folk. There were so many Texans around that I remember one pilot at the great new airfield in Agra saying, plaintively, "I'm just a Yank in the Texan Airforce."

The homesickness that Americans, more than any other race, take with them to the far corners of the globe seems especially acute in India. It is the furthest an American can get from home, and the voyage takes from one to two months on a transport. At first the Americans are so happy to get off the ship that anything looks good. I happened to be in Bombay on March 4, 1943, when a troop transport arrived with thousands of soldiers and hundreds of nurses.

They took Bombay over for some ten or twelve gay hours, until the inexorable taps at 10:30. India looked good after many weeks at sea in a crowded ship that had sailed through intense tropical heat. There was a lot of steam to be let off, and things sizzled in Bombay that day. Fresh blood and, above all, fresh American womanhood was what that country needed, judging from the complaints one heard in American camps. A few hundred nurses all at once was something lots of soldiers had been dreaming about, but hardly dared hope would materialize. Everybody may have been biased that day, but the percentage of attractive nurses did seem extraordinarily high.

At noon I found soldiers, officers, and nurses straining at the leash in the converted Atlantic luxury liner, with all its luxury removed. Transports had improved a little since we went over in World War I, but then we thought eleven days to reach Europe was an ungodly length of time. In the recent war, time was counted in weeks, not days, and those youngsters had put up with some real hardships. So when the commanding officer gave the word "Go!" they went like arrows shot from bows. Within an hour you could not go anywhere in Bombay without seeing swarms of Americans—black and white, male and female. That strange, friendly land fascinated them, and it would have been cruel to dilute any of their enthusiasm with the prediction that soon it would be all too familiar—and not very fascinating.

Bombay was a boom town all day. Anybody that had anything to sell got rid of his wares at those abnormally high prices with which Americans are always greeted. Candy, cake, beer, and steaks were merely *hors d'œuvres* in the day's feast. Then came more serious things in the souvenir line, with feminine interest turning to the beautiful cloths of Benares and Kashmir. And at the top were the jewelry stores, each of which quickly gathered its quota of soldiers pricing everything from moonstones to star sapphires. Within a few hours it was rare to see anybody without a package.

It was a great day, too, for those fortunate Indians who had monkeys which could dance or snakes to be charmed. Here was India as the Americans had always imagined it. Fakirs with long hair and almost naked bodies covered with ashes were a curiosity to stare at, and often to give a few annas to, but horrible monstrosities and swarms of child beggars gave a distressing introduction to India. That universal mendicancy which is one of India's shames was new to Americans, but it was something they were not going to be able to shake off until they boarded another transport homeward bound. As evening fell, dance halls and movies began to fill. The pictures they had seen long before, but they still looked good. They did not know, and we could not tell them, where they were going from Bombay. Some opined they would like to go to Delhi (they pronounced it "Dell High"), whose fame as the best spot in India had reached them. They little realized that the weather in New Delhi and elsewhere was soon going to make them long for the comparative comfort of Dante's Inferno.

I do not mean that nurses and other young women in the

services are to be considered in terms of the white slave traffic in writing about how welcome they were in India. They went to that far corner of the world to do a very trying and necessary war job, and they did it there with the same gaiety and gallantry as everywhere else. But human nature being what it is, the average soldier was obviously overjoyed in seeing some American femininity around. The scarcity of white women is one of the most distressing aspects of soldiering in India. There were no Wacs there in the first year and a half, and few U.S.O. shows. The nurses and a few Red Cross girls were the only American females to be seen. In India, as in the Pacific islands, the long absences from America and the inevitable fact that all the girls and young wives could not be expected to wait patiently, were serious morale factors. India was far worse than the European theater in that respect, since there are white women by the millions in France, England, and Italy.

The G.I.'s in Assam or Burma nearly forgot what a white woman looked like. "After the war is over," one pilot remarked, "I'm going to get black sheets and put a white woman between them, instead of the other way around." There was a corporal whose wife had sent him her latest photograph. "My dear," he wrote back, "how pale you look!" However, one soldier began to get so used to it that "the girls kept getting a shade lighter every month." One of the really delicate problems for the higher command was the Anglo-Indian girls, who are half English, half Indian. When they had dances at Agra many used to attend— among them some very pretty ones, too. Their mothers were by no means averse to getting them married off to American soldiers. The restrictions against soldiers or officers marrying while on foreign duty were enforced with rigid strictness in India. While I was there, even for an American to marry an English girl required "Uncle Joe" Stilwell's permission, and he was not easy to persuade. If a soldier became too involved with a girl, he was gently but firmly banished to another post where the girl could not follow him.

It was always a touchy business to make those youngsters realize that they were not getting the worse end of the stick. There was always a feeling that they were being forgotten, that they were not appreciated, that everybody thought India did not count, and that nothing was being done there, anyway. One officer put it like this: "When you are playing a football game, you like to feel that all the students are behind you. You want them to come out and watch the game, cheer their heads off, and give you something to make you want to play like you never played before. But when you are playing to empty grandstands it isn't so easy."

When even the Britisher has never found himself at home in India, after two hundred years of rule, how can an American from Main Street feel happy? There is a strangely prophetic note for us Americans in the barrack-room song:

'E littul thought that we, from far across the sea
Would send our armies up to Mandalai.

Kipling might have said of our soldiers as he did of his own in "The Incarnation of Krishna Mulvaney," in *Life's Handicap:* "Their fate sent them to serve in India, which is not a golden country, though poets have sung otherwise. There men die with great swiftness, and those who live suffer many and curious things."

How often have I heard Americans wondering why the British or anybody else should want a country like that, where every time you eat you consider whether you are going to get dysentery, or if that last mosquito which bit you did not carry malaria germs? Broiling sun, torrential rains, filth, squalor, disease, insects—are these all that India means, he asks himself? But gradually a new world takes shape before his eyes—still not his world, still nothing like "God's country," but human, colorful, kindly, with an age-old wisdom. He will never like it, and he will never understand it, and he will always be homesick, but some day he is going to realize that he would not have missed it for anything. There were American boys out in the Naga Hills, on the edge of northern Burma, watching month after month for Japanese planes. Let me tell you something about them.

No Americans knew better that it was a world war than the

group of soldiers I saw at Jaboka, on top of one of the highest
of the Naga Hills. There they were, surrounded and living with
almost naked headhunters, and being relatively happy about it.
At least, they did not want to leave, and, best of all, their Naga
friends did not want them to go. Those soldiers, and others in
scattered posts throughout the hills, were providing a warning
network which the Japanese planes simply could not get through
without detection. The job was a really tough one. It is hard to
imagine a more inaccessible territory for a warning system, and
it had to be put up by crews from our fighter squadrons. All the
old surveys and British records indicated that it could not be
done. There had been almost no white men in the territory since
the 1870's, and the last man had had his head cut off, so it was
considered dangerous terrain. Lieutenant Colonel J. E. Barr, of
San Antonio, Texas, who was one of four in our party the day
I went up (there was also a lieutenant named L. L. Hall, and
Preston Grover of the Associated Press) said that when he dis-
cussed the matter with the New Delhi command he was told:
"There is no use studying the reports. They say it is impossible.
So you go in and do it." From the beginning the British obstructed the American efforts, and when we went ahead in spite
of them, they complicated matters by forcing the Americans to
take Ghurkas and Assamese "Rifles" as guards, and they got into
trouble. When we were organizing the system, a message was
sent to British Headquarters about it. Three weeks later an
answer came, saying that the matter would receive consideration.
The District Commissioner had made up his mind that it was
dangerous, and he forbade tea planters to help the Americans.

The look-out station I saw in the Naga Hills was reasonably
accessible. It took a three-week trek to reach one of the outer
stations, and there was a nip and tuck struggle with the Japanese
and Burmese "traitors" at that time. We had to take a long automobile ride from an American airbase to one of the many tea
planters' bungalows which dot the area. This one stood where
a trail came out from the mountain top (although they are called
the Naga Hills they are really a mountain range, branching down
from the Himalayas). The road twisted through endless tea plan-

tations and across bridges marked "Wheeled traffic and elephants prohibited over the bund," until the car could go no further, and there a group of eight Naga tribesmen were waiting to carry our luggage up to the American post.

They grinned in friendly fashion, through betel-stained mouths. These were real savages, as picturesque as any that Hollywood could dream of, naked, except for a tightly wound bamboo thong around the waist from which hung the briefest of loincloths. Their faces, necks, and shoulders were tattooed in evidence that they had their heads from enemy tribes. Inside the pierced lobes of their ears were odd ornaments including, in one case, cellophane from an American cigarette package. Their black hair was cut in a bang in front, and looped around a flat bamboo slab behind. The shape of the face was almost Tibetan—small eyes, high cheekbones, the nose without a bridge. But what distinguished them, above all, was the heavy, hatchet-like knife, with a long bamboo handle, stuck into the waistband, for they were headhunters, and it takes only one slashing blow from the keen-edged weapon to add another head to the village collection.

We went up with them hour after hour, through the sort of jungle that overpowers a man. Plants taller than we, trees that seemed to reach the sky, bamboos soaring to eighty feet. We climbed five solid hours, and the last two were heartbreaking, for the ascent was as steep as a ladder, most of the time.

The village of Jaboka, in a dip of the mountain top below the American camp and our radio station, had been warned of our arrival, which was important, for the only incident connected with the stay of our unit up to that time occurred one day when the natives were not advised, and as the American party approached, the women scattered into the jungle and the men prepared to fight. All was well upon identification, but it took the husbands days to collect their wives from the jungle, and this did not please them.

We walked into the American camp just before dark, to find a dozen Ghurka soldiers busily erecting a stockade. After living on the friendliest terms with the natives for six weeks, the British authorities had sent Ghurkas to protect the Americans, who felt certain that they did not need protection. That was an excellent example of the difference between the British and the American dealings with the natives. Because the British distrusted the Nagas, there was mutual distrust and fear, and hence enmity. The orders to the Ghurkas from the District Commissioner were to build a stockade around the camp, keep the Nagas out, or disarm them as they entered, reduce the area of the encampment if necessary, and there were other similar instructions which the Americans considered nonsense, and which were simply bewildering to the natives. Because the Americans were friendly, the savages were, too, and genuinely so. There was no conceivable reason why they should have changed—unless British interference made them change.

It was the simplest sort of camp, consisting of a long, bamboo hut, open to the winds, with a palm-leaf roof. Otherwise there was only a little mess hall, which the Ghurkas were using, and a kitchen. The ground, the houses, and all the bamboo that was needed cost the American Army the large sum of 15 rupees, or $4.50, monthly. Shortly before, King Tong-am had come up from the village to ask for three months' advance. He said he was going to marry for the eleventh time, and wanted to buy a good wife. Sergeant Leon F. Meyer, of Fresno, Cal., who was in charge of the ten men there, compromised with a month's advance. The main entertainment the soldiers had had was that marriage, for they were honored guests. However, they had to leave before the ceremony was over because the Nagas were beginning to get drunk on rice beer, and King Tong was afraid that some of them might forget themselves—and when Nagas forget themselves heads begin to fall, quite literally.

The village "lost a head," as the natives put it, a few days before we arrived, when one of their old men was caught alone in a field by enemy tribesmen. He could not run fast enough. That made the Nagas hopping mad, so the headman went to see Sergeant Meyer and proposed that the Americans and Nagas ally themselves in a punitive expedition against the enemy. Meyer had to explain that he would defend them if attacked, but the

American Army had come to India to defeat the Japanese, and nobody else. Since the Nagas did not have the slightest idea who the Japanese were, they were disappointed, but the incident did not mar their genuine friendship for the Americans.

The Nagas had their own blockhouse on top of the crest, where a path came in which they guarded at night. Down the trail were pits, camouflaged so that anyone stepping on them fell upon spiked bamboos. There was also another trap which, when stepped on, released a poisoned arrow from a bow fastened in a tree. In front of the blockhouse was a ditch with rows of bamboo slivers, upright, to cut the bare feet of the enemy. Their equivalent of barbed-wire entanglements was a mass of criss-crossed bamboos.

It was hard, when the Nagas walked past or behind one, not to feel a tingling sensation in the back of the neck, but there really could be no question of their friendliness. Mess Corporal Thomas J. Baldwin, of Roswell, New Mexico, nearly had a row with one of them who was blocking the door to the mess room and could not be made to realize he must get out of the way. Baldwin pushed him out, and next thing he knew the Naga began waving his hatchet around. However, he really wasn't that mad.

The Ghurkas, who had arrived only the evening before we did, were infinitely more cautious than the Americans, and the Nagas did not like it. They could not understand why the stockade had to be built to separate them from their American friends—nor could the Americans.

We all sat around the bamboo campfire at night, swapping tales as soldiers always have done, and at least a dozen Nagas squatted there with us. There was the headman, wearing an ancient top hat and a tattered coat, and just about nothing else. There was old Jojo, too, the chief errand boy. There was a flat-nosed, chunky friend of one of the privates, who could mimic English, including the unprintable variety, with parrot-like accuracy but without understanding a word. The G.I. said the next thing he was going to teach him was "Onward, Christian Soldiers."

The Nagas were in a continuous state of hilarity, and they hated to go home. They smoked our cigarettes, made themselves tea in the hollow of a bamboo, and finally fashioned torches from bamboo slivers. Then they trailed off into the darkness, the jungle closing greedily around them, the torches lighting the bamboos that arched high over their heads. No Naga dares to walk alone in the jungle at night.

The next morning we climbed to the radio station on the peak of the mountain. It commanded an immense view south over the mountainous ranges running deep into Burma, and north to the Himalayas beyond the Brahmaputra River, with the morning mist veiling the peaks. The last time the Japanese had come over, that station gave warning fifteen minutes before they reached our airfields, and the American fighters were waiting for them.

After lunch we paid a ceremonial visit to King Tong-am, who had been duly advised of our coming. He lived on the lower peak, in a great house with huge beams. One of his brother's wives had died the day before and we passed the bier, covered with palm leaves and a red cloth. The women hid in flimsy huts built for the occasion, but we could hear their monotonous, chanting dirges for the dead princess. Sometimes they would stop, and then we would see their heads peeking through the palm leaves at us, and hear giggles in place of songs of mourning. Naga women are shy, not because of their nakedness but through simple timidity.

The King's bodyguard was resplendent with crossbows, poisoned arrows, and spears. We walked into a darkened room where we found the king alone, but we were placed at a careful distance in four dilapidated chairs whose history it would have been interesting to know. Each one was entirely different and no second hand dealer would have touched any one of them. The King was a tall, thin, handsome young man, at first dressed like the others, but when Grover and I said we would like to photograph him, he put on a great deal of jewelry and a decorated headdress. We told him through an interpreter that we were sorry his brother's wife died and we hoped he would have many more wives, which apparently was the right thing to say.

The King had to be addressed through a sort of chamberlain, and he remained dignified and solemn until he turned around to shout at his wives, behind the wall, to be quiet. Evidently they were peeking. One of the headmen passed around pieces of cinnamon which we solemnly chewed, and the King accepted an American cigarette. The only time he spoke was when he complained that with the arrival of the Ghurkas too much water was being used. He wanted to know how long the Americans were going to stay. Lieutenant Colonel Barr replied, "After many days, we shall go."

After posing for his photographs, the King had us shown into a hut where the village heads were kept, apologizing because there were only about one hundred left, another hundred having been destroyed in a fire about a year before. In disposing of their own dead, they cut the head off and feed it, as if it were alive, for two years. The body is exposed, not buried. The enemy skulls were on a rack, in rows. Some showed split skulls. There was, in the same hut, a war drum about 15 feet long, made of a hollowed trunk, with two heavy bones to beat it with.

The headman came back with us to camp and sat down with a number of other Nagas to talk somehow with the soldiers, and laugh—and ask for more money. He said the Ghurkas had cut a lot of his bamboo for that stockade. At first he named an outrageous sum, but compromised on 30 rupees and a promise from Barr that no more bamboo would be cut. Normally, opium, cut into small pieces, is used for money in that territory. Otherwise you must have silver, since the Nagas do not take notes.

The headman made a long speech, which the interpreter said meant that he would like a written assurance that the Americans were not going to stay on his land forever. Sergeant Meyer solemnly got out paper and pen and wrote this official document:

> Roses are red,
> Violets are blue,
> When the war's over,
> We will skiddoo.
> (Signed) LEON F. MEYER, Sergeant, U. S. Army.

The headman just as solemnly tucked it away, and everybody was happy. Old Jojo opined he would like to go to the United States and see our king. And so, with laughter and stories the hours passed around the campfire. Late in the evening (nine o'clock is late when you eat supper at four in the afternoon) someone had the bright idea of opening a can of "wienies." We each cut a bamboo sliver, speared a sausage, held it over the fire, and produced hot dogs that had a flavor equal to any eaten on Broadway or Main Street that night.

Lieutenant Hall asked the soldiers whether any of them would like to be transferred back to the airbases. Weren't they tired of living on top of the mountain with no companions but headhunters, and no amusements but to laugh with and at their Naga friends? The answer was "No." Nobody wanted to go back.

That was shortly before Christmas, 1942, after Grover and I had come back "over the hump" from China, and afterwards we spent some happy days in Cooch Behar, along with a number of American pilots and ground crews, for we had a little airfield there in that period. Cooch Behar to them was a happy interlude between dangerous jobs and hard work, and they were grateful to the young, fun-loving Maharaja, who played tennis better than any of them, was a cricketer on the Bengal team, loved American jazz, and danced like a professional. He and his mother, the Maharani Regent of whom I have already written, sat down in the card-room of their great, red-brick palace many a night to play poker with our pilots, and they more than held their own. Meals in the state dining room were happy family gatherings, attended by a bevy of beautiful bejeweled Indian princesses. There could not have been less formality or more friendliness, and Americans were as much at home in the great palace of the Maharaja of Cooch Behar as they were in their neighbor's house on Main Street. Pilots and mechanics used to call the Maharaja "Chief," and he addressed them by their first names.

So, it was a strange war in some ways, and one day two of the pilots, not to mention Grover and myself, went on a leopard hunt from the backs of elephants. Leopard hunting is not only a sport; it is a defense of the cultivators and their livestock. That morning, peasants from the nearby village of Charaker Kuthi sent a runner to the palace to say that a leopard had killed a calf the night before. The Maharaja ordered his elephants out, collected us, and the hunt was on. Cooch Behar has been famous for generations for its hunting, and there is always a large group of trained elephants. We rode out to Charaker Kuthi in automobiles, and then climbed aboard padded elephants which took us into the jungle where the leopard had been sighted. There we transferred to elephants with howdahs atop of them, and double-barreled shotguns were given to us. The padded elephants were taken over by the beaters.

The leopard had been seen in a thick patch of elephant grass, wild plum trees, and shrubs of wild cardamon higher than a man but well below our towering monsters. We lined up across a slight clearing while the beaters came slowly toward us, the drivers shouting their "Hup! hup!" to encourage the elephants, which were somewhat timid that day because at the last hunt, a week before, five of them had been mangled by a wounded leopard.

It was an excruciatingly tense moment as the beating elephants neared the edge of our clearing. But no leopard came out. He had slunk through or passed them, somehow. Four times that exciting process was repeated. We knew we had him because he had been spotted, and was trapped with the river at his back while we executed a pincers movement. The natives from Charaker were watching breathlessly at a distance of three hundred yards, undeterred by possible danger to them if the leopard should bolt their way, and heedless of the Maharaja's shouts to go back.

The fourth beat got the luckless animal. He suddenly dashed straight toward the right-hand elephant, from which my elephant was separated by ten yards. The Youvraj of Dewas Junior, the Maharaja's brother-in-law, had a clean shot from no more than a dozen yards, and the leopard stopped. He was badly, perhaps mortally, wounded. As he thrashed about, I got a glimpse of his spotted hide and blazed away, but it was the Youvraj who gave the *coup de grace*. As the excited villagers dashed up, shouting, the Maharaja's bearers ignominiously dragged the animal out into the open, by his tail. He was 7 feet 6 inches long, which was large for a leopard.

Life is always like that for maharajas in India. The ruler of Cooch Behar is typical of many of the younger princes. Unlike the old-fashioned Maharaj Rana of Dholpur, he is willing to leave much of the government to his Prime Minister, and takes less personal interest in his individual subjects. He is less autocratic, more receptive to progressive ideas, much less bound by religion, and bears the strong marks of Harrow and Cambridge, without being Anglophile. No Englishman lives in Cooch Behar. The chief disappointment of his people is that although the Maharaja is twenty-nine years old he is not married, and has not provided his State with a successor to the *gadi* of his ancient, illustrious line. His mother twitted him about it at Christmas dinner when I was there, and he answered jokingly that he would like to marry an American heiress so that he could use her millions in his public-works department. The Maharani said that every time a good astrologer comes their way she asks him when her son is going to get married, but they always aim to please royalty and say, "Within a year or two." They had been saying that for ten years, she added ruefully.

There was one very exciting interlude of work there that provided a corking story for me and Grover. Captain Johnny Payne, crack pilot who was one of the first to demonstrate that a ferry plane could be taken over the "hump" into China at night, casually mentioned at breakfast that he had to make an altitude-test hop in a C-47 Army transport. He did it, and it took me and some others nearly 22,000 feet alongside unconquered Kanchanjanga, second highest mountain in the world. But for the Maharaja of Nepal's prohibition against planes flying over his territory, we would have gone on a little further to where Mount Everest towered above the surrounding giants and climbed that. American soldiers did strange and wonderful things in that ancient country, just in the course of the day's work. Since the test hop had to be made, Payne could not see why he should not make a trip that was about as spectacular as any this world can provide. Kanchanjanga is 28,168 feet high. Its great ice wall has baffled every expedition, and its summit was, necessarily, going to baffle us, since transport planes are not meant for the stratosphere, but we were going to get a better and closer view than anyone else ever had of it.

"This thing will climb like a homesick angel," said Co-Pilot Captain Lloyd E. Hubbard as we clambered into the plane, hoping he was right. Two other pilots joined us as observers, Captain Jacob Peter Sartz and First Lieutenant Fred K. Darragh. All four officers were famous among Americans in India for having flown the "hump" more times than seemed theoretically possible to do and still be alive. The Maharaja came with us.

Kanchanjanga stands sentinel over the whole Assam plain, and we caught sight of it not long after starting. By rare luck we had a perfectly clear day, and the whole mighty range glistened in white and gold against a pale blue sky. Payne set the nose of our Douglas straight at the summit with its slightly sawed-off edge. Far below us, Darjeeling was obscured by clouds, and soon nothing existed but those mighty, jagged peaks rising from brown to gray to dazzling white. Here was the most spectacular scenery in the world—and all in a day's work!

At 15,000 feet we had to sit down and stay down, for only the pilot and co-pilot had oxygen masks, and at a high altitude the least exertion may knock you out. We fought off a dangerous sleepiness, swallowing hard every few seconds while our lungs gasped for breath and our hearts pounded until they literally hurt.

Now we were 18,000 feet. The winter sun sharpened the tops and ridges that cut into the sky, barren and awful in their loneliness. Beyond that sharp-edged range must be the end of the world, complete nothingness! The brain becomes foggy in that rarefied atmosphere; the notebook dances before your eyes as your hand traces wavy words on a blurred page.

Payne sent back word that we would have to move forward, in order to keep the tail of the plane up as it fought for altitude in the treacherous currents. We crawled forward. Bands of steel seemed to be tightening around our foreheads, but the sturdy transport was getting us there. I looked at the Maharaja and saw his eyes glaze. Later he admitted that he had passed out. It was 20,000 feet, and Kanchanjanga loomed near.

Some time before, Everest had raised its gigantic silhouette over the lesser monsters around us. It stood serene and unclouded against a sky which it surely must have touched—mightiest of all mountains, the top of the world!

Twenty-one thousand, seven hundred feet, corrected, and now we were skirting Kanchanjanga itself, hardly ten miles away. It was the plane's ceiling—and the pilots knew, anyway, that they had to get down quickly, or they would be bringing five corpses back with them, for human beings cannot stand that altitude, without oxygen, for more than a short time. Besides, we had reached the Sikkim-Nepalese frontier, where people believe that the gods of the mountains rise in anger when mere mortals violate their untouchable heights.

Payne banked, and swung the plane around, fighting the tricky air pockets that tossed us up and down. Once on the way back a down current caught the plane and threw it about like a feather, while we hung on for dear life and the pilots struggled for a few breath-taking seconds to keep control. It is said that air blasts in the Himalayas can be strong enough to tear a plane apart, and we were inclined to believe it, after that. Only a strongly constructed machine can take such punishment and get away with it.

As we went down we opened our mouths to suck in great draughts of air, swallowing again and again. Heavy weights seemed to be lifted from our heads and we could move about once more, taking last glimpses of that sharp-angled west wall of Everest which no human being can ever hope to climb, and the 700-foot wall of ice which defends Kanchanjanga's unconquerable summit. Around them were other great peaks—Jonsang, Lhonak, Pyramid, Talung, Dongkya La—so famous to mountain climbers the world over. After months of preparation some of them have toiled and struggled, sometimes not successfully, to conquer one of those peaks. And here we had them all around us just because an American transport plane had to be tested for altitude!

Then came Christmas, and dinner was another kindness from Cooch Behar to the American pilots and newspapermen far from home. Thanks to that delightful family, we all had turkey and plum pudding in India. And then Grover and I flew down to Calcutta, where I filed a homesick story of one more Christmas at the wars, away from Nancie and the children. There have been two others since, with the 5th Army in Italy, and maybe they will be the last.

"Christmas is here, and this big, sprawling, misty city of Calcutta is welcoming hundreds of American soldiers and officers who will do their best to forget 'the black, dividing sea and alien plain' which separates them from home," I wrote. "It isn't an official welcome in any sense, but it is enough for Calcutta to be its cheerful, busy, colorful self and provide all those comforts of modern life which airfields and camps never know—hot baths, electric lights, good food, entertainment, horse races, spring beds with mattresses. Life, gaiety, and luxury may be poor substitutes for Christmas at home, but they are something.

"This city gives a superficial appearance of being invaded by the army, for it is full of British and Indian soldiers as well as Americans, and they all stay around Chowringhee Road, where you can buy zircons and catseyes, ice cream and chocolates, where you can dance with real, live white women, smoke Manila cigars and eat steaks two inches thick.

"Here tattoo artists ply a busy trade from morn to midnight, needling flags or nudes, portraits or monsters, as you please. You can go into the Metro Cinema and see *Mrs. Miniver*, or to the Globe Theater and hear Tchaikovsky's *Fifth Symphony*. Shops display all the wealth of the Indies to buy as souvenirs for sweethearts and wives.

"Uncle Sam's doughboys rub elbows in the street with Tommy Atkins and Kipling's 'Hurree Chunder Mookerjee, pride of Bow Bazaar,' while their officers jostle British and Indian counterparts on the crowded dance floor of Firpo's restaurant. Out in the opalescent, moonlit street beggars creep around like leeches and hang on, block after block, whining the invariable formula: 'No mamma, no papa, no baksheesh,' until the harassed soldier either buys them off or runs away. Fortune-tellers swarm along Chowringhee Road, pouncing on soldiers, wheedling, cajoling, promising them wealth, women and luck, but they get no business from the Americans, for it is against regulations to dabble in that fertile field for espionage.

"A young Indian sidles up and whispers temptingly: 'Wanta nice girl?' But he cannot supply that one girl or woman in the world who means anything to the lonely American walking along Chowringhee Road or Connaught Place in New Delhi or any other street in any other Indian city or village from the west coast to Burma."

Were we not all, Englishmen and Americans, as in Kipling's day, exiles on "Christmas in India"?

Oh, the white dust on the highways! Oh, the stenches in the byway!
Oh, the clammy fog that hovers over earth!
And at Home they're making merry, 'neath the white and scarlet berry—
What part have India's exiles in their mirth?

However, Kipling's Englishman—for all his homesickness— really wanted to stay and keep this India as his own, but if the prayers of all the thousands of Americans there on Christmas Day in 1942 had been heard, not one of them would have been an exile in India when Christmas next came around.

We Americans do not know what heat is like until we go to a country like India and wait, gasping and dull-eyed, for the monsoon to break. New York and Washington, St. Louis or wherever you please, knows nothing remotely comparable to that torture. I literally "sweated out" the first monsoon break of 1943 at some of our airfields in Assam at the end of May. As the monsoon approaches, the air becomes heavier and heavier with moisture, and you sit about panting and covered with prickly heat and sopping wet from perspiration. The nights bring no relief, and sleep is impossible until sheer exhaustion sets in. And then the monsoon, like manna from heaven, breaks.

It is something that has to be experienced to be appreciated.

The air is still hot and steaming—but, oh, what a difference from the day before! As the weeks and months pass and the rains keep coming, with their millions of insects, and everything turns moldy and you, yourself, feel like a wet rag—supposing you are not laid up with malaria—the blessings of the first day will turn to curses.

We lost some correspondents in India, and few escaped malaria and dysentery. I was one of the lucky ones, and ended my eleven months with nothing worse than dhobie's itch, prickly heat, eczema of the ears, and five or six attacks of "Delhi belly."

I think that in all my stay in India I met only two Americans, aside from the missionaries, who really liked to live in India. One was Margaret Wilson, daughter of President Woodrow Wilson. I found her, as I have written, at Sri Aurobindo's *ashram* down in Pondicherry, the tiny French colony on the east coast, south of Madras, and she told me that she was happier than she had ever been. For four years she had been a *"sadhak,"* or follower, of Sri Aurobindo, perhaps India's most famous mystic.

Her name at the *ashram* was "Nishta," a Sanskrit word whose meaning Aurobindo explained to her in mystical terminology. She begged me not to publish the meaning, as it was too personal and sacred to her, and I did not do so in my story for *The New York Times.* But now she is dead, and there can be no harm. "Nishta" means "one pointed, fixed, and steady concentration, devotion, and faith in the single aim, the divine and the divine realization." Not being really an adept in Eastern philosophy, I am sure that Miss Wilson never fathomed its meaning, but it gave her comfort and satisfaction.

In a sense, she had renounced the world, but she was the same Margaret Wilson that her friends had known in New York and Washington, in the same Western style of dress, with that same gay smile which gave her so startling a resemblance to her father. She read newspapers and magazines, and was keenly interested in the war and politics. Once she had been a pacifist, she said, but yoga had helped to confirm her natural instincts in the other direction.

She told me about her "experience," as it is called. She had never been religious, and, indeed, had left her church in the middle of communion, one day in girlhood, and never returned. However, the Indian religious classics and the writings of mystics had begun to interest her some ten years before. Then, more than four years before our meeting, purely by accident (for she had never heard of him) she picked out a book, *Essays on the Gita*, by Sri Aurobindo, from the card catalogue of New York's Public Library, and began to peruse the book in the main reading room. It enthralled her, and at closing time that evening the library attendants almost had to put her out, and each day after that she returned, until she had finished the book. It made so great an impression on her that she resolved to join Sri Aurobindo's *ashram*.

In speaking to me of her experience and her happiness at the *ashram*, Miss Wilson said she had often tried to discover why a person like herself should have been so drawn to mysticism, and should have developed such a capacity for it. One explanation, she thought, was to be found in her Irish blood, for she said her father had always remarked that he was of half-Irish, half-Scottish extraction. At any rate, upon arriving in Bombay she immediately felt at home, and wanted to say to the people on the street, "Don't you realize I am one of you?"

Aurobindo, who was then seventy-three, was a leader of the left wing of the Congress party in the first decade of the century, and was imprisoned several times by the British. In 1910 he left his native Bengal, settled in Pondicherry, withdrew from the political field, and devoted himself to spiritual work. He evolved a new way of *yoga*, different from the old Vedantic philosophy of renouncing all material things and considering only the spirit as reality. Aurobindo's *yoga* aims at bringing the spirit into life and transforming it. That was one of the reasons why his *yoga* could appeal to a Westerner like Margaret Wilson, for it did not demand too radical a break with life as she had known it.

As always happens in India, disciples gathered around the teacher, and in 1920 a remarkable woman joined the *ashram*, who was now known to all the devotees as "Mother." Her full title was "Mother of the Universe," and she ruled the *ashram* with an organizing ability and a flair for drama which kept everything running smoothly, and won for her an adoration which in Miss Wilson's case impressed me as almost as great as that extended to Sri Aurobindo. "Mother" is a French woman named Madame Alfassa. She was then sixty-six, dressed always in Hindu *saris* that framed her carefully made up face and formed the background for her beautiful jewelry. Every morning at 6:30 she shows herself to all the nearly 300 *sadhaks* as she comes out on the balcony and salutes them, Hindu style, with palms together.

Sri Aurobindo shows himself only thrice yearly to devotees who come from all over India and even from abroad, and on one other occasion shows himself to the members of the *ashram,* but he never speaks to any of them, and all the rest of the year remains shut up in his room. *Sadhaks* may submit questions in writing, which he answers if he considers them worthwhile; otherwise everyone struggles along for himself or herself.

There are no monastic rules. Every evening the disciples gather in a little courtyard for half an hour's meditation, which should be accomplished with a calm, peaceful mind, but for the rest of the day they can do anything they please. Miss Wilson mentioned her difficulties in preparing for that meditation, and described herself as only in the kindergarten stage of *yoga,* which everyone at the *ashram* must practice. Aurobindo's *yoga,* as he himself wrote, "is more difficult than any other." Consequently, "for my restless Western mind to get into the necessary state of peace and quiet is extremely hard," Miss Wilson said. At meditation she was the only one to sit on a chair, for she never learned to sit Hindu fashion, which is knee-breaking.

Her life was so completely wrapped up in the *ashram* that she could not show me any of the sights of Pondicherry as we drove through the town. She lived outside the *ashram* proper, which was too small to hold all the disciples. She had a simple, spacious suite in an eighteenth-century colonial mansion, with a great balcony overlooking a garden. The bedroom was comfortable, with nothing different from a typical Indian room fixed up for a Westerner, except a low, table-like altar with photographs of

Aurobindo and "Mother," surrounded by flowers. Aurobindo has flowing hair, and all the men at the *ashram,* many of whom were young, copied his style. There was a community kitchen, for Aurobindo does not permit caste or creed differences in his *ashram.* Miss Wilson said she began as a vegetarian, like the Hindus, but became ill, lost a lot of weight, and "Mother" put her back on a meat diet. She then weighed about thirty pounds less than when she arrived, but said she felt well, and evidently had no forebodings of the death that was not far off.

She had retained her American citizenship, and the only time she left Pondicherry was to go to Madras once and have her passport renewed. She did not have to give up any personal habits. Smoking and drinking are not done at the *ashram* itself, but Miss Wilson had no objection to accepting a cigarette over the luncheon table. However, hers was a life apart. According to Aurobindo's own published statement, *"sadhaks* have no claim, right, or voice in any matter. They remain or go, according to his will. Whatever money he receives is his property. . . . All depends on the teacher and ends with his lifetime, unless there is another teacher who can take his place."

Neither Sri Aurobindo nor "Mother" told Miss Wilson to go away. She seemed so happy to see an American that I interpreted it as nostalgia, and asked if she did not have longings for her native land.

"No," she said. "I do not want to return to the United States. I am not homesick. In fact, I never felt more at home anywhere, any time in my life."

And there she died—happily, one must suppose.

And the other American? Do you remember Nancy Miller? Once upon a time a pretty American girl, just out of college, was married to the Maharaja of a great Indian State—which would seem to have been the answer to any maiden's prayer. I do not know whether it can be added that "they lived happily ever after," but perhaps it would not be too great an exaggeration.

One afternoon in Indore, Nancy Miller (or, as she was known there, Her Highness the Maharani Sharmishthabai Holkar) received me for an hour's talk in a room of the magnificent Lal

Bagh Palace, where she had lived all those years since her marriage in 1926. It had been a nine-days' wonder throughout the world, for the Maharaja Tukoji Rao not only had two other wives, but had been involved in the sensational murder of a dancing girl's lover which had led to his abdication, when he refused to face trial. (Incidentally, his friends were convinced that the murder was committed without his knowledge, by attendants overanxious to please him.)

I asked the American Maharani whether all that sensational publicity had not been rather distressing, and she said it had, indeed. "I was just a girl out of college, and it seemed so unjust! I would not have minded if they had written the truth, but things were twisted so!"

After seventeen years, there was little to write about Nancy Miller. When I said to her, "You won't mind if I write something about you?" she answered, "Why should I? I lead such a simple life!"

Outwardly it has been just that. She sees a few people and her British friends, who speak of her in the highest terms and complain that her husband keeps her in a modified form of *purdah*. They were surprised that he let her see me. In seclusion, years pass uneventfully. There are four children now, all daughters— a tragedy in a country where only sons are desired. They were educated in Switzerland and want to go back as soon as they can, for they hate India. Except for visits to them in Switzerland and a trip to the United States in 1932, the former Nancy Miller has remained in India.

Everyone, Indian and British alike, spoke of her with glowing praise—of her integrity, simplicity, charm, and kindliness. When her car goes along the streets, even pro-Congress agitators stop respectfully and salute her. She has won a solid place in the affection of the people of Indore.

So, outwardly, it was a picture of an attractive, cultured, quiet woman, living a home life with her husband and four children. It was only when one stopped to think that this was an American woman that the picture began to get complicated. The Maharani is now a Hindu, which is very rare, for, generally speaking, one is born into a certain Hindu caste as a result, it is believed, of innumerable previous incarnations. But there is a special (and, needless to say, rather low) caste into which outsiders are admitted. I was told that no high-caste Hindu can be expected to marry any of her daughters. As a Hindu maharani, she wore a *sari*, which that day was of white silk with a silver border. The end of it, in customary style, was draped over her black hair, parted in the middle, while on her forehead, between the eyes, was the tiny red caste mark, which serves Indian women as well as the old-time beauty spot. She invariably wears *saris*.

And there she lives in a wonderful palace with its immense grounds—but only in part of the palace, for another part is occupied by another maharani who is His Highness's second wife. She and Nancy Miller, it is said, never meet. There is still another wife, in a palace of her own. She is Tukoji Rao's first wife and the mother of the present Maharaja, whose marital and love affairs have made him as well known as his father. Anyway, that is the hierarchy—one, two, three, with the American wife ranking lowest.

One would not think all these things are ingredients for a happy, married life of an American girl, but everyone in Indore said that Nancy Miller was happy and one can leave it at that. But those two cases, of Margaret Wilson and Nancy Miller, are exceptional.

The average American soldier hates India and tries to shut it out of his life, living in his barracks, listening to the radio, going to American movies, eating at his own American mess, seeing only other American (never British) soldiers and officers. He has the best of all the service newspapers to read, the *CBI Roundup*, started while I was there, on September 17, 1942, under the brilliant editorship of Captain (now Major) Fred Eldridge. It will be "evil enough to make you chuckle and clean enough to get through the mails," he promised—and it was extraordinarily good to boot.

But there is no escaping India, and sometimes even American officers deliberately walked through the looking glass to seek aid in that other world so strange to them. Here is a story that was told to me by a high American officer as we sat in Nagins, on Dal Lake, outside Srinagar:

"At our Agra camp, months ago, a very secret and extremely important batch of documents, in a brief case, was lost. It was so important that the commander immediately closed down the camp. No one was allowed in or out; construction on the runways and buildings was stopped, and all the workers were set to searching every inch of the grounds. Soldiers went through the buildings, exploring the most out-of-the-way nooks and crannies. The brief case was not there. Hundreds of men were then detailed to work slowly along the roads and fields around the air base, and all the way into Agra. Still no brief case.

"Days passed, and one afternoon an Indian foreman said to the commander, 'Why don't you consult an astrologer?' Being at his wits' end, the colonel was willing to try anything. Four of the local pandits were consulted, but in vain. Word came of a famous pandit in a nearby village, and some officers were sent to see him. However, it happened that he was down with malaria and a high fever, and he could only say that if they were still looking for the brief case when he felt better they should come back. The sixth astrologer also failed.

"The seventh said to them, 'Look for the case at the crossroads of such and such a village.' They searched the crossroads and every house in the village, but could not find it, so they returned to the pandit. He said: 'I know that the brief case was there. It fell out of an automobile and was picked up by a young boy. You must try again.'

"It seemed hopeless, but the automobile had passed that spot, so they tried again, this time inquiring for a boy who had been there on the day in question, but was no longer in the village. And then one man said, Yes, his nephew had been there and had since gone back to his own village, which he named. The officers went there, and after a short inquiry found the boy—and the brief case! It had fallen out of the car and he had picked it up. The papers were of no use and he had given them away. Some had been used for wrapping parcels, by the local shopkeepers; others had been thrown on the village garbage heap. With patient searching and the help of the whole village they recovered every one of the documents that had been secret and important."

That is, to the best of my knowledge, a true story, and it shows you the sort of world in which the Americans were living. In this instance they had to enter that world in order to achieve a purpose.

Yet there was one way to escape—from India and the war and the world, and I did it for one happy week. If you close your eyes and make a wish to get away from everything, your dreams should take you to the Vale of Kashmir. It is good that there should be such a place—better still, that dozens of American officers should have found respite there from bombing and fighting or the dreary routine in the sweltering plains to the south. Kashmir is the only region of India where the climate is really good for the white man. There you find the fruits and flowers of our own temperate clime, all brought together into one enchanted valley, surrounded by the snow-capped Himalayas, and they stretch north to the Karakoram Mountains where once three mighty empires met—India, China, and Russia. There you will find some of the grandest scenery in the world, but down in the valley man has added to the beauty which Thomas Moore sang about but never saw. Here is where the River Jhelum rises from a sacred well, and where Alexander the Great, whose traces we found in Afghanistan, crossed by stratagem to beat the Rajput, Poros. Here is where Jehangir built three lovely pleasure gardens for his Empress Nur Jehan, "Light of the World," and the loveliest of these is Shalimar, whose fame has spread, in poetry and song, over the world.

It is India's playground, where princes, princesses, wealthy industrialists, and British officials on leave ride side by side in houseboats on the river and the surrounding lakes.

You go home in Kashmir's version of the Venetian gondola. It is called *shikara*, and, by some droll custom, each boat has an odd name, followed by the boast that it possesses full, or lovely, spring seats. And so you find "Mae West with full spring seats," "Love Comes to You, with full spring seats," "Careless Rapture, with lovely spring seats," "Dancing Girl with full spring seats," "Cautious Amorist, with lovely spring seats," and others with names too *risqué* for this book.

It is one of those rare places in the world, like the canals and lagoon of Venice, where the atmosphere breathes romance as you ride down the lake, seeing temples in the moonlight through feathery gray willows and the cones of deodars, and up above you the steady beacon on the hill called "Solomon's Throne," and beyond and all around, the snow-topped mountains of the Himalayas. Then the boatman tries to cheat you outrageously on your fare, and you remember the warnings you received about the Kashmiris. That remark your acquaintance made to you as you drifted through an unwholesome village comes back: "Kashmir is like that. It looks beautiful and smells awful."

Britishers almost invariably add, whenever they mention Kashmir, "Where every prospect pleases, and only man is vile." You are hounded for *baksheesh* in a way that would put Neapolitan beggars to shame, and in shops where lovely things are sold you will be cheated shamelessly if some knowing friend is not with you. One of the most important shopkeepers is called "Subhana the Worst," and he himself who put that on his sign tells you, chuckling, that it means "Subhana, the Worst Rogue in Town." One shopkeeper, whose name was Safdar Hussain, was dubbed by an Englishman, years ago, "Suffering Moses," and that is now his trade appellation. It was so successful that others followed suit, and you will find "Joyful Jacob," "Cheerful Charlie," "Jolly Joseph," and "Walnut Willie," who makes furniture.

So Kashmir is like a beautiful apple with a rotten core. Its people live in a Garden of Eden, but are so utterly poor and miserable that one's inquiries must pass from what Emperor Jehangir called his "heaven on earth" to the hidden hell beneath it. The combined States of Kashmir and Jammu are as big as England, Wales, and Scotland together, but as they are largely mountainous, the population is only 4,000,000, crowded with incredible density into a few fertile valleys. In a country where misery is the common lot of the people, Kashmiris are the most wretched of all.

In Kashmir the position of Hyderabad is reversed. In the latter a Moslem minority rules over a Hindu population. In Kashmir the Hindus are only 20 per cent and the Moslems 77. About a century ago the British, with a cynicism which shocked even the political morals of those days, sold Kashmir to a Rajput Dogra family for 7,500,000 rupees, in return for services rendered during one of the Sikh wars. Since then, Hindus have monopolized the ruling power and the wealth, with Brahmin families such as the Nehrus, the Pandits and the Saprus providing all India with brilliant, aristocratic talent. The present Maharaja of Jammu and Kashmir, Hari Singh, is a descendant of the first Rajput prince. Since 1925 he has been ruling over a people whose lot under the Moguls, Afghans and Sikhs has been one of dreadful enslavement —but it must be recognized that he has done some things to better the condition of his people.

It is one of those regions of India where the Congress contention that there is little difference between Moslems and Hindus holds true, but that does not alter the fact that the Mohammedans are treated as low-caste, with the Brahmins sitting securely upon them. The misery of the people has resulted in serious uprisings, with a genuine rebellion after World War I, and both Congress and the Moslem League have made Kashmir a target for their criticisms. However, it is hardly to be expected that Congress would seriously embarrass a Hindu-ruled State, while Jinnah has always made it clear that his Pakistan excludes the Princely States. The Maharaja, like the Nizam of Hyderabad, carefully and for obvious reasons eschews communal problems.

I talked to political leaders in Srinagar, getting a good idea of their helplessness under a genuinely despotic rule. Both the Hindu and the Moslem political organizations, however, profess loyalty to the Maharaja, asking only for constitutional government under his aegis. As things are now, there is a legislature of seventy-five members, of whom forty are elected, but the Maharaja has absolute powers to override them and make laws by his fiat, and they cannot in any way interfere with his rights and prerogatives. He is a law unto himself, living on a scale which is impressive even in India, for he takes fully 15 per cent of the yearly revenue of more than 37,000,000 rupees. Kashmir is, in a sense, like his private estate, and he is not partial to for-eigners. He especially dislikes having Kashmir made the center of a rather fast social set of Britishers, with women nicknamed "the Charpoy Cobra," "the Amorous Haystack," and "the Per-sian Kitten."

Hari Singh has done a good deal to improve the lot of the Moslem cultivator—which fact makes one wonder how they even existed before. In the cultivable areas there is a density of popu-lation running as high as 1,600 per square mile, compared to 800 for India, and 85 for the United States. Literacy is less than 7 per cent, compared with nearly 13 in British India, and when it is considered that virtually all the Brahmins and Kashmiri pandits are educated, the percentage for Muslims must be even lower. Only 2 per cent of the females are literate.

Kashmir's woolen textiles, papier-mâché articles, and wood carvings are famous throughout the world, but they represent sweated labor of the worst sort. The 1941 census reported the average laborer's wage as between 5 and 6 annas (10 to 12 cents) a day, and in the urban areas 6 to 8 annas. Skilled workers get 10 annas to 2 rupees daily. Any number of clerical workers are available at 20 rupees (about $7) per month. Kashmir's grains, fruits, and flowers are the envy of India, yet her cultivators live on the verge of starvation. All authorities agree that the laborers and cultivators live throughout their lives in a state of perpetual indebtedness to their employers and owners. Debt, extravagance, ignorance, excessive fragmentation of lands, sweated labor, misery and more misery—such is the only picture one can give of Kash-mir's people.

It is hard to see why it should be so. They are taxed only 25 to 28 per cent of their produce, which is not excessive for India. They have a rich land where it is cultivable, and the healthiest region in India where, alone, there is no malaria. One can only conclude that, in addition to suffering from oppression, there is something wrong with these unhappy people, who are cursed with a disposition for wretchedness, along with defects of character which make them the least attractive of all Indians, to put it mildly.

I went out to have tea with the man who rules over these unhappiest people in the world. The Maharaja received me in his little palace, and nothing could better symbolize his position as ruler of one of the largest and wealthiest States in India than that beautiful and expensive house. It stands only a few hundred yards from the main palace, which is not much smaller than Versailles, and both are set in widespreading grounds just outside Srinagar. And there you have that extreme contrast of dreadful poverty and fabulous wealth which is so characteristic of India—not that Hari Singh Bahadur has done anything which his people would not expect or which other rulers have not always done before him. For them, the narrow, dirty, overcrowded slums of the unwholesome native city; for him, beautiful palaces and gardens on a spot which the Moguls, with their eye for landscaping, had chosen before him, where one's heart is gladdened by a superb view over the Vale of Kashmir and on to the snow-covered Himalayas.

As maharajas go, Hari Singh is decent, well-meaning and hardworking, and although he is extravagant he is not comparatively more so than the average ruler. His Minister-in-Waiting, R. C. Kak, and his political adviser, Sir Kailash Haksar, were present at the tea, which lasted three hours. The Maharaja is a striking figure. Once a six-goal-handicap polo player, he has permitted himself to put on too much weight to continue playing. His face is extraordinary—wide, typically Indian eye sockets, long-lobed ears, small mouth, curved Rajput nose. The cast of his head is really long and narrow, but the heavy jowls and double chin make it appear round.

The talk was partly frivolous, partly serious, with the main topic of conversation being the appointment of Marshal Wavell as Viceroy. The consensus among the guests was that it was an unfortunate choice, which offered no relief for unhappy India. And then we got on to fishing, having heard that the Maharaja had caught a nine-pound trout a few days before. He keeps immense fishing and hunting preserves for his private use, which the English understand, since that is what they do in Scotland. He told us proudly about that catch, and sent for his rod, which was a beauty.

And by then it was time for the pre-dinner Scotch and soda. "I was a fool at the beginning of this war," His Highness said. "I could have had all the whisky I wanted, and now I have only three years' supply left!" We spoke of famous Indian drinks made of fresh and dried fruits, fermented with partridges and black buck. He told us enviously about a Maharaja of Jaipur who eighty years ago laid down a large stock of real, unblended Napoleon brandy, of which much was left. Surely it must be pretty well unique.

But in the end the conversation got around to the most serious problem of all in India, that of food. In the best of times his people live on the edge of starvation, and there were bad crop prospects. His table would not suffer, and since he and his people believe that his *Karma*, or actions in previous incarnations, earned him his place as Maharaja of Jammu and Kashmir, no one was going to complain for India is like that.

In some ways it was not unfitting that Kashmir should have been my last trip out of New Delhi before I left India for Algiers and the long Italian campaign. That was an accidental ending, for I had made plans to visit Ceylon, Travancore, Cochin, and Orissa, the only one of the eleven provinces of British India which I did not see.

In Kashmir I saw what was wrong with India and why it was wrong—the incredible wealth of a few and the abysmal misery of the many; the yoke that religion and *Karma* and the British paramount power put upon the masses; the aristocratic, cultured Brahmins and the ignorant, despised low castes; the beauty and the filth, the corruption and the suffering patiently borne.

Perhaps, in some far off Utopia, matters will be different. I learned many lessons in India, but none that I value more than the knowledge that all a man's idealism and liberalism and democracy are of no value if they are not capable of practical application. Freedom is not something that you can give away,

like clothes or food. It is something which has to be fought
for and earned, and, in so far as it is given, the recipient must
be capable of maintaining and defending it. Freedom is, in weak
hands, like the Chariot of the Sun that Phaethon tried to drive.
It would run away to license and to new masters.

India should and shall be free, but not today or tomorrow, for
the British will not now set her free, and the Indians are not yet
capable of winning their freedom. Both are bound by that Gordian knot I have written so much about. Some day it is going to
be cut—perhaps by the British, perhaps by the Indians, perhaps
by both together. It is my personal opinion that the British
should take a chance and cut loose—but one lesson I did not
have to learn in India is that my personal opinions, when they
are divorced from personal responsibilities, are very easily given
and of no great value. The which, perhaps, goes for all Americans who are giving advice about India.

I left the country gladly, but only because I was going nearer
to home, with the chance of returning first to the Italy that I
always loved, for we had finished our campaign in Tunisia, and
it was an open secret that the invasion of Europe (that part
which Churchill so inappropriately called the "soft under-belly")
was about to begin.

India had attracted and interested me as much as any other
country I had ever visited. I knew I should want to go back, that
I shall always want to go back, and I did not need a last letter
from the Maharaj Rana of Dholpur to tell me so.

"Your fond reference to my motherland is touching," he wrote,
"and I am sure you will come back to this country again, because
I believe that the call of the East always proves strong enough to
get many people back to India on one pretense or another. Soon
you will be thousands of miles away from my beloved motherland, separated by many countries and large expanses of seas,
where faint and muffled echoes may reach you from my beloved
India. But I hope, wherever you may be, you will carry with you
the memory of her children here, who are different, with their
own peculiarities of deep religious faith and various customs and

ways, but entirely friendly, truthful, and humane in every sense of the word.

"Of this I am sure, that when you do return to my beloved country again, you will find India keeping up her never-forgotten traditions of kindness and hospitality to all her friends."

Post-Graduate

Italian

Campaign in Sicily

I ARRIVED in Algiers on the afternoon of July 9, 1943, and early the next morning we landed in Sicily. That may sound like good timing, but I certainly did not consider it so. It meant that *The New York Times* had no correspondent on one of the most important amphibious landings of the war, and anyway, I always hated covering a military campaign from headquarters. It is a necessary job, and it has been done in this war with brilliance, but the fact remains that it is highly inaccurate, for headquarters receives a correct account only days after the event, and it is certainly unsatisfactory to work from mimeographed handouts which everyone gets. Since I hated to do it, it was inevitable that I should do such work badly, and that brought even less satisfaction.

For those who liked their names on the front pages every day, there was no more certain way of hitting it than writing up the headquarters stories. One of my few quarrels with the news editorial staff was that preference, or at least partiality for the story written dozens, or even hundreds of miles behind the lines. It invariably received more prominent display than the front line story, and often more credence. My own test of journalism is still and always that which Von Ranke, with less justice, applied to history: "to expound things as they really happened is the sole purpose of history." Journalism, as I said before, is not history; it provides the material for history. A man who went to the front and saw what "really happened," if only on one small part of the line, provided something factual which historians will forever be able to use, but Lord help anybody who tries

to write a history of this war based on the handouts at headquarters!

What interested me most during my brief stay in Algiers was
the possible political effect of the invasion on the Italian Fascist
Government. The Sunday editor of *The New York Times,* Lester
Markel, asked me to write a piece for the Magazine Section
which proved to be an interesting lesson in both journalism and
politics. I am not repeating it here to claim a cheap triumph over
those who laughed at me when the article appeared, but because
it was the first evidence in a persisting chain of belief that Fascism
was destroyed.

"The eyes of the world are turned on Italy now, and one can
imagine what question lies behind those millions of speculative
glances," I wrote. " 'Is Italy going to crack, at last?' It is not a
fair question, really, for one ought to ask not whether Italy is
going to collapse but whether she can collapse. When the German people broke down at the end of World War I, it took the
heart out of the German military resistance, but thanks to Fascism and Nazism that does not work out the same way now. . . .

"Like modern Atlases, Fascism and Nazism are balancing dying worlds on their shoulders and it is they who must collapse.
. . . One can narrow it down even further, for the Fascist Regime
is being held up solely by the Germans, and as you study the
whole intricate structure you can see how it is held together. . . .
It was all exceedingly brilliant, worthy of Italian genius at its
best—or worst. . . . All Mussolini needed was a race of people
who fit into that beautiful mold.

"Unfortunately for him and for Italy, his people were not in
the slightest degree suitable material for Fascism. But the Germans were. Using very much the same formula, Hitler created his
terrific instrument of Nazism, which has come close to destroying
the modern world. And because his people were strong where
Mussolini's were weak, he is now in the position of having to
hold Mussolini's structure together. . . . Mussolini was no longer
master in his own house, but at least the house was kept standing and he was maintained as major domo. All the servants were

made to realize that if they did not obey, the house would come down over their heads as well. . . .

"But let us suppose that enough feeling is aroused to make the people want to rise and overthrow the Fascist Regime. What could be done about it? In thinking about an answer to that question you realize the diabolical cleverness of the modern authoritarian regime. There is nothing that the people can do. Those who have arms are under military discipline in the Army or Black Shirt Militia. The rest are unarmed."

I went on to describe the inescapable weakness of the opposition. "The widespread nature of the Fascist structure brings into the fold even those elements which might want to destroy it," I said.

"Above all, there is the temperament of the Italian people. They are not the stuff of which revolutionaries are made. They are not hysterically inclined. There will be no mass hysteria in Italy and no such collective morbidity as overcame the Germans at the end of the previous World War. The Italian is eminently a sane, civilized, intelligent individual. He does not take himself or anybody else seriously. He accepts everything with a philosophical shrug of the shoulders behind which lie millennia of history when Italians went through every emotion known to man and races. He has no tendency toward racial or individual suicide, like the Japanese. He is blasé, cynical, worldly-wise. The very qualities which make him a bad soldier under ordinary circumstances will permit him to bear defeat, suffering and humiliation with a fortitude that the Germans could not begin to emulate.

"Such a man does not crack, even under such a terrific strain as he has been subjected to in the past few years. He may flare up hotheadedly and do enough damage before he settles down, to pave the way for revolution, but the decisive act must come from outside, through military defeat of the Axis on Italian soil.

"To count on anything else would be to play into the hands of the Fascisti. To expect Mussolini to give up until he is deprived of every instrument of power and every hope is banking on something that may be possible, but is highly improbable.

One reason the world is in its present state is that the democratic statesmen underestimated Mussolini and Hitler.

"We are entitled to speculate on what the Duce will do when he is faced with defeat, as he is going to be. One thing he will not do, unless he is completely broken in spirit, is to commit suicide. It would be consistent with Hitler's temperament to do so, probably by getting himself killed at the head of his troops, but Mussolini must be counted upon to go on fighting to the end. Even his worst enemies cannot accuse him of cowardice. He may end up as an exile in Germany, trying to fight on from there or he may attempt to desert the sinking Axis ship to save something from the impending wreck. But it is hard to conceive of him surrendering unconditionally so long as he lives.

"Mussolini is not a typical Italian—fortunately for Italy. And until the last trumpet sounds from the Allied bugles, Mussolini will have the upper hand in Italy. We must always remember that. He may only be Hitler's puppet now, but that is enough. With the whole Nazi structure behind him he can keep going against any internal development that we can foresee today. Italy must not be expected to crumble by herself.

"It is when we go into Italy that the real weaknesses of the Fascist structure will show themselves, just as they have already in Sicily. We will find a people who in their hearts, as well as their actions, will be glad to see us and glad to feel that the whole Fascist nightmare is ending. As each part of Italy is cleared the feebleness of the Fascist façade will be made manifest to the world. It will go as so many other governments and dynasties have gone in Italy's long history. The Monarchy may or may not go with it."

The article appeared on July 27, 1943, two days after the Fascist Grand Council had voted against Mussolini, and he was captured ignominiously and the Badoglio Government was installed. Nothing that I have ever written appeared, superficially, to be so silly, and there was much amusement at home. The *New Yorker* printed it as a news break under the title, "The Cloudy Crystal Balls." Yet nothing else that I ever wrote was more true, and I am repeating it here because it was such a good lesson in journalism and history. From the journalistic point of view, it was proof that if you know what you are talking about it is impossible to go fundamentally wrong, even though you cannot predict the unexpected and surprising events with which history enlivens its pages. But the political lesson was infinitely more important. We made the great mistake at that time, and later at the time of the Italian armistice, of believing that Italy and the Fascist Regime could collapse more or less by waving a magic wand and saying that it had done so. For that belief we paid a high price. An even more fundamental error is still being made—believing in the death of Fascism and Nazism because Italy has been entirely liberated and Germany entirely defeated. But of that, more in its place.

I confess to having been both chagrined and puzzled at the end of July, 1943, and until the facts seeped through. All I could think of was that Mussolini must have been much more ill and broken than we knew, or that Hitler had, for some inexplicable reason, turned on his henchman.

'Meanwhile, the campaign in Sicily went on, but before I joined it I had a chance to go on one of the greatest stories of my career, the first bombing of Rome. Hitherto inviolate, because it was the sacred city of Catholicism and all Christendom, it could no longer be ignored in the military strategy of the war, for it was the chief bottleneck for supplies from Germany and northern Italy. In view of the peculiar quality of the story, I did something which I have rarely done in my journalistic life, and that was to write it as explanation and propaganda. It was of such importance to the war to demonstrate that it was simply a raid against a military objective, which should not have offended the sensibilities of Catholics throughout the world, that a good half of my story was a defense of the motives behind the raid and a claim that we knew we could and would avoid any destruction of sacred edifices in Rome.

I regret to say I was somewhat misled. I had not had an opportunity, up to that time, to see much of the effects of bombing in this war, and when I was told (as we were the evening before by an American brigadier general) that bombing had become an instrument of precision and hence we knew exactly what was going to be destroyed, I believed it. Later, I learned that there is no such thing as precision bombing, except perhaps by dive bombers flying under ideal conditions, and we were going to do high-level bombing. Moreover, in the excitement I did not study the photographs closely enough to realize that our bombing run was directly over the very important and sacred basilica of San Lorenzo Fuori le Mura. It was inevitable that we should damage it severely, and the Fascists and Nazis made great capital of that fact. Moreover, we destroyed a lot of tenement houses around the San Lorenzo marshaling yards, our main target, and killed some 4,000 Romans.

So that part of my story did not stand up, although it was true that the high command did everything it could to avoid damaging Rome itself. The precautions were extraordinary, but, in the nature of things, they could not be highly effective. However, the story itself was a humdinger, from the purely professional point of view. Few stories that I have ever written have given me more journalistic satisfaction. Personally, it was a bit of a triumph to return like that to Rome, from which I had been turned out only two years before, with other Americans. As a demonstration of Allied power the bombing did more than any other single thing to show the Fascisti that their game was up. As it happened, Mussolini was, on that very day, at the Brenner Pass in conference with Hitler. We had hoped that he would be in the Palazzo Venezia.

Seven war correspondents had the privilege of going on that raid, Raymond Clapper of Scripps-Howard, Richard Tregaskis of the International News Service, Joseph Morton of the Associated Press, Richard McMillan of the United Press, J. H. Nicholson of Reuters, Tom Treanor of the *Los Angeles Times*, and I. If I wanted to be superstitious I could say there was something of a hex on that assignment. Of the correspondents I have listed, at least four met with grief in this war. Clapper, Morton and Treanor were killed, and Tregaskis was very severely wounded. But there are some stories that no newspaperman would miss for any reason or any danger, and that was one of them.

We thought it would be very dangerous, because the Romans were warned the evening before that the raid was coming, and they had a hundred fighters available around the capital. But as it turned out, only five planes were lost out of nearly six hundred, and the ack-ack was only moderately heavy.

I suppose there are few excitements in the world greater than the last minute or two when you are dead set on your bombing run, the bombs about to go, and you a fair target for the enemy below. I rode with the leading plane of the second wave of Flying Fortresses which were to bomb the marshaling yards, one of three targets of the raid. General Doolittle, incidentally, led the final B-17 wave.

The crew of my bomber was, doubtless, less excited, and certainly less thrilled, than I. There they were, almost without knowing it, doing something which future ages would record and remember so long as the Eternal City stands on its seven hills. We flew over the Atlas Mountains and out to sea well west of Sicily. Then, at a specified point, we turned north, and for a long time had the coast of Sardinia on our left.

As we drew near the point where we were to cut across the shore of Italy, the plane rose steadily. At 10,000 feet we donned oxygen masks, and shortly after that "May West" life preservers and parachutes. It was all terribly cumbersome, particularly for a newspaperman who had to move around. What with those three things and earphones to follow the talk between the crew members and finally, as we got over the target, a helmet perched on top of it all, I felt as the knights of old must have in their armor. A newspaperman, anyway, ought to have four hands and eight eyes when he is covering a raid, for there are an amazing number of things to see in a very brief length of time. Not the least of his difficulties is keeping out of the way of the crew.

We hit our landfall "on the nose," just north of Civitavecchia. By then we were well past the 20,000-foot height and we stayed there, making our bombing run at 23,700 feet. It was 11:25 A.M., July 19, 1943, when we cut across the shore of Italy. Under all the paraphernalia I could sense the tension rising, and it kept rising to that most exciting moment of all, when we were over the target. Soon we were above Lake Bracciano, twenty-five miles north of Rome, with the visibility crystal clear.

And then Rome swung into view, with two huge clouds to catch the eye before anything else—one caused by our first wave, which had already dropped its load on the marshaling yards, the other by a smoke screen over Guidonia Airfield, which the Italians mistakenly thought we were going to attack. It was Ciampino Airfield that our B-26's went for and put out of commission.

As the navigator peered tensely into his bomb sight, I glanced in all directions at Rome below me. There were the winding Tiber and the Mussolini Forum. St. Peter's stood out so clearly that it dominated the city. I picked out landmark after landmark, all so famous. The house where my family and I had lived was just down to the right, as a reminder that Rome was my city, too, and that I did not really wish it harm. The irony of fate and journalism had brought me back, watching with "no satisfaction," as Roosevelt and Churchill put it, a triumphant Allied force, landing something more than 1,000 tons of bombs in the heart of Italy's capital.

We made our bombing run at a 165-degree angle north to south. By then flak was all round us, looking like so many harmless puffs of smoke—if you did not know otherwise. It was moderately heavy, but not too accurate, with a tendency to hit under us as we held a steady course. At 11:40 precisely I saw the leading wave of our squadron drop its bombs blindly into the cloud of smoke covering the railway yards. A minute later our bombardier released his, and the plane bounced into the air, lighter by the weight of twelve 500-pounders, which was what every Fortress carried.

As the bomb bay doors closed, we made a sharp turn to the left, and just in time, for a well-aimed burst of ack-ack puffed out off our right wing. Again, in accordance with orders given at the briefing in the morning, we swung right to head out to sea, and this time that same battery would have got us, according to the pilot, if we had kept on going straight.

The bombardier took to his gun again just in time to see an Me109 flash by us within a hundred yards. It was a red plane and going so fast he could not hope to hit it, but he gave it a burst just to show that he had seen it. A minute later it made another pass and got another harmless burst. Other gunners saw some enemy planes, but no more than twenty or thirty, in all, rose to defend Rome.

At 11:45 we were crossing the coast again, after having been over Italy only twenty minutes, which seemed like so many hours. Our job was done, and a thick sandwich of American cheese tasted good. There is nothing like a bit of danger passed, to whet the appetite. I returned, for the last few hours of the ride, to the detective story whose exciting thread had been broken as we approached the shores of Italy.

Back at our base, which we reached as scheduled about three o'clock, the pilot let the plane down gently, and the adventure was over. As I thanked the crew I said to them, "You've made history today in a very large way." It had not seemed to occur to any of them. It was just another raid against a military target, another mission ended.

The next morning I made a broadcast in Italian for the P.W.B., which I knew would be heard by friends in Rome, among others. "As we turned toward home," I said to them at the end, "I ran my eye along the Corso Umberto, through the Piazza di Santa Maria del Popolo to the Via Pasquale Stanislao Mancini, where I spent a few happy years from 1939 to 1941. I am going back there soon, and I look forward to seeing my old Italian friends, real Italians, who love their country and hate Fascism."

However, it was to be nearly a year before I would go into Rome with the Fifth Army. We were then still in Sicily, and I went over to watch the last three weeks of the campaign—but I did not go in an ordinary fashion. There were ways and means in those days of getting to Sicily from North Africa, but none was more exciting or punishing than taking one of our speedy motor torpedo boats, the P.T.'s, that were so "expendable" and so famous in the early months of the war. The four of us who made that trip in different P.T. boats of Squadron 15—Quentin Reynolds of *Collier's,* Farnsworth Fowle of the Columbia Broadcasting Company, Alfred Newman of *Newsweek* and I—had the ill fortune to strike the foulest weather that the Mediterranean had seen in many weeks.

There were supposed to be "easy pickings" for P.T.'s off the coast of Italy in those days, and that was why the group under Ensign Richard O'Brien of Vandegriff, Pa., was willing to brave weather that was not made for 78-foot, 50-ton craft which are all engines and guns. Those boys wanted to get there and get into action, and they were not going to let a mere matter of a strong head-wind stop them. At least, they thought they weren't, but on the first night it was the elements and not the P.T. boats which won.

We started out, seven boats strong, despite the unfavorable weather reports, at nine in the evening. The wind was north-easterly, always a bad sign in the Mediterranean, but we were hoping for one of those sudden shifts which are not uncommon. There was no shift. The trouble that first night was the load of 100-octane gasoline which each motor torpedo boat carried on what little deck space she had and which made her topheavy.

I was in one called "The Big Seven," with a pair of dice painted on the side. The skipper was Lieutenant (junior grade) Frederick Rosen, of Dalton, Ga., and the second officer was Ensign Giles Peresich, of Biloxi, Miss. There was also a crew of ten, somehow managing to squeeze themselves into odd corners of the tiny craft. They were gunners, engineers, radio operators, and some took turns at steering.

"This is a helluva time to go out to sea," someone muttered as we got going, and he hit the nail on the head. We all put on waterproof suits with hoods, for everyone aboard is drenched from the moment the open sea is hit until the end of the voyage. It may also be stated there is nothing so conducive to seasickness as riding a P.T. in heavy weather. Only three men in Squadron 15 had not been seasick in the eight months of their service, or in their lives, but two of those were to lose that distinction before we reached Palermo.

We went out calmly enough, past sunken hulls of German and Italian ships from Bizerte, Tunisia. Hardly had we struck the open sea than it was evident that the going would be extremely heavy. Water began pouring over in sheets, with every wave. The salt in it blinded you, dribbled into your throat to make it sore, and flooded like a heavy shower over your whole person, into pockets and shoes.

I took refuge in the tiny radio room, connected with what passes for a bridge. It was dry, but stuffy and difficult on one's insides as the ship rolled and dipped and pounded. Still, it was fun watching the radar, that delicate and marvelous instrument which tells when other ships or land or even airplanes are within range, and exactly where they are.

The time passed slowly. It was like being shoved, pounded, and milled around with nothing to do but to take it and hang on. Because of our high-octane cargo, the group leader, O'Brien, decided not to risk the run through the minefield, straight around Sicily, so we made our way along the African coast—and then it was obviously impossible to strike across the Mediterranean in the teeth of the wind. Some time after one o'clock in the morning we anchored off Cape Ferina, hoping for better luck in the morning.

And there we took what little rest we were to get that night. Our boat literally bobbed like a cork. The officers' cabin swung and spun drunkenly. At five, our anchor line broke, and the wind almost swept us ashore. There was just time to get the engines going and pull clear. Still, O'Brien was not beaten so easily. The sea was even rougher than the night before, but he was determined to try. And try we did, twice taking a terrific beating for several hours, until it had to be given up, and we turned with the wind, letting it carry us swiftly back to our port of departure, where we landed tired and sore, twelve hours from our starting time.

The motto of Squadron 15 was pretentious: "The difficult we will do immediately. The impossible may take a little longer." So, the next night we did the impossible, but we did it without that dangerous cargo of spare high-octane gasoline. The weather forecast was even more unfavorable, but O'Brien could not contain himself. "We will start at seven this evening," he said to his officers, wheedlingly, "and if it is too bad we will turn back in time to be home before dark."

However, all knew perfectly well that nothing short of a gale was going to turn O'Brien back—and they were with him. As a matter of fact, as a landlubber, I would have called it a gale. Certainly, it was about the maximum punishment those sturdy boats and their crews could take. In eight months of operations they had never been out in such weather.

We literally sailed off the tops of the waves into the air, and then struck bottom with crashes that lifted us and everything in the boat off their perches. If you were human you hung on to something with all your strength; if you were inanimate you just bounced, slid and jolted. Those boats did everything but stand upright on their sterns. We were hitting 20 to 22 knots, which was nothing to those speediest of all vessels, but in such weather it seemed a miracle that the boats were not torn apart. It was not a miracle, of course, and O'Brien knew what he was doing, but he put a terrific strain on both men and ships. This time we went straight through the minefields, taking the chance that we would not hit anything. The boat with Newman in it narrowly missed a hit, just at daybreak.

Literally every wave washed a solid sheet of water over us. For Rosen, Peresich, and the men who took turns at the wheel it was a grim, exhausting fight. I have never seen two more tired men than the officers, who barely managed to stand up in the gray light of dawn—a grayness still streaked with lightning from the heavy rainstorm which we ran into during the night, and which had added to our miseries.

The P.T.'s, which had started neatly, seven in a row, just like in a picture, were now scattered to the winds. O'Brien had pushed on ahead, as we learned later. We had lost him in the minefields, which gave him something to worry about. Three other ships gathered about us in the dawn, and later we picked up a fourth, limping along with one engine and its radar knocked out. The weather was less rough then, and when the heavy, beating rain stopped, it was a great relief compared to that awful night. A trip that in normal times should have taken seven hours had taken sixteen.

"We ought to get submarine and air pay," one of the crew said to me, at the end. "Half the time we are under the water and half the time we are in the air."

Allied Military Government was getting its first real test in Palermo, which had been taken a few days previously. The system was still very much in an experimental stage, but, with adaptations and variations, it was to carry on, much abused but always useful. Palermo was the first job of Lieutenant Colonel Charles Poletti and his able assistant, Captain Maurice Neufeld, and they were to stick together through Naples, Rome, and Milan, with considerable success.

I joined the war at Second Corps headquarters. General Omar N. Bradley was then winning the fame that led to his later appointments. It was my first job of real, front-line war corresponding in this conflict—the first, in fact, since Spain—and the simple truth is that I was bored. Had I been romantically inclined I would have said with Dante, in Byron's "Prophecy":

> I am old in days,
> And deeds, and contemplation, and have met
> Destruction face to face in all his ways.

Certainly, there was no zest or romance left in it for me, except at odd moments. There were only weariness and dullness. I tried to persuade myself that since this time it was my own country and my own people who were fighting I should be thrilled, but it was no use. I suppose one's capacity for that kind of excitement is limited, and I had exhausted mine. Only now and then would the excitement of some story take hold of me and sweep me off my feet, but it had to be a good story. Sicily left only two memories with me, and those not very acute—the fall of Troina and the capture of Messina, which ended the campaign. I am afraid one result of my boredom was that I did a pretty poor job of coverage for *The New York Times*.

When I got out to the Second Corps the Germans were already penned up in the northeastern corner of Sicily, and a hard fight was about to begin for the hill town of Troina, the hinge of the whole Nazi position. That gave me a mildly good story, as there were six days of the toughest fighting that the Americans had been up against in the Mediterranean. It afforded me an excellent opportunity to see the American fighting man in action in the war, which I had not been able to do before, and that was something to make one proud. Of course I did not know it at the time, but we were to have nearly two years of that kind of mountain fighting before V.E. Day.

Each day I went out to watch our lines creep closer, to see Troina shelled and pounded to death, and to enjoy again the comradeship of other correspondents in our daily dangers and fatigues. Bob Capa, best and bravest of all war photographers, was there to remind me of Spain. It was the first time I worked with Homer Bigart, the *New York Herald Tribune's* ace correspondent, and one of the best the war produced.

When, finally, we took Troina on the morning of August 6, I went in with the mine-detector squads and reconnaissance parties, to find a town of horror, alive with weeping, hysterical men, women and children who had stayed there through two terrible days of bombing and shelling, seeing their loved ones killed or wounded, their houses destroyed and whatever was left pillaged ruthlessly by departing Nazis. That, too, was to be a familiar pattern of those days, all the way to Bologna—torn streets, heaps of rubble that had been houses, grief, horror, and pain, and, mixed with it all, relief and gladness that the ordeal was over.

In Troina it was ironical to reach an open square and see facing one, in huge letters, one of those ubiquitous mottoes from the Duce's speeches which "adorned" innumerable walls throughout Italy. "Only God can bend the Fascist will, men and things never!" it said, and underneath was a fac-simile of Mussolini's signature. It was a startling reminder of Shelley's sonnet:

> My name is Ozymandias, king of kings:
> Look on my works, ye Mighty, and despair!

We looked on the works of Mussolini all right—ruin, misery, and death. I had seen just that same mixture in many Spanish villages, only then it had been done by the bombs and shells of Mussolini and Hitler.

The capture of Troina gave me my first experience with mines, for in Spain we had been mercifully spared that invention of the devil. I should think that more deaths were caused during the Italian campaign by mines than by any other weapon. Millions and millions of them were sown by the Germans all the way to the Po Valley, and millions still remain in the ground, to take their toll of unsuspecting peasants and children in the months and years to come. It is a nerve-racking business to walk or drive in terrain you know or suspect to be mined, and I often wondered that there were so few deaths among correspondents from that weapon. We lost two colleagues at Cassino when they ran off the highway to take cover from a German plane and tripped a teller mine. I remember vividly how I felt that day we took Troina when our jeep drove gingerly down the road ahead of the de-mining squads and into the town. And at no subsequent time did I ever feel any easier or get used to the sensation.

The campaign folded up quickly after the fall of Troina. I followed it along the main coastal highway with the Third Division, then under General Lucian K. Truscott, which had taken over from the Forty-fifth after the latter's remarkable dash across Sicily and through Palermo. The afternoon of August 15, three days before we took Messina, I remember getting out in a jeep with two other American correspondents, well ahead of the infantry and catching up with our "recon" units. It was a thrilling chase, affording us that exultation which comes with the sense of lunging forward at the enemy, as American troops did with fair consistency throughout the war. Never have they known the bitterness and demoralization of continued retreat or defensive fighting, as the British, for all their bravery, did during three years. I almost felt like acknowledging the waving handkerchiefs, hand-clapping, saluting, and shouts of *Evviva!* which came from the Italian civilians as we raced along. It all seemed, somehow, deserved, although not by mere newspapermen.

And then we took Messina, with General Patton roaring behind us because the engineers had not repaired a road-block during the night of August 17 in time to take the port before morning—but, anyway, the Germans had got everything and everybody over to the mainland. It was a well-fought retreat. Patton was then somewhat in disgrace with the newspapermen and many G.I.'s who knew of the face-slapping incident, although it had not then been divulged. I am glad now that I was one of those who deplored the incident but felt it should not be publicized and cause us to lose the services of a first-rate general.

Through bad co-ordination my story of the fall of Messina reached *The New York Times* a day late, much to my unhappiness, for it was a good story, and I had spent an exhausting and dangerous twenty-four hours in getting it. That misfortune was a fitting climax to a campaign in which, I felt, I had generally done rather badly, so I returned to Algiers bored and disgusted.

The best thing the Sicilian campaign had done for me was to make me acquainted with the American doughboy who had just come very well through a grueling test.

I had plenty of time for thinking in Algiers while I waited for the invasion of the continent, which we all knew would be coming soon. It was my only opportunity to study the Free French situation, and I learned just enough about it to become pro-De Gaulle and quite unhappy over the way in which President Roosevelt and our State Department were antagonizing him and many of his supporters. I did not feel that France was finished as a great power. On the contrary, I was always certain that she would again, after the war, become as great an influence and power in Europe as she had been. No one has been more critical than I of the political corruption and weakness of France or the demoralization of her people, but I knew the French too well to believe that they were unregenerate. Moreover, our pro-Giraud policy smacked too much of conservatism and reaction, in a situation which clearly demanded the reverse.

The correspondents drew lots, as is customary, to see who should go on the next amphibious landing, and in what order and place. I was lucky and won one of the top choices, but was not on the small committee which alone knew which units were going. I should have been placed with a unit making the initial assault but was, instead, assigned to the 45th Division, a tactical reserve to be sent in after the first wave. It was just as well for me, partly because the 45th proved to be a crack unit with which it was a pleasure and privilege to work, and partly because I was so ill before, during, and after D-Day that I did not care a great deal what happened to me or the American Army.

Something I had eaten in Algiers just before I went over to Sicily at the beginning of September to join the 157th Regiment of the 45th Division must have made me ill, but for a while I did not know what was wrong. All I knew was that I felt very ill and did not dare to let on, for fear the doctors would not let me go.

General Montgomery and the Eighth Army landed at the toe of Italy on September 3. Then the ships used by them came around for us, as we were always terribly short of shipping in the Mediterranean. I somehow managed to get aboard my LST and out to sea before announcing that I was ill. On D-Day I had a high fever, with bacillary dysentery, so I am not going to write you a thrilling story of our landing at Salerno. It was hard enough, for ten days or more, to turn out, each day, one to four stories of a mediocre nature for my newspaper. My belongings were lost in the landing, and I had no mosquito net or other protection in one of the most malarial spots of Italy at the height of the malaria season.

The Armistice of September 8, came and went without making the slightest difference. It had been badly handled on both sides. Politically and militarily we made the great error of believing that the Italians could help us materially, although we should have known better. We planned an airborne operation to capture Rome, which had to be called off at the last moment because Marshal Badoglio and his aide, General Giacomo Carboni, had neither the imagination nor the nerve to accept a marvelous opportunity. It was a chance for Italy to enter the war as an ally, fighting with Americans under the command of their own generals—and they threw it away! They were not ready and could not furnish the help which their emissary, General Giuseppe Castellano, had promised.

There was a flurry aboard all the ships when the news was broadcast which was psychologically bad, because the Germans were waiting for us, and they had signed no armistice. Those who thought the war was over had a rude awakening.

Ill as I was, I had no illusions, although nothing would have pleased me better than not to go through with the landing. It all still has something of the quality of a nightmare to me. I can think of Salerno in terms of bacillary dysentery only.

The Geography of Italy

ONE OF the theses which military historians are going to have a lot of fun debating until the end of the world is whether the campaign in Italy was necessary and successful, or whether it was a colossal mistake. We spent twenty heart-breaking months slogging our way from mountain to mountain, at a high cost in human lives, not to mention the material destruction of a great deal of Italy and, in the world of art, a loss unequaled since the barbarian invasions. The south-to-north campaign had never before been made, for the simple reason that the greatest generals always considered it impossible—which it really was. The Germans held us below Bologna virtually until the end of the war, following the collapse in Germany. They chose two great lines, one at Cassino and the other south of the Po Valley, and held us for about six months at each point. And they chose to remain in Italy; they could have fallen back to the Alps at any period of the war and held the line there with half of the divisions they used, or even with fewer. The Po Valley gave them food and the industrial cities of the north afforded war matériel, which were tangible advantages, in addition to the prestige which Italy represented from beginning to end.

This was one side of the picture. The other we heard constantly from Eisenhower, Alexander, and Clark. It told of satisfaction at drawing a regular twenty-five to twenty-seven German divisions down into Italy and holding them there when they could have been used in France and Russia. It told, too, of the immense value of Foggia as an airbase from which to attack the Balkans and southern Germany. The Allied advance through Italy was made with inadequate troops and artillery, against an enemy always in powerful positions and numerically equal. The campaign had to be made on a "shoestring," and—said General Eisenhower—we struck at Salerno because it was the best we could do with the matériel we had at the time and considering the need for haste.

Marshal Badoglio, who has a first-rate military mind and naturally knows his Italy, told me one day that he considered the whole campaign to be a great miscalculation. According to him, we should have ignored Sicily and gone straight for Sardinia and Corsica. With those islands as bases, we could have hit Italy far to the north, and forced the evacuation of Sicily and southern Italy without a campaign. Or, if desired, we could have gone straight on to France.

Marshal Alexander confessed to me and others, early in the campaign, that his original idea was to take Naples and Foggia, and then strike across to the Balkans. Evidently, Stalin vetoed that idea and the Americans backed him, although Churchill apparently wanted to go through with it. Many strategists believe that we should have stopped our campaign after taking Naples and Foggia, which represented the major prizes in Italy—or, at most, after taking Rome and providing a good cushion for them, as well as capturing an Axis capital. That gave us control of the Mediterranean, a great port, and a great airbase.

My own opinion (again divorced from any personal responsibility or expert knowledge) is that the Naples-Foggia-Rome idea was the sounder, granting that it was to be considered necessary to attack Italy in September, 1943. In the end, the north would have fallen, anyway, just as it did eventually. A great many lives were lost for very little gain.

I remember how much we were criticized at the time we landed at Salerno. Eisenhower said then that we could not have attacked further north, as we needed fighter cover and there was the usual lack of shipping. Certainly the Germans were waiting for us, and they hit back so hard that during one critical period of twenty-four hours we were hanging on by our eye-teeth, with only five miles to the shore behind us.

The 157th Regiment landed right at Paestum on D-plus one.

It was a great thrill for me to see those lovely Greek temples in the moonlight, which, as vacationists, my wife and I had visited a few years before. The officers with me had never heard of Paestum, which gave me the first of many surprises during the campaign. I remember having to explain later to the G-2 of a division which had gone into the lines below the Abbey of Monte Cassino that his unit was about to attack one of the most famous and sacred places in the world. He had never heard of it. Perhaps it was naive of me to expect anything else. The fault lies in our system of education. No French officer, for instance, would have had to be told about Paestum or Monte Cassino.

The 45th Division moved in to take up a position along the Sele River, which was to prove the critical axis of the whole beachhead. The Sele and the Calore meet five miles from the shore, and it was down that space between the two rivers that the Germans struck and broke through on the night of September 13-14, reaching the fork in the river and threatening to split the beachhead in two. It was the 36th Division's sector at the time, and for some reason it was unable to cover the ground adequately.

Two factors turned the tide against the Germans. The 45th Division's artillery was just south of the fork, and when the Jerries reached it, in the middle of the night, the artillerymen not only fired at zero range, but dashed in, to fight as infantry. In the dark the Germans did not dare to cross the Calore. The other factor, which proved to be the decisive one, was that the 157th Regiment, along the north bank of the Sele, had stood its ground. Pounded frontally, it hung on, and only when the commander, Colonel Charles M. Ankcorn, found that the Germans were across the river below him on the right was he forced to "refuse" his right wing to face them, but during the night the 157th actually regained whatever it had lost.

Nevertheless, that day of September 14 was highly critical. At eight in the morning the Jerries launched another attack against the 157th and 179th Regiments (both parts of the 45th Division under Major-General Troy H. Middleton) and also at the axis where the British 56th Division touched the 141st Regiment of the 36th American Division, which was also under General Middleton's orders at that time. The German tanks met overwhelming resistance from American tanks and tank destroyers, now right up in the front lines awaiting them. In front of the 179th alone, thirteen tanks were destroyed in less than two hours.

I was with Ankcorn at about noon that day, when General Clark came out to check the situation. "Now, there is no falling back," he said. "Hold that line." I heard him, a little later, say to the 179th commander, "If you go back any more we won't have any beachhead." Ankcorn later muttered to me that he did not have to be told such things. The lines held.

All along there had been help from the sea and air. The fleet was opening up every night with steady fire, that tremendous double-crack over our heads of the naval shells making sleep impossible as they split the heavens. But it was a welcome sound, and even more welcome was the rolling thunder of our bombs as the terrain on the northern edge of the beachhead took a tremendous, incessant pounding from the air. Meanwhile, our artillery was asserting its superiority and firing with devastating effect.

So the beachhead was held, and the Germans had shot their bolt. To me, the great privilege and satisfaction of those anxious days was to be always at the elbow of one of the greatest soldiers it has been my pleasure to watch in four wars, Colonel (now Brigadier-General) Charles M. Ankcorn. He was then a veteran of twenty-six years' service in the Regular Army and I saw him at his best—calm, wise, and brave, and adored by his troops who would have followed him anywhere. In October the jeep in which he was riding struck a mine, and Ankcorn was wounded in the right leg, which had to be amputated. On the day he was wounded he was named Brigadier-General and the Distinguished Service Cross was awarded to him for bravery in the Sicilian campaign.

The 8th Army came up and made a junction with the 5th on the evening of September 15, and then both forces began to swing in a great fan-like movement that soon broke the German resistance and began to sweep the enemy backward all along the line. For a while they held along that ancient line of defense covering Naples—the Sorrento ridge—and I had one pleasant and exciting interlude, doing the famous tourists' "Amalfi drive" in reverse and under war conditions. Some of us had a happy evening at Caruso's hotel in Ravello, drinking his famous wine to the accompaniment of an excellent meal and sleeping in soft beds for the first time since leaving Sicily.

A half hour after leaving Ravello, the next morning, a few of us were in one of the grimmest spots of the front—the pass to the plain up above Maiori, where a regiment of Rangers was still hanging on after ten German counterattacks. It was always dangerous at that pass, but it was gay in war's twisted fashion and highly exciting, so I enjoyed it. Bob Capa was there, hilariously happy at the pictures which, as he put it, were being delivered right to the door as the Germans slammed mortar shells in at us. Men know how to live when any moment may be their last. You squeeze humor out of trivial incidents, and comradeship is especially precious.

Our peep drove up a winding dirt road to the pass, by a lucky coincidence in between German shellings. At the top, the road abruptly came out into the open and descended into the plain of Naples in clear view of the Nazis, so there was no going down it. One of our half-tracks, mounted with a 75-mm. gun, was about to "do its stuff." For many days, and often during each day, it and other half-tracks shelled German positions in a novel way and with more accuracy than our artillery behind them. A German camouflage net near the bottom of the mountain had been spotted by an observer, and the half-track prepared, if necessary, to take ten shots at it. The gun was loaded in the lee of a cliff, and a gunner sat on the edge of the truck, with another shell in his lap. The rest of the crew crouched tensely in their places. The driver speeded the motor, then drove straight through the pass out into the open and faced in the direction of the target. One man aimed the gun and when he gave the signal another pulled the lanyard and the shell was off with a roar. The soldier who had aimed stood up and peered through his binoculars to see where the shot would fall. It was a little short. They aimed and fired again, and again, and then a fourth time, and that was a clean hit. The half-track backed as fast as it could into the lee of the cliff again and the crew jumped into foxholes, and so did all of us—either into foxholes or a solid-looking house which had often been hit but not penetrated by the 88's the Germans were using.

Always it had been the same way. The half-track would go out ai d shoot, and then return before the Germans could reply, but they never failed to reply with interest. For our four shells they must have sent back twenty. Everyone laughed when they started coming, just because it was such an invariable performance, and always too late.

Major James L. Land, executive officer of the unit, who was later killed by an artillery shell, north of Naples, explained the situation to us. The setting was dramatic—a room in a dark old farmhouse with three wine casks in the corner and begrimed soldiers sitting or standing around, some eating their noonday rations out of the inevitable cans. A shell screeched down close by, and we all ducked or winced. "That is why this place is so romantic," Land said, smilingly. Outside, where soldiers were lolling about before, not a soul was to be seen. Everyone was in his foxhole, where there was relative safety, although just at that moment, as we soon learned, one shell landed in a foxhole, killing a lieutenant and wounding two of his men. They had just been "relieved" from front-line duty in a most dangerous spot where they hung on for thirteen days. War has lots of little ironies like that.

It cast a gloom on our crowd, when we learned about it, but just then another shell landed, and a piece of rock which its blast picked up hit a G.I. standing in the doorway in the middle of his back. Ruefully he rubbed the spot. It was just the sort of thing needed to relieve the tension, and everyone burst out laughing. Capa and I agreed that we liked it all so much because it reminded us of Spain.

And then I retraced my way along the Amalfi drive. The highway will always be there, for more tourists and many more centuries, but it will surely never again be what it was that day, nor will it ever again mean as much to us Americans.

Capri was another tourist spot I visited in those days, but it was, in most respects, the same old Capri, beautiful and slightly vicious, and if it had not been for the joy of seeing Professor Benedetto Croce, Italy's greatest philosopher, and meeting his charming family, I would remember it as only a welcome interlude of peace and luxury in a very uncomfortable time. That was the first of many encounters with Croce and his family— long, fascinating talks and pleasant luncheons, presided over by his charming wife and made gay by the presence of their four daughters. Elena (Signora Raimondo Craveri) was later to translate my book on Fascism, at her father's request, and she did me proud. Alda is the chief scholar of the family and her father's right hand man, so to speak. Lydia and Sylvia were, quite understandably, being wooed by American soldiers. Alberto Tarchiani, who was to become post-war Italy's first Ambassador to Washington, was there at the time, and other friends used to drop in, for the Croce house, wherever it may be, is always an "open house." In Capri the family had the beautiful villa of the Albertinis of Milan.

Age has not dulled the quickness of Croce's mind or his ability to call upon his profound wealth of historic detail to bolster an argument. A conversation with him was always a stimulation and a joy. That first day he put forward an argument which he continued to uphold later and which I always considered unwarranted—that Italy had suffered her disease of Fascism and was now immune. He denies any greatness to Mussolini, and believes that there will not be a "Mussolini myth" comparable to the Napoleonic one. Fascism left nothing and created nothing, he said; it only destroyed. He always referred to it through the years as "activism," and that first day quoted his favorite author, Goethe, as saying that the worst thing in the world is "active ignorance."

In my book on Fascism I referred to Croce's early sympathy with the movement, and told how the Fascisti used to claim him as one of their forerunners. In the beginning he did place hope in the movement, as did so many other sincere patriots, but, later, for nearly twenty years, he was, in Italy, the outstanding intellectual enemy of Fascism. Mussolini did not dare to touch anyone so famous, for Italy, unlike Germany, reveres its great men of culture.

I had read most of Croce's books before meeting him, being particularly interested in his political philosophy of liberalism and of liberty. It was interesting to see how strongly he had turned against King Victor Emmanuel III, but he made it clear that he was not anti-monarchical—a distinction which any liberal must honor, since you can have democracy and liberalism under a monarchy just as well as in a republic. At a time when monarchy is a burning question in Italy, that is something which is forgotten by many. I was to stress it often in my writings in the ensuing months. No one had been stronger than I in condemnation of Victor Emmanuel and his links to Fascism. I thought just as little of the Prince of Piedmont, at the time, too, since his career up to the invasion of Italy had been nothing but acceptance of Fascism and obedience to his father and Mussolini.

Those first few talks in Croce's library were, among other things, a great consolation to me, who loved Italy. "If I had space or descriptive art to convey the atmosphere in that living room overlooking the sea, with its shelves of books and its cultured, gentle people who sat and talked," I wrote to my paper, "it would do more to give news of Italy—the true Italy—than anything that Croce said or Badoglio and Mussolini have done. It is in such gatherings that one finds the permanency of all that is good in Italy. Whatever is destroyed in Naples or elsewhere, no one can doubt that the future must be better than these twenty-one years of Fascism, and that is because Croce, for one, is more truly Italian than Mussolini ever was or ever could be."

There are only two ways of living, I remember Croce saying one of those days—one under authority, the other under liberty. Under authority the people are ruled like animals; they are fed, told to do this and that, ordered around, and others do their thinking for them. Under liberty they live like free men, and one can have this freedom with any form of government except authoritarianism or totalitarianism. You can have a government where policemen force their way into a house, take out the children, carry them to school, and make them stay there—and that is liberty.

But Croce has written books on the subject, and this is not the place for an analysis of his philosophy. The appeal of his system to me lies partly in its practical value. One day he said to me, laughing, "In spite of the fact that I am a philosopher, I have some good sense." In fact, that day he gave me a definition of philosophy which he said had just come into his mind: "The intensification of good sense."

There was an aura of rejuvenation about that gentle old man which it was a happy thing to see in those early days of the invasion. He was to lose it later under the impact of all the discouraging things that happened in Italy, but in Capri he was happy. For more than twenty years he had fought almost alone among those of his generation and class in Italy. Rarely did any of his associates stand by him as the Fascisti expelled him from one academy and society after another. Now it was his privilege to see vindicated the ideals for which he stood, and it was doubtless that sense of a life well lived which gave the impression of personal happiness, amidst his sorrow over Italy's plight.

That was less than a week before we took Naples. The final break-through came with startling suddenness when the Germans suddenly pulled out from the Sorrento range. September 28 was an almost unbelievable day for me, and one of the luckiest of my life. Fate has never been kinder.

We knew there had been a withdrawal, but we thought we should be lucky enough to reach Nocera, on the main road to Naples through Salerno. The road had an unending traffic jam. For five days the British had been slogging grimly through the pass at Camerelle, making about a mile a day, with both sides paying heavily. That morning of the 28th the British were determined to force an armored column through the pass, and we went to see what would happen. (Sometimes you make a great effort to push open a door that you think is stuck, and it swings easily, pitching you forward; we felt like that.)

The pass through Camerelle is not high, like the one above Maiori. It is more like two gentle, broad valleys, one descending to Salerno, the other to Nocera. It was as we approached the latter town that we realized the lid was off, and that the Germans had fallen back much further than expected. Already civilians were lining the streets or gathering in cheering, applauding groups. Conquerors could not wish more heartfelt greetings, which were uncomfortably accompanied by flowers and fruit thrown into our cars. They hurt. On the edge of Nocera, a man whose face was desperate with grief shouted curses against the Germans.

Several times we stopped to ask British officers about the situation ahead, but they could not tell us. Their orders had been to take Nocera, cost what it might, but Nocera was now behind us and it had not cost anything. Then we reached the head of the British armored column, just outside Pagani. We were too exhilarated to stop. It was a case of fools rushing in, but it seemed so easy! The civilians were, in a sense, egging us on, cheering, clapping, and throwing flowers at us as we passed. Since every now and then the road was covered with flowers as we drove along, I felt reassured.

At any rate, we breezed merrily through Angri, to truly great applause, and sped on to Scafati. There, on the edge of town, some Italians waved frantically to us to stop, which we did, and it was a good thing for our group of five that I could speak Italian. Several inhabitants waved rifles and all talked tumultuously at once, and what they were trying to tell us was that two hundred yards ahead was a bridge, and at that bridge there were Germans. One of them explained to me excitedly that if we would go with him we could outflank the Nazis and take them prisoners. I pointed out that we were only journalists, and unarmed.

That set me to thinking. Here we were, miles ahead of our army, with Germans in the same town! I turned to the others who were waiting for me to translate, and said, "Boys, it looks as if we have taken Scafati."

That was not the time to advance, so we sat still, and about twenty minutes later forward elements of the British motorized force caught up with us. I told them what to expect and they moved ahead cautiously, with us this time placing some bren-gun carriers and tanks ahead of us. Sure enough, at the last bend before the bridge the leading car met fire.

The Italians kept pestering me, saying that they wanted to encircle the Germans; they knew where they were, and would lead the troops there and it would be easy as pie. I passed the word on, and one group did take an Italian along with it on the right, to effect a crossing of the Sarno River that later was to prove helpful as a flanking movement. Other troops were soon sent around on the left.

Three men with machine guns dashed across the street in front of the bridge into a house, in order to get on its roof, and I followed them, beginning to get that same glorious thrill of the Spanish days. The roof had a low parapet and a lieutenant with two noncoms crawled out, peered over, and saw an anti-tank gun in the piazza across the river and a few Germans in a house dominating the bridge. The lieutenant fired three bursts with his tommy gun into the house.

I heard tracks coming up the street, and went down to see what was happening. Here was some real street fighting, such as I had not seen since the Spanish Civil War—and there is nothing more exciting. The bren-carrier and a Sherman tank had come up. This was shortly after twelve o'clock. The bren-carrier poked its nose around the bend, and the gunner let go with both guns, but ineffectively. A tank officer ordered him back and sent in the Sherman instead. The bren gunner climbed out and shook his head. "Give me the wide open desert," he said mournfully.

Just then the tank blasted away with its 75-mm., making a deafening roar in the confined street. The concussion caused rubble to fall from a bombed-out house next to us. Two heavy explosions answered. They had fallen short and we speculated whether it was German fire or whether Jerry was blowing up the bridge, but a British colonel said it was mortar fire, and he was right.

While they talked things over, I again dashed across the street and up to the roof of the house. The lieutenant was firing his tommy gun again. "There was a bloke in there, and I shot him," he said, pointing to an alleyway in the square across the bridge where the anti-tank gun's muzzle protruded. Later we found he had killed two Germans and that anti-tank gun was not used again.

That lieutenant was the first to spot one of the German Mark III tanks. It started toward the bridge, and when it came into sight he blazed away. Tommy guns cannot make a dent in tanks, but the crew was rattled and backed off hastily. We all laughed at the spectacle. The lieutenant sent down word, giving the range, and from that time on, our mortars shot 25-pounders over our heads and into the Germans.

Someone crawled into view of the bridge and came back with word that it must be mined since he could see rubble in three places in the center, where the bricks had been dug into. We wondered why the Jerries did not blow it up.

Obviously, our forces were stymied, and it seemed a good time to get some lunch. We started to eat our K rations in town, but Italians gathered around so insistently—and, to our minds shamelessly, for that was in a rich agricultural region and they were not hungry—that we decided to go back clear of Scafati for some relative solitude. Those civilians were always getting under our feet—giving advice, tugging at our clothes, waving their guns dangerously around and, in general, behaving like so many flies. Now and then some hysterical man would rush up, and before his unsuspecting victim knew what was happening he would get some frantic, slobbering kisses on both cheeks. I narrowly escaped once, and thereafter kept a wary eye open.

Outside, on the main road, we saw and heard two explosions a few miles to the north and when I asked an officer what was happening he said that the Germans had expected to retreat in leisurely fashion along this main road, but we had pressed in so fast that they were forced to take a side road. So, ironically enough, the enemy was pulling out just a few miles away, parallel to us and in the same direction, since he had to get on to the roads from Torre Annunziata, inland and along the coast.

When we got back near the bridge it was to find that a young British tank officer, whose deportment during that morning had been admirably brave and cool, had been wounded. He lay stretched on the ground behind a house with a bullet wound through his stomach and side, cheerful, but grimacing with pain every now and then. A little while before, as things had quietened down, he and a few other officers had walked up to the bridge. It was a short bridge, hardly more than twenty yards across, as we discovered later, going at an angle to the river so that a house with a balcony on the other side jutted quite close to it. Ivory or shrubs gave the balcony perfect cover, and some Germans were hiding there. As the officers stood on the bridge, a German stuck a revolver out and shot the lieutenant. He had won a Military Cross at El Alamein, and he deserved another for that day's work.

In the excitement, the Germans had run out, and escaped, so the bridge was at last clear. A few of us crept up to it and watched two platoons of infantry make their way along on the left, through the trees down to the water's edge. Somehow, they got across.

The German tank was giving us trouble by coming up, shooting, and then pulling back. An officer sent orders that two bren guns be taken up to that same roof to watch for the tank and let him have it the next time it came forward, so I joined the little party on the roof. We waited in vain. Two young American soldiers whom we had found on our return from lunch came up with me. They had been ordered by their officer to go ahead from Nocera and get a German prisoner for questioning, and that was their monomania for the afternoon. One was Sergeant Don Graeber, of Salt Lake City, the other Private John Priester, of New York City. They had a lot of fun that afternoon.

The tank did not show up again there, so I gave up and returned to the bridge. Our artillery was lobbing shells over our heads, which burst just across the bridge. Sometimes we would watch the mortar shells making a high parabola above us. The British had brought up a little General Stuart tank, of the kind that Americans called "Honeys," and it and the Sherman tank covered the bridge. As the infantry came up on our left, the officer in the Stuart poured volleys of machine-gun fire into the house where the Germans had been, just for safety's sake.

Graeber and Priester came running up to say they had seen a group of Germans, bearing a white flag, come out of a house across the square, and they wanted one of them. A minute later a British officer across the bridge waved, and shouted, "Okay! okay! the Germans are surrendering." He had a Jerry with him who was gesticulating that the bridge was not mined. The officer motioned him to go ahead toward us, which he did. When he came to the holes in the center he stamped in one of them, to show there were no mines. Across the square a group of Germans ran toward us, followed by Tommies who wanted to get them back of the lines quickly. When the first prisoner reached us we could see his face covered with blood. That had been from a 75-mm. shell which hit the house he and the others were in. Priester, who hoped to get him, volunteered to question him in German, which he spoke fluently. The soldier said he was from the Hermann Goering Division and that they had orders to blow up the bridge at four o'clock. But we had come in at noon, which showed how hard the Germans were being pressed.

So we crossed that bridge at last and on to the Piazza Vittorio Veneto, where an officer motioned us to the shelter of a building. "I should take it easy if I were you," he said; "there is an armored car still around that corner." He was optimistic. There were three tanks, not an armored car.

Soon we walked on ahead. Civilians surrounded us and dogged our footsteps, shouting, gesticulating, urging us on, trying to tell us where the Germans were. Fortunately, they were getting in the Germans' way as well as in ours, and they were lucky, indeed, that the Germans let them alone. An Italian led a soldier out into plain view of the Jerries and everybody shouted joyously and gathered around—until a shell crashed near them, when they scattered like the wind. Perhaps like birds would be a better simile, for they flew in chattering, fluttering flocks every time the gun went off, which was often.

One Italian said to me, "Come over here and I'll show you some Germans." I followed him across to an alleyway which gave a clear, straight view down the road to Pompei. And there were three German tanks, those Mark III's with turrets off and the 75-mm. guns which had been giving us so much trouble. It was amazing to look straight at them and realize the Jerries were probably looking at us. Farnsworth Fowle of CBS, who was with me, ran back to notify a British tank officer, and soon shells were hitting around the Nazis. We thought one of them was crippled, for we could clearly see Germans jump out and run across the road, but the driver stayed, and backed the tank out and around.

That game of hide-and-seek with the artillery went on for more than an hour under our eyes. I went ahead to the inside of the curve in the road about 100 yards ahead which put me between the German and British tanks, but gave what seemed like a comparatively safe view. The German took a shot, which fell a little short but uncomfortably close to me, so I moved back to the alleyway, which was soon to become tragic in the journalistic history of this war. Some other American correspondents came up from the rear to join me. Then four British correspondents arrived, and called from across the street to ask whether anything interesting could be seen from where we were. I shouted back that I had been watching for an hour, and it was a lot of fun. So they, too, joined us.

It was a dangerous spot, but it was impossible to make the civilians realize it. They would not keep away. They were just like so many hysterical children—and, for that matter, there were children running around.

The Stuart tank was acting as an artillery observation post, and I played the role of interpreter for an officer trying to locate on the map that tower in Pompei before which the German tanks stood. Our first calculation was too long, but soon shells were falling among the tanks and it looked as though we had got two of them. We again saw men running from one of the tanks.

That was when fate stepped in—at least for some of us. There was no special reason for my choosing that moment to decide that perhaps, after all, I could see a bit better if I went up ahead to the spot on the inside of the curve. So without saying anything, I dashed across to the lee side of the buildings, and began moving up alongside their walls to the house I had been in shortly before. Fowle apparently wondered where I was going, and came right after me. Seymour Korman of the *Chicago Tribune* and Relman Morin, of the Associated Press, hesitated, but decided to trust in my experience, and also crossed the street to follow me. The four British correspondents stayed in the corner of the alleyway.

Korman and Morin had just got across the street, when the shell struck. It hit the edge of the wall at the corner of the alleyway, about three feet up, giving the effect of the "tree burst," the most dangerous type of all shell explosions. Of the seven men standing there, only one remained alive, and he was wounded. Three correspondents, a British soldier, and two civilians lay dead. This was the worst single tragedy involving newspapermen since Teruel, in the Spanish Civil War, when three correspondents were killed by artillery fire, and, of course, it was amazing that an even greater tragedy did not occur. Stewart Sale, of the *London Daily Herald,* A. B. Austin, of Reuter's, and William Mundy, of the Australian A.P., were killed, and B. H. T. Gingell of the British Exchange Telegraph slightly wounded.

I was blissfully ignorant at the time of what had happened, for I was approaching my doorway when the shell burst, and just dashed in. I could see that the mortar had landed more or less where we had been, but I thought it had hit the bren carrier. The other three American correspondents had run back, and therefore had not joined me. When I looked at the Mark III, I realized what had happened. At the instant when I walked away from the alleyway the tank must have started moving in toward us, and it came on brazenly to within 600-yard range, from its previous 1,000. Had the correspondents been experienced enough they would have realized that it was coming in to fire, and that there was time to run up the alley to safety. Instead, they must have stood and watched it.

I did wonder why no one joined me, and I realized that someone may have got it, but things were pretty exciting, and I forgot everything for a half hour watching the duel between the

Mark III and our Sherman from a point between the two con-
testants, which was quite an experience. Shells fell all around
that German, but he stood his ground, and our tank could not
come around the corner to get him because it would have been
blasted apart before it had a chance to aim and fire. It was a
beautiful object lesson in tank tactics, for the German dominated
the situation, although he seemed so vulnerable, standing as he
did in plain view in the middle of the road.

One of his shells hit the building I was in, which somewhat
dampened my enthusiasm. Glass rained down, but none of the
many civilians inside was hurt. It was clearly not a good place
to stay in, but I had to wait ten minutes until the firing let up,
and then I made a dash back around the curve to relative safety.
There I found Korman and the others, who were fairly sure I
had been killed, and there I saw the bodies of our colleagues.
What had been a joyous and thrilling day until then, was now
one of intense sadness.

It was late in the afternoon, and a heavy rainstorm came
up to make visibility bad. We had to get back to write our
stories. Next day, on coming back through Scafati, I noticed that
the doorway in the curve, where I had been standing for that
half hour, had received a direct hit some time after I left. Moreover, another shell had taken away the bottom of the stairs of
that house from whose roof I had three times watched the Britishers shooting at the Germans. In eight years of war corresponding I had never overworked my guardian angel to such an extent.
I had had many close calls before, and there were more to come,
but that day took all prizes.

Three days afterwards, on October 1, 1943, we took Naples.
The reception was a wonderfully joyous one. For three days
before our arrival, Neapolitan patriots had fought the Germans
in the streets, in what I called, with justice, "an episode of genuine heroism." Italy was to be like that all along the line, and it
was a marvelous contrast to the reception our soldiers got in Germany the following year. Here were brave help and genuine joy,
and for those of us who liked Italy it was a great satisfaction to
be able to say so.

The port was totally destroyed, but our engineers soon had it going again. The worst part of those early, thrilling days was the German delayed-fuse mines, the largest of which exploded as late as October 10, killing a few dozens of our soldiers. All's fair in war, and no doubt the delayed mine is a legitimate enough weapon, although it kills many more civilians than it does soldiers. However, the German record in Italy, as a whole, is and will be forever shameful. I was always very careful to check on atrocity stories, and used them only if I knew they were correct, for they can be boomerangs, and there are always people who insist on blinding themselves to such truths—even now that we know what the Germans did in their concentration and wholesale murder camps—but there were real atrocities in Italy. Moreover, there was some blind, senseless destruction of cultural monuments and treasures, and this will also contribute to blacken the German name forever. How can one ever erase from history the wanton shame of the burning of the Royal Society's library in the University of Naples, or of the incalculably precious Neapolitan archives at Nola? In each case, because one German soldier was killed the world has been deprived forever of a part of its irreplaceable heritage of culture. Such deeds set mankind back in its struggle toward better things, and there is no greater crime.

Those of us, who are legion, and who have drunk the giddy wine of that basic source of Western culture, Italy, can only be saddened and infuriated at the realization of what we and our children and our children's children have lost. It is not only because some brutal, ignorant officers could think of no better way to "punish" Italy than to burn and loot her treasures, but it is also because men like Hitler have so used the instrument of Fascism as to bring Italy and the world to this pass. The Huns and Vandals knew no better, but we could have hoped for more from men whose ancestors only a few generations back produced Kant, Goethe, Schelling and Schiller.

There were fruitful and busy days in Naples, during which I renewed my acquaintanceship with the politicians and returning exiles who were building up a liberal and left-wing opposition to the Badoglio-Victor Emmanuel regime, then ruling in Brindisi, with Allied backing.

One day I did something which I had never bothered to do in all my years in Italy. I climbed Vesuvius, to its very top, and I have rarely if ever in my life got such a thrill. I hung on to the edge of the topmost crater, peering fearfully into the seething, glowing mass below, that every few seconds exploded molten lava into the air all around me. It is surely one of the most fearsome sights in the world. Clouds of steam obstruct one's view, but now and then they thin out to show the red, writhing mass of lava whose fierce heat comes at one in gusts. The steepness of the sides, yellowed with sulphur, surprised me. They sheered off below like a cliff. And every thirty seconds came that roar and explosion as the angry mass shot its lava into the air. It is a fearful thing to lift the veil from nature's face, and what I saw was more than nerves could bear for long. So I dashed back between the showers of molten lava, thanking my stars for steel helmets, and casting contemptuous glances toward the Neapolitan plain, where man's puny bombs and shells were still bursting.

And that was Vesuvius on an ordinary day. Readers of *Arabia Deserta* will recall the wonderful passage in which Charles M. Doughty describes the great eruption he witnessed in the 1880's. There was to be another like it that winter, but I was away at the time. The ancients would have said that the gods were angry. Certainly we moderns were giving them cause to be.

Mars, however, was enjoying himself. The Germans made a delaying stand on the Volturno River, but we forced a hard-fought crossing in a three-day battle, from October 11 to October 14. Then they made another stand, and I took advantage of the lull to drive over to Bari and Brindisi for my first contacts with Badoglio and the Government. There was much anti-monarchical agitation at the time, but Croce and others pleaded, at first, that the issue should be put aside until the Germans were driven from Italy. However, someone suggested the possibility of a regency for the grandson of Victor Emmanuel, with Badoglio as regent. Croce, Sforza, and many others supported the idea for some weeks, until it died under Badoglio's refusal to adopt it and the Allies' continued support of the King.

Between us and Badoglio the House of Savoy was saved. By "us" I mean the Allied Military Mission, which had been hastily set up in Bari after the King and Badoglio had fled from Rome, which they did very hastily and ignominiously, the morning after the announcement of the armistice. The Americans would have preferred to deal directly with Badoglio, as they had with Darlan in North Africa, but the British insisted on including the King. We Americans did not care enough, since the State Department was taking the line that Italy meant infinitely more to the British than to the Americans, so the decision was left to Eisenhower. He did not care one way or another. So the King was recognized and supported, and then he began a skillful, tenacious fight for his throne, which made all of us change our minds about his character. He proved himself extremely intelligent and very stubborn, and he fought on until he had saved the throne for his son, Prince Humbert.

At that time, in Bari, the Military Mission, which was soon to become the Allied Control Commission, was acting as a sort of pretorian guard. Politics was taboo in occupied Italy and, of course, anything revolutionary or institutional was out of the question. All the liberal, democratic and leftist forces in the liberated zone were against the King, and if they had been allowed a free hand, Italy would now be a republic, or, at the least, have a regency for the young Prince of Naples. But the British would not permit it, and Badoglio stood effective guard on the Italian side.

Mark Watson of the Baltimore *Sun*, Gerald Norman of The *Times* of London, and I had the first official interview with the Marshal. It was a long talk, in which he freely answered most of our questions, defending what he and the King had done, and also defending Italy. Not knowing the Roman background at that time, I felt rather sympathetic with the old man, to whom I had not talked since Addis Ababa. I reminded him of our last encounters. "Those were better times for Italy," he said ingenuously, and I had to agree.

"Do you remember Termaber Pass?" he asked, eagerly, "and those three days we waited while the road was being repaired and the Negus fled? I suppose he would like the Allies to turn me over to him."

He was clearly still very proud of his title of Duke of Addis Ababa, and he made the point that the title should remain his, even though Addis Ababa was lost, and with it Italy's Ethiopian Empire. "Some people have asked about my title," the Marshal said, and then he raised himself proudly in his seat and added emphatically: "I am the Duke of Addis Ababa! Historical facts cannot be canceled by political events. Napier was called Baron of Magdala, although Magdala was retaken by the Abyssinians. No one thought that Marshal Ney should not be called Prince of Moscow because of Napoleon's retreat."

Badoglio had always been an ambitious man, and I always said so—tenacious of the wealth and honors which had come to him through Fascism as well as through the liberal governments of the first World War. He was a soldier and a monarchist, not a politician. In his old age he has served his King well, but his country badly.

Count Carlo Sforza came over from the United States and landed in Bari when I was there. I saw him at the house of Giuseppe Laterza, the publisher, where he was staying, and the first thing he did was to give me a statement for *The New York Times* which made clear his opposition to the monarchy. He did not, at that time, oppose Badoglio, although he would not support him. Later he was to pay for that intransigency, in the famous incident when the British refused to let him become Foreign Minister. He and others were disgusted and discouraged by the survival of many ex-Fascist figures, some of whom had gathered around the Court. There were too many links with Fascism left in Apulia, and liberals, like Laterza, were being arrested for exercising the freedom of the press which they thought had now been earned. To be sure, neither Sforza nor the others did much better, later on in Rome, when they all tried to "epurate" Italy of her Fascists. It could not be done.

Badoglio, with Allied blessing, had such tainted figures as

Generals Roatta, Ambrosio, and Basso as his chief aides. Roatta, it will be recalled, was finally arrested and made a sensational escape. Badoglio never had any scruples about using such men, because he was completely apolitical. To him they were simply military officers, and he never thought of his own activities as if the Army were an instrument of politics. Unfortunately, the United States and Great Britain were likewise permitting their generals to go ahead as though the military campaign were being fought on maps instead of in a real live country. The British were more aware of it, but we went on to the end ignoring the political consequences of our activities.

Italy afforded the first great test of the United Nations' policies for the reconstruction of the world—and the democratic nations made a signal failure of it. Only Russia took proper advantage of her possibilities. Allied policy consistently discouraged the liberals, democrats, Leftists, and anti-Fascists—the very elements we wanted to see in the ascendancy, the elements which have come to the fore in Italy almost despite the Allies. It was partly military fear that politics might somehow harm security, and partly the fact that, as we had begun by accepting the King and Badoglio, every political move and everything which happened after that was conditioned by their presence, opinions, and following. Moreover, the Allied attitude was based upon the expectation of reaching Rome quickly and settling the whole affair there, but many months were to pass before Rome was taken. What we did was, in effect, to bolster the forces of conservatism against those elements seeking revolutionary or institutional changes. It was inevitable that the discredited generals and admirals, the vested interests, the men whose records made them fear that a new regime would ruin them, and everyone who feared that any drastic change would lead to civil war or a radical revolution, should rally round Victor Emmanuel and Badoglio.

Fortunately, the sound, new elements in Italy, supported by the former exiles, hung on and ultimately formed governments that had little power, but were at least expressive of the liberal and democratic, as well as the radical forces. The Monarchy survived in Prince Humbert, who has been trying, with some success, to place the House of Savoy at the disposal of the new forces, much against their will.

But I am getting ahead of my story. In those stormy months in Naples, the British and Americans sat firmly upon the political lid until the Russians came along and calmly took the initiative away by themselves bolstering Badoglio and the King with diplomatic recognition. From that time on, Palmiro Togliatti, the Communist leader, was the dominating force in the successive governments. However, that, too, came a bit later than the period I am writing about, which was the autumn of 1943.

The Germans had made another stand, this time on the Garigliano before Monte Cassino, and with some gradual variations they were to hold on all through autumn, winter and part of the spring, during which Clark and Alexander threw armies and divisions at them in fruitless, costly attacks. The 5th Army became a heterogeneous force. Italian soldiers entered the line at the side of Americans on December 7, and made an attack on Monte Lungo, at Mignano Pass, which cost them 400 casualties out of 1,000 men—probably the heaviest proportional casualties of the campaign to date for any single engagement. The attempt failed, but at least it demonstrated Italian willingness to fight and die to free their country of the Germans, and as such it had great moral value.

The French, too, were now back in Europe, but the so-called French Army which fought in Italy and later made the landing on the Riviera was never really French; it was composed of Goums, Moroccans, Algerians, Senegalese, and Annamites, with French officers and technicians. The really French contribution was made by the patriots inside France.

For the Americans the campaign was proving the toughest and costliest of their military history, and no story about Italy would make any sense unless you realized what they were up against in those interminable months when they fought through mud and cold from one mountain to another, until the final break through into the Po Valley in April, 1945.

The Italian campaign was a triumph of the ordinary doughboy over terrain, elements, and generals. I do not mean to minimize the part that the other services played, nor do I doubt the judgment of Von Rundstedt in asserting that the decisive factor in the campaign against Germany was the bombing. So far as Italy was concerned, the air attack could not play anything like the most important role, because bombing in the mountains is not very effective. Nothing really counts but the steady, dogged drive of the infantrymen, occupying one hill after another on their tired feet. I am not, either, criticizing the generalship, which was doubtless sound; it is the over-all strategy of which I am thinking.

There was a fight south of Cassino, for the Monte Camino massif, in December, 1943, that was so typical of the Italian campaign from beginning to end that you can take it as a classic. It was won under conditions hitherto unparalleled in American military history. The hardships in the jungles of the South Pacific were undoubtedly just as great in their way, and there is no intention here to draw invidious comparisons. In Italy it was mountain fighting, like the storming of Quebec, or of Longstop Hill in the Civil War—but worse, very much worse, and that is why one can call it unparalleled in our history.

The first thing to do, as always, is to forget about the glorified fighting you have seen in the movies and too often read about. Forget about gallant charges and handsome, picturesque soldiers doing incredible feats with a song or joke on their lips. If war ever was like that it isn't now. A battle is a long, slow process—in this particular case nine days. And the picture you want to get in mind is that of a plugging, filthy, hungry, utterly weary young man, staggering half-dazed and punch drunk, and still somehow getting up and over and beating the Germans and hanging on against the enemy's counterattacks. That is what wins battles and war, and only that. No doubt there is glory in it, but you had better not talk of glory during a battle to men who fought for mountains like La Difensa or La Maggiore on the Monte Cassino massif. Glory is something that comes afterward. During, there are only fear, pain, discomfort, fatigue.

While the British were going through exactly similar experiences on the southern side of the massif, the Americans, on the night of December 2, began their assault on La Difensa and La Maggiore. Do not think that even then the doughboy was fresh, rested and clean. One thing is inevitable—he goes into the fighting already tired. In preparation for the attack it had been necessary to build supply dumps as high up on the slopes as possible. That is horribly fatiguing work, and there is heartbreak when the enemy puts shells into some of them and blows them sky-high, as he is bound to do. The Germans had every yard, every trail, gully, and draw on those slopes registered. Troops had to be pushed up as close as possible before the jump off, and they were shelled in the process, and shelled again in their line.

To get there they had to plod through mud. Everybody must have read about the mud of Flanders in World War I, and everybody is going to read about the mud of Italy in this war. No mud could be deeper, stickier, more persistent. On the flat ground you plow disgustedly through it, often sinking over your ankles. But on a climb you do worse. You slide, slip, and fall all over yourself, getting covered with mud from head to foot. The more tired you become, the more you slither and fall, and the harder it is to stand up again and plug on. Every trail you make is a slimy mess of mud. You walk in it, sleep in it and, if you are an infantryman, you never get rid of it, not even in the rest areas—for they, too, are seas of mud.

Supply problems were so difficult in the battle area that there was not enough water to drink, so, needless to say, there was no question ever of washing that mud off. Your hands and face and ears and hair and clothes were caked with it, sodden in the rain, stiff in windy, dry spells, and always cold. It froze at night on those mountains, and pneumonia became one cause of casualties.

It was a maddening business, but the G.I. and his officers had to take it. They were covered with mud when they began that assault. La Difensa is about 3,000 feet high, with straight ledges, toward the top, that run from 100 to 200 feet. Climbing it would have required great effort, even without rifles, machine guns and equipment in the best of weather. To do it in rain and mud, laden with equipment, and with the enemy firing steadily down upon you would seem to be asking too much of any man—but the doughboy did it.

The artillery barrage which the Allied force laid down in advance was the heaviest of the campaign to that date, and it stunned the Germans, in their deep caves and dugouts. But it did not kill them. It would have meant nothing in itself if the infantrymen had not scaled the peak and spread over the whole position.

They got there at 1 A.M. Most of the fighting in the war was done at night, in order to avoid observation, and that is an element which contributes to fatigue. Soldiers stumble and fall much oftener in darkness.

All night our men stayed on the peak, and with dawn they began to clean up the German positions, under sniping and artillery fire. Anyone who was killed or wounded lay where he fell until nightfall, and then it took six men, who had climbed six or eight hours before reaching the top, to carry down one litter.

And that went on for nine days. As one unit took a peak, another would pass through to storm the next, and then the first would hop over it to the further peak. They began the day tired, and ended it almost dropping with fatigue, and then mopping up would begin or a counterattack would have to be fought off. Every night some of those weary soldiers would have to go on patrols, and often they would get back just in time to fight off a German attack at dawn.

Death, wounds, broken limbs, pneumonia, frostbite, thinning ranks—and still the survivors went on or hung on. So long as they could stand they could fight. It took youth and strength, but, above all, it took guts—not the quick, exalted, daring kind, which is much easier, but plodding, steady courage in the face of unutterable misery.

When you get a combination of hunger, thirst, cold, and fatigue you have not much encouragement to fight. To be sure, the hunger and thirst were relative. There was always enough to keep going, thanks to some heroic work in maintaining supply lines. A case of C rations weighs 48 pounds, and a five-gallon can of water 43 pounds. Each one is awkward and difficult to handle, at best, and so are fifty rounds of ammunition. Strap one of those things on your back and climb a steep mountain with it for eight hours, and you have done something, especially in mud and rain and under mortar and artillery fire. Then walk eight hours back, and repeat the process next day and the next, for eight or nine days.

That is what soldiers did during the battle for the Monte Camino massif. Horses and mules could make only a little of the distance. It was too steep, and animals tend to become panicky under fire. There was one open spot that had to be crossed—and the Germans knew it. They kept it under constant artillery fire. Supply parties were often delayed, but never stopped. Once the firing was particularly heavy. The captain leading the party had seen his men scattered twice, each time losing some supplies and precious time. He said, "Boys, this time we have got to make it, whatever happens." They got across, but the captain was killed. All the way up, that party was shelled, and it took them fourteen hours more to reach the top. But they got there.

That sort of thing takes guts, too, and each day you need more because you are more tired. The first twenty-four hours you are fresh, and you seldom fall. The next day you start out tired, and by the end of the day deadly fatigue sets in. You can see it in a man, for fatigue is poison, just like a noxious drug. Yellow face, bad breath, rivulets of sweat, glazed eyes— these are only some of the physical symptoms of fatigue, and from them come other, more disastrous effects.

As the hours and days pass, you fall more and more often. When you have a load on your back, that sometimes means a broken limb, and it always means a further accumulation of fatigue. Your resistance to cold becomes less; your digestive organs work badly; your nerves become ever more frayed. You lose weight, sleep, confidence. Every day more and more men go under from heavy colds, pneumonia, stomach trouble, and various types of shell shock. New G.I. shoes get torn to pieces in a few days, and men walk with raw feet until they drop, or, somehow, get another pair of shoes.

In every evacuation or base hospital you could find cases which were due simply to fatigue, although they took the form of insomnia, shell shock, broken arms and legs. So it was a great problem, one that all armies fight as they do illness. Wherever possible, troops were withdrawn to rest areas and replaced as soon as they became too fatigued. Under normal conditions soldiers would not be kept more than three days on the actual summits of front-line mountains. However, conditions during a campaign such as the Italian one, with its scarcity of men, were not normal. For instance, the 45th Division fought from D-Day on the Salerno beachhead for forty consecutive days. The 3rd Division, which came in later, did fifty-seven consecutive days. "Rest," after such periods of fighting, generally meant five or at most ten days back of the lines, with opportunities to bathe, get fresh clothing, and a few days in the nearest city to have a fling.

Everything is relative in this world. Just to get out of danger for five or ten days was a great relief. To have hot food, plenty of sleep, nothing to do, seemed like heaven—for a little while. Then other factors began to operate—boredom, homesickness, restlessness, moodiness. Brooding and griping increased until the troops were back in the lines, where they felt they were doing something and getting somewhere.

If there was anything that I stressed in my war dispatches, from the Burma hills to the Apennines, it was that the American soldiers were sick and tired of the war. The United States is "God's country" to any doughboy, and he does not go fighting all over the world from choice, and the sooner it is over with the better. World War I lasted nineteen months, from the time the United States got in. This one took forty-one months to end the European phase. Separation from home, hardships, and dangers become harder and harder to bear as the months and years pass. Whatever there was of romance or glamour or idealism in war to begin with tends to fade away, and it is replaced by fatigue of body and mind. For the average soldier, as World War I proved, war does not leave a permanent mark, and he even comes to look back on it wistfully, on great days of heroism and comradeship, on that joy which every normal man takes in a battle well fought.

But all that comes later, at least for most men. Only speculative and imaginative souls, or natural-born fighters, appreciate the greatness that accompanies war while they are still fighting. The longer the war lasts, the harder it is to be philosophical or detached about it.

There again it is fatigue of all kinds which works upon the soldier. The older men feel the physical strain sooner and go under more quickly, but their nerves, generally speaking, are better. Higher officers, like regimental colonels and divisional generals, are fortunate if they can see a campaign like the Italian one through without physical disabilities. That is the primary excuse for officers receiving better treatment than their men, although in the front-line fighting there is no distinction. However, platoon, company, and battalion leaders are young men, who can take it physically.

As a general proposition, we can say that war equals fatigue, and the longer it lasts the greater does the fatigue become. What I have written here about the Monte Camino massif goes for the whole Italian campaign. Almost every line of mountains had to be conquered under the same conditions of danger, discomfort, mud or dust, and fatigue. Do you wonder that it took so long to drive the Germans out of Italy?

Day after day I watched that fight for the Monte Camino massif, and then I saw the murderous attacks on unimportant little villages like San Pietro, at Mignano Pass below Monte Cassino. Out of one company of American "Mexicans," no officers and only twenty-three men came back. Everywhere it was the same story. Rome seemed very far away, and I, too, after a year and a half away from home and family, was fatigued. I had been at the wars, so to speak, for eight years even then, so I spent Christmas at the front, and then went off for a vacation.

While I was gone the Anzio landing, which was to prove of little value, took place. The Abbey of Monte Cassino was destroyed in a bombing raid which will have to be considered one of the black marks against American civilization, for it was not necessary, and the evidence showed that the Germans were not occupying the abbey. We were not prepared to follow up our raid by an immediate assault, and for months the ruins provided better shelter and observation than ever for the Germans.

At last, almost all our forces in Italy were massed on the Garigliano, bolstered by two fresh American divisions, the 85th and the 88th, and in May we broke through and were on the way to Rome. I also was on my way to Rome by that time.

The Eternal City

I ARRIVED in good time for the break-through in the Lazio Hills, at the beginning of June, 1944, which signaled the end of Rome's existence as a Fascist and German-occupied city. I had left the 5th Army literally bogged down in the mud before Cassino, and I now found them plunging triumphantly, through unending clouds of dust, to their greatest prize in Italy, the goal which had beckoned conquerors for many centuries. But the roads to Rome were not majestic; they were roads of dust and blood, of wreckage and the stink of bodies—and through it all millions of bright red poppies, such as the fathers of those doughboys saw in Flanders.

The stretch from Gaeta to Rome was an unending scene of desolation. Towns like Velletri and Cisterna had all but ceased to exist. The Pontine Marshes, whose drainage was the proudest accomplishment of the Fascist regime, were now flooded, and dismal. German thoroughness had destroyed similar parts of all the intricate, scattered pumping machinery so that it could not be repaired. It was a typical example of Nazi ruthlessness, for the Allies were not slowed down since the roads are raised above the fields.

The cruelty and ferocity of the Germans toward those Italians who opposed them lay partly in their feeling of racial superiority. It was a flowering from those evil seeds of race and blood which arè at the core of the Nazi philosophy, and which are not new to German thought. They can be traced back to the days of the barbarian invasions of Italy, and, in modern times, to the Napoleonic domination of Germany, which aroused a patriotic sense of Germanism as contrasted with everything outside. The philosophy of the superman, leading to a superior, dominating race predestined to rule, was a natural growth from those seeds.

That was one of the things which made the Axis such a monstrosity in history. The Germans despised the Italians, and accepted them as allies only while they were useful and faithful. To Germans, the Italian collapse was hardly more than they expected, and it earned their contempt, but when the Italians turned on them and at last gave vent to their pent-up hatred of everything German, it was accounted base treachery. It brought out, among other things, a vicious, sadistic cruelty, mixed with a cold fury that led to many sickening atrocities. Germans, down to the lowest soldier, had the feeling that Italy betrayed them, and many even went so far as to feel and assert that they lost the war because of that betrayal. So they took it out on the Italians, their cities and even their culture.

To be sure, in the northern half of Italy, where the Fascist Republicans stuck by the Germans to the end but where the great majority of the people simply minded their own business, the German command had the sense to treat Italians with condescending decency, wreaking their fury on the partisans and innocent hostages. The memory of those peaceful, relatively comfortable months before the war ended is going to plague the new Italian regime for years, although history will record the atrocities and the hatred as the unforgivable sins.

We fought our way finally into Rome on June 4, 1944, when the New World came to conquer the Old. Never before in history had the capital of Catholicism, and the world's most historic city, been conquered in a campaign from south to north—and it seems safe to predict that it never will be again, for our conquest was only an exception to prove the rule that the task is fundamentally impossible. What Hannibal and Napoleon did not dare to try, Alexander's and Clark's troops accomplished, in as difficult, bloody, and heartbreaking a campaign as military history can record.

Americans had the honor of leading the way, because it was in their sector that the break-through occurred which permitted the sudden dash into the capital, but almost every one of the

United Nations was represented, except Russia. There were Britishers, Canadians, New Zealanders, Indians, French Moroccans, Poles—all but the Italians, who were denied the honor of taking part in what for them was a reconquest of their capital. Every American unit was somehow represented—the veteran 45th, 36th and 3rd Divisions, which had fought their way north all the way from Salerno, the 34th and 1st Armored, and, newest of all, the 85th and 88th, which were the first selective service divisions to see action. Their record is certainly unique in American history, for in three weeks from their baptism of fire they helped to conquer what has always been one of the greatest prizes in the world. Here were boys from farms and Main Streets, marching in triumph along the path Saint Peter trod 2,000 years ago.

The entry was not without its excitement, for the Jerries made a stand at Kilometer 8, where Highway 6 enters the city. That thrust into the mountain ridge behind Velletri, three days previously, permitted the flanking of Monte Cavo and Rocca di Papa, and cooked the German goose. Faced with the certainty that their positions along the coast were going to be flanked quickly, the Germans fell back swiftly to positions just before Rome, playing desperately and successfully for time, until darkness fell.

I lit out for Rome from Anzio, at five o'clock on the afternoon of June 3. The Hermann Goering Division was being "steamrollered" back, but every available German was being thrown in, even veterinaries, in an effort to stem the Allied rush. The three-quartered moon was a blessing, as it was the night before we took Messina. There was an eerie tenseness in the air as darkness came on. We got over the Alban Hills in the dusk, and our eyes searched vainly through the haze for the Rome we knew lay on the Campagna before us. Excitement gripped everyone, but it was a grim, silent and deserted countryside, except for our advancing columns.

Our pathetic little jeep wound in and out of the cars, and soon we reached the infantry filing along both sides of the road. The wounded were coming back steadily, and there were prisoners, too. Each moment we expected the Germans to react, but still we kept going. At Kilometer 18, dead bodies began cluttering the landscape—our dead as well as theirs. Suddenly we struck a clear, unpeopled stretch, and sped on alone through the darkness, almost holding our breaths. We knew there were some reconnaissance units ahead, as well as tanks, and—how could we know?—perhaps the way to Rome was clear. At last we reached the leading "recon" unit.

"You had better watch out," said the officer in charge. "You've come through lots of Jerries. They are all over these fields, and there is nothing up here except armored cars."

So we had done one of those foolish things which correspondents cannot resist in the heat of getting a great story, and there was nothing left to do but hope for the best. We were at Kilometer 13, a little more than five miles from the outskirts of the city. A tank fight was going on just a mile ahead, which was the furthest our forces were to go that night. There was a short side road to a group of three farmhouses, and we went in there. It was none too soon. Within a matter of minutes we heard the Jerry planes come over. They took their time, flying tantalizingly in circles, and getting their bearings. An important crossroads was only a hundred yards away, and we knew we were in for it. Sure enough, they began dropping flares. Then came strafing, then bombs, as Will Lang, of *Time* magazine, and I flattened ourselves on the floor of a stone hut. One flare dropped next to it, and for what seemed like ages we dug our heads into the ground and held our breaths, waiting, waiting—and then it came! Two bombs crashed beside the house, which shook dizzily as plaster from the ceiling fell upon us.

Only then did we learn that the farmers had built a refuge just outside the house, and we dashed into it. There we were relatively safe. Within a few minutes, four jeeps of ammunition carriers dashed up, and the men jumped out and into our refuge. Then began the strangest night which I had spent since I was ambushed out in Dankalia with an Italian flying column. We were surrounded by Germans, and we knew it and dared not move. Two G.I.'s came in with us, while their comrades went up the hill to another refuge.

Acrid smoke still filled our shelter, from the bombs which had dropped almost squarely on it. Outside, more of our armor was trundling down the highway, which gave us some comfort, but our worry was the Nazis who had been left scattered in the fields. Being correspondents, we were not armed, so the doughboys had to keep guard. One of them had a tommy gun and the other a rifle. They took turns of an hour each, while we sat uncomfortably in the pitch darkness, being eaten up by fleas with which all Italian peasants, judging from my experiences, are afflicted. At one time I found it so desperately uncomfortable that I decided it was better to sleep on the ground, whatever happened, so I went out. Just as I emerged from the refuge I saw our guard crouched, with his gun pointing toward a house in the rear. "I just saw four krauts," he whispered. "Go get the other guy, quick! The safety catch was on my gun, dammit, and I couldn't get it released in time."

The other G.I. rushed up, after I had dived back into the refuge and we waited, but the Germans had got away. Once more in the night we had a similar alarm, and, when daylight came, just before five o'clock, we found hob-nailed tracks of German boots.

Somehow the night dragged away its weary length, with me draped uncomfortably over the rough-hewn dirt steps of the refuge. A peasant woman heated some water for our coffee, which we hastily downed, black, strong, and comforting. Then we went on. Tanks and infantry were now ahead of us. Tough, bearded, dirty youngsters sat astride the tanks as we passed in our jeep, aiming for the head of the column.

Peasants were beginning to come out and line the roads, but they were not cheering, as they had before Naples. They were stolid but curious. Rome was being conquered again, but at first they showed no emotion. Then, as we drew nearer to the outskirts of Rome, enthusiasm began to rise, and a few even threw flowers at the tanks.

A German *volkswagon* came back, careening perilously as the driver tried desperately to keep his hands up in the air and direct the vehicle. Behind him sat a white-faced, horrified youth. At a crossroads was a big, German truck with a trailer. It stopped; Americans rushed up with guns handy, and the Germans tumbled out with their hands raised. Fifty yards away was the most horrid sight of the day—a Nazi with half his right wrist shot away, but somehow keeping that hand as well as his left one up in the air while an Italian peasant roughly searched him. He approached our jeep with imploring eyes, pain and fear written all over him, but we motioned him back to where the Red Cross cars were.

It was 6:30, and we were almost at the head of the column. Two tanks were in front of us. And there, at last, was the road sign, ROMA, just at the bend in the highway. The first tank clanked around it, and then came a crash and a vivid flash as it was hit by an 88-mm. shell from a self-propelled gun which had been waiting. The driver was killed, and two other men were wounded. Everybody else dashed for the ditches, for we knew what it meant. The infantry deployed.

By that time a large group of American correspondents had joined us. They had spent the night at various points along the highway behind us and we were all ready for the kill. However, hours were to pass before it came. That S.P. was a vicious one. He had our range, and shell after shell came in. They have a low trajectory, and when one comes close it gives you the impression of having gone over your shoulder. Once I went to watch our tanks deploying in a field on the left and just as I arrived a shell whizzed overhead, cut the top off a telephone pole near me, fortunately without exploding, and blew up as it hit the next pole.

About eight o'clock I walked down to the head of the column where our tank was still blazing, and put myself a little beyond the ROMA sign, just to be able to say technically that I had been in Rome early that morning. Journalism is like that. Civilians were foolishly running in and out of the houses, oblivious to danger, but they scattered wildly when shells came over.

Just then a sniper opened up. He could not have been there before, but now he had a bead on us with a machine gun, straight down the road, and it was not pleasant as I ran and crawled back. There was a low ditch next to the road, and as I

realized how badly I was in for it I flattened myself in it while
bullets whizzed so close overhead that I dared not look up. However, the firing stopped momentarily, and without rising I began
making notes. Just then a bullet plunked into the ground right
in front of my nose. It did not explode or ricochet—otherwise
this book would not have been written—and when it cooled off
enough to be picked up with my handkerchief, I took it away
as a souvenir of a historic day. Later, I was to think of that when
Ernie Pyle was killed. He should have kept his head down, for
the world needs such men.

There the Germans held us until nightfall. And then Rome
was conquered. Never was there such a Roman triumph as that
next day—jeeps on the Campidoglio, tanks rolling past Saint
Peter's, almost under the windows of the Pope's offices, G.I.'s
buying flowers for Roman lasses on the Spanish Steps, and excitement everywhere! Romans had seen conquerors galore in three
thousand years of history, but they came to devastate the city. We
were welcomed as deliverers, and those most blasé of all peoples
overflowed with happiness to make a joyous Roman holiday.

Best of all, the city had been unharmed by the war, except for
those unfortunate residential districts around the railway yards
and stations, and the Basilica of San Lorenzo, which we had damaged in the first raid. Otherwise, all its glorious churches and
monuments were intact. The Germans had, in a sense, defended
Rome, but their defense was only a screen, and when it broke
the evening before, the whole city was ours for the taking.

It was the day of Sunday, June 5, that counted, for all Rome
came out with the dawn—laborers and patricians, young and old
—to cheer the army which now entered and swarmed over its
streets. Romans, who are so cynical, so world-weary, so cosmo-
politan, were unrecognizable that day in their wild joy. I recall
the day as a kaleidoscope of vivid pictures. There was Mark
Wayne Clark, the conquering general without which no Roman
triumph is possible, and he stood, like others before him, in the
heart of ancient Rome, atop the Campidoglio. Just below the
steps, and all over the square, were those incongruous jeeps, and
below that the Palazzo Venezia, now forlorn, its empty balcony

still draped with the Italian tricolor. Once, that morning, an American G.I. got up there and made a mock harangue to a different sort of crowd than Mussolini used to address. The main entrance of the palace was barred, and nailed across the door was a sign of one of the partisan groups: "Death to traitors!"

It was *Viva!* for the whole world that day, except for the Germans, who left a trail of hatred that was almost palpable. The Roman citizens did not rise at the end, as the Neapolitans had done. It was not in their temperament to do so, and, anyway, they had received a terrible lesson from the Germans a few months previously. Some misguided Communist partisans killed a number of German soldiers on the Via Rasella. In reprisal, the Nazis shot at least 400 Italian hostages, in horrible circumstances, in the Fosse Ardeatine outside the city. For Rome that vile deed will forever remain the symbol of German bestiality.

There had been much valuable underground work for us during the nine months of German occupation, and through it all, the political leaders who were now to come to the fore had organized and carried on their work. Most remained safely in Vatican buildings protected by extraterritoriality. They were old men who could not be expected to fight, but some of them roamed about furtively, hiding in one house after another, and meeting short shrift when they were caught. It had been a period not without its heroism and danger, and Romans will never cease talking about it. Again and again the story of those months is told, until now the outsider almost dreads to spend evenings with Roman friends.

For me there was the great joy of finding all my old, anti-Fascist friends safe and sound. They had been brave and active, as I knew they would be, and now they were among the leaders of the new Italy—the Carandinis, Ruffinis, Albertinis, Fenoalteas, Rollis, and others. Many of them were standing in the Piazza Venezia to cheer the troops and for once I was glad to be hugged and kissed by men whose affection I returned.

From everywhere people were coming out into the open light of the Allies' day. A mob more or less stormed the famous old prison of Regina Coeli, but the guards were all with them, and threw open the wings in which political prisoners were kept by the Fascisti, and the tragic cells full of Italian Jews who had been under SS guards. The Germans had previously let loose all the criminally insane, and some were never recaptured.

It was the same old Rome which gladdened my heart. It is on days like that, days which even for Rome are great, that one sees and senses, as never before, its eternal quality. I knew that our wave of strange people and vehicles would quickly pass, and that Rome would again look as it has always looked. Monsignor Enrico Pucci, cynical head of the famous semi-official Vatican news agency, put it with typical Roman wit that morning when he said, "Oh, it is just another 'changing of the guard!' "

No one could drive through that ancient city on the morning of June 5 and fail to sense its greatness. Here were the Spanish Steps, with lovely flowers still to buy at the bottom. And the bridges, all intact—for, contrary to expectation, the Germans did not blow them up, or any hotel or other building. We found large stores of explosives around, showing that the Nazis were prepared under certain circumstances to use them, but Pope Pius XII gave the Germans credit for sparing the city, and no doubt history will do the same.

I crossed the Tiber, most famous of all rivers of the Western world, over which our troops had passed the night before, in pursuit of the Germans. Soon you come upon the massive Castel Sant'Angelo, once a Roman mausoleum. Then Saint Peter's rises to view, with its majestic dome, beyond the ugly, wide Via della Conciliazione with its modern buildings erected by the Fascists. And with the Vatican you know that nothing is changed or ever can change in Rome, even though a Piper Cub observation plane flew overhead, and jeeps careened around the piazza.

We drove back to the well known restaurant of San Carlo, where Umberto Storci, its proprietor, fell on our necks for joy. He had served me with my last meal of liberty in Rome on December 11, 1941, a few hours before I was thrown into Regina Coeli jail as a prisoner of war. Umberto had been serving German soldiers until five o'clock of the day before, and from then on he was serving American G.I.'s, but with a different heart.

The Corso Umberto was lined with people, as I had seen it lined innumerable times during the Fascist regime, but with what a difference now! The populace did not have to be ordered out for this celebration. They did not have to cheer, *Viva gli Americani! Viva l'Italia libera!* We had just missed a Communist parade, with red flags waving and everyone singing the *International.*

Down at the foot of the huge white Victor Emmanuel monument, an Italian military band was bravely trying to drown out the noise of armored cars, jeeps, and shouting people. That was when General Clark stood on the Palatine Hill. Behind him was the Roman Forum, that eternal reminder of the greatest lesson which Rome has to teach—that conquerors come and go, but Rome goes on forever. Childe Harold had spoken well:

> O Rome! my country! city of the soul!
> The orphans of the heart must turn to thee,
> Lone mother of dead empires! and control
> In their shut breast their petty misery.
> What are our woes and sufferance? Come and see
> The cypress, hear the owl, and plod your way
> O'er steps of broken thrones and temples, Ye!
> Whose agonies are evil of a day—
> A world is at our feet as fragile as our clay.

There is something about Rome which makes one want to be philosophical instead of journalistic. Everyone who has ever been to Rome and lived in it and written about it inevitably succumbs. Its atmosphere is redolent with ancient things that somehow never seem to change. And yet your reason tells you that Rome must have changed. I had seen it, year after year for a score of years, but the changes did not register in my mind. All that I could see and feel and understand was that everlasting quality that made colossal forces like Fascism and conquering armies blend into its neutral background. Yes, indeed, there is something special, something unique about Rome which was there in the days of Augustus as it is today.

It took the acute French mind to invent the saying, *Plus ça change, plus ça reste la même chose.* That is Rome for you in the past quarter of a century, for it has changed, just as you and I and the world have changed. It is true that in essence we are the same people and the same world, but within limits there are differences and distinctions to make in us, in Rome, and in the world.

Just twenty years before we took Rome, the Socialist deputy Giacomo Matteotti was brutally murdered by Fascist gangsters, and things were never quite the same in Italy after that. Mussolini almost had his Fascist regime shot out from under him, and its survival was due solely to weakness and lack of unity among his opponents. On January 3, 1925, he thumped his fist on the rostrum of the Chamber of Deputies, and shouted that he was going to be boss, and a tough one at that. It was six months later that I first saw Rome as a student.

Romans were still blinking their eyes in helpless, bewildered fashion. No one quite like Mussolini had come along since Cola di Rienzi in the fourteenth century, and that was a long time to think back, even for Romans. In normal circumstances, the Roman is just about the most blasé, world-weary, cynical individual you could hope to meet. Plenty of Romans throughout the ages have been sharp and unprincipled enough to have earned the jeers of their fellow Italians despite many noble exceptions. Faced with something they did not understand, but which seemed new, clever, and capable of bringing tangible results, the Romans shrugged their shoulders and let events take their course. Those who fought against it were being mowed down, and that was painful to see. They fought for liberty, which is, after all, a good Roman tradition, but the disposition of minds and hearts was such as to stir up a little maelstrom in Italy, which was later to spread from country to country.

Now it would seem like destiny, but actually, in 1925 and 1926, Mussolini was feeling his way, in hit-or-miss fashion, toward that extraordinary conception of the one-party system and state which was to permit a tyranny undreamed of in the past. So much went by the boards in those days—political opposition, freedom of the press and speech, the right of labor to strike or to form autonomous unions! It should have been amazing to see it all happen, but actually, an outsider like myself, little interested in politics and deeply immersed in the study of Dante and medieval Italy, saw almost nothing. Now and then someone would take a pot-shot at the Duce, and then the people would all come out and cheer misguidedly because the assassin had missed. Then, of course, there were always Fascist-arranged demonstrations, but they were merely a new kind of Roman holiday which nobody took seriously.

Those were the days when Rome appeared to have lost its soul. A small group chose exile, or were expelled. Others withdrew into a shell, but most either accepted the regime cynically or applauded as Fascism went on from one triumph to another. It had reached its Golden Age when I returned to Rome in 1932, which was the tenth anniversary of the March on Rome. The capital was being partly transformed, with its new Via dell'Impero, its excavations and restorations, its elimination of some of the slum districts. The evil effects of the revaluation of the lire in 1927, and the repercussions of the world-wide economic crisis, were only beginning to be felt. There had been the conciliation with the Church which had given Fascism such great prestige in the Catholic world; statesmen from England, France, Germany, and Austria were flocking to Rome and praising Mussolini as a champion of peace; in Germany a National Socialist movement modeled on Fascism was about to take control.

Rome, it appeared, had again become the capital of a great power, and Romans strutted in uniforms, saluted, paraded, cheered—and then went home to laugh a little at themselves and shrug their shoulders. Fascism was in its heyday and few there were to say, "Beware of Nemesis!"—that goddess who was also a good Roman citizen and who could never be exiled.

Mussolini, living in the clouds, was surrounded by flatterers and was deluding himself with ideas of grandeur. He plotted war while peace was on his lips. Three years later he struck, in Abyssinia, the blow that was to lead by inevitable progression to the second World War—and the Romans applauded more than ever. Had not Italy become a great power? The whole world, they thought, feared and respected Fascism, and many countries were imitating its forms. Those poor democracies, England and France, were members of a dying order.

If Rome could have been given a collective physiognomy in those days, when I returned from conquered Addis Ababa, one could say that it looked like the cat which swallowed the canary. Then you saw Romans at their worst, applauding a success that had been won at the expense of morality, ignoring the signs of economic collapse, deluding themselves with the belief that they were a great, martial people, worshiping the Duce who, they thought, would lead them to new and greater triumphs. Even fewer there were now to beware of Nemesis!

And yet that was the period when the decline began. Mussolini was hitching his wagon to the shooting star of Nazism, and their first joint adventure was in Spain. There, as I told you, I saw Italians routed ignominiously at Guadalajara, in Fascism's first military defeat, the Baylen of the twentieth century. I saw them pay heavily in blood, matériel, and money for a hollow victory that brought nothing but the delusion of prestige, and I was back in Rome to see those same soldiers return for their poor triumph while Romans, this time under orders, lined the streets and cheered indifferently.

That was the fateful year of 1939, and already something was wrong with the picture. To be sure, a victory had been won, but the price was staggering. It was all becoming a hollow show, and effort and an extra dose of cynicism were required to make believe that all was well. Now Romans were calculating not on their own strength but on that of Hitler and on the weakness of the democracies whose statesmen were then reaching depths of shameful appeasement. The laughter of the Romans was false; their skepticism was genuine, and if they shrugged their shoulders, it was ruefully and with the knowledge that it was much too late to do anything about it. Rome was at last anti-Fascist, but, since nothing could be done, Romans became "realistic" and hoped that the Duce might save them, somehow, from the impending wreck.

The only genuine outburst of enthusiasm that I was to see in twenty years (until June 5, 1944) came when Mussolini announced, in September, 1939, that Italy was not going to enter the war. He was furious about his "martial" nation being so obviously pacific and anti-German, but, anyway, he took some comfort in the popularity it brought him—his last spell of real popularity.

Those of us who were in Rome at the time of the "stab in the back" which the Duce delivered at France were sick with disgust over the indifference and cynicism with which all but a few Romans took the development. The people were sure the war was almost over, since Mussolini obviously felt sure. They knew how immoral the declaration of war was, and condemned it intellectually, but they were clearly prepared to accept any benefits that might accrue. That is the worst accusation which can be made against Romans, and Italians generally, in the whole war, for it gave evidence of a widespread moral corruption. Those were unhappy days for Americans—days made livable only by the loyalty of many good Italian friends, who stuck despite risks.

Things went from bad to worse for the democracies, while the Romans were never (in their opinion) more realistic. Since the British were going to be beaten long before Americans could do anything about it, there was nothing to be done. Only now there was a subtle change in the general feeling, for bitterness had set in with the Italian defeats in Greece and North Africa. The length of the war, the material distress and moral shame, and, above all, the palpable failure of Fascism and the Duce's policies, were all, collectively, teaching Romans salutary lessons and bringing out much good in the midst of adversity. Now Mussolini had lost his popularity, and so had Fascism, and the culminating blow came when he stood on the balcony of the Palazzo Venezia and declared war on the United States.

I stood directly below him, and marveled that something so monstrous to every Italian could be taken so calmly, for this time I knew how badly they felt. It made me wonder if anything could move these world-weary people from that impassive, eternal, unchanging acceptance of whatever happened.

Three years were to pass before the answer came, and then Rome seemed to rise from its ashes. That attitude of indifference, cynicism, world-weariness, proved to be only a mask, after all, even though it is a mask that is almost never removed. Here were fervor, excitement, joy, a friendliness that flowed like the Tiber itself to welcome not conquerors but deliverers. Best of all, new spiritual and moral bases were being laid, and although many were Romans in the bad sense of the word—scheming, treacherous, and cynical—very many more had found ancient virtues in themselves.

That condition, at least, was new in the Rome of recent decades. Not since 1870 had there been such an awakening. To see Rome alive with hope, courage, and determination was a strange and wonderful thing. I suspected that it might not long remain so. There was so much about Rome that had not changed, so much dead weight that could not be thrown off, so many reminders that Rome is eternally the same. Fascism had come, but had not entirely gone, and that devastating wave of war, more cruel to Italy than any invasion by Hun or Vandal—although made for a different purpose and not against the Italians—will soon subside, too, for the war is over in Europe. Then we shall see whether Romans will again start shrugging their shoulders, withdrawing deeper and deeper behind their masks, until the world looks again upon the apparently unchanging face of the Eternal City.

But nothing will erase the greatness of the day when we liberated Rome. The world forgot it almost immediately, for the next day, June 6, the Allies landed in Normandy to begin the liberation of France, and we took a back seat. But the war was far from over. The Germans got across the Tiber and fell back swiftly to the north, with that skill which never deserted them even in their worst days. We routed one army in taking Rome, but the German force as a whole was never routed until the final break-through into the Po Valley. In Kesselring they had probably the greatest of all German commanders, and history will have to record that when he left Italy he was undefeated.

Italian politicians came up from Naples to join those who emerged from hiding. Some of those in Rome I was meeting for the first time—Ivanoe Bonomi, who became Prime Minister,

Giuseppe Saragat, Alcide de Gasperi, Giovanni Visconti-Venosta, Alessandro Casati. Others were old friends, such as Nicolò Carandini, later appointed Ambassador to Great Britain, Sergio Fenoaltea, Eduardo Ruffini, and Pietro Nenni whom I knew in Spain. I may also have met Palmiro Togliatti, then "Ercole," when he was representing the Comintern in Barcelona at the end of the Spanish Civil War, but I cannot remember having done so.

They all formed the first of several Bonomi governments, on June 9, when Marshal Badoglio gracefully withdrew after the opposition to him, was expressed in strong fashion. Churchill was furious. He held up the Allies' approval of the new cabinet for eight days, much to the discouragement of the Italians and of those who were anxious to see a genuinely anti-Fascist, liberal government in Italy. The British Prime Minister was afraid that a new set of men would not abide by the very onerous armistice terms which Badoglio had signed. It was the first of a number of moves that supported conservative forces in Europe. At the end of August Churchill himself visited Italy and talked to the new men, and he went away with infinitely more understanding and sympathy than he had before. From then on Italy had a genuine friend in the old Tory.

The Monarchy appeared to be very shaky in those days. Victor Emmanuel III, although remaining King, had delegated his powers to his son, Humbert, Prince of Piedmont, who became Lieutenant General of the Realm. The Prince, still unable to assert himself, and still new in the game of politics, came out badly in the first exchanges. The populace, on the whole, had shown a moderate amount of friendliness, but the politicians were nearly all against him. The Socialist and Action Parties were strongly republican, and so was the newly reconstituted Republican Party, under the leadership of Giovanni Conti and Randolfo Pacciardi, commander of the Garibaldinis in the International Brigade and cherished friend of mine from Spain. The Communists still supported the House of Savoy, but Togliatti confessed to me that they would turn republican, once Italy was liberated. Only the Christian Democrats (the inheritors of Don

Sturzo's Popular Party), the Liberals, and the Democracy of Labor Party were mildly favorable and determined to put aside the institutional problem until Italy was entirely free. Republicanism in Italy, I decided in the course of time, is not really a positive force, except for the Republican Party, which remained somewhat out of the main political current, oversimplifying an immensely complicated situation by interpreting everything in terms of republicanism and monarchism.

When the first government was formed Humbert was not consulted, and a new oath of loyalty to the country, instead of to the Crown, was formulated. He could still count upon months of activity during which the institutional problem was to be shelved. Among the Allies, the British were strongly for him, and in the Vatican he had benevolent good wishes, partly because the Vatican by tradition is in favor of the conservative force which monarchies represent, and partly because he and his wife, Princess Marie José, are devout Catholics. The Vatican, however, does not like to be on the losing side, and it was up to the Prince to demonstrate that he could save the throne. He began a patient, tenacious, clever fight, whose primary object had to be the living down of the disgust and hatred aroused by his father and his father's Fascist record.

It was not long before I had to write that, as far as Rome and the Allies were concerned, "the honeymoon was over." Within ten days the wits were grumbling, "Rome was never like this," and asking when the soldiers were going to leave, why they were eating up Roman food, and whether Italians were supposed to enjoy the way Roman girls and women were throwing themselves into the arms of the American soldiers. For several reasons, some of them justified, Rome did not consider itself a conquered but a liberated capital. Nevertheless, their first experiences with politics frightened a lot of Romans, who from then on began suggesting that the Allies remain in Italy indefinitely, to stave off Communism, a revolution, or new forms of totalitarianism. Those were Italians who had no faith in Italy and I never felt any sympathy with them, and I felt even less for the many thousands who are only waiting for the day when they can desert their unhappy country for the material comforts and order of the United States. Twenty-one years of Fascism, capped by nine months of German terrorism, had left ineradicable marks of moral weakness.

I am not going to discuss here the long series of dispatches in which I expressed an opinion, bolstered by innumerable facts, that we Allies were making as serious errors in Rome as we had made in Naples—errors which had the result of handicapping and discouraging those very democratic and anti-Fascist elements which represented the principles for which the United Nations were supposed to be fighting. The British remained consistently hostile to Italy and Italians, for the understandable reason that Britain had not forgotten Mussolini's contribution to the war or the conquest of Abyssinia. It was a short-sighted policy, since Great Britain needs a friendly Italy as a bulwark against Communism, and because of her own position in the Mediterranean, yet everything which London did was calculated to weaken and antagonize Italy. Those who hoped for a different British foreign policy from the one which led to World War II found no comfort in Rome. The Americans stood supinely by, getting no directives from President Roosevelt, who was too busy with other problems. If Italy avoids Communism and a link with Russia (which I believe she will), it will be in spite of Anglo-American policies, not because of them.

Life in Rome was busy and fascinating in those months after liberation. I dropped war corresponding for a while to concentrate on politics and history, with a bit of philosophy thrown in. Italians do not talk in the straight, matter-of-fact terms of the Englishman or American. A conversation over the dinner table and coffee is always brilliant and always concerned with abstractions. I used to sit, helpless and envious, listening with pleasure and profit, but unable to join in the talk because my own mind moves along precise, concise, and material lines. I could talk about specific events and practical developments, but not in abstract, universal terms.

In lieu of Croce I had Santayana to visit, although the one could no more replace the other than their philosophical systems could be exchanged. When I was with Santayana, whom I found, living and writing peacefully, up on the Celian Hill, in the convent of the English Blue Sisters which is near the ancient church of Santo Stefano Rotondo, I was taken out of this world and into an eternity of the spirit which the Indians might have envied. I had left my own ivory tower many years before, but here was a man past the age of eighty who still lived in one.

During my first visit he spent most of the hour interviewing me. The first volume of his autobiography, *Persons and Places,* had recently been a best seller in the United States, and he was astonished when I told him so. He opined it must have been because people liked *The Last Puritan,* his only novel. "Nobody reads philosophy," he said. I had the impression that he hardly realized a World War was going on, or that Rome had been conquered again.

"I live in the eternal," he said to me with his wide, infectious grin and gleaming eyes that seem almost to pop out of his head. So I had to tell him about Italy, Fascism, Russia, and the war in all of which he seemed only mildly interested; time had ceased to mean anything to this man, who is a philosopher of the old tradition, living apart from the world.

"I've just been re-reading Racine and Dickens, because I've had no new books for years," he told me, "but they are new to me because they are eternal. There has been so much killing, so much suffering in the world's history! It is always the same."

I could see that it had all passed him by (quite literally, in that particular period) as sounds in the street to one safely at home—in this case his last earthly home. "I shall never leave here," he said to me. He had just finished the second volume of his autobiography, and he showed me the typescript. It has since appeared under the title, *The Middle Span.* The third and last volume was completed before I left Rome, but he told me he would not permit it to be published until after his death, because it contained the names of too many living persons.

He asked me whether Russia was really going nationalist. I answered, at some length, in the affirmative, with qualifications and distinctions, and he remarked that personally he had no feeling, either of opposition or approval, concerning Communism or Fascism. "Doubtless there are good things in both, as well as bad," he went on. "I think it is right that there should be new movements, suitable to new generations and periods. They shock and disturb those who are attached to old institutions, but they are not meant for such persons. It is true that although the Communists and Fascists intend to be 'for the people,' they end up by being for those men who are running the state.

"The trouble with applying Fascism to Italy is that the people are undisciplined. They often make good Fascists, from eighteen to twenty-five, but after that they become individualists again. One can say that they are not on a high enough social level to become good Fascists."

He asked me to lend him my book on Fascism, which I took to him the next time I saw him. A few weeks later, on another visit, he returned it, saying that it had taught him much about the history of Fascism but, "of course, I would not agree with your analysis in the last half of the book" (which is concerned with a critical account of the decline and evils of Fascism). In his talks with me he never hid his sympathy with the movement, and one day said that perhaps he felt that way because he was Spanish and naturally inclined to authoritarianism.

Indeed, Spain was the only contemporary question in which he showed keen interest, without knowing what was happening there, or (in my opinion) realizing what the Civil War had meant or what Franco stood for. He felt sure that the British were backing Don Juan for king. However, even Spain was primarily a part of his autobiography, something that was alive in the past but was now only a memory.

Santayana used to reside at the old Hotel Bristol in Rome, during my first sojourns in the city, and he made it a place of pilgrimage for students and philosophers from all over the world. "That used to be a good hotel," he said, "but it declined, and I stayed on long after all the nice people had left—not that I ever saw them. I have always lived apart, and now I am so out of touch with things! A few months ago someone sent me a copy of the Harvard *Lampoon*. They must speak a different language now. I could not understand a single one of the jokes."

It was like visiting a ghost from my youth. You left the world when you entered the convent, and he was out of the world, too, but visiting him was pleasant and charming.

My researches into contemporary history were more fruitful, when judged by newspaper standards. I dug up things about the armistice with the Allies, the international crimes of Fascism, odds and ends about Mussolini, and, most sensational of all, the trial and execution of Ciano and others of the Fascist Grand Council who had dared to vote to overthrow the Duce.

That story had the quality of a Greek tragedy with Mussolini as an implacable, revengeful *deus ex machina*. "For those who had a sneaking liking for that debonair, sophisticated, hail fellow well met," I wrote in my dispatch concerning Ciano, "it is unpleasant to have to state that he did not behave well." At the trial he backed down ignominiously and tried to say that he did not want to ruin the Duce, that it was an error but not treachery, and that he wanted only "a wider national block intimately tied to Fascism." But the sentence of death was a foregone conclusion, although he could not believe it. In prison that night he wept hysterically while old General Emilio De Bono tried to calm him. In the morning he had to be dragged to the chair into which he was tied, and then shot in the back. Galeazzo Ciano, playboy of Fascism, had toyed lightly with his country's fate, but he valued his own life too highly to die with dignity and courage.

Later I unearthed facts which showed that he was a dyed-in-the-wool scoundrel and even an assassin. His were the orders which led to the assassination of Carlo and Nello Rosselli in France in June, 1937. He had a veritable "Black Chamber," connected with the Ministry of Foreign Affairs, which was guilty of all kinds of nefarious deeds and was involved in the assassination of King Alexander of Jugoslavia and Barthou. Ciano kept a diary in which is entered sensational material for historians of Fascism. His widow, Edda, daughter of Mussolini, fled to Switzerland with the only copy.

And, of course, the war went its slow, painful way. The Germans were withdrawing gradually. I was at the taking of Siena, with Reynolds and Eleanor Packard of the United Press. We had been interned there at the beginning of the war, and we wanted to have the satisfaction as well as pleasure of seeing the place and its people again. It was taken by the French. General de Montsabert, with whom I had dined the evening before, told me flatly that whatever happened he would not fire a shot into Siena. He knew every stone in it. So that lovely, medieval city was captured without a scratch on July 3. Siena and Assisi were the only towns of first-rate importance to come out unscathed in that entire region. The towns and cities of Tuscany suffered irreparable damage to their monuments, and I spent a great deal of time investigating what had happened to the art and culture of that cradle of the Renaissance.

Florence gave me a great shock when I went there after returning from the invasion of southern France. My story was the first to tell that the heart of that unique gem of a city was gone forever—its bridges and old palaces and winding, medieval streets around the Ponte Vecchio, the part that made Florence Florence to those who knew and loved her—although tourists will still find the famous monuments of their guide books.

One of my personal pleasures in Florence, aside from seeing my old friends alive and well, was to find Bernard Berenson, most famous of living art critics, safe and sound in his house at Settignano with its marvelous collection of art intact. It was a joy to sit before the fire and talk to that wise and charming old man, whose mind has become as enriched with age as his house has with the treasures of Italy.

Of all the Tuscan cities, Pisa was the most damaged. Not a single important monument escaped damage or destruction. Four shells from an American battery south of the Arno River landed on the roof of the Campo Santo, causing a fire which all but destroyed the great frescoes. It was perhaps the greatest single loss to art in Italy, where so much was lost.

My first story on Florence aroused the fury of Italians and Italian-sympathizers in the United States, because I said that history would forever condemn the Florentines for not having lifted a finger to save their great bridges and the heart of the old city. The Office of War Information later issued a story that four patriots tried to save the Ponte Santa Trinità—which may or may not have been true, but which did not alter the main fact that the partisans did not really defend their bridges. They were badly organized and undisciplined, and, as Berenson put it, they were not *passisti*—they had no feeling for the past. Later, as told in my stories, they had fought with great bravery and sacrificed many lives, perhaps as many as two hundred, fighting the Germans on the northern edge of the city. There was no lack of courage, but even there General Alexander was angry with them because their activity forced him to change his plans and go to their rescue. History, as I wrote, will have to lament the fact that the Florentine patriots were so brave and so futile.

We hit the Gothic Line, which ran along the mountain range south of the Po Valley, at the beginning of September, broke through it by the end of the month, and found that it meant nothing and we were still frustrated. Everywhere the Germans were fleeing back to their frontiers except in Italy, and there they held until nearly the end of the war. Clark, who was made commander of the 15th Army Group, containing both the 5th and 8th Armies, did not get the troops and matériel to drive the Germans north. Had ships been available for amphibious landings, Alexander and he could have cleared Italy much earlier. Some of his best divisions were taken away for the Southern France invasion, and were not replaced. He had to save up artillery shells for months before he could make his last offensive. These are things his critics should keep in mind. I have not the military knowledge wherewith to judge his skill as a commander, but it seemed to me, from what I saw, that he and his brilliant Chief of Staff, Major General Alfred M. Gruenther, did as good a job as possible under great handicaps.

Back in Rome—and in New York—coals of fire were being heaped upon my head for the stories I wrote about the lynching of the Vice Director of Regina Coeli jail, Donato Carretta, on September 18, 1944. The mob was out to get Pietro Caruso, Fascist Questor of Rome, who was to have been brought to trial that morning. The High Commission for the Punishment of Fascist Crimes had been shockingly frivolous in its precautions and preparations for the trial, and it even invited relatives of the Fosse Ardeatine victims to the Palace of Justice. The mob would have lynched Caruso if it could have got at him; instead, it lynched an innocent man, under conditions of the most sickening cowardice and atrocity. I happened to be the only correspondent to be an eye-witness, from beginning to end, and although I have seen much that was terrible in this past decade, and was hardened to bloodshed and brutality, I was shocked and infuriated—so much so, that I swore that morning to write a story which would forever blacken the name of contemporary Romans and do the Government as much harm as possible. The story almost burned through the paper on which it was printed. I remember having been so furious only once before, during the "blitz" of Barcelona on March 17-18, 1938, which I have described.

The average reader was shocked as much as I wanted him to be. Roosevelt and Churchill both issued stern warnings to the Bonomi Government that such things must not be permitted again, and in Rome the A.M.G. and the Allied Control Commission gave similar warnings. I had been the only outsider to see exactly what happened, although the official investigation later brought out all the facts, with exemplary frankness. However, that morning I was the one to go to Count Sforza, then High Commissioner, who dismayed me by the relative lightness with which he took the matter, and to Colonel Poletti, to tell them the entire story. So I suppose I did a lot of damage.

Before the smoke cleared away, a barrage descended on my head. My old friend Randolfo Pacciardi was warned that morning of my intention, and tried vainly to reach me by telephone to dissuade me. Being unable to do so, he replied, in advance, in one of his brilliant editorials in the *Voce Repubblicano,* asserting that "some foreign newspapermen, and among them some who had understood everything in Europe, the Spanish Revolution, the Jugoslav radical revolt and the present sanguinary installation of the Fourth French Republic, but who never understood that even Italians have blood and souls, were horrified by the Carretta episode, and in their dispatches will cause further harm to our poor country." He meant me.

The *New York Times* was deluged with letters, and printed one complaining of my smugness and inability to write a detached story. The writer explained that it was natural to expect an overwrought, embittered people to give vent to their righteous wrath, and journalists were wrong not to take such things into consideration.

It was agreed (with one exception) that the lynching was a bad thing morally, both that particular one and lynching in general, but it was felt that the attitude of the Romans should have been understood. The exception was the Communist organ, *Unità*. For the Italian Communists the mob is always right, which is one reason that Communism in Italy made such a consistently bad impression upon me.

The day after the lynching I had calmed down, and felt a little contrite. To be fair, I sent the greater part of Pacciardi's editorial, but the next day there was space in the paper for only half of my dispatch, and that in the first edition only. In general, however, I felt that my story was completely justified, and I would do it again. My critics were overlooking a simple matter of logic—you cannot condemn something in general and condone it in particular. If lynching is bad, as they all admitted, then the lynching of Carretta was bad. Moreover, it was easy for men, sitting comfortably 3,000 miles away over their newspapers and their bacon, eggs and coffee for breakfast, to say that I should have been cool and impartial. They seemed to forget that even correspondents can be human, and that under the emotional strain of seeing anything as bestial as the way in which Carretta was lynched, it was hardly possible to be cool. Had someone put a pistol to Carretta's head and shot him, it would have been different. On that day I took it for granted that Carretta was guilty and deserved to be killed. It was the way in which he was killed, and the shocking lack of governmental authority, which I was criticizing. Later the official investigation established Carretta's innocence, the report saying that he even took "the gravest risks to favor political prisoners."

The whole incident was, among other things, an illuminating lesson in journalism and ethics. It showed the influence of personality upon news. Perhaps it also showed that I am becoming too moral in my middle age, and am not making sufficient allowances for human failings. Later it also sickened me to read about the way in which the Milanese mob treated Mussolini's body after patriots had courageously, and deservedly, executed him. I see no reason to condone such things, especially as it was the same mob which for years cheered and saluted the Duce. Roman mobs have not changed since the days of Coriolanus, and, while one should not expect them to change, I cannot see why bestiality should not be condemned and fought wherever or whenever it occurs. If that be "smugness and hypocrisy," I must plead guilty.

I was feeling very thoughtful in those days of violence and justice, and keenly conscious of the fact that I was witnessing something typical of the world in which we are living—a world of violence and political justice. Perhaps that is why the execution of Pietro Caruso, the hated Questor of Rome who had delivered fifty hostages to the Germans to be shot in the Fosse Ardeatine, moved me so deeply. He was not conscious of having done wrong, and nothing could have been more typical of the moral decay induced by the totalitarian mentality than that. His excuse was that he was simply obeying orders and carrying out the job to which he had been assigned by the State. Millions of Nazis and Fascists have made the same excuse, and in all sincerity. The State, the totalitarian system, is always right. Those who execute its orders have no moral responsibility; they are merely functionaries, carrying out orders as soldiers would do, for they must obey. Such is the argument, and I was convinced, after attending the trial each day, that Caruso sincerely believed he had done no wrong. I do not think that anything else so impressed me with the evil of Fascism and the totalitarian way of life than that realization. On a much greater scale, it explained why and how men such as Quisling, Henlein and Pétain had no consciousness of having done wrong.

Curiously enough, the case of Caruso taught me another lesson for which I shall always be grateful. I am going to tell you the story of his execution exactly as I sent it to *The New York Times* —partly so that you will understand what the lesson was, and partly because I want to offer it, without any modesty, as one of the best stories I have ever written. At any rate, I thought so at the time, and I am willing to stand by it and present it for judgment as a test of journalistic experience in covering a specific story within the limitations of time and space of the daily dispatch. There was no room in the next day's newspaper to print it nearly in full, and I supose that as far as the Cable Desk was concerned, it was just another execution. To me, it was an unforgettable experience.

"At 2:08 P.M., under such a blue sky as only the Roman countryside can provide, Pietro Caruso was shot in the back, expiating as bravely as any human being ever could those terrible crimes he had committed in the name of Fascism," I wrote. "Justice at the end was quick and merciful. Only a few peasants in scattered houses around the medieval Fort Bravetta on the Aurelian Way knew what was happening and they smiled when the hearse with his body was later driven from the grounds.

"About a dozen newspapermen and an equal number of American and British photographers were present, aside from officials, officers and soldiers. Lieutenant Colonel Harry Pollock, A.M.G. police chief, and his assistant, Major Percy E. Coxhead, as well as three British officers, represented the Allies.

"It was a terrible thing to have to see, but the world is like that now and one should look at it with open eyes. Many, many thousands of men and women are going to die in Europe even before this year ends, just about as Caruso died today. As his trial and the mob killing of the innocent Donato Carretta before it were symptomatic of the new world we live in, so was Caruso's execution today. Who knows how many of us who write this story today and read it tomorrow are going to be stood up against walls some day and shot?

"Now what Italians are waiting anxiously to see is whether the Fascist Republican threat to shoot forty hostages for Caruso will be carried out. One of those hostages, said the German Transocean Agency yesterday, is José Togliatti, brother of the Roman Communist Minister Without Portfolio.

"Fort Bravetta is one of a ring of ancient fortresses around Rome that in recent generations have been used for training purposes and to store munitions. It stands on one of those rolling hills, three miles to the northwest of Rome, and often in the past it has been used for executions. In fact, it looked as if it had been used recently, for the ground behind the fatal chair was torn with many bullet marks.

"You might have thought it was just an ordinary, cheaply made wooden chair, except for the crossboard at the top which had a 'U' shaped dip where one who might be prostrate or faint could lay his head. It was not necessary today, not for Caruso, who lived badly but died magnificently.

"It was a flat, wide segment of a circle formed by old stables on one side and breastworks on the other in which Caruso died. His chair was placed at the foot of a solid dirt bank that looked like a huge golf bunker, 30 feet high and perhaps twice as wide.

"No doubt it was especially hard to die on a day like this, which was a bright, beautiful, slightly cool day with just a touch of autumn in the air. The Roman countryside could not have been more lovely. So perhaps we journalists who prolonged his life some twenty minutes need not have felt remorseful. There had been some misunderstanding. An official from the *Questura* came along to say that without authorization from the Minister of Justice there could not be any witnesses. It took some time to get Minister Tupini on the telephone and straighten things out.

"Caruso could not see the countryside, however. He was at that time seated in a closed, gray, hearselike police van with only a small grille at the back, and in with him were a dozen metropolitan police and the Regina Coeli prison chaplain. The priest was like a ministering angel. We could see that when they came out and in what followed.

"The prison van came around the breastwork and drove some

ten yards beyond the chair. Behind it was an open bus with two platoons of armed *carabinieri* who had followed Caruso from the time they took him out of Regina Coeli. That was two minutes to two, which gave Caruso just ten minutes to live.

"A platoon of twenty *carabinieri* under two officers had been waiting since one o'clock behind the bunker and now they marched out in a column of twos. As they approached the spot, the doors in the rear of the van opened and the metropolitan police tumbled out, one carrying Caruso's crutches. They were ordered over to the other side, and the one with the crutches stupidly followed, so when Caruso was helped out he had to stand a moment on his broken leg without them.

"That was when we saw how calm he was. During the trial his face had been haggard and strained but now it was different. He looked like a man who had paid his price and won peace of mind with it.

"The guard ran over at last with the crutches and Caruso put them under his arms. He was not going to be like Ciano, whose execution in Verona he, himself, had supervised, and who had to be dragged to the chair. He gave the crutches gently to the guard, put his hands on the back of the chair and tried his best to get astride it, but his broken left leg would not go well and a *carabiniere* had to help him get it settled.

"They tied him in place, first his legs, then a cord twice tightly around his chunky body in that same crumpled blue suit he had worn at his trial. He watched them do it and helped as much as he could. It was then that the priest went around and stood in front of him behind the chair. It was a young priest, bareheaded, in a black cassock with a gold and magenta stole. He put his hands gently on Caruso's cheeks and Italy's first great war criminal looked up at him. The priest's hands went to Caruso's shoulders in a soothing gesture, and we could see they were talking. Twice the chaplain pressed his crucifix to Caruso's lips.

"The cords were tied and a man went up to the chair with a sash to blindfold Caruso. He shook his head, and the man stepped back. Caruso looked again at the priest and must have asked, for the chaplain again extended his crucifix. We could sense that they were saying together the last 'act of sorrow.'

"The time had come. The priest, still praying, backed slowly away, Caruso's head turning avidly for a last look at the extended cross. Then his last comfort on earth was beyond his vision.

"His voice rang out so clearly and loudly that it startled us. '*Viva l'Italia!*'

"The *carabinieri* lieutenant drew his sword and gave an order to the two ranks of police lined up not more than five yards behind the chair. Caruso turned his head to the right as far as he could. '*Mirate bene!*' ['Aim well!'] he said firmly.

"They did—fourteen through the back, six at his head, and it sounded like one shot. His brains were literally blown out, and we could see spurts of dust behind the chair where the bullets hit after going through him. At least, there is no quicker or more merciful way to die.

"His body slumped over to the right and the weight on the cords made him bob up and down slightly as if still alive, so that someone thought the *coup de grace* might be necessary. But he was truly dead and the prison doctor so pronounced him.

"The gray van had driven away and now its place was taken by a black hearse, whose doors quickly opened and a few men began taking out a plain, rough pinewood coffin which seemed too small and flimsy for the thick body they were now gingerly untying from the reddened chair. But they squeezed him into it, shoveled up his brains from the dirt and threw them into the coffin, too, and took the chair away. It came to pieces because the legs were buried in the ground.

"The priest knelt beside the open coffin and prayed, and at 2:14 they put the cover on. A few of us went up to the chaplain and asked what Caruso had said while he sat in the chair. 'He asked forgiveness for his sins,' the priest told us, 'and he said: "I only hope my death will be of some use to Italy."'

"I happened to drive out just behind the hearse and the van of *carabinieri*. A group of peasants lined the road outside, and in front of every gate and every house were other groups of people, mostly women and children, but also men, and everybody smiled when the hearse went by. Those who walked along did not salute, Fascist style, as Caruso would have expected some time back. Only one old priest raised his broadbrimmed black hat. Everybody else smiled, like the Roman countryside and the sun and the fleecy clouds and the blue sky.

"They drove the hearse past the Basilica of Saint Peter's and then turned toward Regina Coeli prison. Caruso was going to an appropriate last home."

(Back home, on the desk in New York, I know they were shocked and perhaps amused by my suggesting that. any of our readers might be stood up against a wall some day and shot, and, of course, that passage was deleted. Perhaps some of the readers of this book feel the same way. But it was not silly. Never think so—for, if you do, you do not understand what is happening in this world and what Fascism, Nazism, and Communism have made of justice. Caruso died because he was a criminal Fascist, but men and women have died by the thousands and millions, and will die, because of their political beliefs. You and I, who are, let us say, democrats and liberals, could conceivably some day find ourselves opposed to some new form of Fascism or to Communism—and for *that,* people are shot.)

But that was not the lesson I had in mind. Strange and sentimental though it may seem, Caruso taught me how a brave man can die. He was a beast and a criminal, and he deserved to be shot, but no man could have died with more courage and serenity of spirit. It seemed so easy. When he waved away that bandage I thought of "Prospice":

> I would hate that death bandaged my eyes, and forbore,
> And bade me creep past.

He made it seem so easy to die! He stepped from life into death as one would cross a threshold from a harrowing world outside into the peace and quiet of home. I only wish that when my time comes I can behave half as well as did that despicable brute, Pietro Caruso.

The Lesson of Fascism

Wₕₐₜ the chronicle of Rome needed in those months after liberation was not a journalist, but another Ferdinand Gregorovius to write a history that would parallel, in an astonishing number of respects, his *History of Rome in the Middle Ages.* The whole of liberated Italy provided the same picture of misery and lawlessness—natural and understandable enough, but none the less distressing. Romans were wretched, and the most characteristic and famous expression of their bitterness came, appropriately enough, from the slum district of Trastevere. Someone painted on a wall: *Arivolemo er puzzone,* which, literally translated, means, "We want the 'stinker' back." The "stinker" was Mussolini.

By that time the word "liberation" had become a mockery. Throughout the war well-meaning Americans and Britishers really believed that Italians and others should have been thankful for having their countries used as battlefields and turned into shambles. Had we looked upon this as punishment and retribution for shameful policies, it would have made sense, but to go into Italy, destroy it, and then tell the people they ought to be grateful, was hypocrisy. The cynical usage of the word "liberation" showed what everyone thought of it. When an automobile was sequestrated or a house requisitioned we said we had "liberated" it. When a town was ground into dust and the inhabitants no longer had houses, shops, churches or monuments, then we said that town was truly "liberated." The people had nothing left and nothing to do; they were indeed free.

There was no need to wonder why the Italians were not grateful and why the picture that we drew was one of riots and bloodshed, black markets and thievery, and widespread immorality. There was a desperate economic situation, with industry paralyzed, prices skyrocketing and a currency inflation that became daily more perilous. Our military occupation necessarily increased the economic distress, although we were bringing in a certain amount of food. An unfortunate promise by President Roosevelt to raise the bread ration from 200 to 300 grams was not fulfilled for four months, despite his definite orders. What was even more unfortunate, although obviously unavoidable, was the fact that Italians in the German-occupied zone were living better than in the Allied zone.

Allied political policy was in no sense calculated to encourage the resurgent democratic and liberal forces, as I have written. "You are driving us into the arms of Russia," one cabinet minister said to me. Italian spirits became so low that when the British editor of the P.W.B. newspaper, *Corriere di Roma,* asked me for an article, I wrote one on the theme, "We have not forgotten." I mentioned Italy's contributions to culture, the charm and the goodness of her people, the nobility of her anti-Fascists, the strategic position of Italy in the Mediterranean, and other assets of the Italians.

"Italy has her contribution to make in the post-war world," I concluded. "She is not going to be isolated. She is needed. Your great assets, tangible and intangible, will not be lost unless you throw them away. . . . Do not believe that the world is against you and that we have forgotten all that Italy has meant and all she can still mean. And never for one moment believe that Italians have not great and powerful friends everywhere, who want to help and who look forward to the day when Italy will be one of us again, respected, strong, beloved."

I was not being only sentimental, for I believed what I wrote. Even the British, who dominated the Allied Commission and were blocking every move in favor of Italy, were only responding to a hostile public opinion in which most of the political leaders (Anthony Eden was an exception) did not share. We saw at the end of the campaign how the British rushed troops into Trieste, in an effort to save that great port, if not for Italy, at least for western Europe and the British Empire. Manifest destiny will again some day make Italy and England friends and allies.

But in the fall and winter of 1944 in Rome every politically conscious Italian who knew what was happening behind the scenes was anti-British. Mussolini was having his last fling in the north, and made an outstanding speech in Milan on December 16 to a large and enthusiastic Milanese mob, some of whom four months later were to defile his dead body. For my sins I have had to read all his speeches, and I have no hesitation in saying it was one of the best he ever made. That was the time Von Rundstedt made the last, desperate German counteroffensive in the Ardennes, with its initial successes. In Rome there were so many evidences of renascent Fascism that everyone was asking whether there was not a real fifth column operating. Fascism was not dead in Italy at the end of 1944, and do not be so naive as to believe that it died a sudden death in April, 1945.

I went up to Florence and the front, for Christmas. It snowed heavily up in the high Apennines beyond Futa Pass, just south of Bologna, so the landscape looked like a postcard, on Christmas Eve—but it did not feel much like it. My dispatch on Christmas Day was not very full of Christmas spirit, perhaps partly because I had contracted a streptococcus infection of the throat in Florence on the way.

"There is no use writing wishwash about this particular Christmas in the Apennines," I radioed *The Times*. "It is one helluva Christmas and why not say so? It is bitter cold and dull and forgotten, and it is far away from home. Yet these bare, forbidding mountains, with their snow and icy winds are strangely and pathetically full of Christmas spirit. One could find no stronger tribute to the appeal of this holiday than the fact that men who might logically be bitter and sarcastic about Christmas are somehow celebrating it today cheerfully and enthusiastically."

Then I went off to the hospital, where I discovered that penicillin is really all it is cracked up to be. And then I went to Sicily to do a series of stories on that unhappy island. I found a grave situation, what with crime, the reawakened Mafia, and the Separatist movement which had become very powerful. It was a seething cauldron in which Sicilians were being allowed to stew in their own juice, with little help or control from the Allies or the Bonomi Government.

On the way back to Rome I stopped off in Naples and dropped in to have a talk with Croce—a very different Croce from the one I had seen in Capri a year and a half previously. This was an old, tired, and unhappy man.

"Dear Matthews," he said, "I have done what I could in this world, and I am entitled now to close my eyes. In a few weeks I shall be seventy-nine. I am going on working all the time, because it is an old habit and I must work, for if I stop for a little while and think about the state of affairs now, I cannot stand it. When I think of the Italy that I saw created in the 70's and 80's! It was a good Italy. There were difficulties and there were bad things about it, but we went ahead, struggling and creating. We quarreled, and people even fought duels. It was a survival of the old, chivalric ideas. And now—

"The worst thing about Fascism is what it has done to us morally. The youth of Italy are good, but they have an ignorance of things that we took for granted which is frightening. The men of forty or forty-five are all right because they were brought up in an era when decency and morality still counted."

Croce was then being strongly attacked in the United States by the eccentric Salvemini-Borgese group, and he was bitter about that, also. He felt very profoundly that this was no longer his world, and work was his only consolation—work, and that charming family of his. "What is there left for me to do," he said as I bade him good-bye, "except the final sleep?" He was like the one whom George Meredith wrote about who had learned "to walk gently in a world where the lights are dim and the very stars wander." The lights of the world are now garish. They are not good for old eyes.

Curiously enough, I had that same impression of discouragement and helplessness when I saw Pope Pius XII in a long, private audience before I left Rome—except that His Holiness had, of course, a religious faith which sustained and inspired him with hope, and the skeptical Croce could not have a similar inspiration. This Pontiff is going to be the center of great controversy in the years and centuries to come. I have heard him strongly criticized by Catholics in Rome, and even by priests of the Holy See, for having been so completely diplomatic during the war and holding the scales even as between the Axis and the United Nations. Fascism, in all its forms, threatened to be an even greater anti-Christian force than Communism. The Church has taken a strong, open stand against Communism, but it never has done so against Fascism. I can see the practical reasons for that, and there is no reason to doubt that the Pope was, personally and behind the scenes, anti-Fascist, yet I, like millions of others, could only feel discouraged that the most important religious figure in the world felt it was not desirable or possible to condemn in public an evil which he deplored in private.

The difficulty (although it may seem paradoxical and sentimental to say so) is that Pius XII's character has all those elements which in the course of time will almost certainly lead to his sanctification. No one can question his piety, goodness, humility, charity, self-sacrifice and other characteristics which go to make up a saint. However, a saint in this wicked world is about as much at home as a man from Mars and when you are dealing with men like Hitler, Mussolini, Franco, Pétain, and their ilk, it is not saintliness you need, but the whip which drove the money-changers out of the temple.

Now that the Fascist governments have been ground into the dust (although Fascism as an ideology is by no means dead) Pius can concentrate on Communism which, as everybody must know, is the chief worry of the Catholic Church at the present time. Here the Pope is on firmer ground and his diplomatic skill is highly necessary. From the doctrinal point of view he need only fall back upon condemnations that started with Pius IX when Marx, so to speak, was a pup. But diplomatically it has been necessary not to antagonize Stalin, who now has under him many millions of Roman Catholic Poles, Lithuanians, Croats, and the like, and who has been busily organizing the various Orthodox churches for political purposes.

In Italy, however, since the Pope is Bishop of Rome, there was no difficulty in condemning Communism. A number of young intellectuals tried to foster a "Catholic Communist" movement, and were firmly squelched.

The Communist Party in Italy has not been calculated to rejoice the heart of anyone like me who hopes to see the country take the road of liberalism—but, then, they would not be Communists if they did so. Of course, they claim to be within the democratic fold, but what a Communist understands by "democracy" is vastly different from the modern tradition of democracy of Europe and the United States. So long as you define your terms you can call yourself anything. Professor Giovanni Gentile, the Italian philosopher, actually demonstrated to his own and others' satisfaction that Fascism was truly liberal. Nevertheless, both democracy and liberalism have certain rather definite modern connotations—and they do not fit either Communism or Fascism.

The Communist Party in Italy, even under the mild and conservative rule of Palmiro Togliatti, pursued policies directed against freedom of the press, speech, and meeting, for a party militia and a politically controlled army, in favor of the masses, or even the mob, in every circumstance, and, in general, followed the rigid dogmatic faith and principles of their creed, regardless of the right or wrong of a particular development. I am not registering surprise because they did so, but I am merely saying that as a liberal and a friend of Italy, I would not care to see the country go in that direction, and I presume most Americans would feel the same way.

The danger of Italy's going Communist is considerable, although it has been exaggerated abroad. The movement is not winning a broad mass basis, but it has skillful and well financed leadership, and it may easily develop the same sort of "mass of maneuver" which the Fascisti built up between 1919 and 1922. The Italian people are as little suited to Communism as any other in Europe—but they were little suited to Fascism, and they fell for that. It is, naturally, much easier to go from one authoritarian movement to another than it is to go from Fascism to liberalism or democracy as we understand it.

The Italian Communist Party, which only assumed importance with the arrival of the Moscow-trained Togliatti at the beginning of 1944, has not tried to seize political power, although at all times it held the dominating position in the successive Badoglio Bonomi governments. It began by supporting and bolstering the King and Badoglio, and only gradually extricated itself from that anomalous position. It is still nominally on the fence with regard to the Monarchy, but a controversy over an interview I had with Prince Humbert forced their organ, *Unità,* to proclaim the essential republicanism of the Communist movement.

Its support has, if anything, been an embarrassment to the throne, since a monarchy can and does exist with all forms of democracies as well as with absolute governments—as witness England, Norway, Sweden, and Denmark—but it is a contradiction in terms to have a Communist monarchy. It was inevitable that the anti-Communist and anti-revolutionary forces should be among those to rally around the Lieutenant General, Prince Humbert.

In the interview, published on November 1, 1944, which Humbert gave to me and which has become a historic document since it was an extremely carefully formulated statement of the Crown's position, the Lieutenant General said that the Monarchy in Italy must move to the left, even, if necessary, as far as Socialism. However, one might as well expect to see a Communist pope as a Communist king.

That interview, which caused me more trouble to get than any other in my career, incidentally contributed greatly to the government crisis of November 26. Through gross carelessness and a breach of confidence on the part of the Allied Control Commission's press bureau, it was divulged that Premier Bonomi had seen the text and had passed on it before publication, although he had previously denied having done so. The resulting furor, added to other factors, was enough to send his first ministry toppling. I and *The New York Times* were exonerated of any blame, but it was a highly embarrassing incident.

It showed the extraordinary touchiness of the monarchial question, among other things. However, by that time (the end of

November, 1944) Humbert had greatly strengthened his position. He had spent the intervening months since the liberation of Rome wisely and well, on the whole, and had gained a certain amount of respect from a number of politicians, as well as a considerable popular following. In view of his reputation, I was frankly surprised—and I said so—to find him intelligent, well-informed, and quite determined to put up a terrific scrap for his throne. My interview dismayed his opponents because it showed a carefully worked out and highly intelligent program to save the House of Savoy. Personally, I did not care one way or another whether it helped or harmed him. That was not my business. I wanted the readers of *The New York Times* to get a presentation of the Crown's case, just as I had given them the republican side.

What was more important than having surprised me was the fact that Humbert has been surprising a lot of important Italians, not to mention foreigners. However, the monarchy in Italy has only a slim chance of survival. King Victor Emmanuel once told Theodore Roosevelt, who visited Italy after his presidential terms: "I am raising my son in such a way that he can be president of the Italian Republic."

That was a wise father, in some ways, but if there is a republic it will be because of the political sins of that father. Humbert's hardest task will be to make Italians forget and forgive the past, in which his own role was far from creditable. His next hardest task will be to fight off support from elements tied to that past—men seeking a haven of safety in a revolutionary storm. He can use the support of the vested interests of church, aristocracy, land, and industry, but, as he himself put it, he cannot build a safe structure without moving to the left.

It will be extremely difficult to hew to that line, nor will it be possible, really to shake off the past. Nothing has been so pathetically futile in this era of liberation as seeing Italy try to "epurate" herself of Fascism and the Fascists. It is like a man trying to cure himself of tuberculosis over night.

Victor Emmanuel Orlando, last surviving member of the "Big Four," of Versailles, held that Italy never became Fascist in the sense that Germany became Nazi. The Allies were wrong in thinking that Fascism had been strong in Italy and must be eradicated. There was nothing to eradicate. The falseness of that belief was complete, as was Orlando's identification of Fascism with dictatorship, tyranny, and intolerance, not with a philosophical or political system. Yet the old man (he was then 85) was not in his second childhood, but, on the contrary, retained an extraordinary keenness and vigor.

Where Orlando was on solid ground was in his basic tolerance. He is a liberal from way back, and he holds that everyone is entitled to his political opinions. If a man was a Fascist at a time when everybody else was, it is juridically inadmissible now to say that such an attitude was illegal and hence punishable. Punitive laws of that sort, Orlando told me one day, would be his idea of Fascism. He took the line that for the next fifty years Italy would be faced with the problem of survival, and a multitude of political parties, with their varied programs, was a luxury which Italy could not afford. In short, his plea was "forgive and forget"—which, as a general principle, was not unwise.

There was a great deal of wishful thinking and rationalization going on in Italy, involving some of the best minds in the country. It was an effort, conscious or otherwise, to escape responsibility for Fascism and the crimes committed in its name. There were two theses. One was the Orlando theme that Italy never really was Fascist; the other was put forth by returned exiles such as the Socialist, Pietro Nenni, and the Republican, Randolfo Pacciardi, which held that they and other high-principled, brave Italians who consistently fought Fascism were the real representatives of Italy during those twenty-two years, and that the country was with them. Hence, punish the Fascisti but do not punish Italy.

Neither thesis had any basis in fact, nor, to my mind, was there more validity in Croce's efforts to demonstrate that Fascism was a passing fancy in Italy which had been cured. He claimed in an article written at my request for *The New York Times* that "Fascism is not definable according to a determined political idea, because it has no such idea and boasts of having none, being a revolution which leads to a realized idea and which gives itself a system, but of being a revolution that continues to infinity." For me—with all due respect to a very great thinker—this is incorrect, and the facts have proved it to be so. Fascism is definable, and it survives because it is a determined political idea and force. The Fascisti boasted of their lack of a system (Mussolini said a system would be a "shirt of Nessus") only while the Duce was feeling his way, hit or miss, to the finished expression of those feelings and desires of the twentieth century of which Fascism was the result. In the end, Mussolini was strangled by the very "shirt of Nessus" he himself wove.

To me, after all those years in Italy, nothing could be further from the mark than to say, as Croce does, "And now Italy is free of the Fascist infection, and although still in grave danger she can die any kind of death but no longer that death." Fascism is not dead in Italy or in the world, and of all the lessons I learned in the war and in these years of work, the most important is precisely this survival of Fascism, which, being totalitarian, must be linked to the triumph of that other totalitarian concept, so much like it and yet so very different, Communism.

However, Croce does admit that "the ideological danger of Fascism persists" and that men are still "prepared to adopt Fascist methods," and he concluded his article by saying that Fascism should not be judged as a *morbus italicus* but as a "contemporary sickness which Italy was the first to suffer."

So, then, what is Fascism? I caused some heartburnings in Italy by preaching my conviction that Fascism still survived, and it would be a grave danger for Italy or the world to lay down the arms that had been taken up to fight it. A monthly called *Mercurio* printed an article of mine on the subject which aroused an enormous amount of controversy. I had written much the same article for *The New York Times*.

"My thesis, years ago, was that Fascism was a natural development in Italy and the world," I said. "My thesis, now, is that Fascism still survives in Italy and will continue to plague you for at least another generation. I believe it is wishful thinking for your statesmen and political leaders to claim that Fascism has disappeared from liberated Italy and that it will from the northern zone as soon as it is freed. You and I and everybody in the world who have any claim to being liberals or democrats will be fighting Fascism all our lives. It is our *mal de siècle*. When Mussolini said that 'this is the century of Fascism' he was right to a considerable extent, even if he was wrong in thinking that Fascism would triumph. The year 1348 was your year of the plague, and to have called it that, in those dreadful months, would not have meant praise of disease. Fascism is the plague of the twentieth century, and if you start from the comfortable thesis that it has gone because you have chased Mussolini out of the Palazzo Venezia, or have six parties instead of one, or have waved a magic wand called 'democracy,' the chances are only too great that you will fall from one kind of dictatorship to another, from one form of totalitarianism to another.

"That mouth-filling word 'defascistization' is not only hard to say; it is infinitely harder to do, and I do not need to tell you that. Like all foreigners here I have watched with mingled sympathy and dismay your efforts at epuration. They are not succeeding and it is my personal opinion that they never will, except in odd cases and superficially, and that is because complete epuration is impossible. It is always possible to cure a disease by killing the patient, but not even another Black Plague could kill enough Italians to rid you of Fascism.

"It is not for an outsider like myself to deliver a lecture on the deep roots of Fascism in Italy, but nobody who studies your history from—let us say—Cola di Rienzi to Crispi, or reads your philosophers from Machiavelli to Gentile, can escape the conclusion that Fascism was to a certain extent a natural phenomenon in Italy. Moreover, I must repeat, Fascism is a world force. As has happened before in history it was for Italian genius (in this case an evil genius) to give expression to a powerful and previously unformed urge of the contemporary spirit."

I did not claim for one moment that we Allies had been particularly intelligent, sensible or practical about it. We started out happily from the principle that if we eliminated the Fascist Party structure, put the hierarchs in jail, suppressed various associations, administrations, syndicates, and organizations, abolished racist laws, and then shouted from the housetops that Fascism was dead, it would really go to some lonely cave and die. But all these things are only the trappings of Fascism!

Why say that a Fascist was a man who made the March on Rome, and so forth? A man could have done that, sincerely and patriotically, in a mistaken idea of what Fascism would do and bring to Italy, and then, with equal honesty, could have changed his mind when he understood. Why should it be taken for granted that a Fascist was an evil man and an anti-Fascist a good man?

"It is my contention (and I fully appreciate the bitterness of this statement)," I said at the conclusion of my article in *Mercurio*, "that twenty-two years of Fascism, of which sixteen were totalitarian, have left a mark on the vast majority of Italians up to the age of, say, forty-five, which can never be erased. As the Allies advanced northward we found everybody to be self-proclaimed anti-Fascists. Thousands posed as martyrs; all told how they really at heart never believed in Fascism, which for most of them was true. But genuine, active anti-Fascists were very few. The Communists in twenty-two years did nothing of any importance in the underground movement until the overthrow of Mussolini, and the other parties did less.

"Now, many of these genuine anti-Fascists, some of whom are returned exiles, protest that Italy must not be confused with Fascism, that Fascism represented a small clique of criminals and did not represent Italy. History will not support that contention, nor does any objective observation of Italy today support the contention that Fascism has disappeared. It has not, and it is going to take a generation of Italians, led by high-minded men such as Croce, Bonomi, Sforza, Casati and younger ones like Carandini, Saragat, Fenoaltea, Pesenti, La Malfa, Pacciardi, Vinciguerra (just to pick some names at random) to bring Italy back to its rightful place in the European comity of nations.

"It is not easy to restore health to the body politic when it has suffered such a disease as Fascism, which has left you a legacy of corruption, moral rottenness and the inability to think for one-self. This, surely, was the greatest crime of Fascism."

But let us retrace our steps, and see if we can find out what Fascism is. The eighteenth-century Germans invented the word "superman" and its modern connotation of a man above and beyond humanity who yet condescends to put his genius at the service (at least theoretically) of the people. That idea reached its most brilliant exposition in the philosophical works of Fried-rich Nietzsche in the next century. One of Hitler's last gifts to Mussolini in the violent sunset of the two dictators, was a copy of Nietzsche's works.

"In reality," wrote the distinguished Italian philosopher, Prof. Guido de Ruggero, in an article commemorating the centenary of Nietzsche's birth, "one can excavate a gospel, and at the same time an apocalypse of Nazism, from the works of Nietzsche. The repudiation of Christianity as a morality of slaves which weakens the satanic and heroic pride of man in preaching goodness and love of one's neighbors; the disdain for democracy as a triumph of mediocrity and a leveling of the will to power and the vital force which lifts the caste of rulers from the common herd; the anxious search for a new morality, 'beyond good and evil,' which consecrates the right of the strong to crush the weak, and which had as its distinctive mark 'faith in oneself, pride, an immense and ironical aversion for altruism'; the final Dionysiac orgy of one who believes he has discovered that 'life is essentially viola-tion, appropriation, the subjection of all that is foreign and weak, the imposition of one's own form'; this stormy sap of Nietzscheanism entered into the blood of Nazism and fed its mad energy."

Authoritarianism is a principle as old as the hills, older than the Catholic Church, which is authoritarian; as old as kings and tribal chieftains. The military men have been the great ex-ponents of authority throughout history. They demand and en-force order and civic peace as the end of government. It was on the principle of order that Generalissimo Franco built his fol-lowing and won his victory—only to find that order without life, order imposed from above and not coming from the sense of civic duties and the patriotism of the people, is a mockery. Anarchism goes to the opposite extreme, holding authoritarianism to be "the most flagrant, most cynical and most complete denial of humanity." The liberal wants authority, supports it, and demands that it be placed at the service of the best interests of the community. But for the Fascist, authority, imposed through the instruments of fear and violence and by means of hierarchical discipline, is the framework within which the internal and external policies of the state move. It is both an end and a means.

To digress slightly—let us keep in mind that Fascism uses two elements of society, the reactionary forces and a "mass of maneuver" composed of the dissatisfied, anti-social forces of the moment. The reactionary forces are the so-called vested interests —large landowners, big industrialists, aristocracy, monarchy, and even the Church. To them rally all those who fear a Communist or Socialist revolution or chaos. The "mass of maneuver" has been made up of soldiers unable or unwilling to return to the humdrum existence of civil life, of the discontented, economically ruined bourgeoisie, of unemployed workers, of the hungry, miserable, and desperate.

In short, it is the mixture of certain common and ancient characteristics with certain peculiar ones that makes Fascism unique. There is an exaltation of the "State," which upon analysis proves to be a group of men, headed by a leader—Duce, Fuehrer, Generalissimo, Poglavnik, or whatever he is called. Their aim is not wealth for themselves, but power and the aggrandizement of their country.

The technique they use is totalitarian—the control of the armed forces and police, of every branch of government, of all modes of expression (press, radio, speech, public meeting, books), of education and the professions, of every part of the civil services, of big industry and economy in general. Fascism has a one-party system, which furnishes the man-power and hierarchy for this control.

These are the outer trappings, the framework, the structure, the instruments of Fascism and we can—and doubtless shall, in time—destroy them. But the heart of Fascism does not lie in such externals, and it will continue to beat. The externals are expressions of deep-rooted impulses, philosophies, and historical traditions. The haphazard way in which Mussolini built up the Fascist structure deceived many into believing that it was mere opportunism and would change with any wind. However, the changes were only the tacking and filling of a boat going toward a shore in the face of a storm. Mussolini was, in those formative years, partly the shrewd appraiser of opportunities and partly the puppet of great historic forces that drove him inevitably in their way. No one has yet made a comprehensive study of the philosophical background of Fascism. The road is a long and fascinating one, through the precursors of Romanticism and the Romantics themselves, through the German philosophers of the mid-nineteenth century to such diverse thinkers as De Gobineau, Sorel, Pareto, Houston Chamberlain, and Haushofer. The first World War broke down barriers of security and morality which had made nineteenth-century liberalism possible, and out of the pieces grew two kinds of totalitarianism, one deriving directly from Marxism, the other from currents of thought, such as Hegelianism, which Marxism also utilized.

But neither Communism nor the various types of Fascism were sudden, spontaneous developments of the twentieth century. They were the flowerings of thoughts, hopes, and aspirations—or simply of urges and instincts—which had been shaping for generations and even centuries.

So far as Fascism is concerned, we are not going to wipe it out easily, and least of all can we do so simply by eliminating the men who were the exponents and instruments of Fascism, or the institutions through which they worked or the techniques they used. Fascism is not only a method of achieving and exercising power; it is a way of life, an attitude of mind, a philosophy of government, and even a religion. It is "the great modern heresy," as Baudelaire called Romanticism a century ago. "For we wrestle not against flesh and blood but against principalities, against powers, against the rulers of the darkness of this world, against spiritual wickedness in high places."

It is in the philosophical background that the key to Fascist doctrine is to be found. There are the violence, the racism, the all-powerful State, authority and regimentation, discipline and militarism, nationalism and imperialism. None of these doctrines was conjured out of thin air. They have deep roots in European thought, and it is those roots which must be torn up. These are the real reasons why Fascism survives in Italy, as the Nazi form of it will survive in Germany, and other forms elsewhere. These are the reasons we are going to be fighting Fascism for a long time to come.

In *The New York Times*, on more than one occasion, I warned that Fascism was a hydra-headed monster—or, even worse, is like Antaeus who derives his strength from deep-rooted forces. We can beat him to a pulp, but unless we eradicate those profound sources from which Fascism draws its nourishment, this modern Antaeus is going to get back on his feet and come at us again. Mussolini, in the definitive article on Fascism which he wrote for the *Treccani Encyclopedia,* said, "Fascism now has in the world the universality of all doctrines which, in fulfilling themselves, represent a moment in the history of the human spirit." That was not merely bombast. Fascism is an organic sickness of which the Fascism itself is more effect than cause.

Let us briefly recapitulate what Fascism is, so that we may identify the factors which are going to survive. Like all other political systems, there are two sides—the governing or ruling class, and the governed. A Fascist government is a one-party system, highly centralized and authoritarian, with rigid control over every phase of a nation's life. Hence it needs a loyal party hierarchy, thoroughly regimented and disciplined, through which force is applied, to maintain order. This government is militaristic, nationalistic, and imperialistic, and it proclaims a dogmatic political faith.

In a word, the governmental structure is totalitarian, and does not differ, in that respect, from Communism. We are going to destroy the Fascist governments in those countries which opposed the United Nations, so there is no need to worry much about the survival of that feature of Fascism (although it may continue in countries beyond our control, such as Spain, Portugal, China, and a number of Latin-American states).

It is not so much a survival as a revival which is to be feared, because the spirit of Fascism will live in the minds and hearts of the millions of the governed. They remain possessed of a state of mind which can be called the Fascist mentality. Let us study it.

The faith that was placed in the rulers will become a myth, comparable to the Napoleonic myth in France a century ago. The inevitable misery and turbulence of the post-war period will strengthen the desire for security and order, which Fascism considers as ends in themselves. So men will yearn to place their destiny in stronger hands, so that they do not have to act and think, but need only trust and obey.

The young have been deeply ingrained with a love of soldiery and its attendant uniforms, medals, pomp and glory, and defeat has not eliminated that feeling. Least of all will the emphasis on physical prowess and physical courage yield to admiration for brains and the sedentary virtues of civic life. Fascism has taught a whole generation to believe in violence, force, and the right of might. With that has existed a contempt for what is called "the bourgeois life" and "the bourgeois morality." Whatever is done on behalf of the "moral idea" (which has been the State or the Race or the Ruler, and which will be the survival of one or more of them) is good, whether it be murder, torture, violence, or some form of suicide. Private virtue or morality becomes secondary, even undesirable. You start from the Machiavellian thesis, so heartily approved by Mussolini, that "all men are bad"; you deny the validity of the Christian philosophy of natural law. You proclaim the inequality of men, the value of the "elite," the necessity of considering people qualitatively not quantitatively.

Where you find these ideas you find Fascism. You may find them in an American industrialist or a union leader, and you may find them in hundreds of thousands of German war prisoners—but, wherever they are, there you have Fascism, and there you have the true enemy of liberalism and democracy—and, for that matter, of Communism, which has very different aims and ideas under a similar governmental structure.

The Communists, as a matter of fact, give Fascism a class interpretation which fits neither the historic facts nor the present reality. It serves the Communist program and the sincerity of the motives behind the struggle of Communism and Fascism need not be questioned, although we saw during the two years when Hitler and Stalin were allies that they could accommodate their systems to practical ends. However, no one can doubt now that the Communists are completely anti-Fascist and earnestly desire and fight for the destruction of Fascism or for the conversion of useful Fascist elements into Communism. But there is a decided difference between what they understand by Fascism (or democracy, as I have remarked) and what the liberal considers it to be.

"Fascism was really an organization to defend the interests of an imperialistic caste," wrote the Italian Communist Party organ, *Unità*, "and it is still, in the measure that it exists, the expression of these interests. The terroristic forms of Fascist tyranny were merely the defensive measures of plutocratic groups who, while smothering every workman's aspirations to freedom and well being in the country, carried on a policy of brigandage and robbery abroad."

It is on the basis of this understanding that the Italian Communists have been fighting Fascism, very effectively and sincerely —but in reality they have been fighting capitalism and a certain number of men who were, among other things, Fascisti. As the Fascist Republicans demonstrated in northern Italy, and the Falangists in Spain, it is possible to make great and radical strides in the direction of Socialism and the welfare of the laboring classes—and still remain Fascist.

In short, the enemy was not only underrated; he was misunderstood. The term Fascism was made synonymous with dictatorship, reaction, militarism, imperialism, or even just capitalism and conservatism. It became merely a label of reproach or a loose epithet with which to berate one's opponent.

Let us look again, briefly, at the situation in Italy, where Fascism began its disastrous career. Every man and woman to the age of forty-five, and every child, has lived his whole life, or the best part of it, under Fascism, which shut him out from the world. It was all-absorbing. Even if a man saw its evils and limitations, he did not know the rival methods of life and government. Democracy and liberalism, whether regarded as enemies or aspirations, were unknown in a practical sense. Democracy is not to be acquired now by simply assuming labels like Republicanism, Communism, Socialism, Liberalism or any other "ism," but by profound and fundamental spiritual changes. So now there is no alternative to Fascism, no substitute, nothing to go back to except by a long, arduous, and dangerous road that can lead not only to our type of democracy, but more easily to Communism, and possibly to anarchy or even a new form of Fascism. And Italy, at least, had a large group of anti-Fascist leaders as the war ended, but Germany showed there were no anti-Nazi forces of any importance worth a hoot in the whole country.

Both Italians and Germans are infinitely worse off after "liberation" and conquest than they were before. Fascism was like a jail where the individual had a certain amount of security, shelter and daily food. When you throw habitual prisoners out on the streets to fend for themselves they sometimes starve, and then long for jail again. When we freed the slaves in the South, thousands of them regretted the security and relative well-being they had lost.

So, now, millions of Italians and Germans, who have lost their false security and are not intelligent enough or politically conscious enough to realize that Fascism brought them to this pass and was on the toboggan slide even before the war, sigh for "the good old days" of Fascism.

We can see from the horrors of the German prison and concentration camps how effectively Nazism inculcated the philosophy of violence. Those who lived abroad in the last year or two of the war could not help being impressed every day by the breakdown in morality which came in the wake of Fascism. "We refer to the decay of public order, misery, and hunger, the relaxing and brutalizing of customs and usages, the lack of discipline among the youth"—to cite Pius XII in his broadcast commemorating the end of the war in Europe. Youngsters literally have to be taught the simplest principles of social morality and ethics, which are taken for granted in other countries. The civic sense—the determination and willingness of a citizen to work and sacrifice for his community—has to be recultivated. Respect for law and order is going to be a painful reconquest in the war-torn countries.

International morality, as the world knew it before totalitarianism, is a thing of the past—or else one must give it different definitions. We know now that treaties are simply matters of temporary convenience, that international obligations have no validity unless there is going to be force behind them, that justice and right among nations, also, can only be achieved by force, or by the threat of force. The technique of foreign policy, or international dealings, has changed, and whether we like it or not, we must recognize it. Neville Chamberlain dealing with Hitler and Stalin was like a stripling in a bout with catch-as-catch-can wrestlers. One need not argue whether it is better to conduct foreign relations in the manner of English gentlemen or as catch-as-catch-can wrestlers. Even the English gentlemen have the same ends in view, and in their day have done as "realistic" things, as any Fascist or Communist.

Machiavelli's "Prince" is not dead; he has merely changed his methods. One does not now use poison or the dagger, generally speaking, but the results are achieved by other means, perhaps just as immoral. We want certain things—peace, international trade, prosperity, and the like—and that is fair enough. But this is "the century of Fascism." We shall not gain those things by isolationism or by sending out untrained, inexpert diplomats who have no power to represent a strong nation. Any nation is as strong as it wants to be. To have strength means nothing in itself, but to have it and use it is the only thing that makes sense in a world which is rapidly moving backwards to a modernistic version of the Dark Ages.

All that I am driving at in this digression is that we are living in a new and different world, conditioned by totalitarianism. We have fought and defeated the Fascist countries, but ideologies are so much harder to kill than men and institutions. There is going to be an invisible gate-crasher at the peace tables, a sort of ghost, the Spirit of Fascism. It will live to plague us all and make a mockery of those complacent gentlemen who will think it dead because its leaders and governments and titles have been swept away.

When Germany went down in a real "Götterdämmerung," it was not a form of national suicide or an accident of fate. It was a calculated, if monstrous, policy to perpetuate the glory of Nazism and German militarism. Those who thought that the devastating military defeat of Germany will teach a final lesson of futility or a consciousness of sin to all Germans were thinking as democrats and Anglo-Saxons, not as Nazis and Germans.

As far back as August, 1944, when I was in Rome, I heard something from a reliable source which I sent to *The New York Times,* and which was to prove remarkably prophetic. In the previous summer of 1943, when we invaded Sicily and were preparing to invade the continent, Hitler saw the writing on the wall and called all the most important gauleiters of Europe to his headquarters.

Germany, he said, was not going to be able indefinitely to hold off the immensely superior forces which were being massed against her, and it was inevitable that in the course of time her armies would be driven back to their home territory. However, that need not mean defeat, the Fuehrer continued, if plans were laid and every German did his duty. It was necessary to defend every German city, one by one, as Stalingrad had been defended. If that were done, it would give Germany such moral strength, such pride in her heroism and such a great place in history, that for a century no foreign power would dare to treat her as anything but equal. The youth of Germany would be so inspired and the United Nations would pay so high a price for conquest that the rebirth of a new Nazism and a Greater Reich would come quickly.

And so Germany was defended, and so she has gone down to defeat, but that defeat is, to the Nazi mind, a glorious one. They were betrayed by their allies, they will say, but they fought to the end against overwhelming superiority, and they never surrendered. This—and not the defeat itself—will be the myth, along with that other one of having tried to defend European civilization from Eastern Bolshevism. That very remarkable document, the last official communique of the German General Staff, is not going to be a record of shame but an inspiration to future generations of Germans.

Which brings us to a simple conclusion: Fascism was not and is not an Italian or a German or a Japanese phenomenon. It is world wide; it had many decades of development behind it; it has trained a whole generation of our contemporaries in a number of countries; it has millions of unwitting exponents in democratic nations. The real enemy of the twentieth century is not nations like Fascist Italy, Nazi Germany, or militaristic Japan; nor is it men like Mussolini, Hitler, and Hirohito. It is the whole evil complex of thoughts, feelings, beliefs, desires, and aims which gave rise to Fascism and which will persist until their defeat in the minds and emotions of all men.

And to me, just as the end of the war in Europe was not the end of Fascism and Nazism, so the deaths of Hitler and Mussolini were not the ends of them. Each died as he had to die, as the history, traditions, and character of the German and the Italian peoples demanded. But each will live again as surely as the spirit of Napoleon rose from his ashes to create the Second French Empire and foster that Napoleonic myth which will forever be a force in France and in Europe. One ended in ignominy and the other in cosmic defeat, but their fate had been linked for a quarter of a century—and do not forget that it was Mussolini who showed Hitler the way to catastrophic glory.

Unfortunately for the world, Hitler had at his command the most diabolically perfect instrument for Nazism which could have been devised—a brave, disciplined, military-minded, dull people, with enough brutality to provide the necessary measure of terrorism and propogate an adequate amount of fear. Mussolini used to lament that the Italian people were such poor instruments for Fascism, and he was right. Hitler met no such obstacle,

and in his hands Fascism came to be the most powerful and destructive force known to history.

So the two dictators handcuffed themselves together, and so
they went down, the one as an Italian, the other as a German.
Mussolini died as Cola di Rienzi died. Hitler died in the holocaust of a *Niebelungenlied* twilight, and in so dying he created
his myth. Mussolini's ghost went to join those of Cola di Rienzi
and the two Napoleons, for he was in their tradition. Hitler's
went to join those of Bismarck, Hegel, and Treitschke, for he
stemmed from them. Their god was Wotan and their ideal Pan-
Germanism.

That ill-assorted pair, those strange political bedfellows, are
going to haunt this world of ours until we lay their ghosts—if we
ever can—by instilling democracy into the hearts and minds of
Italians and Germans. In olden days it was enough to kill your
enemy and display his head, but that was because leadership was
personal or dynastic. Today you can kill your enemies, but you
do not thereby kill the ideas for which they fought and died.
Hitler and Mussolini are dead, but Nazism and Fascism still
live, and we must go on fighting them, as Germans and Italians
will have to do in forming their new governments and rebuilding
their countries from the ashes left by their ill-fated dictators.
Years of misery, perhaps of chaos, lie ahead for those two countries, and, in the weakening of memories, those malevolent
spirits, Hitler and Mussolini, will tend to take on an ever more
beneficent aspect. They were the enemies of mankind in life,
and so they are and will be in death. We have only begun to
fight them.

I had come a long way since those careless, carefree, ignorant
days of 1925 when Fascism swam into my ken, a vaguely romantic, ill-understood movement which the world applauded.
I was slow to see the danger, but not so slow as were some others,
and I have fought it as well as the next man. The pen is not
really mightier than the sword, but it is a potent weapon, none-
theless, and I shall not lay it down. Indeed, it is for us now to
carry on the good fight, for the soldiers of the United Nations
have done their part.

Reaction is to be feared, much more than revolution. There are times when revolution is young and wholesome and brave, like a fresh breeze coming over the lightening fields after a weary night. Let me, before I, too, lay down my pen, relive some hours when the spirit of the *Marseillaise* sang in the air of awakened France.

Recess on the French Riviera

I HAVE been lucky on the draw in my newspaper career. When the number of correspondents on a given assignment is limited, they draw for places. In Abyssinia I won the right to go with a flying column through Dankalia, and it provided the best story of the war. In Algiers I won a top place for the Salerno landing. And now I was to win twice for the landing on the French Riviera—first, to be able to go with the infantry assault wave, and second, to get the choice of the central division with which the radio transmitter was going. It was my old division, the 45th, now commanded by Major General William W. Eagles, and I got an especial kick out of being with them.

We hoped and thought it would be the decisive blow in Europe. The break-through from the Normandy beach-head occurred as we were waiting in Naples for the start, and Bradley and Patton were galloping toward Paris while we were on our way. The landing had been planned since the previous December, and active preparations were under way for ten weeks. It was as great an armada as the war had seen and we struck with more than 800 ships, without counting warships and not reckoning airborne troops. Most of the commanders thought it would be tough going, for the whole coast was heavily defended, although not in depth.

The spearhead was 100 per cent American, but a French force followed on our heels. In reality, it was a North African army commanded by the French. Already the false optimism which was to cost the Allies so dearly had spread its insidious propaganda. "You will be fighting like hell for three weeks," a naval officer kidded us at breakfast on D-Day, "and somebody will catch up with you and yell, 'Hey, boys, this war has been over a long time!'" But we went on plowing through an isolated, unknown world like the caravels of old-time explorers who never knew what they would find at the end of their journeys.

Granting success, we felt sure that this would be the last great amphibious operation of the war in Europe—and it was, despite the way the conflict dragged on. That was one reason I was so keen to go. The night before we landed, all the officers were sitting around the dining salon writing to wives, sweethearts, and mothers. On the eve of a D-Day almost everybody writes, and you cannot help feeling somewhat sentimental. You know that some of those (and perhaps you yourself?) writing with studied casualness are not going to live to see another night. It is the time to say nice things and to leave the memory that you would want to leave.

Normally, I never felt any such urge to write my wife on the eve of perilous events. I had never done it before, but somehow that night I felt I should. I do not think I had any forebodings of death. Long ago I learned that presentiments of the sort generally meant that your liver was out of order or you were tired. It took me a long time to realize that. Often in Spain I had the feeling, "This is my unlucky day," but, of course, nothing came of it. I am quite sure now that, all unbeknownst, some day as I am carelessly and absentmindedly dreaming my way to somewhere, Death will come up and sock me on the back of the head. And that will be *that!*

But the night on the *Ancon,* as we were approaching France, I thought I was being sensible. I had stretched my luck inordinately in the previous nine years. In a sense, I had no right to be alive. Like the character depicted by Sergeant Bill Mauldin, I was beginning to feel like a fugitive from the law of averages, and we thought the coming "show" was going to be hot stuff. Besides, when you do something for the last time (remember, we thought the war was almost over) you have an especial feeling about it. You hold your breath and cross your fingers.

In my letter to Nancie I quoted what a young lieutenant at my elbow had just said, "We're going to give Lady Luck one more kick in the behind." The Navy lived up to its honorable and commendable custom of serving a bang-up dinner for a last meal, the night before. It always made me a little uncomfortable, for it seemed a bit like fattening pigs for slaughter, but it isn't a bad feeling to go into battle with some good roast beef and pie à la mode under your belt.

I always felt I could do without getting the "thumbs up" sign on starting a flying mission, or to be wished good luck on leaving for the front. They are reminders that you are going to need luck.

And then, on the morning of August 15, 1944, we went through them as though they were a paper hoop. That landing will go down in history as the nearest thing to perfection in amphibious landings in the war. Despite its extraordinary intricacy, and after months of planning, our assault forces hit the beaches at H-plus two minutes!

There have been many accounts of amphibious landings, and most of them a whole lot more exciting than the southern France operation, so I will not bore the reader with details. Journalistically, it was the best break of the war for me, for by an accident of fate I was the only newspaper correspondent to reach the radio transmitter on the beach-head the evening of D-Day, and thus the only one to get out a full, first-hand story of the landing. That was one of those satisfactions which give an unusual fillip to newspaper work, and, besides, it pleased my vanity that in my old age I should still be able to demonstrate how to be a war correspondent.

The personal thrill was to have landed at a part of Europe which I knew and which held only the nicest memories of happy holidays with Nancie during the Spanish Civil War. The 45th hit the coast just outside St. Maxime, and on the succeeding days I was driving in all directions—through St. Raphael to the edge of Cannes, to St. Tropez, to Aix-en-Provence, where I spent a night in the very Hotel du Roi Réné where, in the winter of 1938, we had a blissful week. Surely, the French know how to live better than any other people in the world! The walks in the rich fields or through picturesque, winding streets, the little casino where we gambled, the cafés where we drank vermouth cassis, the marvelous food, washed down with Rhone wines and capped with an old *marc de Bourgogne*, the records of Spanish music that we played, the sunlight and the mild air and the laziness. . . . Will the world ever be like that again?

I wrote a nostalgic piece, from before Cannes, on August 21. "It isn't only a Frenchman whose heart jumps at the sight of Cannes lying bright in the sunlight across the Gulf of La Napoule," I said. "All of us who remember it in the great days when it was the most fashionable spot in France, if not in the world, are entitled to skip a beat or two at seeing it there and thinking that soon the world should regain some of its sanity, and we can sit again on the terrace of the Carlton Hotel and order cocktails such as only its famous bartender can make, and then eat such a meal as none but a French chef can concoct. And afterwards we will go again to the casino that this morning I could almost throw a stone at, and perhaps see a ballet or perhaps play a little roulette.

"These were daydreams today, because the Krauts were across that ridge in front of us shooting in our direction, and yet the thrilling and wonderful thing about it all and about this flaming invasion, that within a week has taken us this far at one end and to Toulon and Marseilles at the other, is that they are dreams which are coming true."

And then we went back to the siege of Toulon, where Reynolds Packard of the United Press and I spent fruitless and dangerous days, hoping and expecting to get in. And then Marseilles fell.

It was a French force under General de Lattre de Tassigny which took those cities while our own American 7th Army moved north in that great sweep which was to take them up the Rhone Valley to a junction on the Rhine with Patton's forces.

To see France rise again from its shameful past was of all things in that campaign the most satisfactory and the most thrilling to one like myself who knew the French and had lived in their beautiful capital. The *maquis* were superb. They, as much as we, liberated southern France. There was a new spirit, young, joyous, brave, and, for the first time in all the years I knew the country, Frenchmen were happy to see us. It was a heartfelt welcome whose sincerity could not be dimmed, even later, when that "honeymoon" ended. For once the Frenchman, who is not on the whole inclined to show the best of himself to foreigners, took off his mask, and in those weeks I felt that I had got to know the French better than in all the years since 1925, when I visited and lived in their country. What we did on that invasion, among other things, was to rediscover France—the real France.

A French armored unit burst into Marseilles on the morning of August 23, and a few glorious days of real "liberation" began. If anybody had told us as we approached the beach-head early on the morning of August 15 that on D-plus eight Allied troops would be in Marseilles, it would have caused hearty laughter. Toulon was scheduled to fall in something like three weeks, and Marseilles about D-plus fifty or sixty.

What a pleasure to write the story of Marseilles, that grand old port which celebrated its 2,500th birthday more than a half a century ago, which gave France the name of its hymn in revolutionary days, and which has always been a place of such life, color, and gaiety that every foreigner who knows it has learned to love it as Frenchmen do. That evening it was gayer than ever, because it was free at last, but down on La Cannebière and at the Vieux Port the shells were still pouring in, snipers were firing away, and that atmosphere of death, danger, and excitement which had become so familiar made it all throb with emotions that the Marseillais had not known in a century and a half. Even for those of us who had seen many such sights it was a great thrill, a fitting climax to the first and most important part of our invasion.

The Germans tried to defend it like Toulon, which was still resisting all French efforts to reconquer it. The enemy manned the roads, hills, and forts in the port and on the little Island of St. Frioule, next to the famous Chateau d'If, but they were not in enough strength. The Americans had cut off their retreat, blocking every road, the evening before getting down to Martigues on the Étang de Berre.

A fight that lasted more than two days had held the French back at Aubagne, but by the previous night the town was cleaned up. The break came at dawn on the morning of the 23rd, when a French tank column was thrown first down the main highway from Aubagne, then around by a secondary road that skirts the city on the north, and finally wheeled due south through the suburbs of St. Julien and St. Barnabé and straight into the heart of the city along the Boulevard de la Blancarde.

There were not many Germans to resist them as the column swung left into the Boulevard de la Madeleine, which in its lowest stretch is La Cannebière. The enemy reacted as best he could. From two forts which he held on the edge of the Vieux Port—St. Nicolas and Le Pharo—he sent shells crashing into the Boulevard Madeleine. Anti-tank guns blazed away down La Cannebière, and many snipers manned windows. They made it hot and difficult for a while, and they were still there as night fell, but it was a suicidal last stand whose outcome was never in doubt.

Many of those snipers were Frenchmen, the equivalent there of the Italian Fascist Republicans who fought it out at the end in cities that we took, because they knew that no mercy would be extended to them. In France they were the followers of Jacques Doriot, ex-Communist who had betrayed his followers and his country to collaborate with the Germans. I had seen signs written by his men on the walls of some of the villages around Toulon and Marseilles. Coming through Aubagne on the way to Marseilles, we saw a typical one which read *Vive Doriot! We do not want to be the slaves of Stalin!*

Three other American correspondents and I followed the route of the French tank column into Marseilles, but it was not until late afternoon that we were able to get down to the Cannebière. We had been almost mobbed by the Marseillais all along the route. The Germans, no doubt, had many thrills in their conquests, but they did not have our kind, for we who had made the long campaign through Italy to Marseilles, men of many nations, did not come to conquer but to liberate and if it was a proud day for the French who returned to their native country, it was also a proud one for the Americans whose army had made that conquest possible.

The Marseillais seemed to sense that, for it was not imagination which made us feel that those few Americans who got into Marseilles that day of liberation—mostly war correspondents—received a warmer welcome even than the French.

There was a mad quality in the atmosphere of the city that day. The Marseillais are noted for their excitability, and they were effervescence incarnate. As we drove through St. Julien a young patriot ran toward us firing an ancient pistol that sounded like a popgun. He shouted something about Germans being in a house a few blocks away, and wanted us to help him and other patriots to kill them. But we dashed his enthusiasm by explaining that we were correspondents and unarmed.

Never, outside of a museum, have I seen so many antique pistols and revolvers. Every man seemed to have one, and everyone waved it menacingly or joyously in all directions. Never, either, have I seen so many trigger-happy people, and we were to learn before the day wore out that there was at least as much danger from excitable patriots as from Germans.

For ten days there had been sporadic street fighting between Germans and the Free French. Two days previously, the Germans had known the game was up. They stopped food supplies and all transportation, and began mining the port. The day previous they had begun their usual thorough job of destruction, which left the port a shambles. To be sure, Allied bombings had likewise done plenty of damage. One group of civilians told us about two especially bad raids on May 28 and August 14. An old woman said bitterly, "There were six thousand dead," and then walked away abruptly. That was the only jarring note we heard.

We were by then sitting in our jeep at the upper end of the Cannebière. It was about six in the evening. The famous boulevard was a scene of desolation—rubble of masonry, broken glass everywhere, people huddling in doorways or dashing madly across the street. Not a single vehicle stood or drove between us and the Vieux Port, for the Germans were down at that end and in some of the side streets to the right of the old port. That section, which contains the Cathedral, the Bourse and the Post Office, was the last corner of the city where they were in any force, except for the forts I have mentioned.

A fusillade of shots cracking near us on Les Allées Léon Gambetta sent us scampering quickly into the nearest doorway. "Those are the men of the P.P.F. [Parti Populaire Français, of Doriot] who are firing," we were told. The shooting quickly died away, and just then a column of six French tanks came down the Boulevard de la Madeleine and began moving along the Cannebière. It was our chance to get down under its protection, and we moved fast, hugging the walls on the left side until we reached the crossroads of the Cours Garibaldi. As I walked along that scene of destruction I could not help thinking ironically of the famous Marseillais boast which one used to hear so often in Paris, "If Paris had a Cannebière it would be a small Marseilles." The glories of La Cannebière were temporarily eclipsed.

Hugging the lee side of the Astoria Hotel, we saw two American naval officers, and dashed across to join them. Both had come in as observers and were waiting impatiently a chance to get down to the port and see what damage had been done. The two best known hotels in Marseilles—the Grand and the Noailles —which were just around the corner on the Cannebière, were intact, but the former still had Germans in it, and while we were there they shot an old Frenchman who seemed to me to be dead when four patriots dashed along the street to carry him back to where we were.

A young patriot standing next to me talked seriously and happily. "Paris and Marseilles both liberated! What a great day for France!"

We were determined not to go away without seeing the Vieux Port, which is the real heart of Marseilles, but it was impossible to get down the Cannebière. So we moved around to the left, hoping to get down the side streets. Just then a car came by with patriots distributing the first newspaper of liberated Marseilles. It was *Le Provençal*, organ of the Socialist and Republican Patriots. They had beaten the Communists to it although the latter were quite strong in Marseilles. Under a banner headline

Vive la France! were photographs of De Gaulle, Roosevelt, Churchill, and Stalin. In the upper left-hand corner was an editorial outburst of joy at the deliverance of Marseilles. On the back of the page, in a corner, was a stop press: "Paris is freed! The news reaches us just as we are going to press." As a matter of fact, it was the first, premature claim of the seizure of the capital by patriots.

That walk down to the Vieux Port through back streets was an odd sort of triumphant journey. Every ten yards, women would rush up to embrace and kiss us. After the first half-dozen or so had knocked their heads against our heavy helmets we learned the proper technique, which was to lift the casque up as far as the chin-strap would allow and receive the kisses with pleasure on both cheeks. Those who know Marseilles and the particular section of it we were in will realize what sort of charming young ladies most of those were who kissed us.

We got so much confusing, over-willing advice that we did not know what to do, but we gradually drifted toward the Vieux Port until we were less than a block from the foot of the Cannebière and two blocks from the port itself. We could see the port, jammed with its usual little fishing smacks. A drunken patriot finally stopped us and kept sticking his old pistol literally under my nose as he warned us against going any further. It was there, and from then on, that we realized the peculiar danger of our position, for, as we started back and passed a narrow street, another drunken young patriot saw us and made an impulsive gesture with his rifle to his shoulder. *"Nous sommes des américains!"* I shouted hastily, and when he sheepishly put his gun down I delivered a lecture on the advisability of looking before shooting. Again and again on that walk back to our jeep we were startled by looks of suspicion, accompanied by obviously itching fingers on pistols or rifles, followed by grins and shouts of welcome when they recognized us as Americans. For obviously we were the first they had seen.

Scattered at random in many of those streets were hundreds of amazingly good counterfeits of dollars. When you picked them up you saw they really formed two sheets, with anti-Semitic propaganda inside. "This dollar has paid for the Jewish war," it said, among other things. The Germans had scattered them about from trucks, before leaving.

It was 7:15 o'clock and the Germans just then started shelling the Vieux Port and surrounding streets with 6-inch cannon, so we lost no time in getting back. I went up the Cannebière from the Cours Garibaldi several blocks ahead of the others, and again got a scare when a patriot reached for his pistol on first seeing me. "You look so much like a German," he said apologetically. Obviously, any American going around the streets of Marseilles in the dark that night would as likely as not get shot deader than a German before he knew it.

At one point the glass of a door that stuck out just ahead of me broke and tinkled to the ground, although I had not heard the sniper's shot. More tanks were moving down the Cannebière, and shells kept crashing down at the Vieux Port. On reaching the jeep I foolishly stood out from the buildings to look down the street. A sudden whistling sound came directly over my helmet, and then an explosion about thirty yards behind me. The other correspondents coming up the Cannebière said a tracer bullet from what must have been a 50-caliber gun had gone over my head. We piled into the jeep and sped up the Boulevard de la Madeleine to safety. The Germans were having their last fling.

The next day was one of the great ones of my career. There was a surge and sweep to that day which caught me up and lifted me on its rushing current. It was one of those moments which held within itself the end of one era and the beginning of another. If you can catch such a moment, you have, indeed, caught history on the wing.

When I returned in the morning, Marseilles was still throbbing with its new-found freedom, still crackling along dozens of streets with exchanges of shots between Free French and collaborationists, and still crashing to the thunder of German heavy and light cannon that made La Cannebière as unhealthful as the day before, not to mention that whole section around the St. Charles Railway Station and the new port.

It was, in short, as interesting and exciting a spot to be in as any in the world that day, not so much for the thrill of being right in the fight, which is after all a personal pleasure on the part of war correspondents, but because of its atmosphere of intense, revolutionary life. If I related in *The New York Times* a few of my personal adventures that day, it was simply because it represented something that had much significance for the future of France. What we correspondents saw with our own eyes was part of the burgeoning of a new life. We could not escape it.

Take the newspapers, for instance. Two more that had been clandestine came out openly in the morning—*La Marseillaise,* organ of the National Front, and *Le Rouge Midi,* the Communist organ. They had little in them but paeans of praise for the Free French and also, in the case of the *Rouge Midi,* of the F.T.P.F. (Francs Tireurs et Partisans Français, the Communist patriotic organization). They had banner headlines: "Marseilles, conquered by the F.F.I., is entered by Allied troops"; "Allied armies, led by the F.T.P.F. and French troops of North Africa, entered Marseilles yesterday morning"; "F.F.I. frees Paris from the yoke of the invader." In other words it was, according to that belief, the French patriots who were freeing France, not the Americans, the British or the De Gaullistes. Those newspapers, and even more, the attitude of the people themselves, made it clear that the future of France was in the hands of the patriots and not of the exiles.

A scene typical of revolutionary France was taking place in the Lycée des Sciences, off the Cannebière, which had been converted into a temporary police station that morning when two colleagues and I walked in. We were following a group of patriots and gendarmes escorting a white-faced, protesting couple, who were led into the buildings amidst the mutterings and curses of those standing about. Every one of them was armed with a pistol or a rifle. We asked a gendarme what it was all about. "He was a police officer who worked with the Gestapo, and she helped him," the gendarme replied. "They will soon be *kaput.* Do you want to see the bodies of the ones we executed this morning?"

When we said yes, he took us around the back, pointing first to two bodies lying at the base of one wall and then to three others beside another wall. "They were P.P.F.'s," our guide continued. "We shot about fifteen since last night. Come here and I will show you some live ones." He took us to the iron-barred window of one room and pointed to three women. A girl with eyes swollen with weeping stared sullenly at him as he cursed her. In the next room, four men, roughly dressed, were lying on the floor. "*Kaput! kaput!*" he shouted at them, and, then turning to us, "*Tous Gestapo Français.*"

"Don't you give them a trial?" we asked.

"Yes," another gendarme answered. "We try them and then we shoot them."

An obviously responsible young member of the F.F.I., noticing that we were getting an odd impression of patriotic justice, intervened to ask us to come upstairs and meet their leaders. There we were told a different story about the reformation of the police corps, and about thousands of denunciations which were going to be investigated and disposed of on a strictly legal basis, with the suspicious ones held for trial and the guilty ones shot or imprisoned. In short, we were seeing the results of popular justice which was still going on all over Marseilles, but they intended to organize it legally.

One of the three leading organizers of police resistance, Marcel Renoard, delivered to us a serious if rather boastful speech. The prisons of Marseilles were full of P.P.F.'s, he said, and he expatiated on the bravery of the police and young men. "Spread the news that France did not lay down her arms in 1940," he said. "She has always fought. And tell Americans that we like, admire, and thank them. Many German soldiers here want to surrender, but they fight because they are afraid of being killed. We do not kill soldiers." That was one of the paradoxes, significant of the revolutionary feeling. The French were not especially going for the Germans. They were after the collaborationists. We saw dozens of clashes between patriots in the streets and P.P.F.'s barricaded in apartments. Hatred between Frenchman and

Frenchman was infinitely greater than between the French and the Germans.

We had a thrilling example while we were in the police building. There had been a constant crashing and crackling of fire all around the building. German heavy shells were falling in the neighborhood, which we understood, but whenever we asked about the small-arms fire the matter was shrugged off as inconsequential.

"There are some P.P.F.'s in the building across the lot," one patriot finally told us. "They are firing into here, as they are doing against the police at the St. Pierre Prison, because they know we are taking P.P.F.'s." At one moment a patriot strolled to the window, lifted his pistol and blazed away several times at the building in question.

"There is no difference between Laval, Pétain, and Doriot. They are all the same clique," Renoard was telling us. "The P.P.F. got prizes varying in size, according to the importance of the prisoner, for those they delivered to the Gestapo, just as if we were beasts. They had torture chambers," and he explained in lurid detail some of the things that had been done to men and women.

Just then somebody shouted down below. The noise grew to a roar, and then the whole building seemed to flame with excitement as dozens of patriots and gendarmes poured shots into that offending building. Some in our room threw themselves on the floor; others rushed out with pistols drawn, edging up to windows that looked on the Hotel de la Lycée from which the firing had come. We three correspondents picked what seemed like a safe corner and stayed there, I being reminded vividly of many such scenes in the Spanish Civil War. This went on for fully a half hour that was full of excitement, shouting, and noise, with no results, until a party of patriots went around to the front entrance of the hotel, dashed in, and started cleaning it out.

Again and again patriots would come up to one of us asking for ammunition. Lack of munitions, and above all of machine guns, had been a constant complaint. Judging from the amount of shooting which had been going on, one could not wonder that ammunition kept running out. We had to explain each time that, being correspondents, we were unarmed, which always aroused wonder. I suppose we were the only unarmed men in Marseilles.

Some of their pistols sounded like popguns, but others in the confined building made a noise like cannon. The P.P.F.'s had machine pistols, and once, peeking through a window, I could see a shuttered window with a hole in it for the muzzle of a gun, which was one of those used to fire on us. It was all rather exciting and, to tell the truth, somewhat hysterical with a touch of comic opera, but men were being killed in the process, and the intensity of the feeling involved was significant for the future.

When the firing died down and we went out, it was to find similar scenes on a smaller scale in many places. The Cannebière was again no-man's land. As we went down to investigate a shell crashed into a tree across the street from us, so we turned back and drove our jeep by a circuitous route to the Boulevard de la Madeleine.

It was lunchtime, and to that city of famous restaurants and *bouillabaisse* we had brought C-rations. Looking for a place to get them heated, we spied a wine shop with its shutter half up, and a timid old woman peering out. When she saw we were Americans and heard our desire, no persuasion was needed. No people could have had a more royal welcome than we three correspondents and the jeep driver. Like everything else that happened, it had its significance. There were three old spinsters there who took us back to their little kitchen and living room and served us with a courtesy, generosity, and friendliness that were touching to strangers far from home. Friends, hearing that we were there, kept dropping in to talk to us and, above all, to thank us because of what America had done. Here, indeed, was to be found the goodness which lies at the heart of bourgeois France, its solidity, simplicity, and courage. Such people were not going to be kept down.

But what was most significant was the special welcome accorded to us because we were Americans, and that we found everywhere we had been since D-Day. The French who came from Africa received no such welcome.

Driving around after lunch, we saw the Chief Civil Affairs Officer of the 7th Army, Colonel Harvey S. Gerry (an old Paris friend of mine), and followed his car to the Prefecture. There the Committee of Liberation had set up headquarters. The Acting Prefect told us that F.F.I.'s had stormed the Prefecture four days before, and "from then on we were in command of the city."

The streets of Marseilles were continually swarming with cars of partisans dashing madly in all directions, with flags flying in the breeze and guns bristling on all four sides. Trigger fingers were very light. In one such car that went by in the morning we saw a pretty young girl, helmeted and with a businesslike pistol sticking over the side of the car. Coming out of the prefecture we ran into her and her young companions, one of whom had to juggle four hand-made grenades precariously in order to shake hands. The girl kissed each of us, *à la française,* on both cheeks, and, I learned more about revolution from her, in the next half hour, than from all I had seen since landing in France.

Mlle. Geneviève Fouré was twenty-three, she told us, and she had brown eyes and brown hair and a mischievous smile and everything else that Hollywood might want. She was one of two young women, she said, in the "Patriotic Militia," which she had joined four days previously, since which time she had killed two Germans and wounded several others. She was dressed in gray slacks with a sort of pajama top that had a tricolor sash around the waist and the tricolor armband of the patriots. Each of the two pockets of her slacks bulged with a gun which she took out to show us, and had she been less attractive it would have been hard not to think of "Pistol Packin' Mamma."

"I'm so tired!" she said to me. "All last night we stood guard over some French tanks, and this morning we have been patrolling the streets."

"But tell us about the Germans you killed," we said.

One of her companions suggested that we adjourn to a quiet office in the prefecture, where he promptly produced a magnum of *Côtes du Rhône* wine. The second girl in the patriot group joined us there. She was Mado Delsarte—"call me Madelon," she said—a short, chunky, broad-faced young woman of the people whom any German would clearly have been sorry to meet. After the now customary embracings we all sat down around a desk. Geneviève reluctantly took off her helmet. "I haven't combed my hair in five days," she protested.

"Tell us how you killed the Germans," we insisted.

"It was on Monday," she said, "during some street fighting at the corner of the Rue des Saintes and the Rue Paradis. There were two Germans with tommy guns around the corner firing at us, but they did not want to shoot at the women in the street, so they made signs to them to take shelter. I was the only woman with a dozen of my patriot companions, so I said to them: 'Wait, I'll go to see the Germans.' I walked up the street and joined the other women. The Germans were directing them into the shelter of a house. I said to the women, 'I'll go first.' So I started inside. Just then the Germans turned their backs to start firing again, and I shot them both in the back."

"And how did you feel when you shot them?" one of us asked.

"They got what they deserved after the way they treated the French," she replied.

Mado insisted that they all get going on "an urgent mission," so after more embracings and handshakings we parted with our exciting company.

"*Bonne chance!*" one of us said as we separated.

"*Chez nous on ne dit pas 'Bonne chance,'*" a young patriot replied. "*On dit 'Merde!'*"

Of the many reminders of Spain that day, the parting shot was the most vivid. "This," I thought to myself, "is 1793 all over again. This is what the youth of France is feeling and doing." Marseilles was conquered, as far as the Free French were concerned, by its youth. The patriots were mostly young men and, in some cases, young women. Their spirit was clearly revolutionary, although for the most part not consciously so.

"Anyway," I concluded my dispatch to *The New York Times* that night, "whoever thought France was dead can ponder over these few incidents of a day in Marseilles. France is vibrating with life—new, young, brave life. No one can say where she is going, but she is back on the map of Europe, with all the fire and dash of her great days. Marseilles alone is proof of that."

And so I "signed off" on the invasion of southern France and—so far as this book is concerned—on war corresponding. We all thought the war was virtually over, as you thought. So did the Allied General Staffs, thereby making what was surely the greatest miscalculation of the war. Eighteen divisions that were about to start for France were diverted to the Pacific. And when Von Rundstedt struck in December he caught us off guard, and there were anxious days, saved not by our generals but by our G.I.'s, whose defensive stand was, in my opinion, the greatest page of soldiering which the Americans wrote in the whole war in Europe.

But from then on there were only odds and ends of war corresponding for me—two brief flights to France on special stories, a trip to Florence while it was still being fought for, a visit to the front at Christmas time. They were all anticlimactic, and I was not in Europe for the final smash through to Berlin and victory.

So the memory I want to keep and to have remembered—my own "farewell to arms"—was the taking of Marseilles. It was the right sort of note, a note of youth and hope and high resolve, the promise of a future better than the dark and terrible days which had gone before.

Examination

ALL ROADS lead to Rome, and this account may just as well end there as anywhere else. The war is over, and with it a dangerous decade also ends for me. The education never ends, but in life as at school one should pause to take an examination and to put down the sum of things learned.

It had been a hard school, and some courses I flunked and others I passed, according to the point of view. I would not think of denying that I had made many errors and have my share of "D's" and "E's," but it is the average which counts, and that is what I have given you here so that you can specify the final mark.

I know that some will say, more or less regretfully, that I failed, for that has been said in print more than once. While I was in Italy in the last period, the *Nazione del Popolo,* organ of the Committee of National Liberation of Florence, published two attacks on me. The second was headed: *Italia Misconosciuta* ("Misunderstood Italy"). The writer, Bruno Archi, said he had received a letter from an American friend "in which he told me about the correspondence of American journalists in Italy, and about the place which Italy has in the press of the United States."

"The news which arrives here is for the greatest part due to the correspondent of *The New York Times,* Matthews," this friend had written. "If you could only see the evil that this one man can do to the cause of those who love Italy you would be painfully upset. In every article, every day, he loses no occasion to make the most unjust and indirect accusations, the most shameless defamations, against all Italians, with a malignity that makes you boil. There is no way of combating it, because Matthews has become the oracle which admits of no contradiction.

I do not know if you have the means or time to read *The New York Times*. If you can, do it, because the campaign of Matthews against Italy is incredible."

The word "incredible" was in italics. There was more in that vein, after which Bruno Archi gave his own opinion.

"About Matthews," he wrote, "there is nothing to be done. It is not the first time that he makes a propaganda about Italy which serves Fascism and the reaction. The only act which can serve any purpose, and it would be a sign of dignity on the part of anti-Fascists, would be to cut oneself off from all relations with that man. The 'very able' journalist Matthews boasts not only of having interviewed the Lieutenant General, but also of being the personal friend of various anti-Fascist leaders, and this is due to the only non-reactionary period of his career, the period during which he was correspondent in Spain. . . ."

I offer that as a typical viewpoint, although I do not consider it justified. Those Italians whose judgment I respected and whose characters I admired were indignant at the attacks against me, and as far as I am concerned that settled the matter.

The thrust concerning Spain, however, which was not a new one, sometimes distresses me. Have I changed? But it is ridiculous to ask whether, faced with a similar situation today, I would react as I did in the years 1936 to 1939. There could not be such a situation today. The world has changed, and if we have not changed with it, then we were ossified a long time ago and are out of pace.

History does not repeat itself. It is dynamic. Franco is no more savory in 1945 than he was in 1936 or 1939, nor is Falangism, but the solution of Spain's problems surely does not consist in turning the clock back to 1939, even supposing it could be done. It is not my idea of consistency to take an attitude (such as, let us say, pro-Communism in the Spanish Civil War) and maintain it whatever happens in the succeeding years. When Russia is doing what is right, as she did in Spain and at Munich, she deserves applause. When she does what I would consider wrong, as in her pact with Germany in 1939-1941, she deserves condemnation.

When there are two sides to a very complicated situation, like that of Poland, one should be free to say that the Soviet's actions are in part bad and unjustified and in part reasonable. Either of two categorical attitudes is as harmful as the other: Stalin is always right, Stalin is always wrong. It would be hard to say which class of well-meaning Americans is more dangerous to the future peace of the world, the Red baiters or the doughty champions of the Soviet Union.

The liberal recognizes that he need not and should not take either stand. As a liberal, he is naturally anti-Communist and anti-totalitarian in every form. He must hate and fear any way of life which deprives men of freedom, even in order to raise the general well-being or distribute social and economic justice to a somewhat greater extent. If it has done that in Russia, and the majority of Russians are satisfied, then the liberal should say, "They are welcome to Communism." But if, in one's own country, the Communists, by due process of law or otherwise, should seek to gain power, it is the duty of the liberal to fight back as hard as he can with the same weapons. And if, in between, one sees Communism expanding by methods which are purely nationalistic and imperialistic on the one hand, and expressive of an internationalization of the Communist ideal on the other, then the liberal has to say:

"On guard! There are limits beyond which such expansion and such more or less forcible proselytizing are jeopardizing the happiness and peace of the world. You are entitled to security, but you have no right to claim that security means the domination of Europe. You are entitled to your way of life, but you have no right to foist it upon us. If we recognize your right to security we are not going to be hypocritical enough to say that you are bringing sweetness and light to Estonia, Lithuania, Poland, and other countries which do not want you. Moreover, it is not the part of liberalism to believe in peace at any price, although the liberal will pay a very high price for it, indeed, since liberalism is anti-militaristic."

This is, of course, the great liberal problem of our era. Wilhelm Roepke asked if it be admissible that liberty can be killed in the name of liberty; whether tolerance should be practiced even in the face of intolerance, and whether the liberal game can have as one rule that of not observing the rules of the game.

In Rome, in February and March, 1945, there was one of those typical, philosophical controversies which are to be found in the continental press only, where journalists are often highly cultured and where the habit of abstract thought is general. Benedetto Croce started it by asking whether it made sense "to grant liberty to those who use it to annul your liberty." This, of course, is exactly what Communism seeks to do, and what Fascism did in Italy. Mussolini rode to power in the free and easy atmosphere of competitive politics, but once he reached the top he frankly stated that he had no intention of allowing his opponents the same freedom which had been granted to him. In fact, he heaped scorn on the weaklings and the fools (as he considered them) who permitted him to ride roughshod over their bodies to dictatorship. To be consistent, Communists would take exactly the same line. They "demand liberty in the name of your principles, but deny it to you in the name of theirs," as Croce put it.

The international problem is much the same. Those nations which act and must act according to principles which have their bases in democracy and liberalism are handicapped in dealing with nations that have no principles—or, at any rate, principles with totally different ethical bases. When the dictum of war that "all is fair" is applied to international politics, then the liberal countries have to adopt the same procedure, or go under. To do anything else, as Professor Guido de Ruggero wrote during this discussion, would be not liberalism but imbecility. You cannot, he rightly pointed out, avoid one *sine qua non* of liberty, which is that the rules of the game be obeyed, and he who acts otherwise has no right to liberty.

The liberal problem, in a nation, is what to do when faced with a threat from anti-liberal elements which use constitutional and liberal forms to destroy freedom, and externally, what to do when faced with an anti-liberal (in this case a totalitarian power) which uses the formulae of international liberalism and requires you to act on them while its own actions are those of a ruthless struggle to impose on others its special nationalistic and political aims.

There are two answers, one on the philosophical plane, the other on the political. Philosophically, liberty is an absolute which no empirical process can destroy, as Croce and many other philosophers have always pointed out. You cannot destroy goodness, let us say, no matter how much bad is done. Neither can goodness destroy itself by being good, so it is theoretically ridiculous to say that liberty or liberalism can destroy itself by being liberal. That, to repeat, would be imbecility, not liberalism. At the same time, liberty can be temporarily overcome, as it was in Germany and Italy and as it is in Russia. In other words, the men who exercise liberalism, and their institutions, can be defeated, even though "liberty" lives on as an idea and aspiration.

So you get to the practical problem of "protecting liberalism," to use Roepke's phrase. The answer, simply and brutally put, is that liberals are as entitled to use force and to fight for liberty as their opponents are to destroy them. Secretary of State Cordell Hull, in his last definitive statement of United States foreign policy, on March 21, 1944, put it as neatly as any liberal could wish.

"There is no surer way for men and for nations to show themselves worthy of liberty than to fight for its preservation, in any way that is open to them, against those who would destroy it for all," he said. "Never did a plainer duty to fight against its foes devolve upon all peoples who prize liberty and all who aspire to it."

The Girondins of the French Revolution (to use a classic example) did not use force to defend their principles, and they went down before the Jacobins who did. Jean Jacques Rousseau had earlier given the world a key in his celebrated dictum that one must "force men to be free" if they do not understand or if they forget their supreme good.

Of course, the Communist asks (quite properly, from his viewpoint): "Against whom is force to be used?" Velio Spano (Paolo Tedeschi), the editor of the Rome Communist paper *Unità*, asked that very question in reply to Croce last February. "For us," he said, "political propositions, in order to have efficacy, should be translated into actual directives of practical action." This is sound realism and it suits the totalitarian mentality which, whether Fascist or Communist, is "activist." Actions count, not words. What Velio Spano meant was, "All right, boys, but don't try to use your force against us." He was willing to pay lip service to liberty, but he was, quite understandably, unwilling that he as a Communist should be deprived of the liberty to seek a Communist regime in Italy.

The answer to him was to make a distinction. So long as he and the Italian Communist Party pursued their aims by the legitimate method of legally winning a popular majority at the polls, they all had an absolute right to go ahead—and no one is stopping them in Italy. If, however, their methods should change to those of revolutionary violence, then it would be legitimate for the liberal and democratic elements in Italy to oppose them with force.

On the international plane, although in practice the principle is by no means so easily applied or even so desirable, it is fundamentally the same. As long as Russia achieves her expansionist aims by political means she must be opposed on the same plane, but aggression is to be condemned and when, or if, it becomes dangerous enough, it must or would have to be fought. In any circumstances, the liberal must oppose that expansion if he is to remain consistently a liberal. That does not imply enmity to Russia, nor does it mean preparation for World War III. On the contrary, friendship with Russia is a keystone of the international peace we all, including Russia, want. Each nation has its national rights, and even if they cannot be precisely defined they reach a practical limit on the political battlefield of the world. Russia has indisputable rights to national security and even to expansion, but there are limits beyond which security and expansion become aggression, and there one would be entitled to cry "Halt!" The rules of the game should be followed, and if they are violated, the liberal has a right to protest and condemn, if only for the record.

To be sure, you can argue that the rules have changed and

that wrestling (to return to that figure) has changed from Graeco-Roman to catch-as-catch-can, and therefore the catch-as-catch-can wrestler is not breaking any rules. But then, to make that admission is to abandon liberalism. All you can consistently do is to fight catch-as-catch-can style against your opponent in order to restore your own method and your own rules of the game after the match is won.

This is not only the century of Fascism, as Mussolini boasted; it is the century of totalitarianism. The two movements have the same roots and methods, although very different aims and ideals, and, between the two, I frankly admit, give me Communism any day. But until I am faced with that choice I will oppose Communism—in national affairs by the active propagation, in anything I may write or say, of liberal and democratic ideas, and, in foreign relations, by a plea for vigilance and a policy consisting of the encouragement of liberal and democratic elements throughout the world and opposition to the forceful spread of Communism beyond the frontiers of Russia.

So long as Mussolini abided by his assertion that "Fascism was not an article for export," no foreign liberal had a right to quarrel with it, except to express his general aversion to authoritarianism. In the same way, so long as Communism remains a fundamentally Russian phenomenon which, one assumes, satisfies a majority of the Russian people and improves their lot, the non-Russian liberal has no right to complain, whatever he thinks of Communism. But when Communism becomes an article for export he must actively oppose it, or abandon his claim to being a liberal.

A few weeks before taking power Mussolini said, "Fascism cannot be transported outside of Italy any more than Bolshevism can be transported outside of Russia." He was wrong on both counts, and later he was to repudiate the limitation for Fascism that, he said, "now has in the world the universality of all doctrines which, in fulfilling themselves, represent a moment in the history of the human spirit." But Communism has that same "universality" now, and one would be blind not to realize it. It does not follow that because it is universal it is good, or that the liberal, in opposing it, is going against the trend of his time, and hence is an obstructionist. Liberalism also has a universality in this world, and one with infinitely deeper roots than Communism, for it springs from the eternal aspiration for liberty.

However, do not misconstrue my ideas about Fascism and Communism and a possible choice between the two. The inevitability of that choice has never existed, but it is one of the alarmist pieces drawn out of the bag by neo-Fascists whenever they want to frighten us about Communism. That happened in Italy after the Armistice of 1943, when the reactionary forces which had gathered around Badoglio and the King were supported by the Allies because the latter feared a Communist revolution. That bugbear is one of the things which will contribute greatly in the future to the survival of Fascism. When the German Army went down, its last gasp, you will recall, was that it was fighting to stem the westward rush of the barbarian hordes of Communism. That myth will also rise to plague us, and it will be the task of the liberal to avoid both the Scylla of Communism and the Charybdis of Fascism—although, as I said before, if the choice ever were forced upon me I would take Communism.

It is not war-mongering to point to the obvious fact that the world is being split into two great political camps. The conflict which has now ended in Europe had two ideological aspects, that of the democracies against Fascism, and the fratricidal struggle of the two totalitarian concepts of life. It was a triangular war in which two opposed ways of life joined to destroy the exponents of a third way that was inimical to both. And now this leaves the democracies and the Communist power facing each other over the stricken field of Fascism. They need not settle their differences by war. This is still a fairly large world, and there is room for both doctrines. But war, as we have learned to our sorrow, is not avoided by appeasement; it is avoided by possessing the strength to hold your own and by using that strength for political purposes. What this world needs is mutual accommodation and respect for the rights of others. The liberal problem, in the international field, is to apply and insist upon that accommodation and respect. If we cannot get them for ourselves and for others, then this world is not going to be much worth living in, and in any event, an armed clash will be inevitable. Anyone who predicts the certainty of such a clash is talking without adequate knowledge or responsibility, for it is in no sense inevitable. Anyone who fails to work to prevent it is a dangerous fool—and the only way of prevention lies in friendship with Russia if such friendship is accepted and loyally returned.

All these remarks stem, of course, from my observations, experiences and beliefs. This is my examination paper, and I am putting down what I have learned. The things I have seen and done in my career forbid me to accept any dogmatic, all-inclusive political faith, such as the economic interpretation of history in particular or Communism in general. I try to fit things into the picture of my experiences and knowledge—such as they are—and Communism does not fit.

Democracy and liberalism do fit in with my ideas, for I feel that through them liberty of a sort is realized on the political plane—not perfect, abstract liberty, but the nearest thing to it which modern political institutions can provide. I want a government which will respect my rights as an individual as long as I obey its just laws and do not harm my neighbor and fulfill my legal obligations as a citizen. I want freedom of speech and press and all similar freedoms. I want the right, in so far as it is feasible, to choose the men who will run my government, and to turn them out if they run it badly. I want to feel that the ruling minority is open to the pressure of public opinion, and that its ranks are open to new men coming from below—even to me, if I should ever prove my worthiness and desire to play my part in government.

These things are all a part of a liberal credo and a liberal way of life, the only way that now satisfies my desires after these ten years of work. Because I feel that within certain limitations and despite lamentable failings and dangerous threats for the future, my own country, the United States, comes close to satisfying these needs, I am proud of being an American. My life abroad for

fourteen years has not made me "anti" any country, for I have
seen the greatness of which nations like England, Spain, France,
and Italy are capable. Least of all would I claim that the United
States has anything to teach that mother of all democracies, England. All I say is that no amount of living abroad could make me
blind to the ideals for which the United States, in its blundering
way, stands. Our liberal and democratic institutions, however im-
perfect, are real and precious, and I will defend them wherever
I am and with whatever weapons my age may permit.

Perhaps our fight is one for survival only, but that is as good
a thing to fight for as any, if what we wish to protect, and see
survive, is liberty. One must become reconciled to the idea that
this is a period of wars, violence, and revolution which will long
outlive us—and perhaps the best thing one can hope for is to go
down fighting on the right side. This is not pessimism; it is a
recognition of the fact that the history of humanity is nearer to
tragedy than to happiness. There have been other dark and tormented ages when liberty lay buried alive under the weight of
authoritarianism, and ours threatens to be another such age
unless authoritarianism is fought tooth and nail. Political virtue,
in these times, must consist in that struggle upwards toward the
light and air of liberty, a struggle which humanity can never
lose, however many of us may individually fail and die.

By the eternal dialectical process of history one can feel certain that the evils of totalitarianism will engender the forces of
opposition that will overthrow it. But if you merely say that,
and sit back and wait for it to happen, you are an immoral sen-
timentalist. At best you have passed a historical judgment which
has no ethical value—and even its historical truth is based upon
the fact that men have always fought tyranny and have not
merely recognized it as evil.

The true liberal says, "Give free play to all the contending
political forces of society," but then he goes in and fights for
what he feels to be the right, so that sometimes he is the conservative, sometimes the revolutionary (as you have seen me be,
in this book) but he is never the spectator. As Croce so profoundly writes, liberty is not a fact but a process, not a possession

but a conquest, a victory which one must go on fighting to maintain—not by authority but, if possible, by unimpeded, open discussion, not by forceful imposition but by education and voluntary acceptance.

I feel that my attitude has hardened into a sort of anti-Romanticism and anti-Illuminism; that it could (if I were philosophically inclined) be systematized into a neo-Classicism and neo-Rationalism, which surely is the only direction that offers hope in a world that has run amuck, after its long, disastrous journey from the days when "Nature," "Science," "Reason," and "Progress" started humanity on the road that was to lead to Fascism, Nazism, and Communism.

If that makes me a conservative, I am not afraid of the accusation. Indeed, the liberal often finds himself politically on the right in these disordered days. That does not mean he has moved to the right, but merely that the forces which brought the reaction to Fascism have pushed the axis of political thought to forms of "leftism" that are not necessarily the more advanced or desirable for being new. There is nothing in liberalism to prevent social and political programs as advanced as any which the "radicals" are advocating—so long as "advancement" is not made to consist of practices such as the abolition of private property, nor made synonymous with Communism or Socialism or some other dogmatic political faith.

The utilitarian basis of liberalism can never be abandoned without abandoning liberalism, although it is not the sole aim and there are qualifications about the means used to achieve it. The aim can never be the glorification of a State or a Race or a Superman or a Dictatorship in any form. It must be the good of the greatest number. "I regard utility as the ultimate appeal on all ethical questions," John Stuart Mill wrote in the essay "On Liberty" which still remains a classic expression of liberal thought, "but it must be utility in the largest sense, grounded on the permanent interests of man as a progressive being."

The path is not an easy or simple one, and sometimes you feel you are involving yourself in contradictions. In writing of the Italian conquest of Abyssinia I posed that perennial problem, whether one has a right to use violence to force a better status upon a people low in the scale of civilization. The violence, *per se,* is immoral, as it was in that case, but the result was of benefit to the millions of Abyssinians. Mill, you will recall, had no doubts about what to do. "Despotism is a legitimate mode of government in dealing with barbarians," he wrote, "provided that the end be their improvement, and the means justified by actually effecting that end." Allowing for the fact that along with the evils of Fascism the Italians brought much that was good to Ethiopia, you have a similar situation. So you see that even by the definition given by so good a liberal as John Stuart Mill, it was possible to have doubts—of a practical, not an ethical, nature—about the conquest of Ethiopia. History is continually putting such posers to us. Was it not better for Greece and the world (even to this day) that Philip, the cynic, the despot, the corrupter of morals and the man of violence, should have won, than that Demosthenes, the democrat, the idealist, the patriot should have saved Athens?

However, one must then ask whether it is not right for the Communists to say that by their "depotism" they are forcing good upon millions of persons in the lower reaches of society and improving their lot? The answer, as with Italy and Ethiopia, is both "no" and "yes"—no, because their form of utility is not, in practice, "grounded on the permanent interests of man as a progressive being," and yes, so long as they confine that activity to the proper levels of society in their own country. Not being a "barbarian," or one who feels the need of Communism or who agrees that it will improve the lot of the masses in my country or in other advanced nations, I deny the right of the Communists to impose their system of government on everyone. If anyone tells me that the lot of the people of Estonia, for example, will be better under Communism than it was in the more than two decades of freedom, I beg leave to express strong doubts.

If the events prove me wrong, then I must change my "yardstick" for gauging the good and the bad in contemporary politics. "Complete liberty of contradicting and disproving our opinion is the very condition which justifies us in assuming its truth for purposes of action," to cite John Stuart Mill once more, "and on no other terms can a being with human faculties have any rational assurance of being right."

Everyone has a "yardstick," which varies from day to day and year to year as he grows in knowledge and experience. The ability to judge more or less soundly depends on that knowledge and experience, but it is influenced by many subtle impulses of temperament, character, health, material position—all those things which, in the Freudian term, make you rationalize your thinking. Recognition of fallibility is one of the first steps to wisdom, but if you do not go on from there to the realization that fallibility, like all things, is relative, and that there are those in the world even more fallible than you and less in a position to form judgments, then you are a modest fool.

These past ten or twelve years have given me a widespread view of contemporary politics. I have had a "liberal education" in the political sense of the word, and that is the reply which I give now as I present myself for a degree as a citizen of the world. I am not pronouncing a final, dogmatic credo, for if I did so I would be guilty of the same attitude that I condemn in Socialism, Communism and—perhaps above all—in those so-called professional liberals who, in the United States especially, have in recent years taken the rigid pro-Stalin, pro-Chiang Kai-shek, pro-Gandhi, anti-Churchill line, come what may.

I lay no claims to wisdom in general, but a few wise things I have learned in these hard ten years of fighting and living, of seeing and listening and reading—and one is that the road to truth is only reached by those with open minds who are willing to learn even from the ones who differ with them, and who are willing to change their minds, to admit and profit by error.

I make only one boast in all my career of twenty-three years in journalism: That I have never written anything I did not believe to be true. I have tried to serve no cause but that of truth, and in so far as possible—human nature being what it is— I have followed my reasoning and not my emotions to where it led, regardless of the conclusion. Many of my stories harmed a cause in which my heart lay, but I have no remorse and no regrets. I would have liked to favor the cause of Congress and independence in India, but I would not distort the truth to do so or hold back anything I learned. I am as convinced as anyone else of the necessity for Great Britain and the United States to work together and remain united, but I would not, in Spain, India, or Italy, refrain from criticism or the publication of facts damaging to the British.

The office of the journalist, as of the scholar, is, to quote Ralph Waldo Emerson, "to cheer, to raise and to guide men by showing them facts amidst appearances. He plies the slow, un-honored, and unpaid task of observation."

The responsibility is a heavy one, if only because people have an inherent tendency to believe what they see in print. Do you remember the argument at the inn, in *Don Quixote,* between the innkeeper and the curate?

"I tell thee, friend," says the curate, "there were never any such Persons, as your Books of Chivalry mention, upon the Face of the Earth."

"*A otro perro con esse huesso,*" indignantly replies the Inn-keeper, ["To another dog with this bone."] Why, Sir, are they not in Print? Are they not published according to order? Li-censed by Authority [for this, read: Passed by the censor] from the Privy Council? And do you think that they would permit so many untruths to be printed, and such a number of Battles and Enchantments to set us all a-madding?

Alas, they would, and that is part of the weight of responsi-bility which a journalist bears. But I would not want to end this work without one brief expression of pride that the pro-fession which I follow played its part well in this last war, a better and bigger part than was played in World War I or in any previous conflict in history. The price that was paid in lives, wounds, imprisonment, and shattered health was correspond-ingly high, as it had to be, but it was paid with open eyes. I sometimes like to think that the pace we set in the Spanish Civil War was the one which was followed and kept up in the great war, but it would have happened anyway. There is only one way to cover a war, and it has never been different—to go to the front and from the midst of the battle see with your own eyes what happens. Nothing else in war corresponding is worth more than the paper of the day on which it is printed. Only first-hand news endures, for it is the stuff of which history is made.

I suppose I have done my last such war corresponding. I am an old battle horse, and often in these past few years I felt a weariness—not of the flesh but of the spirit—a sort of kicking at the traces, as if it were time I were put out to pasture and left to browse in peace. I have done my part at the wars in the past ten years, and often I thought I would write *Finis*. But it is not for a man to sign off. That seems a little like suicide. It should not be "good-bye," but "au revoir."

> I cannot rest from travel: I will drink
> Life to the lees: all times I have enjoy'd
> Greatly, have suffer'd greatly, both with those
> That loved me, and alone . . .
> How dull it is to pause, to make an end,
> To rust unburnish'd, not to shine in use!

Some men are born to type—the explorer who suffers the loneliness and cold of the Arctic regions, the entomologist who faces disease and danger in the jungles of the Amazon, the mountain climber who confronts death just to mount higher and higher, to the very summit. A newspaperman is the soldier of fortune, the Ulysses of this poem who yearns

> in desire
> To follow knowledge, like a sinking star
> Beyond the utmost bound of human thought.

Tennyson, you remember, took the idea for his poem from the twenty-sixth Canto of Dante's *Inferno*, where Ulysses tells his stirring tale of adventure and death.

> *Né dolcezza di figlio, né la pieta*
> *del vecchio padre, né 'l debito amore*
> *lo qual dovea Penelope far lieta,*
> *Vincer potèr dentro da me l'ardore*
> *ch' i' ebbi a divenir del mondo esperto,*
> *e de li vizii umani e del valore.*

One always has that urge to learn more of the world and of the virtues and vices of humanity. The way I feel now I do not ever want to roam any more. I do not want to hear the thunder of guns and bombs, to see men die and to live-myself in momentary fear of death. I want peace and quiet and my home and family, for I have earned the right to them. I have paid my price to history, and it is for the younger men to take up the burden, while I sit back and say that we did things better in my time, for "there were giants in those days."

But if there is another war?

Begun aboard the United States Transport *James Parker,* at sea, May 17, 1944.
Finished at Sunnyside Inn, Asheville, North Carolina, June 3, 1945.

Index